God's Quantum Vortex

God's Quantum Vortex

The Secret World of Esoteric Sciences

Volume 2

JIM P. WALKER

authorHOUSE®

AuthorHouse™
1663 Liberty Drive
Bloomington, IN 47403
www.authorhouse.com
Phone: 1 (800) 839-8640

Published by AuthorHouse 10/13/2015

ISBN: 978-1-5049-5551-5 (sc)
ISBN: 978-1-5049-5550-8 (e)

Print information available on the last page.

This book is printed on acid-free paper.

Contents

Chapter 1 1
Chapter 2 23
Chapter 3 48
Chapter 4 55
Chapter 5 64
Chapter 6 84
Chapter 7 90
Chapter 8 117
Chapter 9 132
Chapter 10 144
Chapter 11 205
Chapter 12 224
Chapter 13 311
Chapter 14 323
Chapter 15 340
Chapter 16 365
Chapter 17 394
Chapter 18 438
Chapter 19 446
Chapter 20 454

Acknowledgments 469
About the Author 471

Contents

Chapter 1 .... [illegible]
Chapter 2 .... [illegible]
Chapter 3 .... [illegible]
Chapter 4 .... [illegible]
Chapter 5 .... [illegible]
Chapter 6 .... [illegible]
Chapter 7 .... [illegible]
Chapter 8 .... [illegible]
Chapter 9 .... [illegible]
Chapter 10 .... [illegible]
Chapter 11 .... [illegible]
Chapter 12 .... [illegible]
Chapter 13 .... [illegible]
Chapter 14 .... [illegible]
Chapter 15 .... [illegible]
Chapter 16 .... [illegible]
Chapter 17 .... [illegible]
Chapter 18 .... [illegible]
Chapter 19 .... [illegible]
Chapter 20 .... [illegible]

Acknowledgements .... [illegible]
About the Author .... [illegible]

"Only a person, who has experienced all the possibilities on Earth, can be Aware of, and connect with the Cosmic God, TIH."

Jim Walker

The story evolves from the personal experiences of the writer, from his deep (40 years) research and discoveries of Quantum Cone vortex. Once into Awareness, he reveals the techniques of connecting and triggering the "Act of God" events. He formulates the "mysteries" of self-fate programming. He explains how the Government, Religion, Finance and Science are interconnected, for the first time in history. His research deep dives into the Bible, Yoga Meditation, Wave-Particle Quantum Physics and into occult, the Metaphysics. He is not just theorizing about life events, he is proactively changing the events in biblical proportions. He becomes the miracle creator by thought and by action, the trigger man, who can only relate to the higher dimensions and to Cosmic Intelligence. The formulas he writes may seem similar to previous theoretical physicists, but they are his own concept, given the examples of his work and e mail prior to "God's Particle/Boson" announcement by Peter Higgs on July 4th, 2012. The Quantum Cone Vortex diagram and it's connection to Yin and Yang with annihilation and creation, related to Cosmic Spiral Sequence of 4 Sixes may seem absurd to earth 4th dimensional thinkers, but it is backed by facts by the author. His prediction of the next Flood is backed by errors in time measured by Mayans and Nostradamus. Once a person is elevated to the vortex in Quantum Cone, with zero weight/gravity and when Time stops in Quantum reality, then he/she will able to be awarded with all possibilities to create or destroy. The writer imitates the out of the box thinking of God, but he is not comparing himself to Cosmic Intelligence. He just uses the Quantum Energy (in form of Dark and Light energy, he calls Satan and God for convenience). The examples are powerful and convincing. The reader should not just observe the author's human encounters to get to quick conclusions. It is a manual of how to think without Fear. Once the Fear is eliminated the mind is open to deep into sub consciousness and to build The Awareness, where all possibilities are unrestricted, and to rise to the 6th Cosmic Dimension, God.

Chapter I

He went through his books... Soon he confirmed how things worked. The theory of Wheeler came to help. The energy created of compressing magnetic field lines turns to mass; mass creates gravity. The gravitational theory is about converting mass into energy (hydrogen, uranium). The opposite is true also. The energy (magnetic, explosives) can be converted to mass. The Einstein theory was proving right. There is a relation between wave length of light and mass and Energy!

Energy = MC square.

But that is measured on earth. When the antigravity applies the speed increases beyond speed of light and moves with Universal Speed. The electromagnetic field created of clashes of gravity and the antigravity moves with speed of light on earth to create matter, the gravitational wave....

Black holes are created by implosion of all magnetic fields; wormholes are basically time machines, where two minds can communicate through electromagnetic vacuum fluctuations. When the meditation was applied or some challenging problems occurred, Jim was not afraid to jump aboard that great Time Machine...

His theory started at early age that the positron moving toward you (future) equals an electron moving away from you (past). Present is where the future and the past meet. To connect the dots, in the future one has to accelerate the electrons to the point of meeting the positrons at earlier time in the future. If one wants to go to the past, then one has to slow down the electrons of moving forward. That can be achieved by a different way of thinking. When one breathes and thinks different and place a wish into his mind, his brainwaves are in a mode to see the future or the past. The emotion which has magnetic fields compresses and energy is created which emits in the form of invisible light/plasma/antiplasma from the solar plexus. The creativity starts. The worm-hole, communicates between active consciousness and the sub consciousness. That's where the time machine will tell you if your wishes can come true or your questions of the past can be answered...

Jim, having seen pictures of Studio 54 Club (in a Bulgarian magazine Star, this was in 1976), he thought "it would be nice to have his own club just like that!" At this time he was in his 2nd year cadet program in the elite Naval Academy, in Port of Varna, Bulgaria.

God: "Stop fantasizing young man. Do not forget your priority is to escape from Bulgaria. You are jumping the gun!"

Jim: "Stop challenging me, Father!"

Because of the impossibility of that thought and because he knew he was predestined to a higher society than his original country, he always knew he was different and better than others. Yes, how many eastern European Naval cadets had that desire to enter the most lucrative legal civilian business for an individual in the USA? Possibly most of them but how many would succeed? Living and operating a business near the White House and operating the oldest restaurant, Bellini's? Getting his first club for a 100 bucks and now with $1,000 -- he can twist and turn to make that lease work? Some people would pray to God, would believe in their "lucky star," but not Jim. He believed that whenever he asks his sub consciousness will manifest itself in a success or failure. He believed that God was The Invisible Hand, which would guide or misguide him based on the values he seeds in his brain. Miracles for him were an everyday thing. He was more surprised when the normal things around him occurred. Like somebody honestly asked him, "how are you, Jim?" He was not complimented very much in DC, but then he knew why? Most people demanded much more than they deserved and they felt entitled to benefits, but not committed to a serious relationship. At this time he was not thinking about Amanda, or about his family in Bulgaria. All of his focused was on reopening that thirty year old club. Nobody dared to improve it for twenty-two years. "Yes, not a soul in Washington had tried! What a mystery," he thought? Same lighting, dance floors with missing parquet, ladies' rooms with flooded bent downward floors, second floor with foot deep holes in dancing area. The HVAC was good but as a fan only, not cold. And more things ...remained same since his previous visit in April, 2001.

Jim: "Yes, I am ready for the next miracle, God/TIH!"

God had more under his the sleeve for Jim than he expected. That was the beginning of the end of night clubs in DC.

Nikias: "I know you have a police clearance from the previous application. I need a current one. Mr. Bender is usually a tough guy, I know him from Kilimanjaro night club in which he took the owner's home for not paying his full lease. Looks like he's softened up giving you the lease to sign that quick! What did you tell him?" He looked puzzled...

Jim: "I guess there is a God for some people in DC, because I can't be this lucky always?"

Nikias: "Police don't like you! You operate a whore house. What luck? I am trying to get your hours fixed. This guy Mansur you are partners with, really screwed you up!" He was serious.

Jim: "I would be lucky to get out of that partnership. That is why I am trying to open this club by myself!" obviously was extremely proud of this act.

Nikias: "I will get your deposit from Tony Barros. Too many protestors! They came to the ABC board hearing like hungry wolves to kill. They were disappointed you did not show up."

Jim: "The lesbians and this gay guy Mitch Keller together with under current gossiping words of Council member, Jack Ronan, the dummy mediator Oliver Green, and the out of the woods seventy people protesting who don't want anything around them; no 711, no Subway shop and no straight guys, like me?" He was laughing.

Nikias: "Now you know why you are paying 250 dollars an hour for my services!" He was cocky again and for a good reason.

Jim: "I will pay you more as long I get my licenses and we get the hours at Randevu Club corrected."

Nikias: "People will tell you anything until they get what they want, and then they forget you until the next trouble. Jim, you seem to be a fair man to me, no matter what people say about you."

Jim: "Let's make this work then. What else do you need?"

Nikias: "This is a serious club and the ABC board will ask you for your financials. That is no more some hole in a basement! I need to show them a minimum of 20,000 dollars in your account by tomorrow afternoon!"

Jim: "Give me two days." He would not confess he had only $1,000 cash on hand...

Nikias: "I will stretch your time to get your license up to four months, refund contingency and free four months rent after your deposit!"

Jim: "Right now the deposit and lease signing counts, the license can wait."

Nikias: "Ok. Put the money in the bank for your landlord to see your statement. We need financial information for all parties who issue permits and sign the lease." Smiling, he somewhat thought that Jim was some kind of an opportunist with no money. And even he had it; he was profiling him already as a "marked man," by the government. Yet, he believed that Jim may have chance. The perversity of writing checks was like a whore getting paid even the client was impotent or she would not provide services requested.

Jim: "Let see what the next venture will bring?"

Nikias: "Two days. Don't call. Be here at 3 pm, Thursday."

Next day Wednesday Sept. 5th he went to the 300 Indiana Avenue. He was prepared to see the 180 days detention on his record. He paid the five dollars fee and waited fifteen minutes. The record was printed and finally given to him through a small window by a mean police lady Officer.

Jim: "Thanks!" He grabbed his driver's license ID back and he quickly glanced at the Police record...

Jim: "Wow, no record! God is great!" or, "was it me again?" He thought the miracle was unfolding already. Whatever the mind set he put in motion previous six months it was working now. He almost grabbed the phone to call his lawyer. Instead he called his old roommate and schoolmate, Rafael, in Florida.

Rafael: "What is the news my dear friend!" He sounded friendly and a bit sarcastic.

Jim: "First, the good news. I am getting the club! "The Pier 9," the oldest club in USA, established in 1971. You saw it in April. Second, on U Street it is impossible to get the liquor license; too many protestors!"

Rafael: "What is the guarantee nobody will protest you at the new location?" He was skeptical.

Jim: "There are no residents nearby to protest! It was a club before. Why can't it be one again?"

Rafael: "What can I do for you now? You owe me money from investing on the U Street venture." He sounded agitated.

Jim: "We were partners there. If we'd won, great; if we lost it affects both of us. I paid the lawyer, sound man, mediator, and architect for change of floor plans. My expenses were twice more than yours."

Rafael: "Ok, ok! I am not investing in your new venture, bad location." He calmed down.

Jim: "I need a favor, brother! My lawyer asked me to print my current financial report. I have to show at least $20,000, in my bank statement to get approved by ABC board for the liquor license. If you can send me $9,999 (ten thousand minus one), in two separate days with wire transfer, IRS will not get red flags."

Rafael: "Sure. But I want my money back, ASAP. I am going to the bank now." He puffed in the phone.

Jim: "Great! Now I know why people don't reopen clubs for twenty-two years, ha ha!" He clicked off the phone. Seems everything was falling into place. The landlord will be happy, the ABC board, clean police record... Now he needed to get the money for the 24,000 dollar check? He really missed that money he blew up on Amanda, but he knew GOD would reward him somehow!

Thursday, at 3 pm the meeting with Nikias was finalized with glee!

Nikias: "Dear Jim! Thanks for the financial statement. I see you have $20,000 in your account. I see you have no criminal record! How did this happen? Did you bribe someone at Police record keeping? Do you owe DC taxes and 100 dollars on a water bill?"

Jim: "$100 water bill?"

Nikias: "DC cleans hands" application for a Master license, for liquor establishments is asking this question, not me."

Jim: "I don't owe taxes or water bills, thank you!"

Nikias: "Tony Barros is sending you the check back in the next ten days. The lease is ready with my amendments. Wallace has a copy. Sign your part and wait for Mr. Bender to sign his part. I like your persistence, young man."

Jim: "Ok. I will leave now. I hope we have better luck this time?" He pushed the chair backwards and stood up, feeling ten feet tall.

Nikias: "Success in this town needs more than luck. We need a miracle sometimes. You remind me of me at a younger age. Aggressive, smart, educated and not fearing facing any challenges. You are entering a completely different game now; the cut throat game. They are few like you here with night club licenses. I represent one of them and he is always in trouble."

Jim: "Who?" extremely curious to be given the name.

Nikias: "Phantom, Vibe guy, Rogbin. They are changing the name from Vibe to Urban next year."

Jim: "Maybe they can give me some promoters?" laughing.

Nikias: "I know him, he will not talk to you, but he will talk to me," saying with that smirking face again.

Jim: "Lets sign the lease tomorrow and get the license first, then we will promote." He walked out the door….

Jim went back to the infamous bar Randevu. He was acting normal. The drinks were served, the Police harassment continued, Officer Bolton was all over the place, finding nothing after visiting twenty-two times without a warrant to search the premises. Jim was also watching the news. They were still searching for Chandra Levy, the missing intern on Capitol Hill.

Wallace: "Hey Jim, come to my office at Newmark on Connecticut Avenue, Mr. Bender just sent me a fax with his signature. I need your signature also to seal the deal. Also, bring the check book, ok!"

Jim: "Be there at 2 pm."

Wallace: "Here is the key for the club. This deal came through amazingly fast." He was truly puzzled and extremely surprised.

Jim: "Hey, nothing should amaze you. I deal with my powers and with God's help!"

Wallace: "I hear you are getting your deposit from Tony Barros. That and the best lawyer in town and your powers, you said... Sounds like you have all the necessary tools in place?"

Jim: "Wallace, read The Bible. This town is Sodom and Gomorra, I don't like neither this town nor the people in it, but, it is the easiest place to start a business for me. No mafia, but plenty of false mouths, who pass gossip, just like DC council member, Jack Ronan!"

Wallace: "Believe me, all this infighting, throat cutting, back stabbing between restaurant and club owners, all that makes my work more difficult." He took the $24,000 check and then smiled. "I hope this time you will not get protested and you will get your license?"

Jim: "I hope the ANC is more lenient towards this business, since we are away from any residential area, but, that is something for my lawyer to deal with. You did a great job so far." They shook hands and Jim walked out holding the key like it was a Faberge egg. It was happening again! Wow! This time there was no partner, and hopefully no Police harassment? Jim decided to head towards the club immediately. He jumped in the Benz and headed toward Buzzard's Point.

Jim: "Miles, time to work! I got the lease. Send me your promoters, ASAP. We can meet at the club in the next thirty minutes to an hour." He tried not to get excited, trying to stay business-like.

Miles: "You got it? I have been trying to get that lease for a year! Congratulations!"

Jim: "You told me you bought it?" laughing…

Miles: "Yeah, I was getting one day liquor licenses here and there, hoping to save enough money for a down payment, but. Mr. Bender is very impatient!"

Jim: "Impatient? You had a year! I got it in one week!"

Miles: "You are European! You should know what has been happening in this country the last four hundred years, buddy! Same thing that just happened to you did not happen for me!" He sounded sad.

Jim: "Maybe you can make money from the promoters?"

Miles: "My man! The money is in the liquor sales. The door pays too many people; the band, the DJ and the security."

Jim: "So how were you making money renting for one day?" He was studying the club business already, while driving!

Miles: "…..Usually the lease holder or the club owner would sign a letter to the ABC board to ask the promoter to obtain a one day liquor license. The promoter pays $300 and shows proof of insurance and what kind of music will be performed; live band or recorded music with DJ.

Promoter has to pay taxes within thirty days on what his revenue is, and he should not owe any previous taxes."

Jim: "Sounds great! Now call your connections and I will issue letters signed for one day events. See you at the club."

The traffic was building up at 3 pm. At around 3.15 pm Jim pulled over in the parking space in front of his new club. 1824 Half Street was a secluded address and to get there one had to know the DC streets, because most street signs were removed or nonexistent. The only sign showing Half Street near Q Street was there but was pointing downward. Jim opened the club and he was amazed to see it empty without anybody talking to him and trying to sell him the space to rent. He felt like many club owners in the past with mixed feelings of having the huge 12,000 square feet to fill with patrons! Euphoria of, the beginnings of success and taking the risk and trying not to fear the failure was overtaking his brilliant mind. He saw a huge fifty year old safe next to the door ticket booth, it was open. "I have to get the new combination for that monster, hopefully to fill up one day." He thought to himself. He saw a lot of ziploc leather bags, around ten, inside.

The black granite bars were the only newer things in the club. Someone tried to fix the club in year 1999, probably Mr. Bender, but it seemed he stopped short?

Miles: "Hey Jim! I brought you some people who are with Addison Band. Another group representing DC Ramble is coming shortly also. The good news is they work with cash, if you don't mind?"

Jim: "Cash is King. It will go to my account anyway, so IRS will know any way. I don't keep money under the mattress."

Miles: "This is Big Greg, promoter for Addison Band."

Big Greg: "Hello." His look was of mixed races, Black and Chinese.

Jim: "I guess you have promoted here before?"

Big Greg: "Yes sir! We work with WKYS and you can hear us on the radio every Saturday night."

Jim: "You know how the business is then! Make me an offer and I will rent you the club with a one day liquor license."

Big Greg: "$5,000 per day. I need two days to reserve, "Halloween" and "New year's" evening."

Jim: "So, you have $10,000 now?" He couldn't believe what he was hearing? But then that is the club business.

Big Greg: "Here is $10,000. Book me. I know DC Ramble is coming and they will probably ask for the same dates?" He pushed an envelope with crisp newly wrapped 100's in bills.

Jim: "Sure, do you have a letter I can sign?" he expected to fill out a form.

Bid Greg: "Look. I just need your signature. The rest I can fill out. Also, I need your full name." Jim was surprised to see a plain piece of paper given to him and the envelope with $10,000 next to it. He did not want to act with resistance and he made the decision to take the money and to put his signature on the paper.

Big Greg: "Here are the dates I reserve." He wrote them on the front of the envelope. Then he wrote his personal cell phone next to those dates.

Jim: "Interesting way to do business! But look what is happening in DC? Nothing amazes me much in these last fifteen years!"

Big Greg: "I will provide my security, my liquor, and the band. The only thing I ask you to do is to keep electricity on, with working toilets and proper fire extinguishers."

Miles was smoking cigarettes and he was quiet. Seems like he made his own deal with the promoters and he was not involved in the conversation. Just about to leave the door of the club was bending from loud knocking. Miles ran to open it. The promoter for DC Ramble go go band was there.

White Mike: "Hey Miles! Thanks for the heads up. Who is the new owner?" A tall light skinned man appeared. He reluctantly entered and he was puzzled, Jim guessed from the look of the young handsome European man.

Jim: "Hello, I just got the lease. I heard many things about your band. It was on the news about a swimming pool party."

White Mike: "Ohh, the underage ladies who undressed in the swimming pool? That was the "Barry farm Groovers," not us. That just put us on the map, even more. We got so many calls since then. Any publicity is good for business."

Big Greg: "Hey Mike." They knew each other. Addison Band was targeting the younger crowd 18 and over, while DC Ramble was 21 and over and their crowd was more mature. The group had been around for ten years. They were respectful when they met, but definitely rivals when it came to bookings in clubs and market shares.

Big Greg: "I am done here for now. See you later. Any problems just keep me posted, ok?" He disappeared through the door.

Jim: "Miles told me about you, Mike, but I know about you, EU, Junk Yard, Total Recall, TCB and Addison Band for years. Here is my business card "Walker's Media." He was almost current.

White Mike: "Interesting. We never allow taping of our performances. How do you know the other "go go" bands?"

Jim: "I did a couple of videos of EU with Sugar Bear and Shorty Tim, before he went to jail." Both of them smiled.

White Mike: "We used to play here ten years ago. Basically we started here as "DC Ramble Go Go band." Everything was fine until one night FBI agents were trying to stop a fight. You know the FBI headquarters were across the street. The fighters turned against the agents and lined them up against the wall and shot them "St. Valentine's Day" style. The Headquarters were moved few months later to Pennsylvania Avenue, NW. Since then police are on our ass everywhere we go."

Jim: "You may need better security?" he stated.

White Mike: "The security is plenty in the club and around. The fights are usually brought on from their neighborhoods. We can't stop the fight beyond the club, but the police will make up stories and link everything to the club. That's what we are dealing with; kids without fathers and police without justice." As they were speaking a low flying police helicopter hovered above the club, beaming with a spot light and observing the SUVs leaving and coming around the club.

Jim: "Politics and history aside what can I do for you before and after I get my license?" back to business.

White Mike: "I will pick a couple of Saturdays here and see if there is no trouble with the cops. If everything turns out great, then we can do it with some kind of rotation. We try not to have permanent days in a club, because police will start harassing us and the club at the same time."

Jim: "They do that to you too? I thought I was the only one they fucked with!" he was concerned.

White Mike: "No matter how they write the laws, you are still a foreigner and we are still black. The worst nightmare for American government employees is to see a foreigner make more money than them, and black people having fun. The worse of the worst is when a black man makes too much money and doesn't pay assumed taxes, then IRS goes berserk!" adamant about what he was saying.

Jim: "When accident happens, are they after the promoters?" he was inquisitive.

White Mike: "No, they go after the club licenses. You guys are easier targets. Promoters are like bartenders and waiters, we can go elsewhere, and owners can't!" That is why we do not want to stay too long in one place. We are at Trade Winds, at the Legend, and at Mirrors. Everywhere! We can make Tuesday or Thursday or Saturday jump up in attendance and sales of course."

Jim: "Ok. I see.... Now do you want to pick some nights here?" he was getting tired of the conversation and he needed to go back to Randevu bar.

White Mike: "I see Big Greg just left. I will take two Saturdays he left open. Here is my deposit of 10,000 dollars. I will let you know within a week what I will choose. Now tell me what he has?" he meant business.

Jim: "He got the Halloween and The New Year's Evening."

White Mike: "Ok, he is not only a fast talker, he is a fast mover!"

Jim: "Miles said the same, but I think in this business it is, "first pays, the first gets the club."

Jim headed to Randevu bar. He felt like he was on cloud 9. The big dream was not only in his head but now it was turning to reality. It took him twenty-five years to make it happen, but he felt he deserved it.

Nathan: "Congratulations, Jim! You made it!" He was puffing a Monte Christo cigar, Jim just kept for occasions like this. The almost ten inch long and one inch in diameter cigar had a great taste.

Jim: "Yes, it was a time to expand after three years in this hole in the wall!" He also has indulged in a Monte Christo cigar. He paused, and then continued:

"It was my unfulfilled dream for a quarter of a century. You know I should write a book about all my adventures and discoveries. There is higher power most people are not aware of, but it is triggered by an individual's mind! I did research in higher physics, like Einstein's special relativity theory, Wheeler's magnetism and Max Planck quantum mechanics. It has to do with the celestial influence matter, energy, speeds and dimensions!"

Nathan: "... or being lucky?"

Jim: "Luck happens once in a while, but when too many successful events manifest themselves, it is like writing a new law? Why did it happen, who helped you, where did it happen, what is the main reason you are doing it, the motive, is the result socially acceptable, who benefits from what you achieved, and are you happy and satisfied, or do you want more in life? Those are the questions in history and eventually only time will judge the legacy individual creates."

Nathan: "So, in a process of doing your things you create your legacy?"

Jim: "Everyone creates biography. Not everyone creates "the legacy." Give me ten people from the last century who could be most important? They don't have to be in specific category of work. They could be writers, explorers, Nobel laureates, politicians, generals?"

Nathan: "Reagan, Mike Tyson, Hitler, Stalin, Sylvester Stallone, Churchill, Einstein, Kennedy, MLK, Clinton."

Jim: "Ok. That is good. No club owners. That is ok. Everyone who creates a successful brand creates legacy. Michael Jackson, Aretha Franklin, Elvis Presley, Henry Kissinger, Tina Turner, Frank Sinatra, Nikola Tesla, Isaac Newton, Archimedes and Aristotle..." As they were deep in conversation a medium height blonde in perfect proportions emerged at the bar area, a not too distant copy of Marilyn Monroe.

Samantha: "Who is the owner here? I heard down in Miami about this guy Jim who is running this place!" In truth, she just got out of jail. She was incarcerated for stealing major amount of merchandise from her employer "Up Against the Wall." After a year in jail she decided to up the game and to join an agency as an escort, but she did not like the 50/50 split pay. She decided to move to advertising herself, on Eros.com website. Someone told her in jail about Randevu's bar and the tolerant management.

Nathan: "You are looking for him!" He pointed toward Jim.

Jim: "Hey, I did not know I was that popular?" he winked at Nathan.

Nathan: "You are a brand!" signaling that both were having the mischievous bonding.

Samantha: "I need some pictures taken immediately for my website. I heard from friends you take pictures of the ladies?"

Jim: "I am almost finishing my conversation here. Have a drink and give me ten minutes, ok?" he did not want to seem desperate or to follow anyone's orders. The blonde seemed sincere, but nobody in bar business would fall for that.

Nathan: "I see your theory works, all those quantum mechanics and Einstein to get pictures of?" He knew he was wrong, but he thought it was laughable to compare the entities of sex and higher physics laws, Jim was referring to?

Jim: "The difference is Einstein was getting hardly any sex from his Serbian wife and she was giving him conditions, similar to what DC women give to me." Both were laughing.

Nathan: "What conditions? I heard something but I don't exactly remember ….alcohol!"

Jim: "Einstein predicted a solar eclipse and they have astronomers observing the fact, when the Furer Hitler ordered all scientists to retrieve to Germany. He was able to prove his point and to get the Noble Laureate and of course the prize. Then he got "some" sex. Rumors are his sons own two buildings now in Manhattan!"

Nathan: "Here you get sex by reference, plus nobody orders you around!" he assumed.

Jim: "Brother, everything in life has a price tag! Everything we breathe and think and do has sequences! I had to trace my path with greatest education, defection, become ship's master, use my charms without compromising with sex, going to jail for a lying lady, operating restaurants and clubs without pay, opening club without money in the bank, with barely 100.00 bucks three years ago and now with really $1,000.00 of my own!"

Nathan: "You can't fool me, you just told me you made $20,000 from the promoters an hour after you got the lease and the keys?" he was appalled. Jim took a long drag of the fat long Monte Christo cigar.

Both were like two cats that were enjoying life! Samantha was drinking the Long Island Ice Tea and she was anxiously looking toward them crossing often her perfectly shaped legs.

Jim: "Nathan, when I make money it is never my money! It is money given to me by God! Or shortly, it is a product of my ability to make my sub consciousness work for me!"

Nathan: "Don't tell me you are God! You are the best pimp I've ever seen!" He took a sip from the single Malt.

Jim: "See, I need to write that damn book. Even Jesus dealt with prostitutes and tax collectors. The world has not changed since. I am talking about how I make events benefit me? It is a process of specific thinking. I tap into mysterious powers which help me in situations where everyone else fails or is afraid to enter."

Nathan: "What makes you so unique entering the night club business?" He laughed out loud.

Jim: "We, the club owners are public figures. Because of the huge potential incomes, the police, the IRS, the ANC, the ABRA, almost anybody can file a complaint about anything. Then the constant scrutiny by not only the normal customers, (before they get drunk), but also by the uncontrollable drunks or some people who are plain high on something before or during the closing of the establishment. I have stories about all of that."

Nathan: "Jim, go take your pictures and we will continue after, where we stopped off. Cheers for my Godly friend!"

Jim: "To God and to future miracles!" Both of them clashed glasses. Jim stood up and grabbed the camera under the register. He always kept a new roll of 35mm film and fresh batteries just for situations like this. Three years prior he was just taking pictures of regular happy hour customers, but later on he would take pictures of ladies of the night. He would select the best looking of the bunch for bar promotion. Many single and married men alike would come and ask the same question," where are the girls?" or "show me the album, the "brown Book."

Samantha: "Where do you take pictures? I do not have too much time."

Jim guided her toward the back liquor storage room which night time was opening as extra drinking space. The small TVs, leather reclining chairs, a champagne color love chair and sofa and the red Lava light in the corner; all that with a large box of fresh cigars by the bar end was giving the lounge a cozy, intimate look. Police were going crazy trying to break the silence code of that mysterious place: a crossover of Playboy Mansion, Mustang Ranch and a two story mini club?

Samantha: "Shoot front positions and rear positions" she ordered; she was comfortable in front of camera. The huge brown painted sliding door kept the crowd guessing what was happening in the liquor storage/ extra room.

The leather sofa and the semi naked beauty complimented each other. She came to the right person. Jim was probably the best photographer that ever was. He had been a professional photographer since 1982 when he bought the all-round Nikon photo camera system. The telephoto, the wide angle, fish eye lenses were doing miracles during his trip in France. His right choice to use wide angle lens was awarded when he took the picture of the Eiffel tower in Paris. They had to walk almost a mile away from it with the second engineer until the camera could take the full height. Jim took pictures of countries around the world, but what was in front him on this champagne leather love seat and sofa was a dream to most men in the world.

Samantha: "I want close ups and great details. I want to be the best on Eros.com." She was undressing herself. Jim was amazed of her easy going behavior. Why he couldn't have a lady like this, as girlfriend or wife? He felt the same way the photographer felt around Marilyn Monroe. The difference here, this woman was by herself and willing to do anything, while the big Playboy centerfold in 1953 was with huge entourage of rich protectors and would be boyfriends and husbands.

Samantha: "Do you like what you see?" She pulled her pink panties down. "Do good close up here!" she directed the camera toward her young nineteen year old flower like opening between her legs. The perfect clitoris was slightly aroused, so it looked like a small nose above the triangle of pink walls under it.

Jim: "Can we do better than that?" he unzipped his pants and the 8 inch rod was fully aroused now.

Samantha: "I thought you would never ask, hurry!" She rolled down condom on his poll with her mouth and started to massage his balls.

Samantha: "Come on Daddy!" she sat on him and started riding him, sitting and pulling him up and down, with bursts of squeezing and relaxing her perfect vagina muscles.

Jim: "I am close to climax. But I will finish quicker from behind. I think you have been selfish, top for you pleases you better?" They changed positions.

Samantha: "True. Now you have a minute. Hurry!" she wanted to leave the room. Jim felt the nervous tension building behind the brown door. Nathan and the five customers around the bar wouldn't stop the Police from searching and shutting the place down. Jim accelerated the rhythm of the intercourse and less than a minute both achieved the climax at the same time. The loud R&B music at the two story lounge prevented everyone from hearing anything inside the room and their screaming voices were unheard.

Jim: "Where have you been exactly in Miami? I used to live nearby and I know it somewhat."

Samantha: "I just made up the story. I was in jail and they kept talking about your spot." She put her all white dress on, then both started laughing, while Jim was opening the sliding metal door.

Jim: "Come back in 48 hours, Monday night. I will have those pictures ready, as he was heading to the bathroom to wash up and to discard the condom.

Nathan: "Hey those must be nice pictures?" he was suspicious, so were the patrons around the bar, but they did act like it was none of their business...

Jim: "Not a bad ending day, I put 20,000 dollars in my account and I just took pictures of a Marilyn Monroe look-alike."

Nathan: "You are proving your theory. You are living your theory. What else is on the horizon? Anything I should be aware of or to hide from, or to expect?" he was laughing, but at the same time he was nervous. The cigar had a calming effect on both of them but the conversation was vivid as it started an hour before.

Jim: "First, I did not get my liquor license yet and I already made $20,000. That seems a bit strange but in the world of business creativity is based on one's thinking and has to be legal. My legality came from signing the lease. Second, what I do as a businessman in my place is to write my own rules. Taking pictures is legal as long as the models are not underage." He puffed the cigar and hid the sex part of what happened in the room. He couldn't trust anyone in the bar to that full extent. "Let them guess," was his motto. It kept him in the business for the duration of ten years, so it worked!

Nathan: "So, you seem well connected! Maybe that is why you are so successful."

Jim: "Yes, I am. I am aware of my surroundings. Are my connections great, only time will tell. I have only three great friends in my business world. My lawyer, my accountant and my IT guy but then I am paying them, so, they are not exactly friends, but necessary connections."

Nathan: "How about your doctor?"

Jim: "I don't think doctors are friends to anyone? They are charlatans and they have knowledge enough to keep you alive but never fully cure you. Otherwise their business will be shut down for good, and their schools would be closed and there would be only emergency rooms. Health care is a business like anything else and expanding. For example: I would ask a doctor to cure any of his patients. He/she wouldn't allow me. Why? It is a simple answer. Every patient is like a bank account, the doctor is entitled to withdraw from as long he can fool the patient of being cured."

Nathan: "Well, so is accounting, law, IT, car repair... They charge you too...." he was about to leave.

Jim: "In the other fields people have somewhat control. In the health system an old person can get lost and screwed. That is where I come and tell people they do not need a doctor as long they are thinking and behaving healthy. Before one asks for "health care" he/she should work on his/her "self-care." The only thing in the human body which one can't fully control is their appendix, broken bones, open wounds.... and bad teeth, at least in my case." He continued smoking.

Nathan: "Basically, we need just ER, emergency rooms? You are not really a health prophet; you smoke cigars and take pictures of prostitutes." He started to leave. "I think you mentioned something about legacy? I hope your legacy is not going to be in some newspaper? I hear they are trying to close, Mustang Ranch in Nevada for unpaid taxes!"

Jim: "Hey, I pay taxes and I am not them, but maybe close to it?" he almost pushed Nathan out of the bar area.

Nathan: "Check, "Sex guide USA." They mentioned you there as prime location in Washington, DC."

Jim: "I will! I do not have enemies for a reason. Next time you come I will explain to you why?"

Nathan: "Great! I can't wait till the next time! There is always something new to be amazed by you, my friend." He was one of the few customers who would buy Jim a drink; in exchange Jim would give him a free cigar (but not always a Monte Christo).

Jim: "Bye Nathan!" he referred to his patrons as "good customers," not "good friends" and very rarely would ask what their names were or what they do or where they are from? That made them wonder, considering everyone in DC was kind of nosey about knowing the patron's whereabouts, building data base, e-mail list, business cards raffle for something free. The only thing which was evidence of anything happening was his, "brown book/photo album" of beautiful hookers. The rejection of taking a picture of them could be because they were undercover Police ladies. Not everyone was asked to the small room, but the ones who rejected were not talked to any further by Jim, assumed; "red flags/undercover/unfriendly/not hookers."

Jim made a mental note to check the website, "Sex guide USA." He knew the danger of too much information about his location. He believed in "any publicity is good publicity," but he preferred his patrons to be more discreet about whom they meet at Randevu bar. There were some dignitaries like UN Secretary Kofi Annan, who happen to be brought there by a transvestite, Leah from Lufthansa Airlines. There were top lawyers who were picking $300 an hour ladies from Randevu. Every one of the ladies had stories to tell… That will be brought to light later. At this time Jim was concerned about opening this forgotten club, for almost twenty-two years! "Shame on you Washington, DC," he thought, "incessant talking, posturing, and no action?" He was interacting with the customers drink-wise but his mind was wondering with speeds of the universe. For a moment he wanted to announce to the universe that against all odds he got the club! He did not call it "mind over matter" like 99 % people would think and say. His motto would be, "Mind over Minds!" Was Mr. Bender, the smartest man from Brooklyn that vulnerable to give him the club so easily? Was he with the philosophy, "one bird in the hand is better than two birds in the bush?" Basically equals to, "better 24,000 dollars in the bank, than 45,000 dollars he would dream about." Mr. Bender also, probably was betting on the business to fail? Ten years lease? When the life span of a club is two to three years, before some trouble starts! Jim was finishing his cigar and also the end of his bar shift. He lived nearby and soon he landed at home. He saw the 20,000 dollars in the safe, he touched it.

Jim: "It is not a dream!" he thought. Then he remembered the pictures he took, "when they developed them on Monday that would not be a dream also! I can't wait to see them, my Marilyn Monroe!"

Sunday would have been nice and boring. He woke up relaxed and optimistic. He looked at his apartment and he felt lonely. He wanted to invite Amanda and ravage her body as he did many times before. He wanted to call his brother and father in Bulgaria, to brag to Alexandra who was his long time lady friend from grammar to High School. Even he wanted to brag to his commander Ganev from The Naval Academy. "See. Nothing can stop me from achieving what I want!" Like a silent movie he was looking at his whole life with images of his mother Loretta, his childhood with dusty summers and constant sicknesses, the yoga books, the fitness achievements, the first desire to escape the old communist country, to prove to himself that he was better than anyone, even being expelled from school, the near death experience trying to escape, then the priests helping him out to find his class mates. Then him becoming ships Master, and then meeting Contessa, Mr. Smith, owning Bellini's restaurant, owning Randevu's Bar and now The Zoro night club!

Then he remembered the failures, everything was achieved in some kind of "make a wish" manner. It was like a game. The dream state of being young and the reality of being old was the, time machine everyone is aware of but not so many people are willing to figure it out. The dream state makes you go to school, to overcome obstacles, to fight biases, to compromise your basic principles, to keep pushing forward. Then the reality comes to light, when everything one works for disappears, and the pain of failure is bigger and longer than the pleasure of success. So was the connection between past, (dream, memories) and future (reality), one huge wormhole, a time machine! Jim was successful achiever, but all that had a price tag; not "money value, but, emotional, mental, and physical" value. What was different between Olympian who gets the world record and one civilian? It is not because of his luck or because he had extra legs or extra hands! It is the drive, the training the mind pushed to the extreme, the victory, the crowd screaming and the medals. What is the biggest disappointment to the crowd? Yes, the voluntary retirement. Why can't he try again two years from now, just like Nikias's secretary suggested? Maybe within those two years he has time to rethink? The government gives you five years after a crime is committed to restart, like a misdemeanor. The central planning society makes five year plans. Jim did not have that luxury to stretch, to twist, to gamble and to manipulate. His mind was working in six months increments. If it wouldn't work in short time, forget about it. He was creating his own statistical law. Just six months before he was upset over Amanda taking all his extra money. Then he believed that if God wanted/allowed it, he would get what he wished for, (now the Wheeler theory applies).

He headed to the bar, he felt like it was his second home. He always thought of his customers as some dysfunctional characters. But they were his base, the mixing bowl of including all people, regardless of race, sexual orientation, rich or poor. That's what made this club work!

He was greeted by anxious and thirsty crowd at the door. His style was never to open Randevu bar before 9 pm on Sunday. Sometimes he would see taxis circling around to find his place. The simple way to advertise was two sided blue and white square signs on the street. He would place two heavy plants on top of the base, so no heavy wind could overturn it. Many irregular or new customers would complain that it was hard to find his place, but once they found it, they were happy and content. They were like lost kittens who finally found the mother cat. One of his somewhat regular patrons was Phil, a lawyer, of forty plus, chubby-friendly looking dirty blonde man.

Lawyer Phil: "The cigars are good but the show here is better than ever!" he pointed at the long legged mixed beauty Eva, she looked Spanish, but in reality she was a nice mulatto lady. Her signature was fish net panty hoses on top of black stilettos, and her long black hair was falling on short upper torso with perfect breasts and her tiny waist above perfect shaped hips.

Lawyer Phil: "I am buying this lady a drink!" he waved toward Eva. She accepted it and they did strike up a conversation.

Eva: "I haven't seen you here! Are you local or a tourist?"

Lawyer Phil: "I am local; I work in downtown, DC." He was enjoying his cigar, Grand Marnier, and the fishnet beauty, near 6 feet, twenty-eight years old.

Jim: "I see you are making friends here!" He was seeing that often at the bar.

Lawyer Phil: "I hope this place last forever, cheers!" he lifted his glass, so did Eva, who was getting uptight. She was maybe willing to get a free drink, but no long drawn out conversations.

Jim: "Tell that to the police." He thought to complain about Officer Macallan, but he stopped short...

Eva: "Phil, you seem like a nice guy, but I need to get to work, you know what I mean?" she opened and closed her long legs coming down from the bar rotating chair.

Lawyer Phil: "Ok, I will drive you to anywhere you want."

He winked at Jim. "I will be back." Both of them knew he was not coming back.

Although nobody was talking about sex, that was happening outside the bar. The code of silence was well orchestrated by Jim. He would never get into personal conversations with anyone about the ladies or the Johns, or he never talked to or about the pimps. He was the envy of the Police and they felt impotent trying to catch him doing something illegal. And they never did. Was he lucky? No. Was he smart? Yes. It was complexed formula to follow and reminded him of FORTRAN computer programming he studied the last year in the Naval Academy (later they named it "Naval war college." Does not Naval mean war? What dummies are Bulgarians?) FORTRAN is programmed in a way to give you specific answer, "yes" or "no."

Jim's name was the nightmare for the government officials, so was his style of doing business.

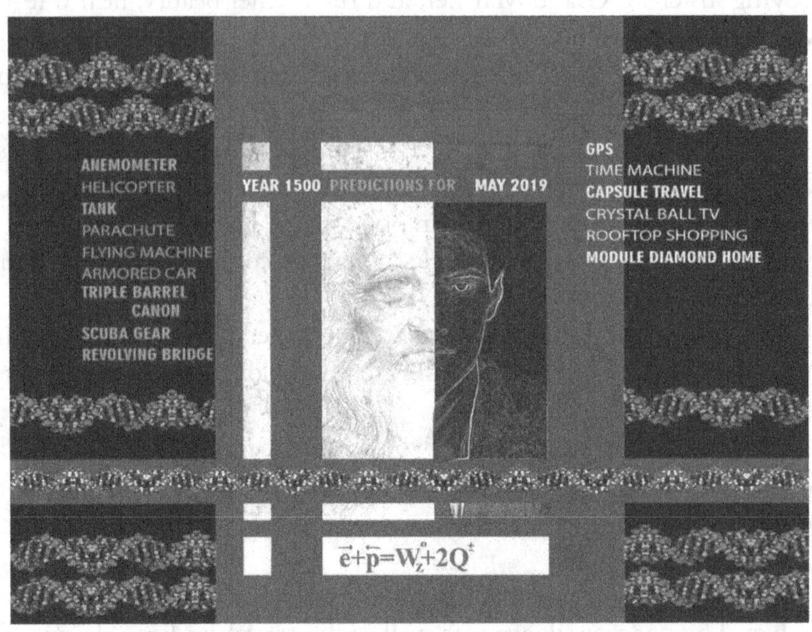
ANEMOMETER
HELICOPTER
TANK
PARACHUTE
FLYING MACHINE
ARMORED CAR
TRIPLE BARREL CANON
SCUBA GEAR
REVOLVING BRIDGE
YEAR 1500 PREDICTIONS FOR MAY 2019
GPS
TIME MACHINE
CAPSULE TRAVEL
CRYSTAL BALL TV
ROOFTOP SHOPPING
MODULE DIAMOND HOME
$\overrightarrow{e}+\overleftarrow{p}=W_z^0+2Q^{\pm}$

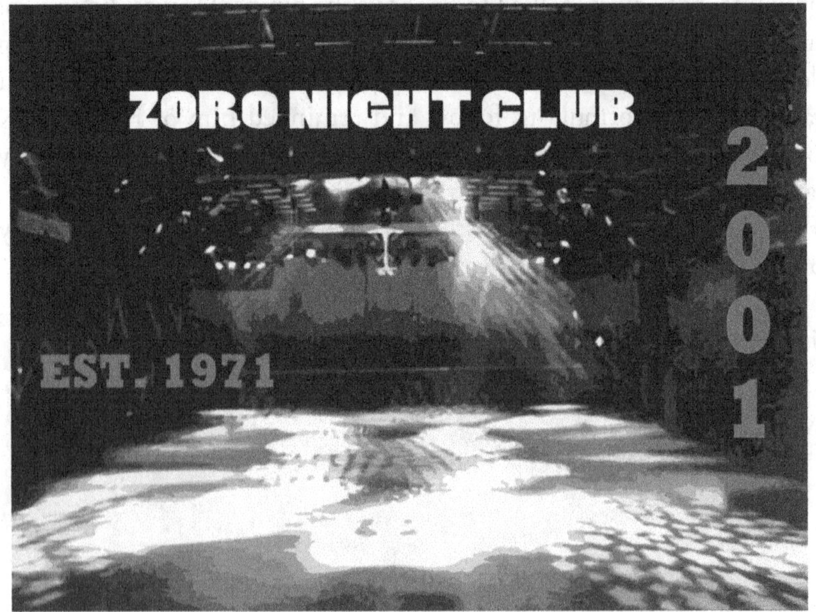
ZORO NIGHT CLUB
2001
EST. 1971

Chapter 2

While the odd couple was leaving other people were coming and leaving also. He noticed a slim overdressed short twenty-five year old Arab looking man.

Jim: "You dress well for Sunday night" he complimented the serious looking guy drinking scotch on the rocks.

Ali: "Oh, it is an Armani suit. I prefer Italian cuts." He spoke good English, knowing it was foreign to him.

Jim: "Where are you from?" Not the usual question he would ask, but he felt that he was one of the irregulars, so he moved forward.

Ali: "I am from Saudi Arabia." He was proud and he continued to smoke a Dunhill fancy cigarette. Jim observed nice silver framed with black mirrored face wrist watch Movado.

Jim: "Visiting or business?"

Ali: "Neither, I am a pilot. I fly Apache helicopters."

Jim: "For USAF, the Air Force?"

Ali: "No, I just graduated from the school. I will fly for my country." He had a demeanor of seriousness, while he was talking. Jim was surprised to hear that Saudi Pilot can fly top secret classified war machines? "Must be the alcohol talking here," he thought. He was used to fake attitudes around the bar. He would have forgotten this man, but, history would not. Two days later he saw Ali's face on TV. He was one of the nineteen hijackers who flew jumbo airplanes at New York World Trade Center towers and at The Pentagon!

Monday September 10th, Jim headed to the bank. He deposited 22,000 dollars in the account. He started to make phone calls to sound people, to construction people, to plumbers and to carpet installers. The answers were vague when he used The Yellow Pages. Some of them listed were out of business, some sounded busy, some were too expensive, and some were sounding like they were sleepy! He started to make appointments at the new club Zoro. The first one was for ADT security systems. "If I could install my sound system and buy the liquor I need a great alarm system first," he thought. Later on he would invest around 150,000 dollars in the next six months; just the liquor inventory was around $60,000. Some of the money came from Randevu bar and from the $14,000 refund from his deposit at 1115A Street, the original Zoro night club.

The sound he requested was from the new Guitar Center, previously known as Venaman music center in Rockville, Maryland. His account with them was dated first in 1987, when he purchased his 2400 Macrotech Crown amplifiers. Now fifteen years later they were to help him restart his sleeping DJ production, but in his own club. Jim was disappointed in not finding his old salesman. "He moved to Chuck Levin's, music on Veir's mills Road in Wheaton, MD" the young "guitar man" said.

Then he made a call to Achim Nikias, his lawyer.

Jim: "I got the keys and some promoters to work with. Now I need my deposit from Antonio Barros." They laughed.

Nikias: "I already talked to him. We can get it in the next few days." He sounded positive.

Jim: "Hopefully he did not spend it?" saying it with a little trepidation.

Nikias: "They are still selling condominiums; I hope they will give your money back." He was positive and convincing.

Jim: "Mr. Bender is fair at business, but, mean when comes to collecting money, I heard."

Nikias: "I will let you know as soon as the check comes, bye now." They both hung up.

The evening was uneventful. Mansur was working behind the counter. Jim was telling him about the club, "and if he wanted to invest in it?"

Mansur: "We have more problems now. We don't need to create more problems somewhere else, young man! I would like to see it, but I will think about it."

Jim: "I can take you there now. I don't have to open early today. My happy hour is almost nonexistent here. You know my business starts after you leave." Traffic was light around 8 pm and soon they were there, within fifteen minutes.

Mansur: "This place is too big," looking at the two story dormant monster club. At 12,000 square feet inside and about 2,000 square feet of parking area outside it was impressive for anyone.

Jim: "One needs high speed here to cover that area on a busy night." He was showing him the six bars, and the second floor office.

Mansur: "Do you have a kitchen? Any good refrigerators you don't need?" He was asking the weirdest questions.

Jim: "I think you should be helping me here, not the other way around?" He thought what irony was that, Mansur was asking him for equipment?

On the way back to Mike's/Randevu the two men were having an honest talk.

Mansur: "You see Jim. We are in trouble again. The construction guy who helped me initially, (Sarkisian), is asking for his balance of money I owe him."

Jim: "How much?" He took the I-395 North exit. The Benz was happier on the highway.

Mansur: "Just 8,000 dollars."

Jim: "Listen Mansur. From day one you always think I owe you money and I had felt the pressure to pay for a new ice machine, to fix your hours of liquor sales, to hire a lawyer and pay for it, to absorb the Police harassment and to deal with the trashy crowd on X Street and to act like everything is normal and to keep paying half the rent, insurance and improvements."

Mansur: "Young man. I took you under my wing poor and now you are opening a club! You are doing great! Now I need to stop Sarkisian from a lawsuit."

Jim: "I see we are on two separate paths in life."

Mansur: "If you don't like it, you can leave the bar. I can always find someone else to partner with."

Jim: "If I did not know you any better, this sounds like a threat?" He laughed of the nerve of Mansur. "I will keep the bar, regardless of my opening the Zoro.

Mansur: "I wish you luck, bye, don't forget I need help!" he said it humbly yet with a little anger. Jim was getting used to beggars of any kind in DC like Mansur, Mr. Bender, and Nikias. Almost anyone whom he met needed something. Although this young man was grateful to Mansur for giving him the break in life, he also felt he was being used. He thought Mansur's behavior was quite similar to the pimps he disliked at Randevu. The more they were meeting and talking, the more the distance and the deeper the division between them grew. The phenomenon of jealousy can't be ignored. Through the human history that part of any vertebrate living body had this stigma of inadequacy. The ten year war at Troy, the hate between the families of Romeo and Juliet, the battle for the heart of queen Cleopatra and most tragedies depicted in operas like Othello or Carmen; all of that drama pertaining to jealousy. Here in this Roman Empire reflective small town, called Washington, DC, the jealousy does not stop there. It is the beginning of action, and usually a wrong action. The entire life of Jim was fighting and wining against that phenomenon. That whole story is how to win against inadequacy of one's opponents. That includes whole society, starting with his brother, then his partner, then his own lawyer, then The Police Department, then the ABRA, then FBI, then the Washington Post, and then the Channel 7 TV. What is left, he wondered that wasn't bias and against him? Oh, don't exclude the other two club owners in town at this time; Mr. Dodson and Rogbin.

Jim dropped Mansur at Mike's/ Randevu and parked the car nearby. The bar was filling up slowly and with usual characters. Some of them were blue color workers, like Amine, the HVAC guy, or the Monaem, the F&B manager at Sofitel hotel. At 11.30 pm like clockwork the bar got fully packed. The music videos were playing and the crowd was happy. The human wave around the bar would stretch hands every now and then with empty glasses to refill, with money in their hands to pay the bar tab, to request cigars, to change the music and to see the "brown book." The ladies of the night varied from eighteen years old like Diamond and Essence, to Tear Drop and Crystal in their mid 20's, and veterans like Heather, Holly and Tyra at around forty. Some of the names were made up, some names were real, but the attitude was the same -- to get money, to catch men. The formula in was the same other clubs were using, "keep some women around the bar, the men will come." If the women are ready to date, that would be even better.

Jim was talking to some of the patrons. The night seemed normal and no Police bothered him. Maybe their attention was preoccupied with investigating all the wrong leads to solve the Chandra Levy's mystery disappearance? He was serving drinks and the ladies were relaxing. He was wondering if that Sarkisian suit was real. He did not see any papers to prove that? Was the envy of him opening the new club factored in this sudden demand? Maybe Mansur was trying to increase the rent? Maybe he was having someone else talking to him and he was thinking to kick him out? They really never signed any agreement and any sublease. So, he felt his staying at the club was really week to week. The irony of life would be that "week to week," would last ten years; while his 2x10 year leases lasted much less. Maybe the theory of creation was working in reverse in big projects? The life expectancy of bigger clubs is always much shorter than smaller clubs in DC. The patrons would say it is because of greed! Yes, they are somewhat correct? In fact greed it is not limited to the owners, who were trying just to pay the rent and a hopefully to make a little profit, greed is mixed with envy that is the worse manifestation of government corruption. That is not a theory; that is real fact in DC.

He closed the bar uneventfully and headed home. He was flipping through TV channels and enjoying the great Nakamichi sound system, enjoying the look of AKAI open real decks and the newly invested Video camera, the JVC 700KY, a D9 digital-S camcorder was a three-chip, industrial TV studio camera, newly bought at around $20,000. At this time, that was a lot of money. He was prepared to start his club, but he needed more sound. He got the sound for one floor, but not all floors. Only time will tell how things will go. He was tired, but optimistic ...for him the glass was always "half full"!

At 10.15 am Tuesday 09/11/2001 the phone rang.
Lora: "Are you watching TV?

Jim: "No, I am asleep... What is wrong with you?" he was about to hang up.

Lora: "Watch New York news. They hit the towers." She sounded surprised and truly shocked.

Jim: "What towers? I am going back to sleep, bye." Thinking to hang up, he decided to listen for five more seconds.

Lora: "They hit the Pentagon also, the terrorists!" She was crying.

Jim: "I do not care about Pentagon or any towers, bye!" He hung up. "People will not let me sleep, damn it." He went back into a deep sleep, but not for long. At 11.30 am the cell phone lit up again. This time Jim was more alert and he was about to get angry.

Jim: "Hello!" his answer was angry.

Michael: "Jim, are you ok?" His father from Bulgaria sounded concerned.

Jim: "Papa, I answered the phone," he was laughing at the tone that people were calling him with.

Michael: "Oh, ok! I am watching the news, USA is under attack."

Jim: "Listen, papa! I don't watch and don't trust what I see on TV. Why do you?" he gave his father a little confidence with that statement, besides being alive. "…And the Pentagon is 12 kilometers away from here, ok?" laughing.

Michael: "Ok, ok. Call me once in a while, son. Better than that, come see us, please! You have been away for quarter century!"

Jim: "I am opening my second nite-club. I may do that after it gets established a bit."

Michael: "Ok, we have our faith in you."

Jim: "I know and I need to focus and make it work, but I have many obstacles and enemies, dad."

Michael: "Son, you did decide to leave Bulgaria on your own, you do everything by yourself, you will succeed, I will pray for you, Jim, my dear son!"

Jim: "Yes, but you make me weak, when there are emotions involved." He almost started sobbing.... "Let me go. If I succeed or fail, it is based on my decision and effort, but sometimes the enemies are organized too well and even miracle workers like me can lose."

Michael: "If your consciousness lets you think the result is what benefits you and you can sleep at night then you are doing the right thing. Good bye."

Jim: "You sound like the famous warrior who said "the result justifies the means," and seems like you are agreeing with my decision to defect in 1980?"

Michael: "I don't approve, and you never asked me. But it seems everything you touch or think does work for you so far. Like being captain, owner of your own business. The only concern of mine is you need to get married soon. I need grandchildren from you, my smart son!"

Jim: "Yes, Caesar, easy to ask, difficult to promise and impossible to do. American women tend to only value money and benefits and no brainy man, like me. I guess I make them insecure in DC? New York women are probably better, also California women are better. How to marry without higher requirements? That is the question?"

Michael: "Maybe a Bulgarian woman can be a better match. They are poor, but smart and healthy!"

Jim: "I will see you soon. Stop worrying about me and let me be myself."

Michael: "Ok, son! Hope everything turns out the way you want it! See you soon. Bye!"

Jim: "Bye, dad. Say to my brother and my stepmother best wishes. Bye!" He hung up and started crying. "How in the world do I only have four friends, God only knows!" In terms of the lack of friends, that one can have…he was a lucky man in many ways.

He thought of his brother, father, Lora (whom he didn't like), and Tavit, (the IT man). During the conversation he started to flip between the channels. Every channel was showing the worried faces of TV hosts and hostesses with the same background, the burning towers before their implosion. Then they were talking about another plane heading towards DC, the Nation's Capital. They were showing the pictures of nineteen hijackers, mostly from Saudi Arabia. Jim jumped somewhere in the middle of the chat with his father and started recording. Just two days before he was talking to the Saudi Arabian man Ali that America was invincible, being protected by two oceans, the Pacific and the Atlantic. Who was insane enough to attack the most powerful nation on earth? The pictures were changing from the firefighters in the burned buildings at World Trade Center One and Two, to eyewitness accounts, to Pentagon officials who lost their lives, to White House evacuations. Seemed the chaos was taking over the best organized capitalist country in the world. Jim was not too much concerned with any terrorist attacks. After he hung up the phone, he realized that what was directly important to him? The new club, he just signed the lease for was in his mind, not the Pentagon, not the White House, not the World Trade Center, and not the Capitol Hill losers.

Nobody ever invited him to any military parade, to any barbecue picnic, to Capitol Hill parties. He felt more related to the Twin Towers' victims, where just seventeen years before he was having drinks with Contessa at Windows of the World restaurant on top of the World Trade Center One. They were surrounded then with young mid-twenties yuppies who were only talking about money. Now they were waving from windows and jumping from the 100th floor, screaming. Yes, Nostradamus was right in his predictions, but he was off by six years and four months. It was supposed to happen May, 1995).

If the Mayans are wrong about Dec. 21st, 2012, then the same error will place the end of the world at May 21st, 2019, something to think about, right….?

Now at 1 pm he decided to check on his investments. He grabbed his US Passport and headed toward Randevu first, which was on X Street. He did not go inside. The building was still standing, untouched by any terrorists.

"Where are all the zealous and perverted Police and vice clowns to protect the city? It is easy to harass foreign born US citizens and hookers and pimps, dear Officer Bolton, Tobias, Morrey, is it not? Why with not the same vigor you couldn't protect the Pentagon, the President or the Towers, you idiots?" Jim thought.

He took H Street eastbound and made a right turn on 6th Street, heading south. He observed empty streets everywhere he turned. He was happy that The Element, a two story club was still there at G Street on his right side and The Rock, a three story pub with billiards was still there on his left side. He was driving slowly. He did not see any Police cars passing him by or any passengers or commercial vehicles. This was usually a busy, hustling corner, the future home of Verizon's event convention and sports center. He couldn't see anybody around the DCFD engine # 2, a fire fighting center on 6th and E was empty of fire trucks and personnel. The doors were open and he saw one man with a blue uniform with a puzzled look on his face who exchanged glances with Jim. "What is going on?" was written on their expressive faces, like a Jason's masked face from the movie, "Friday, the 13th." (The killer with the chainsaw may be funny then, but not funny now).

Jim remembered all his Navy training in the Old Bulgarian Naval Academy (the new "Naval War College,"). If that attack had happened there, all highways and exits from and towards the city would have been restricted by check points! Nothing like that was happening here. The USA was unprepared for an attack like this and was basically paralyzed. Except for the White House and Capitol Hill no plans for civilian population evacuation were enforced. God forbid if the terrorist had used the biochemical or nuclear devices for mass destruction! Where would people go and hide? Shaking his head, Jim drove by the Police Headquarters at 300 Indiana Avenue and the DC Supreme Courthouse nearby. No activities, everything was asleep. He turned into 3rd Street underpass leading toward South Capitol Street and toward his new club Zoro at 1824 Half Street, SW. Within five minutes he was facing his location. This time he entered the club. He climbed to the roof. The hatch was unsecured, just about anyone could hide there and enter from the roof 4 ft x 4 ft opening or exit through it. The buildings were connected and anybody can jump from roof top to roof top. Jim looked around for any signs of terrorists activities and couldn't find any? Next to him was an S&M club The Crucibles. It was a sex club without liquor license also, owned by Mr. Bender. All buildings were owned by him from S Street to T Street.

Jim was happy to see his business intact and after checking the floors and his office he slipped out relieved. "The triggers for Wars are on Capitol Hill and in the Pentagon and in the White House." The history tells about Pearl Harbor. The FDR knew about it, but he didn't take precautions to stop the attack. The news was screaming the name Bin Laden. Then Jim thought and connected the dots.

"Follow the money, young Man!" was his motto. The history tells that the relationship of George H. Bush, the 41st president of USA and Bin Laden went back to 1977, when he was ambassador to China. The Bin Laden's family was one of the highest regarded in Saudi Arabia. The father of Bin Laden had open-door to access to the ruling Palace at any time without appointment. His construction business was so big and his political connections were so strong, he was considered one of the top families in the country. When someone needed construction done in the area, they would refer it to Bin Laden. USA military signed many contracts with this powerful Arab man, including the construction of the military barracks in Lebanon. Bush, the senior was in the picture at many high level meetings. Logically Bin Laden saw his connections very valuable and he went beyond the customary government contracts.

Bush: "Hey, Bin Laden! I am trying to open my oil business in Gulf of Mexico, and I may need some help?" he asked. Being ex CIA officer, he knew how to throw a hook to adversaries. He never liked the Arabs, but they had money and that was his only interest.

Bin Laden: "I don't build oil rigs." He acted offended, but he liked the interest. He smelled the trap, but he wouldn't grab the bait.

Bush: "No, this is not a construction favor as usual. I need a loan, a big loan."

Bin Laden: "I have the capital, but I will need a favor too." He was seeing an opportunity to advance his own agenda. In his own way of thinking he felt more powerful when people, especially Americans, were asking him for favors.

Bush: "500 million to start my oil exploration in the Gulf."

Bin Laden: "Wow, I am rich, but I am not a stupid banker. And even if I was a bank, I'd need some guarantee in some collateral."

Bush: "How about next twenty years I will give you US government contracts? Not only will I repay you, but you will triple or quadruple your 500M."

Bin Laden: "I will think on it and I will give you my word within a week. I will not pay you directly. I will create a Bank in Texas just for you. Then they will not know I am behind the scenes. So, let me talk to a few of my friends." That day, SNL was born. Savings and loan association, which would lose 800 million in people's investments! Also, the baseball team Bush junior will buy would lose money. Where did the money go?

The relationship between the Bush and the Bin Laden families was bumpy. After the 165 US soldiers were killed in Lebanon, the relationship between USA and Saudi Arabia deteriorated. Some people blamed it on terrorists' organizations, but if you look about US foreign policy and everything going on in Central America and the Middle East, nobody should exclude the involvement of Bush connections in cocaine shipments to the streets in Los Angeles and Washington, DC. Do not forget the freedom fighters in Nicaragua that Reagan supported but not the Congress, the Iran-Contra scandal where tow missiles were traded for cash to support the freedom fighters. And Oliver North had to call the Congressmen and Senators to start moving their fat asses and to vote to approve the bills to spread Democracy in Central America. Also, to implement the Monroe Doctrine,

(document of European Colonial nonexpansion in Central America since year 1823). Sounds great until Cuba and Venezuela came into the picture, where the ideology, not the colonial powers were anti American and obviously communist.

Senator John Tower said: "Because of this mix of cocaine for dollars, dollars to buy tow missiles, missiles to be sold to Iran via Israel, cash from Iran to support the "freedom fighters," all of this to circumvent the US congress and the constitution Oliver North, Admiral Poindexter, Secretary of Defense, Gaspar Weinberger and chief of CIA Bill Casey even the President of USA were implicated in the constitutional fraud."

They testified to Congress with, "I can't recall" phrases. Reagan would agree that out of three shipments to Israel he approved only one, thinking it was arms to Israelis, not to Iran, to help release hostages in Lebanon. Some of them lost their lives, some of them lost their jobs, nobody lost his freedom because Bush senior pardon them all at the end of his presidency. The irony for Jim was that because of Bush cocaine game and Eric Holder's "catching and detaining the biggest drug dealer that ever was Rayful Edmonds," he was able to date his girlfriend Nina mentioned earlier on. That was Jim's version of events.

In 1993 some eight months after he lost his reelection against Bill Clinton, Bush senior headed to Saudi Arabia to pay off his outstanding loan to Bin Laden's father. Some would say not paying his loans on time made Bin Laden order the hit on the army base in 1983 at Beirut,

Lebanon, killing 241 soldiers. Hezbollah took responsibility, but who paid for the 12,000 lbs of TNT? The second non payment caused the first attempt of topping off The World Trade Center in February of 1993. Bush was not only out of power as President, but also out of money. It is too coincidental that a year after Bush leaves The White House (in 1992) the WTC becomes a target again? Seems Bin Laden runs out of patience. FBI would blame a blind man of giving orders? Does Bush owe him money too?

The April visit at the Kuwait University by Bush, was to meet with Bin Laden. CIA would make a report that Iraqi plotted the whole assassination attempt. The true story was that Bush had arranged a meeting with Bin Laden to pay off his debt and to stop any terrorist attacks on Americans and American Landmarks. The airplane with all the Secret Service security that was assigned to ex President Bush takes off with Bin Laden on board.

Bin Laden: "Where is Bush?" he shouts, seeing the trap closing in on him.

Secret Service man: "He will meet you later!" He knew that was a lie too.

Ten minutes later the bomb explodes and the plane with this powerful Arab man and everybody aboard gets killed. The revenge of President Clinton is directed toward Sadam Husain, the Iraqi President. Twenty-three tomahawk missiles are showering Bagdad. Two flight attendants in hotel lobby are killed. Out of sixteen Bin Laden children one decided to fight Americans everywhere he can see them, but he preferred large targets; like navy ships, embassies and eventually he will destroy the Towers in NYC on September 11th, 2001.

The intelligence during the Clinton Administration will look the other way, but under tremendous pressure it will reveal Bin Laden name, but not his true motives. They will say it is because the "war on jihad," Muslims against non believers, against non converters... hmm... Instead of taking the truth that is family feud, the Muslims were convinced that it is religious war. When one with tremendous capital like Bin Laden starts a war of faith, he can coach young people to board planes full of jet fuel to crash kamikaze style into anything. "Yes, 40 virgins are waiting for you in Heaven!" Bin Laden would say.

Jim was not a politician, he was not historian, and he was not a leader to million dollar fellowship church. He probably would be remembered in the history books as the loneliest man in the universe, like he counted four of his lifelong true friends, two of them were his blood relatives.

Was he unattractive, was he damned, was he from some disadvantage race, did he have an offensive disease, was he an underachiever, was he living in a remote and hard to find town, was he without transportation, was he bald, fat or cripple, was he unfriendly, introverted, was he selfish, was he a bad dresser, was he someone who had bad odor, was he sexually repulsive, was he educationally challenged, was he using old equipment, was he speaking one language, that couldn't be understood, was he a religious fanatic, did he have an STD, was he gay, was he mentally and physically unstable, was he limited to one business, was he unfair, a cheater, was he a pedophile, polygamist, killer, dating married women, poor, a pimp, a false prophet, drug dealer, mafia, arms dealer, slave owner, racist, a gambler and finally an alcoholic. To all of the above, the answer is a resounding – no!

Then what is the problem, America?

When they asked Churchill "Why do you like history?"

Churchill: "I wrote it!"

When they ask Jim: "Why do you write history?"

Jim: "To explain it."

The evil crowd: "Why do you need to explain it? Is it not better to read it and accept it the way it is? You can't change it or reverse it, or improve it? Who do you think you are, Jesus, God, and a messenger?"

Jim: "I am what you are trying to be, 99 per centers? I told you what I am not first. Now tell me how many have my record? Show me your hands, in the air, be honest, anybody? And you are here to judge me? And I bet every one of you thinks you are better than me! Why? Where? How? No, no. Do not get angry with me. Get angry at yourself! Because if I tell you who I am, where I come from, what I do, how I did it, what are my goals and what I have achieved, you would have two choices. First; you would want to be me. Second; you would run out of this door or you would commit suicide."

Evil crowd: "So, you think you are better than us and we are the 99 percent losers?" booing his analogy.

Jim: "I never said I am better than anyone. I say I am different than you. I am in competition with myself. What I have done in my fifty-four years of living is a text book of most people's wish list.... depends on your drive, ambition and ability. Yet, basically it is all about, what an individual wants to do with his/her life? It does vary."

Evil crowd: "Jesus had goals in life too; things to accomplish and they killed him."

Jim: "Who killed him, the Jews and non-believers? The envious, non-believing crowd cheered his death. Those who worshiped him still cherish him today. What does that tell you about the scared hypocritical crowd?"

The Evil crowd: "We are more educated and aware of who is like us and who our leader is."

Jim: "Having an I-phone or Blackberry does not make you any better!

I bet in Jesus' times, they had scrolls. Everyone in the crowd thought Jesus was nothing but a charlatan, manipulator and they believed the Jewish tribes of government were doing the right thing by punishing Jesus on the cross?"

Evil crowd: "Ok, tell us why we should believe you and be like you?" They finally started to listen.

Jim: "Then you should read my book!"

Evil crowd: "Ok. Be brief, to the point. We will read this book. Tell us in ten words who are you?" anxious, curious and yet skeptical.

Jim felt like Moses and the writing of the 10 commandments and entering some weird Dating Game. Yet, he had to be heard. It was not to brag, but to reaffirm his legacy! He couldn't allow his name to be recognized as many before him, only after his death! He quickly briefed them on his achievements – education, adventures in faith programming, holistic health, club opening and restaurant owner with money excluded, his winnings against any governments mind games, e.t.c. ...

1. Education: Master's Naval Academy, Bulgaria in 1980.
2. Sports: Black Belt Judo/Karate, yoga, running, gymnastics, swimming...

3. Achievements: Master of an Ocean going Ship at age 26, 5 DC restaurants and clubs owner, speaking 5 languages.
4. Licenses: Realtor, Bartender, Lincoln Tech, Food/Alcohol.
5. Presentation: GQ, 6 ft, NYC modeling, actor in movie "Broadcasting news."
6. Attitude: Outgoing, people person, 30 year fine dining.
7. Health: Excellent, teaching others to improve themselves.
8. Arts: Established "Walker's Media" in 1988, 40 videos produced.
9. Alternative sciences: research in health, astro physics, quantum mechanics, dark matter and upgraded it for next 1000 years.
10. Sex life: Popular with most available women, and many partners.

Evil Crowd: "All the things noted in this manuscript that you have done in one single life, huh! Yes, we bow to you, great man! Now, please write the manuscript. Hurry! The manuscript which will encompass health and science, for the next 1000 years, that is a serious statement. What are you talking about?"

Jim: "I am referring to 100 year old science here: theory of relativity, gravitational theory and quantum mechanics and health implementation. Once someone has health, the success in business will follow. Like the Romans say, "strong spirit is in a strong body."

Jim will say, "A smart and successful spirit in an aware body." To succeed is to know your strong points and your weaknesses, and the weaknesses are to be improved constantly only if you are aware of them.

How does one know what their weaknesses are?

First. Observe your heritage. See how your parent behave and look? Unfortunately we can't just say "I look and behave like my father!" The nature changes the code by involving a second person, your mother. The two people will create a better survival code for next generational, evolution.

Second. Observe yourself in the mirror everyday you wake up. Do you like who you see? People will see you the way you present yourself. If you think there is something within your powers to change and improve your image, do it before someone criticizes you.

Three. Exit your door and enter the street and outside world like a winner already, like man or woman ready to be complimented. People will notice your great attitude quicker than your anger; most people are negative, stiff, and angry. A smiling person is like sunshine in a dark room.

Fourth. Always have business cards in your pocket. In life only two or three people will check your ID, Police Officer or bar manager, but your business card will be checked constantly by people who you interact with every day.

Fifth. Don't look for jobs all the time. Once you find a great one try to maximize it. Have an updated resume handy but do not show it around. People get insecure around achievers.

Sixth. Try to diversify your interests and knowledge. A person with licenses is better than someone with just an opinion!

Seventh. When people give you money it is not because of the work you've done, but because of your knowledge. Insist to get respect, before you get money. You will create dependants quicker that way. Person with money can pay anyone, why they should choose you?

Eight. Teach before you make someone look small and unimportant. Always tell your students, "I want you to challenge me and argue you point with me. Not just agree with me! It will make you a better student. Eventually, I want you to be better than me. Most good teacher's goal is just that. Bad teachers do not want you to be better than them. That way bad teacher can control you instead of educating you.

Nine. You need freedom. Have your phone, car, place to live without someone else to co-pay.

Ten. Make one person happy, starting with yourself first and along with seeking the truth about you, honestly. If you can't do that, it's not worth the effort of being alive. You're just taking up space on earth!

Jim left the Club Zoro at Half Street, SW. He collected his thoughts. He was relieved that his business survived but he sensed the dark cloud approaching this great and evil city. These people here are not afraid to kill their own. He remembered senator John Tower, who died in April 1991, after his famous, Tower Report. Bush Sr. left his post as President and pardoned his Republican friends from Iran Contra affair in 1992. Why should they be nice to foreigners now? Like clock work Bush junior announced seizing assets of about 60 billion in USA who financed the terrorist abroad. Next day, Hogates restaurant on waterfront in SW was closed forever. They said it was a front for Al Qaeda financing.

Jim remembered his neighbors spreading rumors about him and his partner Mansur at Randevu, bar and that was some three years before. He was not concerned what Marsha, the bartender at Starlight was gossiping about, while drunk. He was more concerned of whom she was talking to? Being new on the block, he was against a total of 100 years combined restaurant experience of his neighbors. Not only did he slow down their revenues, but he was expanding to a new location.

The news was bad for the next three days. They counted the "collateral damage" at the sites. At the World Trade Center there were around 3,000 people, at the Pentagon 200 and in Pennsylvania 165 people lost their lives. They were showing pictures of the nineteen hijackers. Jim's jaw dropped when he recognized Ali, the Armani wearing suit Saudi Arabian guy, he chatted with on Sunday. He remembered him bragging about Flying Apache helicopters. Jim did not believe him, he thought of him being drunk. The television host was explaining how they got their training in Florida at an Aviation School in Computer Simulators. The Boeing, cockpit was showing them how to fly, but not how to take off or land the airplane? The news was talking about a Boeing 747, taking off from Dulles Airport toward California, but it was diverted toward Capitol Hill. There was probably a fight on the plane and the terrorist Ali, probably directed it towards the Pentagon, flying low above National Airport in a circle to the puzzled residents below.

Jim was in quiet mood. He learned from the previous experience with the security computer he came across, not to contact authorities (even if they were offering $25,000.00 reward). The less visibility to the outside world in DC the longer one would stay in business or would stay alive! Later on Tim Russet would lose his life over a whistle blower scandal, with CIA agent Valerie Plame, in the year of 2008. Jim saw the whole commercial trade in DC was on hold. Bush was talking to New Yorkers through a bull horn that no crime like that would stay unpunished, while the demolition crews were cutting metal and rescuing crews were still looking for survivors. Other buildings around TWC were considered structurally unsafe and they needed to be demolished. Surprisingly there were survivors after so many days of horror. One thirty-one year old mixed race lady was found in the rubble! She would marry her boyfriend later after her recovery.

Jim thought of calling Amanda, but he did not want to. He knew that his anger of six months before was the cause of TWC collapse. He remembered that mid March 2001 his last glance at the greatest capitalist city in the world was towards Battery Park and the Twin Towers! Same buildings he saw first when the old Greek ship "St. Nikolas" was approaching New York Harbor in 1980, on Thanksgiving Day. His asylum was approved next day and he was issued I 94 form and Social Security within a week. Now, 21 years later his first memories were razed by some planes with terrorists. He thought of the process it took those relatively new buildings to topple? Just seventeen years ago he was enjoying drinks with Contessa on the roof top restaurant. Those were the best times, when he was a Captain, GQ dressed, had money, a lot of women around and somewhat connections with the top echelon people in the night life and next to Plaza Hotel. The owner of the club Allure gave him that first feeling of being in the position to have perks and of being in charge. All that would have been great if not for Contessa's assassination and Mr. Smith gay secrets. Then the perfect emotional storm started when Frida and Amanda moved in opposite directions on him. That anger at Amanda was the gravitational wave Jim was able to create to complete the task, terrorists like Bin Laden have been attempting for a decade. The story about God's creation and destruction applies here.

"God will bend you, but he will never break you; you break yourself." All the terrorists needed were a lucky break. They tried and tried to hurt the USA. To pick the date 9/11 was either genius or they were reading Nostradamus too well?

Jim's theory and experience was that life can push one so much until one starts reacting. The rulers and dictators, businesses and government do statistical analyses of how much they can push the masses or the individuals before they revolt, quit or move to another location. The government does that through taxes to suppress growth and through incentives to create growth. Every year congress is changing Tax Codes to put more money in the US Treasury. The Wall Street executives will go berserk trying to sell bonds, mutual funds, CD's, 401K, and any kind of way to fill up their pockets with tax sheltering games. While some investors can wait twenty years, some cannot. Then the crisis starts when too many sellers and few buyers crash the NYSE, DJI or NASDAQ. Bulls and Bears, Fortune 500, blue chips like, Exxon Mobile, Coca Cola, Phillip Morris, IBM, and Apple were always a low risk investment with great dividends, but the mystery here was investments were in insurance stocks, shortly before the WTC attack. Jim's theory in a strange way is to watch any sudden jump in any stocks buying. Maybe there would be a second/political motivation reason, besides the usual profit driven reason!

At this time driving back to his home there were all types of thoughts in Jim's mind. He did not blame himself for the TWC implosion. He was aware of his powers, now he was seeing them at work. What all the terrorists wanted was a legacy. Did he help them by provoking his subconscious God-like powers, creating the gravitational wave to push the Towers down?

This anger towards Amanda brought the whole city economy down. If that was a onetime event in his colorful life he would say, "Maybe it was just a coincidence?" But the sequence of many similar events the next ten years would prove his theory not delusional, but right. He would start earthquakes, tsunamis, hurricanes, floods on many occasions; he would put his rivals out of business or just like Mr. Baldwin and later on DP the Don, out of life!

Was he a "mental terrorist and mental creator" at the same time? He was aware of his God like powers, but his enemies were not. Sometimes he would warn them in advance what would happen to them, and dealing with the expected ignorance. Jim knew they would suffer eventually. His conscious was clear, that he warned them, so he slept well at night. How this works is to make the wish and to oppose it, then to forget it and to wait and see?

Here is the formula: Electron/negative charge meets positron/ positive charge = neutron/zero charge + 2quanta/energy. The Thought can be negative or positive to end with destruction/creativity, as long it is balanced with opposite at the same time.

That applies to religious fanatics too. Most people would say, "Bless you! God be with you. Be safe! I wish you well." Do they really mean it? Jim would doubt that. "When they tell you positive things, you think the opposite. When they challenge you, you prove them wrong!" The government is the biggest brainwasher. To keep you contained and to control you they invent institutions and programs. They are five sectors where most people are kept at: First: Education; School and Colleges. Second: Work places. Third: Military. Fourth: Church or in religious institutions; Fifth: Jail

Based on one's mental state he/she can find themselves in one of those institutions. How long one will survive there depends on how one uses his mind and its manifestation. Or do you want to be out of the box? Out of 320 million USA's population, 180 million were the registered work force, 3 million in the Armed Forces, 6 million in jail, 10 million in school system, 1 million in religious institutions, government regulators are 20 million, so where possibly, is the rest of the 100 million? The phantom US citizens, self employed, criminal element, kids before school, retired and old and ex patriots living out of the country. Control that, idiots!

Jim was wandering how to react to the new tragic situation? Since Pearl Harbor USA has not been under attack for sixty years! The whole economy had suddenly frozen. Everyone was scrutinized. The evacuation of all government buildings showed the one sided USA policy, to protect their own. Civilians did not count as valuable "collateral," looked like on this day of 09/2001 everyone was on his/her own. ANC members usually vocal in business applications and how to renew the licenses on their conditions, those cowards were nowhere to be found? Police harassers of businesses were nowhere to be found?

All the ABC Board and their inspectors were nowhere to be found. Vice squads, with their jump out, paddy wagons were missing. Jim thought at least business owners would be notified with some plan to evacuate. After all doesn't the government need tax collections from 1500 restaurant establishments in the city this month?

Jim put a VHS tape in the VCR to record that day. It was a textbook of chaos and a missing President and Vice President and the missing Chain of Command in the USA government.

Jim had read many books from Tom Clancy. Nothing even close to what was happening here. Where is Ryan, the hero to save the country?

Jim was debating shall he keep the lease? Is this reason valid, being; an "Act of God? Or, terrorism?" No traffic on the streets, no airplanes in the air, no assurance from the government who is placing Anthrax in the mail? Jim made a decision to wait till the weekend and see if other clubs are going to be open for business? Then he would stop the $24,000 dollar check, or let it go through?

He went to Phantom night club, his rival club. He was hoping to meet the owner Mr. Rogbin who he shared a lawyer with, the famous Achim Nikias. What a surprise? The line to enter was half a block long. He did not need to wait at all. He identified himself as a club owner and asked to meet the Manager Jai Mallory, whom he met two months ago, while he was looking for a construction company for his club at 1115A U Street, NW. She was friendly and she introduced him to her contractor Xuan. He talked to him and he (Xuan) turned out to be very unreasonable and expensive. So, the doormen were not hesitant to let him in. Jim acted like an owner, he looked like an owner. The usual ritual at the door was exchanging business cards.

Alain Kalantar: "Nice to meet you, I am VIP coordinator." He led him through the door.

Jim: "I own Randevu bar, at 1426 X Street, but my next club is in South West, Zoro.

Alain Kalantar: "I will open my own club soon; maybe we can coordinate the future events in DC?" Later on he would partner with David Karim, a mixed martial arts champion, who opened Josephine's, Lost Society, Current with some LLC investors. He was friendly and he showed Jim around. The DJ Basaam Haddad was the resident DJ and Eddy S. was the Bar Manager.

The place was full with about 1,000 people. Basement had two separate videos rooms and two bars, with low ceilings and dark, smelly unventilated corridors. The main floor had a mirrored stage with two poles and regular crowd was dancing around them. It was mostly stripper want to-be ladies. Jim climbed up the second floor, which was basically an all around terrace. Open space connected the main floor to the roof. It reminded him the way his own bar/lounge was built with an open space between 2nd and 3rd floors. Jim bought a drink, the usual Single Malt neat and he offered Alain one. He declined and disappeared in the crowd, probably went out to the street?

This new club owner was observing the crowd. It was 99% white and nobody was older than twenty-five. They were dancing to Hip Hop and R&B music. Life goes on…. They did not care that 9/11 just leveled buildings and scared the hell out of New Yorkers, who were waiting for something to happen to George Washington Bridge, to Lincoln or the Holland Tunnel. And here the DC party scene was out of touch with the rest of the country. Ignorance can be rewarding, only to people who do not value life and dignity! If it was his first day in DC, Jim would have screamed from the balcony, "Stop the music! Get out of here, you ignorant idiots!" Yes, that would have been twenty years prior, when he believed he risked his life to escape to a better society. The true perversion of Democracy was revealing right in front of his eyes. They, the dancers, were "the Evil crowd," who were the ones to support you one Saturday and to abandon you the next Saturday. They would follow their promoter or just choose a new club? They would always look for something free or new R&B artist or some movie premiere, depending on what their social network would advertise. Sometimes they have DuPont Circle snow ball fights, in the spring time they have pillow fights at the National Monument ….go figure.

Jim thought, "Who I am kidding, I can't criticize them if I am opening a similar venue. I will exploit their stupidity. After all what brings them here, the alcohol to start, and always something else; drugs, sex and common interests!"

Jim: "God, what I am getting myself into?" He almost slapped himself. "God, do not let me become like them." He asked his sub consciousness …

He was cutting through the crowd. He tried to chat with some pretty ladies, but seemed they were too much into themselves, drinking, talking and dancing. Maybe if they knew him or he was a drug dealer they would have been friendlier, or some of them were just lesbians? Some, maybe, were concerned with his age, but at his bar Randevu they were not. So must be a social thing. "If you are not part of the clustered club group then you are considered an outsider and ignored." Later on, he would find that his status as club owner would change that, "group attitude," to his advantage. And there would be some defectors from "the group." He finally got out and felt the fresh air. There was a much smaller line. He shook a few hands in ritual small talk.

Doorman: "Did you like it?"

Jim: "It was great. I couldn't find Jai, or the owner. One thing, I was very surprised about was that we just had September 11th horrendous catastrophe and it seems nobody cares?" incredulously appalled.

Doorman: "This is not a government building! We do not close for things like that." What an answer. What does the government have to do with it, or with Democracy? Or it was pure greed!

Jim decided to keep the lease. He could have stopped the check, but he was tested and he knew that airplanes would fly again and banks would open on Monday. Nobody should stop the true capitalist machine from spinning and making money, The Great USA. Jim had nothing against Amanda or against the Evil crowd, (the Government and the dancing, ignorant citizens). He respected their functions, but he did not expect them not to do them correctly. Almost twenty years he had bad dreams about his Naval Academy, which took the best years of his young life, 17 to 22, but he always woke up and said "Thank God, I am here in the USA, and not in depressing Bulgaria." He considered this his new country and was supposed to be better than the one he escaped from. For him the USA was the lesser evil, not perfect, but still evil. Maybe being born in USA, Evil is normal?

The irony was that the first flight to Colorado by Fed Ex airplane delivered was his check to Mr. Bender, who suddenly stopped calling Jim, asking, "where is the check?" Regardless of Jim' instructions to wait two to three weeks, Mr. Bender's desperation was obvious! For the richest club owner in SE part of DC, who would make 60 million in the next five years from his $880,000 investment in 1988, that was obviously not good business, especially given the 9/11 situation. It said to Jim that money does not define the rich man in USA. It camouflages habits, desperation, and gangsterism.

Jim remembered all suppose to be rich men and women he came across in his turbulent life like Contessa, Mr. Smith, Marshall Coyne, Molly, Frida and her Mother, the Wall Street Investor, Yannek?

How come some of them acted so desperately cash poor? Except for Contessa and Frida, they basically were acting like haters. Is wealth hidden when there is no love? Jim was very trusting, loving, touchy person. Yes, the typical European most people would say. In business he was fair, but not stupid. He found himself between two landlords, Mr. Bender and Mansur. Mansur would cry constantly about his lawsuits, about shortage to pay rent. He was buying new cars, improving his house, helping his son to buy a condominium, but he was looking at Jim to help him out with licenses, insurance and the latest was that Sarkisan lawsuit. On the other horizon, Mr. Bender was expecting him to fix the twenty year old closed club, to get the license and to pay the rent and the property taxes. Was it worth it? Are the club owners so concerned about their ego and profit, that they would sacrifice everything, including their freedom?

While the rise of the three clubs competing owners in town, IRS had other plans. The same plans to close Mustang Ranch were to shut down anything Mr. Rogbin or Mr. Dodson and Jim would open the next ten years. The lying words of Jack Ronan would turn to harsh reality to Mr. Rogbin, Wesley Snipes, and the Mustang Ranch owner, who was hit with a 16 million IRS bill for unpaid taxes and he would flee the country to Brazil. Eventually his Ranch would be sold for $120,000 dollars ten years later. "Collect this.... IRS!"

Yes, the check went through. Now Jim was concentrating on getting his license and fixing the place. He needed plumbers, carpenters, new ice machine, new oven, new fire suppression system, new dance floor, new carpet, liquor supplier, HVAC check, office computer, sound system, roof repair, and two digital TV boxes. Yes, being the 3rd King in DC needed sacrifices….. No wonder no one touched that club for the last twenty-two years!

Chapter 3

The next day he was busy on the phone and started making appointments to fix the club Zoro. Towards mid-week Nikias called him to pick the red placard for the hearing date for his liquor license.

Nikias: "The location used to be great for a club in the early 70's. Buzzard's Point was the Headquarters for FBI and Coast Guard and a power plant, built in 1936, polluting the land with PCB (polychlorinated biphenyls).

Jim: "Hopefully the PCB will not affect my customers?"

Nikias: "ANC would not object to a spot like this. I don't think they even would want to drive by it. They rely on Police reports. You keep it quiet, you will last there forever!"

Jim: "Ok, let see what they will say at the hearing?"

Nikias: "I will see what I can do with the paper work. Interesting thing, your rival shows too much money in the bank, you show nothing -- $20,000?"

Jim: "Who is, Mr. Rogbin?"

Nikias: "I can't disclose who; attorney-client confidentiality."

Jim: "Mr. Rogbin, I know it." Both laughed and said good bye.

Jim did not know at this time that all club owners in DC were targeted, but only time would tell who would survive, "The Game?" He would find out that by showing less "Cash on hand," he would be scrutinized, but much less.

This manuscript is not a manual on how to become a club owner. It is written to show how one who gets involved in the DC club scene how to survive and come out without going to jail or to filing for bankruptcy. Or worse -- deportation! There are millions of young people in the USA and around the world with dreams and grand illusions on how to start and prosper in the restaurant and club lucrative business. Any promoter would give you ten points of advice on how to run your operation, just to get his/her 20% commission from the bar sales; or some weird door/bar sales cut. Why don't they ever open a club themselves? Do you know why? Because they are never responsible for what their crowd is doing! They (the promoters), don't sacrifice millions of dollars in constructions and licensing. They can move from club to club, leaving proprietors looking for new promoters, or get shut down after an accident. Not all owners have plan B to fall on. The money from the door is often unaccounted for, but the Government assumes, if it is a big crowd, then there must be big money too! The greed involves not only the club owners, but everyone involved in the business, wanted their cut for the following: Liquor/food purveyors; Landlords; Advertisers; Police; employees/subcontractors; IRS; DC/state; Insurance/property/club; Utilities; corrupt officials; family/gold diggers; Mafia; Financiers; Accountant; Lawyer; IT/maintenance/sound; Realtors, when for sale; customers, free loaders; Promoters; Partners; Construction; Thieves and last but not least….. drum roll…profit for yourself!

Think my future club owner. Can you handle those twenty-three points?

Dream as much as you want, but when tires meet the road your car has been tested. The formula of success is to start small and to work the venue yourself. Work with cash if possible. Don't, "cook the books," meaning, "No two sets of accounting."

Studio 54 went down after disgruntled accountant disclosed the true finances of one of the most famous clubs in the 70's (1975-1977). The owner Michael went to jail for saying, "we make more money than the Mafia." Later on he opened the "Palladium" on East 14th and 3rd Avenue in New York.

While the Zoro club was starting to get things into motion, the Police started to harass everyone on X Street. America entered the dark age of Terrorism/McCarthyism. Instead of looking for communists, now they were looking for terrorists. Almost every customer entering or leaving Randevu lounge was stopped, interrogated, but nobody was arrested.

Herbert: "This Police Officer kept me outside an hour after I left Randevu, Sunday. I told them I work at the airport."

Jim: "Did you show them your ID and credentials?"

Herbert: "Yes. They just ignored it and kept asking questions about who is in your place and if I am picking up any prostitutes?" he was almost crying. He was a big bear like, with baby face and wearing TSA shirt and hat to match.

Jim: "I saw you leaving by yourself. Why did they stop you?" he gave him a free cigar, but Herbert declined. He gulped a quick shot of tequila with lime.... guess it was his nerves.

Herbert: "I guess being black and in 9/11 times, they have mixed bias, especially leaving the bar!" a bit calmer.... the drink helped.

Jim: "Did you remember their names or badge numbers?" He needed info in case he wanted to build a case of harassment.

Herbert: "No, they hid the badges, they said they would not make a police report and there would be no charges."

Jim: "Charges for what, for talking to Ecstasy and Lollipop? Next time send the Police my way. We do not need cowboys with Police badges hidden. They may not be real Police if they did not show you badges?"

Herbert: "They did show them very quickly, but not long enough to remember the numbers."

Jim: "Next time ask them to talk to me at the bar, not harass you on the street, ok?"

The priorities in the club Zoro, construction and licenses were distracted by Police so zealous in trying to find something bad going on with Randevu. Unaware of ABRA giving an extra month to renew the ABC manager's licenses in September, the Police with their Swat Team outfits arrived at the bar. Jim was just across the street, when he saw them entering. They did not have protective gear, but they had pistols in their holsters.

Officer Hedley: "Your establishment has no licensed ABC manager" real angry.

Jim: "I have a valid ABC manager license," he pulled out his credentials from his wallet.

Officer Hedley: "You were not here when we checked and her license is expired" he pointed towards Lora. He was wearing all dark blue uniform, the same Swat Team had. No helmet, no shields. Jim thought it looked like a Halloween Costume.

Officer Hedley: "I will write you a citation according to ABRA. Fine is 700 dollars. You pay at 1st MPD; if you think you are wrongfully cited, talk to the Judge." He handed a form to Jim. "Sign here, please."

Jim: "I have the Memo from ABRA showing the extension till Sept. 31st. I don't think you are aware of it?" he almost laughed at his aggressiveness and stupidity.

Officer Hedley: "I can shut you down right now for any reason I can think of, so don't push me."

Jim: "Ok" he signed it. The wolf pack of four blue-color-costumed-Swat team left and Lora was laughing too. "They have issues! Maybe it has something to do with your new club?"

Jim: "Washington politics at their best! You know I read the Bible and my science books with the same intensity. I can see the analogy to the Roman Governor of Judea, Pontius Pilate, whom the Jewish priests demanded that he punish Jesus for falsely claiming he was "King of the Jews." Roman soldiers arrested Jesus. Pilate did not want to punish him and sent Jesus to King Herod, but he returned him back to the Jewish Priests (the Pharisees, Essnes and the Zealots), who believed Jesus was not the true Prophet; a sorcerer, magician, not the son of David and the Messiah). They did not believe in his powers to heal, or to save lives, or bring lives back from the dead, or heal a sick and mentally, disturbed minds and of course, converting water to wine at a wedding because his mother requested it."

The analogy was similar. There would be three kings in DC. One, the real one Jim would be free, no bankruptcies, no jail, no deportation. The other two kings would have just the opposite happen to them. Mr. Dodson would have a second bankruptcy and would owe 9 million dollars (see article at Washington Post by Jacqueline Palank, Aug. 20th, 2010). Mr. Rogbin would file for bankruptcy and would face deportation, after three years of incarceration (see article in Washington Examiner by Bill Myers, Dec. 2nd, 2009). Remember the two thieves accompanying Jesus during his and their crucifixion. Well not paying IRS is theft, Dodson and Rogbin! And who escaped free? Jim did. That was the true answer.

The analogy here is obvious in the present. DC Government is like the Jewish Priests. Attorney General Walter Adams would be representing the Federal government, (Pontius Pilate and King Herod). The betrayal would be done by Judas, Andy Sherman. He would show up later as GM at the club Zoro.

Jim's rule: "When in doubt, hit the books. You will find all your answers there. Do not call friends, family, teachers, or girlfriends. Maybe you are in this situation because of their ill advice in the first place?"

The hearing for Zoro license was for mid-November, 2001. At this time the economy was on pause. The only movement in town and on TV was President's Bush and his military advisers. He sent troops immediately to Afghanistan. His great intelligence was telling him (and the press?), where Bin Laden was and targets were attacked from the air, in caves and by CIA operatives on horses. The news was gloomy and showing widows of men deceased at WTC. Pentagon was grieving over lost comrades. Pennsylvania was creating a shrine at the crash site of Flight 193. One person was happy for not too much attention, Gary Condit. The attention shifted from searching for Chandra Levy to searching for Bin Laden.

Jim was able to install completely a new second floor and also new dark gray carpet, industrial strength. The money came from Randevu and the money refunded from Tony Barros, that 14,000 dollars.

October 31st, 2001 was Halloween night and the Go Go band Addison Band gathered an old crowd of followers.

Big Greg: "It is been ten years since we performed here!" he was not excited, but with some feeling of Déjà vu.

Jim: "I heard the gossip about the shootings outside the club?"

Big Greg: "True. It was after a DC Ramble event. That is why we kept it on a low profile, but Police do monitor our concerts."

Jim: "You have your own security. They must know how to deal with the crowd!"

Big Greg: "We have Big Jamal Security, around fifteen people. Every one of them weighs around 300 pounds. We check everything; hair, shoes, bags. We tap down everyone, man and woman."

Jim: "I hope no one gets hurt tonight?" he was not responsible for the event, but he acted concerned. Jim observed firsthand how to make 24,000 a night. The sound system was delivered early in the afternoon. If one has never been to Go Go concert then you don't know the dimension of sound system they use; at least 4 Quad bass speakers facing the dance floor and the crowd. Mids and tweeters were on each side of the stage like two towers. The instruments were on stage, which were mostly conga drums, cow bells, key boards, horns, and a guitar.

The liquor was mostly cases of Remy Martin, and then the champagne Moet Chandon Nectar, some sodas, definitely no beer. Security was rough. They knew the "bad apples." They knew the underage patrons with fake ID's. The game at the door was $40 for ladies, $70 for men to enter. If someone was wearing sneakers, they would charge him $100. The irony was that ladies would talk to the men with sneakers more than men with dress shoes... The illusion was that sneaker men maybe more financially rewarding to them! In the city where the minimum wage was $6 dollars an hour and good paying jobs were at $12 an hour, you do the math. How much does 100 dollars mean to enter a door and to impress lower paid or unemployed ladies? Jim would remember Blue eyes, a lady hooker at his bar slogan. She said one time to him, "I like criminals!" and she was serious...

Jim: "Why?" laughing.

Blue eyes: "They always have money!"

The crowd grew big and loud, but they were contained following inside the yellow rope toward the club's main entrance. There was also Police presence.

Officer Briggs: "I will make sure this place is bulldozed one day."

Jim: "Why?" he was curious, never expected that from an Officer.

Officer Briggs: "You are having Go Go again?" definitely disapproving.

Jim: "It is not my event, I am subleasing with a one day liquor license" laughing.

Officer Briggs: "If you want to stay longer here, sell food, or diversify."

Jim: "When I open the club with my own liquor license I will have a full kitchen. Now, let the patrons enjoy their fantasies. It is Halloween Night, Officer" he was arrogant and cocky.

Officer: "They may look like they are having fun, but underneath they are bunch of cop killers, if you know, the club history?"

Jim: "This promoter has security of fifteen men and they are checking everything before entering the club. I think you should check them on outside if you recognize any, "cop killers," now he was being a little sarcastic.

Officer Briggs: "We can arrest them if we recognize them, but that would take some data base search and that needs updating."

Jim: "I will appreciate it if the Police would cooperate with the club in advance, not waiting for something to happen? Just give me the pictures of any suspects you may consider dangerous and I will inform you, if I see them" he bluffed and patronized at the same time.

Officer Briggs: "Best for you is not to have them here, ok?"

Jim: "If you can recommend me better promoters I will consider them." He was cat playing the coyote.

Officer Briggs: "Try the gay and lesbians, they are less volatile."

Jim: "This club was gay for eight years and it was still shut down, Officer."

Officer Briggs: ".... But they never killed anyone. Any way, you seem to know all the answers. We will be monitoring the club. Good luck, mister!"

He walked toward the power plant wall where the arriving patrons had their cars parked and started to write tickets. The sign "no parking 10 pm to 5 am," was obscured at the middle of the street -- posted on a wired fence behind an old wooden poll and was dirty and hard to read.

Jim: "Welcome to Half Street, SW with signs pointing downward and parking signs hidden." He thought and he made a mental note to talk to someone about those obvious discrepancies. The crowd was wearing strange outfits and they were moving in small groups, seemed they knew each other. As a whole they were ignoring the police. There was an inherited resentment between police and Go-Go goers, even if they attended those types of concerts, for first time.

Chapter 4

The unique, "DC home-grown" funk culture was born in 1976 by jazz guitarist Chuck Brown, within the next thirty years bands like Sugar Bear, EU, Addison Band, DC Ramble, TCB and the band Subtle Thought self-proclaimed, "grown and sexy" crowd would be still around.

"Go-go music is the soul of Washington" the crowd would say, but Officer Briggs would not agree, neither his entourage at 1st MPD. The bars were quiet until midnight. The crowd was gathering behind the balcony facing the huge two thousand square foot dance floor. There were mostly young 21 plus year old ladies. ID check at the door was strictly enforced and almost full body and bag checking. That made it a bit uptight, but once the music started and the conga drums beat blasted through the 30,000 watts total power of speakers, the human wave attacked the bars. The Long Island Ice Teas and Sex on the Beach individual drinks were replaced by bottles of Remy and Moet, until the band started ordering. That translated to cases of Remy and Moet. Some chasers were coca cola and ginger ale. Jim noticed that with the volume increased and the rhythm of the music, the drinking escalated also.

The crowd moved in some trancelike state. Men would hold bottles of Remy in their hands lifting them in the air and would dance. That was maybe some kind of mating call ritual because usually they were surrounded with ladies, some of them with questionable drinking of the age of 21? The most interesting part on the dance floor was the triple stack of people on top of each other when the music brought them into frenzy. Most people in the media were wondering about that freaky mood of DC go-go followers. It was singing along with the band, water dance type with sexual content with partners behind, very physical, extreme workout like, sweaty. The outside world could only assume what went on at those affairs. Taping was not allowed, even by Jim, the owner.

Big Greg: "What do you think? Anything like this in your old country, Bulgaria?" he was proud of his followers and the whole set up.

Jim: "No sir, I doubt there is anything like this in the USA and in the world! Just leave the place in one piece and the way you found it, clean. Please!"

He walked to his office with a girl who asked him if he had something to drink in there. When one think about the African American women in USA, they will talk to you if you have "a game."

"Game" translates to women as raising their interest in you to the point of some kind of benefits for both sides. Being an owner of a club was beyond the game level; basically the rules have changed to Jim's benefit automatically; the great cigar, the beautiful young lady, and the drinks. She could not stop dancing. For the first time Jim experienced sexual "water dance." She pulled his pants down.

Jim: "What are you doing?" He assumed he will get a blow job? Instead, she grabbed the Remy drink and turned around. Her nice round young and perfect ass was riding his 8 inch pole up and down with the beat of the music a floor below.

Jim: "I wish Amanda could see me now! This lady is not only as good as her, but with the music tempo it puts you in a highest level of experience of sexual pleasure!" He thought. The strange situation here was that Jim was still smoking his Cohiba pumping that perfect and juicy vagina, while she kept drinking the Remy! He was enjoying the view of the pear shaped body, while she kept asking for seconds and third refills.

Jim: "Drink from the bottle if you like?" he was laughing.

Shaquita: "Hey, I am lady, ok!" Very questionable he thought.

Jim: "I see!" He was almost finishing and he did not disagree with her. Suddenly both of them were climaxing at the same time and she almost dropped the half full glass and Jim almost burned her with the cigar.

Shaquita: "Hey, "Clinton," keep that cigar away!" she was convulsing and grabbed his penis and start sucking it for more drops.

Jim: "Thanks, "Monica!" Shall we call a few senators now?" They were making fun of President Clinton and Monica Lewinsky's affair.

Shaquita: "Yes, but I am not drinking Gran Marnier!" her voice disappeared in the Jacuzzi bathroom.

Jim: "Ok, let's go downstairs. Thanks for the "dance." He gave her a hundred dollar bill. "That is your tip."

Shaquita: "Thanks, Daddy!" she ran down the back exit, leading toward the first floor. Jim did not ask her phone number. She was just another fuck, free loader/gold digger and one of the twenty-three octopus-type-hands, he knew that were reaching into his register....

Jim finished his cigar and headed down to the masquerade, which was called, Halloween. The band was resting and DJ Cheno, from WKYS FM 93.9, was playing hip hop music, the same music Jim was using in Randevu bar and recording on his reel to reel, AKAI at home.

Officer Briggs: "No trouble so far! I am surprised?" He was wondering...

Jim: "Not every concert turns into a violent brawl. Some of them "have a beef" at home, but they bring it here."

Officer Briggs: "This time you are lucky." He was one unhappy officer…The history will show only four people will lose lives in a thirty year period of Go-Go scenes. More people have accidents on the roads in USA, but the obsession of relating deaths to club names like Ibex on Georgia Ave, or at Eastside club on Half street, or at club 1919 on 9th Street later on, and anywhere in Maryland, all that was more newsworthy if it is related to Hip-Hop, Go-Go and Clubs.

November 1st the hearing was conducted at ABC board room at 941 North Capital, NE. DC.

ANC 6: "We are opposing the Liquor License at 1824 Half Street, SW to be issued to Solaris Corporation T/A Zoro. The license is CN, for night club..." The protestor was a sixty-eight year old retired Marine.

Nikias: "What is the reason?" he argued for applicant.

ANC 6: "We took helicopter pictures. It shows that the club is too close to residential area."

ABC Board: "Can you come to agreement now or we will schedule another hearing?"

ANC 6: "If this is going to be a go-go club, we do not want anything like that in our neighborhood!"

Nikias: "We can put that condition in "no go-go club" and we can move forward with obtaining the license."

ANC 6: "We know that a major development is coming a few blocks away, the new Baseball stadium. If this club is licensed, it would have adverse effect on business in the area. We know sometimes the lease is for ten years." Obviously, someone was coaching him. He sounded like a lawyer.

Nikias: "We will investigate the argument and hopefully, we will resolve our differences before the next hearing." Jim remembered Lawyer McElroy and Mansur and the unresolved disputes with ANC 2F.

ABC Board: "January 15th is the next hearing date. Please come with your arguments or agreements then." Maria Laban, the chairwoman said.

Jim: "Nikias, please fix my hours at Mike's/Randevu too please, while we wait for the next hearing."

Achim Nikias: "You live a complicated life, young man! Only God knows what will happen, but I will see what I can do?" He was the "Dean of ABC lawyers" in town. If he couldn't do it, then nobody could.

Jim started to see trend in DC. He tried to open the club on U Street. They pushed him out. Now they are delaying him here? And he still needed to be ready for inspection and pay the rent in a two week window, if the January hearing was to be successful!

Yes, without money and with just pure ambition/stubbornness he was trying to accomplish things in DC, nobody was able to accomplish, even with money, lawyers, and a great Police clean record. He went back to the books to find answers. He also started meditation. He needed results fast. He even went to a psychic, the best in the World; Christina of Georgetown. He needed to activate these hidden powers of his subconscious. The meditation was a starter, but the way his energy was projected this time he needed positive results.

He found that in the seven octaves the Mi was the octave of creativity/light. The opposite was next to it, Fa was the octave of destruction. To get respect one can not be seen only as a dark man/destructive. He has to be seen as a powerful/creative man. The fear generated by the police to the population was the result of their own insecurity and dark thoughts. They rather see you as a bad person, uneducated thug, see your criminal record, prove you received your money from wrong sources and skeptical about your intentions, instead of embracing you, giving good ideas and to show any efforts in supporting you. So, the Devine intervention was needed and that is what Jim was doing. Instead of turning around and leaving them victorious, he decided to continue construction and getting his license.

There are three dimensions of time – human, galaxy and cosmic. Human is the 4th dimension; repetition/reoccurrence/Spiral is the 5th. The Cosmos can be Eternal with all the possibilities in the 6th dimension. Most people live in the 4th dimension, the cellular/earth state. Some people develop their extra perceptional ability and awareness by repeating someone's achievements and knowledge, then they move with galaxy speed of light, (here we travel by thought). They are better judges of good and bad (heaven and hell). They are the most educated, better aware, great personalities to follow. Ignorance is the result of skipping the 5th dimension and moving to the 6th dimension.

All possibilities are in the choosing the highest speed possible, where the molecular state turns to electronic, or, matter to light that is the ultimate dimension and highest self consciousness (low radiation, bio plasma, and kundalini). The hydrogen is the element that converts to light, molecular to electronic state. The quantum mechanics by Max Planck describes the movement of light as burst of quanta (bundles of light waves, energy), traveling with intervals of time in between those impulses. Through special breathing the hydrogen converts to helium. The single electron and single positron at the unstable hydrogen will convert to stable two positrons and two electrons element (fusion). At the end result, the energy released can be directed toward any purpose. Basically the humans can mimic the sun and glow with (low) radiation, (the bioplasma, and kundalini).

Here comes the phrase, "Results will justify the means." ….Not always. If praying, meditation, true radiation, fasting, climbing high mountains and all of that give you the result you need….then celebrate!

The problems were piling up. One event with DC Ramble, ended with someone getting shot, dead. The only reason Police did not investigate Jim was because it was a one day liquor license, and belonged to White Mike. He got so scared he decided not to promote at Zoro ever again. That was not the club closing reason and the media did not report it. Jim was thinking about ANC 6, retired Marine Colonel and how he would bring that particular incident to protest even more at the hearing. Would the best lawyer win or lose? Would God assist Jim, through his super subconscious powers again or would he just quit? Quitting is easy. He can blame it on 9/11 terrorists, on the Police, on his strange patrons and promoters, bad luck, Amanda, the government, himself, on Jim's not producing enough money, ABC board and the ANC.

To get into the mind of the business achiever or any astronaut, or any winner of the Olympics, all falls should be expected, and that will give you the reason to try hardest. If one never knows pain, the same would never appreciate the pleasure of winning the full victory. Jim was reopening a land mark in DC, abandoned, but with a great history. If no one had the key to something important in his life, the same one would never have the pain of losing it or gaining it.

Bellini's was a 133 year old restaurant in 1991. Pier 9 or Zoro was thirty years old in 2001. How many foreigners or US citizens would have tested themselves in this torturous way? Jim did not have anybody to turn to for advice. He needed 40,000 dollars to complete the kitchen, soda machines, and the stages on each floor, HVAC, fire suppression system and the ice machine. The begging call from Bulgaria came and it was expected.

Ophelia: "Hey Jim! How are you?" It was his stepmother.

Jim: "Mother! How are you? I am ok. I am surprised to hear your voice! Why is my brother or father not calling me? Are they ok?" he was calling her mother in respect.

Ophelia: "They are ok, but too proud to ask you a favor. Economy is so bad here and we need money!" She was still with sexy voice, he ignored...

Jim: "How much? I need $40,000 here right now. I am opening my new club."

Ophelia: "Can you spare 2,000 dollars for now? Your brother will never ask you."

Jim: "Now I will need 42,000 dollars. Ok. I will send you money. Hope this will help?"

Ophelia: "We have a swift account here. Why don't you come visit us? It has been twenty-one years since you left!" she sounded sincere.

Jim: "Soon. Let me open this new club," he was getting disappointed to see his family asking for money.

Ophelia: "We appreciate it! I can't explain the stubbornness of those men? You know how the Bulgarian men are? Good night, Jim!" She sounded sexy as usual. Her voice was very close to Amanda's cat like low voice…

Jim: "Good night, mother!"

Around Christmas time in 2001 the shopping malls were empty, the Army and Air Force was fighting the Taliban in Afghanistan, trying to capture Bin Laden. Every foreigner and some Americans were displaying, "United We Stand," but the police were still harassing everyone at Randevu Bar.

Officer O'Conner: "Is everything ok, here? I see familiar faces." He was trying to be sarcastic. He was the in charge of vice Squad for prostitution on the Federal Government side. While the war on terror was obvious, the war on Sex was covert.

Jim: "We are fine. And whoever you see here is a legit customer, with proper ID checked." He knew his angle, but did not provoke him.

Officer O'Conner: "Well, I see Diamond and Precious a couple of my old "acquaintances." Do you have valid ID's on you?" he approached the street walkers.

Jim: "This is not a public place, you are bothering my customers, sir!" exasperated by his arrogance.

Officer O'Conner: "Police can enter anywhere where there is a liquor license issued!"

Jim: "I will check that with ABRA tomorrow," suspicious about what he declared. FBI may disguise theirselves as MPD, but they had different powers to investigate.

Officer O'Conner: "ID's please!" Precious did have the ID on her, but Diamond did not.

Officer O'Conner: "You can't sell liquor without checking for proper ID. I want to see your ABC manager's license, sir!" he pointed toward Jim. Jim pulled out his ABC Manager's license, which was just renewed.

"Here. It is extended for next two years."

Officer O'Conner: "It looks ok, just a warning. Don't serve without checking ID first."

Jim: "I have seen their IDs already. I know those ladies, they are my regulars."

Officer O'Conner: "Your regulars? Those are hookers!" he sounded appalled.

Jim: "They are buying drinks. I don't discriminate according to hobbies or professions, sir. I don't see you checking the non hookers and male customers. I think you are profiling here?" laughing at the absurdness of it all...

Officer O'Conner: "I think we will get to know each other, Mr. Walker" he was leaving the bar being sarcastic.

Jim: "I think you should catch terrorists, not waste time on hookers' IDs, officer!"

The FM radio blasted with WPGC station DJ Michelle Wright about the new Cloud nite club. Jim learned about the turf war between Mr. Rogbin and Mr. Dodson for control of the FM Airwaves. While his, Vibe club got shut down in early 2002, he was opening another one under a new name Urban, soon after that. Jim was looking for good DJs, possibly from the early 70's? The long time existing 12 inch Dance Records on the famous gay club strip West of Dupont Circle closed doors forever in mid-November, 2001. That definitely was a bad omen. Jim had bought many records from there himself and he had seen DJs promoting their skills there.

The hearing for the club was on January, 15th 2002. Jim was prepared for either outcome. He knew who he was up against; the guys with helicopters, with law degrees, with tremendous capital, with DC connections, with police, FBI, ANC, with capabilities to support you for life or, to shut you down with a drop of a hat. His construction was complete and his paperwork looked good. He had the best lawyer working for him.

Now the game was, "wait and see." He felt he was in some kind of lottery game. He knew this game and he needed to win. He decided not to go to the hearing.

Instead, he headed to church. That was St. Matthews Church on Rhode Island Ave., NW. It was his hide away; he never attended any masses there. He would usually go there to silently pray to all the icons and statues, which represented some kind of Bible prophets, "for the police and all of them to just leave him alone." He would just burn candles in front of the statue of Virgin Mary, holding Jesus. He always associated himself with Jesus and Mother Mary with his own mother, Loretta. It always worked. At this time he was waiting for the ABC board to say yes or no to his dream?

All his quantum knowledge and yoga and dreams now were resting in some zero modes. Between winning and losing, (mostly wining), Jim knew that the cycle was never closed, it spirals to the next level and it may look like repeats, but in true evolution it never does; similar events but never the same.

If his lawyer is what everyone was saying he was, then he should make his magic! If God was testing him and challenging Jim's subconscious strength, or vice versa Jim's, subconscious was challenging God would, the reward be the fruition of his dreams. Then it was all fair games.

Jim knew being anxious would not make the ANC change their minds, or telling the ABC Board what they wanted to hear, that would not award him anything. The puzzle was like a huge algorithm, like in the Quantum Turing machine.

Chapter 5

There is no one in the physical world that he had known and dealt with his luck or failures. He just waited for the answer. He already advertised for DJs, promoters, bartenders and cooks. He was ready. At 5 pm his cell phone lit up. He was heading towards Randevu bar.

Nikias: "Jim, come to my office. Bring your check book, ok!" he was a bit arrogant.

Jim: "Sure, I am around the corner." He did not want to talk on the phone either. At 5.15 pm Jim was at his office on the 5th floor.

Nikias: "Hey my Bulgarian club owner! You are now in a different league. Congratulations!" He stretched his fat short Greek hand toward Jim.

Jim: "I got the license? Oh, my God!" he stretched his hand and they shook hands.

Nikias: "No, thank me first, then God, ok! Those characters have pulled all kinds of tricks, but I fought them. What helped you the most was the distance from the club? The nearest protestor was beyond the 500 feet minimum."

Jim: "I was in Church and this helped a bit!" he laughed.

Nikias: "Honestly, I have never had a case like yours! Everything was so far fetched and impossible to put it together. Especially, your finances, your criminal background, you running a whore bar? I was afraid that you would quit on me, like you quit on U street, but you stuck to your guns, my friend! I am proud of you!"

Jim: "We both passed, the human test, but only a miracle can explain the outcome."

Nikias: "Remember, you used to work for me in late 80s, now fifteen years later I work for you!"

Jim: "A twist of fate, ironic. By the way, who is this guy Mr. Dodson at Cloud night club? Is that your account also?" he saw an opening, while he was giving a blank check to this great lawyer, signed of course.

Nikias: "Oh, he is an impostor. Michael Jordan has that club with 80% holdings, the other 20 % are owned by ten Ethiopian investors."

Jim: "Now I know why I am paying you 250 dollars an hour. This guy is all over town spreading rumors he owns Republic Gardens and other clubs."

Nikias: "Many promoters in DC are "owners," but without lease holdings and liquor licenses in their names--it is door talk! Now call the Health Department and you need General ABC inspection to open for business, for your Master restaurant license, besides your liquor and occupancy permits."

Jim: "How about Mr. Rogbin at Platinum? How is he doing?"

Nikias: "Stay away from him; he is trouble for many reasons."

Jim will find out in due time IRS was after Mr. Rogbin from day one...

Next day he received a phone call.

Ceaser: "I am a chief investigator at ABC board. I need to inspect your club before opening." He sounded all business-like.

Jim: "Sure. Can you come in the afternoon? Health department is coming at 11 am."

Ceaser: "Ok. See you at 3 pm."

Jim met the Health Department around 11.30 am. She was driving a new Chrysler PT Cruiser. That was a small Al Capone look-alike, black boxy car.

Jim: "Government pays well, I guess?" He was trying to win her over and kind of "break the ice."

Inspector Watson: "Yes, but that is a gift!" That was a classic DC line to avoid any financial disclosure. "Are you ready to open?" she was a chubby forty plus year old, light skin African American lady, who sounded a bit too serious. She headed toward the kitchen. After almost thirty minutes of opening and closing refrigerators and walk-in freezers and checking the brand new kitchen equipment and ice machine, she wrote the report.

Inspector Watson: "You passed for now, but there are few demerits I found, like exposed walls and other minor details."

Jim: "Ok. Thanks!" She disappeared soon after that. Few hours later Ceaser showed on time. He was a bearded African American forty-five year old man, who Jim came across at a hearing, while he was working on substantial change of his nature of operation and his liquor hour extension at Randevu/Mike's lounge.

Jim: "Good to see a familiar face here!" he opened the club.

Ceaser: "Yes, you were represented by lawyer McElroy once at the hearing a couple of years ago, right?"

Jim: "You have a great memory, sir! Now can you see if we can open this club? Rent is due in ten days, no joke."

Ceaser: "That is a short time, but if you have everything lined up, it is doable. You passed!" He sounded surer, than Jim was.

Jim: "Thanks!" It was respectful handshake and beginning of long lasting friendship. Later on they would meet and consult on many occasions for future clubs openings.

Jim installed most of his existing sound. The Ford E350 van moved the 5 amplifiers, the Technics Turntables, the DJ mixer, the fog machines and the special effect lights. He advertised in Washington City Paper and on Craig's list in DC.

Bonnie Heit: "I am one of sale advertisers in City Paper. I saw your ad looking for promoters. I would like to reserve your club for Memorial Day Weekend at the end of May, 2002." She passed him her business card.

Jim: "Sure, but I need a deposit!" He was surprised of his own demanding tone and he smiled with confidence.

Bonnie Heit: "I need two days; Saturday and Sunday!" She pulled out a check book...

Jim: "I need 5,000 dollars. You keep the door!" He got used to getting those deposits for one day promoters. In his mind he saw the window to pay his rent due within a week and he was testing her mind.

Bonnie Heit: "Lock those two days for us, ok." She started to write the check.

Jim: "Can you give me any guarantees at the bar in sales?"

Bonnie Heit: "I am giving you 5,000 dollars. Anything on top is a plus. Usually, promoters get any kind of deals. You are demanding a bit of a high price. My followers are not the greatest drinkers. They are all lesbians and not great spenders. It is hard to get a huge club like yours, because we can't guarantee them any high sales."

Jim started to understand Mr. Bender. He was dealing with those promoters the last fifteen years. Jim needed to negotiate and compromise. When business starts the risk is equal to agreeing to maneuvering chances with a positive outcome. Being careful and cautious is caused of self inflicted fear to lose something.

Jim took the check and walked out. He was rushing to a meeting with Goth promoter Matthew. He represented the Punk Rock subculture which started in Great Britain in late 1970s and against the mainstream. Their fashion for men and women was mostly of black leather and men would wear long trench coats. They booked every Friday for the next six months.

Jim: "How much are you buying the door for admission? Any deposit you can give me?"

Matthew: "I can bring you 200 people. I charge 5 dollars at the door. We pay for advertisement, the DJ and security. There is little left for me."

Jim: "I need bar sales guarantee. At least 5,000 dollars per night! The club needs to pay rent too and other expenses."

Matthew: "That is possible, if they spend 25 dollars, per person."

Jim: "Starting next week, ok? I will need a contract signed. If you do not deliver the guaranteed $5,000 the contract is void."

Matthew: "I need more time to advertise. Then you will see results."

Jim: "Good, let's make it happen!" They shook hands.

January 23th, Friday night, the Goth party arrived. They had a beautiful thirty something red-haired lady at the door. She was charging 5 dollars admission and tall black skinny guy was checking for IDs. Wrist bands were given to 21 of age. It was like a permit to drink. Jim instructed the two bartenders, Arlington Bartenders School sent him, "No band, No drink."

The crowd was weird. Jim observed them dancing on the dance floor individually, holding in one hand a drink and as a ritual a cigarette in the other. Jim wouldn't mind that if they were not throwing lit up cigarettes on the dance floor. He started seeing new and newer burned dark spots on the nice and shiny parquet floors. He went to the DJ booth and announced, "No cigarettes are allowed on the dance floor." That dropped the mood and the drinking at the bar also. Seemed that they were protesting him? On top of that the DJ was blasting the, "Community" speakers to the point that a flame came out of them! That was expensive to repair! Jim observed his register not getting filled to his expectations, (he counted about 1,400 dollars) and his sound speakers in ruins! He needed God's intervention. He closed the doors in his office and started to meditate.

If, the sub consciousness couldn't help him he guessed God couldn't either. Then therefore, nobody else would. Toward the end of the party his cell phone rang. He ran quickly towards the second floor office.

Big Duke: "May I speak with the owner. My name is Duke. I am a promoter, looking for a venue to move my crowd to."

Jim: "I am the owner. Where did you promote before?"

Big Duke: "I have about 500 followers. We were in Jennie's, across from 4th Street Safeway. They lost their liquor license. We are looking for a new location."

Jim: "Where did you find out about me?"

Big Duke: "I saw it in the City Paper ad you were looking for promoters."

Jim: "Which night do you prefer?" He saw his meditation technique working.

Big Duke: "Fridays! I have researched the market. Most of our type promoters focus on Sunday nights. Like DL Sunday's, but, on Friday we have monopoly."

Jim had a quick thought. The Goths were burning his dance floor and blowing up his speakers, and were 2/3 below their $5,000 guarantee. "Fuck the contract of six months! Are you kidding?" He was thinking.

Jim: "Can you come see me tomorrow afternoon?"

Big Duke: "Yes, I will bring my partner with me. See you tomorrow at 2 pm."

Jim: "Great." He clicked off the phone. "I am good, God is good! Thank you, The Invisible Hand!" He was deeply into the wormhole, into the time machine, and into his own mind. He opened the drawer and he lit up a great Cuban cigar Cohiba.

He had a Monte Christo also but they were for special occasions. His legs were resting on the same desk sideways, while he was holding the cigar with his left hand and going through his text messages on his cell phone. After five minutes he decided to go downstairs to check on the Goths. They looked like zombies from Michael Jackson's video, "The Thriller".

Jim: "Amanda, give me the Z report, please!" That was the total of the nightly sale and Z key position clears the register memory for the next day.

Amanda: "The final sales are $1,458 dollars, sir!" She handed him the report. Jim called a quick meeting with Matthew and his partners and the DJ. The door head count was 134. That made 670 dollars.

Jim: "Numbers don't match. I don't see $5,000 sales today or even close to it. I don't see your margin of profit at the door. My rent is due in one week. Can you guarantee me next week 5,000 dollars sales?"

Matthew: "We need more time to advertise."

Jim: "I will move you to the second floor. I need my main floor to bring more people and more income. My landlord is worse than me, I can wait, but he can't!"

Matthew: "We like the first floor. We signed a contract for six months."

Jim: "The contract does not specify first or second floor, also you didn't give me the guaranteed revenue. I will give you one more chance to prove me wrong. If next Friday, I am disappointed, the contract will be void." He stood up and Matthew's entourage also stood up.

Matthew: "Till next Friday! Hope things will improve?" but, both doubted that.

Next day Jim checked Randevu's bar sales. While he was working there the sales were around $600 to $700 a night. When he counted the register the amount was in half, about 400 plus dollars. He was concerned about that major drop and he called Lora, the bartender lady at Randevu.

Jim: "What is going on with the sales last night? That was a big drop!"

Lora: "You know Jim... When you were here it was like a whore house!" Now I am trying to get this place to be a normal bar. Ladies of the night are asking about you. I guess you spoiled them, or they need "pictures taken?"

Jim: "Do you know what? I am not interested in your philosophy! I want the sales to increase, not decrease. You can think whatever you want, but at the end of the day or night the cash counts, not your righteous ideas. Mr. Bender does not care about anything else besides the rent being paid on time!"

Lora: "Jim, you should focus on the Zoro club and let me run Randevu here. I need to make some money for myself too."

Jim: "Again. You sound like Mansur? The moment I opened Zoro, you both act like you want to get rid of me? I am not letting my "brain child" club go down financially and nobody's philosophy can change that. I am coming tonight to get my finances in order. I will alternate between the clubs until I make them profitable!"

Lora: "Feel free, it certainly is your "brain child," but obviously you can't be at two places at once. And I know about rent due at Zoro. Just like rent is due here."

The meeting with Big Duke turned out to be more surprising than it was supposed to be. Quantum Turing machine was working in some strange algorithm. The gravitational wave between the disappointments of Randevu and the great expectations from Zoro that quantum wave created the energy and the reality at 2 pm to his surprise. Jim believed miracles just don't happen; they get triggered and created by The Thought.

Big Duke: "Hey. Jim! We would like to see your spot. If we like it, we have some grand ideas for it!"

Jim: "I do not want to hear any excuses, sorry stories and failures. Tell me what you can do for me, and of course what do you expect here?" He meant business. After almost four years in the business he was seeing a great opportunity to seize the moment. No, he did not want to get rich; he wanted to get awarded fairly, and to be recognized as a true club owner. Here he did not have any partners, nobody to share rent, to discuss future plans, successes or disappointments. Even in Studio 54 there were two partners, at Tracks Club were five partners, here he was by himself.

Big Duke: "We like the spot. We would like to rent it for Memorial Day Gay pride weekend."

Jim: "Sorry, these days are already taken by Bonnie Heit. She made 5,000 dollars deposit. She wants Saturday and Sunday."

Big Duke: "We will buy Friday and Saturday for the same amount..." He was a healthy built tall African American thirty-something handsome man. He was a barber by day, promoter by night. His male friend, who was married, was slim built and tall and his name was Willie.

Jim: "I need bigger leverage. Give me an offer, I can't refuse!"

Jim was challenging the Turing Machine, (his own mind, God/ TIH) and Big Duke was probably the missing card on the gamblers table, in the algorithm.

Big Duke: "Ok. We will sign a contract with you for six months. We will hold the door; we pay you in advance for that. We guarantee you 400 to 500 people a night. You will sell your liquor. We cannot give you more guarantees."

Jim: "Money talks, can you give me a deposit now? I need $2,500 for the Memorial weekend Saturday, also $800 deposit in advance for the door on Fridays."

Big Duke: "I can write you a check now." He pulled out a check book.

Jim: "I am a bit high tech. I have a wireless credit card machine, Nurit. He pulled out a battery operated portable device.

Big Duke: "I have heard of them but I have never seen one! You are ahead of the curve, buddy!" Big Duke was also curious if the machine would work? He was used to seeing credit cards swiped on restaurant computers, at gas stations, at banks, but never in some warehouse looking night club? He looked around the second floor office. He observed a small Dell Lap top, an office phone and video camera on a tripod in the corner.

Big Duke: "Are we recorded here? Do you need to videotape the credit card swiping?"

Jim: "No, this camera is for taking pictures of my contractors 1099ers... Do not worry, Duke."

Big Duke: "Hey, Willie. I need your approval before I swipe my credit card. I will give a full deposit now. You will give me your half ($1,250) after the Memorial weekend, ok?" Willie just nodded. He was the quiet guy.

Jim: "Ok, I will process $2,500 now." He swiped the card, it printed out right away. Everyone in the room was surprised that the machine worked!

Jim: "Just sign here and we are in business!"

Big Duke: "Call me right away if any problems? I will pay you in advance for the next week in cash. Here is $400. We need to advertise at least for the next ten days."

Jim: "Thanks, your contract is for six months, we can renew it later on."

He did not ask for a guarantee. The deposit and the 500 people guaranteed were sufficient. The confidence of this couple was in sharp contrast with the Goths.

Last Friday of January the Goths arrived with about the same amount people, and maybe 10 less; instead of the promised 200 people and guaranteed 5,000 dollars a night. Jim observed a repetition of the event of Friday before. This time they were not burning the dance floor, but they were not drinking much either.

Matthew: "Sorry boss! It is a short time to advertise." He was looking for excuses.

Jim: "Don't give me Spiro Agnew excuses. Either I leave my club or you leave my club first. I don't think you have a choice?"

Matthew: "Ok, President Nixon! You may have trouble finding good promoters here?"

Jim: "Listen, I can give you second floor on Fridays or some other Day? You may need to move to a smaller venue?"

Matthew: "We don't want the pressure on us."

Jim: "No pressure, it is business. All I want is to pay the rent here! I am not greedy."

Later in the decade Scott Royce and Lori Beth will find two basement restaurants to compete in against each other for age over 18 and the age over 21 crowds. The Meeting Place and Recessions, on X Streetwould be a battle ground for Midnight and Spellbound promotions. The latest are considered "upper Goths," who are better dressed and whose music is geared more towards mature Goths. They are still there in 2012. Jim's recommendation was followed well, to choose smaller venues and to last longer. It was amazing how a beginning club was able to pay the first month's rent? Through his business career Jim was able to always meet his financial obligations. He never would have a business closed for not paying rent. This book was not written how to make money, but to be aware of DC politics!

When someone becomes a target the "wolves," working for DC or federal Government are relentless. Jim observed how a pack of lionesses would attack a much bigger single buffalo and bring him down eventually.

The methods that the government would use will be revealed later, but like Malik (Mansur's brother in law) said "going to work and doing business in DC is like going to school, always licensing, hearings and testing and surprise inspections..."

Officer Dwayne: "I heard you opened a second club in SW?"

Jim: "Yes, but who told you that?" he did not want to be sarcastic.

Officer Dwayne: "Your neighbors at Starlight Bar don't think highly of you," he laughed.

Jim: "I know who that person is. It is Marsha. She has been calling me all kinds of names since we opened in 1998! The funny thing was she was looking for a job and she called me at my new location. Once she found out who I was, she cursed me out and hung up!"

Officer Dwayne: "I see the resentment between the businesses. I am here to check on your ABC license and your customers."

Jim: "I am not here as manager. My manager is Lora. Please check her license."

Officer Dwayne: "Hmmm. How many managers work here?"

Jim: "There are three ABC managers here. We rotate. Today MOD (manager on duty) is Lora."

He started to feel some kind of undercurrent here, in slogans, "he smelled a rat."

Lora: "Yes, sir! I am the ABC manager. May I assist you with something?" She pushed Jim aside and stepped forward holding her license in her hand.

Officer Dwayne: "I know who you are and we know "the activities" here."

Lora: "I am not aware of what you are implying and we have been checked a thousand times in the last four years" she was getting perturbed.

Officer Dwayne: "Police Chief Naylor designated your club as the "hot spot," one of fifteen in DC. We have videos and confessions of your customers. We can shut you down now." He was going out of his way, but he looked like a dog that barks, but never bites.

Lora: "We talked to your supervisor on 3rd Street, NE. He said we cannot discriminate on the bases of professions or hobbies, we can only discriminate what the liquor law restricts and that is underage drinking and that the age 21, is the legal age to drink. I think you should catch terrorists, not go after a black woman like me." She threw out the race card.

Officer Dwayne: "Ok. We are not on the same page, Miss Manager!"

Jim: "I think we keep meeting all different types of uniformed and vice Police and they keep talking the same! What you are accusing us of has been going on since 1941. We are just doing business in the wrong zip code, sir!" He observed the Officer's reluctant departure.

With the rent paid on time, Jim concentrated on developing his business concept. The promoters were pouring from everywhere. They were all kinds and coming from anywhere. The club Nations across South Capitol was promoting heavily to a young white crowd and it was called "the Buzz" on Fridays and "Velvet," a gay night on Saturday. Because of drugs sold there Friday nights, it would be eventually closed. The drugs ecstasy was blamed for some weird behavior at a US Marine barracks nearby. In one night police made eight arrests of drug sellers. Senator, Joe Biden introduced a bill later on RAVE (Reduction of American Vulnerability to Ecstasy). Jim overheard that and he did not want to deal with them.

He did extensive research and was able to contact some of the major players in the club scene.

Jim: "Hey Antonis! I am looking for promoters for my club. I can pack 2000 people easy and more on two floors."

Antonis: "I own the Panorama productions. My crowd goes to specific places. What is your address?" he paused.

Jim: "1824 Half Street, SW, Zoro, the old Pier 9."

Antonis: "No way. We only do NW. Sorry! Good luck!"

Jim: "Thanks!" they both hung up.

Jim: "So, DC is still segregated!" he thought. "How can we make this show work?" He was in the world of his own creation. "Beware of what you think, it may happen. Then once it happens, are you able to handle it?" He was contemplating. He remembered his lawyer's words. "Now you are in a different league, young man." Crowds in 2002 were drowned in by new radio waves, by My Space electronic media, by shiny fliers, by big name DJs. Some of them demanded $4,000.00 a night with hotel room reserved in advance. The music was constantly changing. Jim read an article of segregation of races and incomes by music and by street geography.

The article was how the place at the 4th estate restaurant was packed day and night by white young professionals, while the place across the street at restaurant Ascot, was barely half full with an African American crowd.

Sam, one of the owners of, 12 inch dance records, said music is a divider, and not a uniter. Nards, a popular DJ service providing services in Virginia and DC had one of the largest of music selections they claimed around 30,000 titles of different songs.

Nards: "If you want to change the crowd, change the music." That is their slogan. The geography of Northwest, DC at 16th street and U Street was that, West of 16th would be the side for white professionals and east side would be all African American; mostly government and students patrons.

The major clubs in NW in the year of 2002 were: Platinum, Diversite, Coco Loco, 11th hour, 4th Estate, Element, Ascot, Vibe, 1223, U, Cada Vez, 5, Ozio, 18 Street Lounge, Champions, Third Edition, Home, Havana Breeze, Randevu, Republican Gardens and Polyesters.

The SE clubs were: Sodom, Bottoms, 55, Ziegfeld and Secrets, Washington and Nation.

The NE clubs were: Tunnel, Dino's, Aqua, Cloud and W.

The clubs in SW were: Zoro, Zanzibar and Fusion.

Jim was constantly promoting. Every club he went to and chatted with had some promoter who would have the particular niche to bring the specific crowd. The "e VIP list," by Eric Taylor had a great pull at the 1223 Club on Wednesdays. He advertised himself as urban marketer. Mostly his crowd was a mixed bowl of government employees with average salary and some students from Howard University. Same crowd but on a larger scale was at Cloud. The urban patrons at Cloud, were far from the VIP wanna-be's. They were a mixed crowd of students from HU and urban thugs with money, especially from Baltimore area. Although Mr. Dodson was almost living at Howard University, promoting to beautiful tall ladies from African American descent, his second leg was in the courthouse. He would stay at the door at 500 Indiana Ave., NW and greet and pass his shiny VIP cards with advertisement for free admission or free drinks. It worked for him. The New Year's Eve of 2002, he made $120,000 at the door and $270,000 at the bars. He beat his partner Mauricio in the International Square who made $180,000 two years before during the Millennium. The Mauricio concept was identical to Panorama's Antonis. They both advertised and pulled in the international crowd from George Washington University and Georgetown University. They were mostly from wealthy Iranian, Pakistani, and Bangladesh descent.

At Nation the Buzz was changing to Rave parties. Some of their promoters came knocking on Jim's Zoro' club door.

Mr. Tucker: "I am the President of Global House Movement. I want to see your venue." He sounded dry and flat.

Jim: "Do you have a date in mind?" He was strait to the point.

Mr. Tucker: "Cinco de Mayo."

Jim: "May 5th?"

Mr. Tucker: "Yes, sir!"

Jim: "My place takes two to three thousand people. How many can you bring here?"

Mr. Tucker: "One thousand to start; it will increase with time, if they like it."

Jim: "We need a contract, I will need a deposit." He was all business.

Mr. Tucker: "Let me see it first." He asked for directions and hung up.

Some thirty minutes later they met. Mr. Tucker brought a friend with him. They looked around and they liked the space. They liked the second floor, where they would have only VIPs and they signed a contract. Unfortunately, they did not have any deposit down, so Jim became suspicious. They left him a bunch of flyers of future events. At the time they were in office, another promoter showed up at the office.

Mr. Tucker: "Can we look one more time, in case we missed something?" The thieves asked. Jim found out the same night they had stolen his diamond tip needles with cartridges of both "Technics 1200 MKII," turntables he hooked up on the second floor, (VIP lounge). He grew suspicious. The next promoter was Tubb Entertainment. He sounded more diversified, but he was into the Go Go Bands scene. He mentioned all the usual players; Addison Band, DC Ramble, Subtle Thoughts. He said that the Bands have flexibility on some nights. He said that a good Tuesday or Wednesday is equal to a good Saturday night. The irony of the club business is that it takes two to three busy nights a week to consider it a successful operation.

The Zoro club rent was considered high at 12,000 dollars per month. Lora was bugging Jim why he didn't seek a cheaper space?

He remembered the warehouse next to him where Mr. Bender kept his extra speakers and furniture.

Jim: "Hey Mr. Bender! You have a space next to Crucibles, on Half Street? Can I open another club there?"

Mr. Bender: "Sure, but it has only two bathrooms. You may need to build more for a larger crowd?"

Jim: "I like the 24 foot high ceilings. And everything is open space. The loading dock is huge and I like the two story offices built by the entrance. I would block the broken glass windows on the rear."

Mr. Bender: "Yes, that is 1812 Half Street. You can do a lot of stuff there because you do not have a liquor license."

Jim: "I am thinking of non alcoholic parties here, for age under 21 and above 18."

Mr. Bender: "You can have nude shows there if you like? Police will not bother you at all."

Jim: "Give me a good term lease and not too expensive, ok?" They laughed at the thought of it.

Mr. Bender: "This place needs a lot of work! I will give you a ten year lease with $3,000 a month to start." He was a good businessman. The place was 5,000 square feet! Great deal!

Jim: "Whatever they say about you, you are ok in my book, my friend!" they both laughed again at the slight camaraderie.

Mr. Bender: "You see I did not even check your references?" laughing in agreement.

Jim: "..... We did not need a realtor this time! I will give the check to your man at Bottoms club, Eddy, ok?"

Mr. Bender: "Nice doing business with you, Jim! You are different than most people I have known. You just don't talk, you move forward!" he paused for a moment....

Jim: "That is true. If I want something I get it. How? That is a subject for research and history to tell?" both hung up.

The business world was in favor of this genius mind, the risk taker, the money maker. While he was pressing forward the opposite was happening at the Police Department. It was the positive and creativity in Mi octave that was fighting the destructive forces of Fa octave. Of all 35 clubs/lounges listed in 2002 only two would survive during the next decade. They are Ozio and Third Edition. Now, we are getting to the point! How come thirty-three of the actively involved DC night life club owners could not survive? Even by any theory of statistics and probability 6% survival is suspicious. There was a conspiracy here to conduct a, "War on Clubs."

Max Planck wrote the Radiation Law: E = hv (in year 1900).

Intensity of light is related to frequency, where "h" is Planck constant.

Are the club owner victims of the frequency of opening clubs? The more clubs the more radiation the more creativity and money, (Mi octave), the more Fa octave, (the government opposition and therefore destruction)?

Tesla experimented with resonance and destruction. He was able to make earthquake machines. Maybe the Fa octave, (resonance), cancels the Mi octave (creative energy E)? Jim was to write a new Club Law! In 1937 Alan Turing broke the code of Enigma (German military encrypting communication language in World War II). Jim was about to discover the relationship between enormous wealth (E) and destruction of it through government envy, machination and manipulation. The

"American Dream" promotes the idea that "if one works hard, he should be rewarded." They should change it to the "American nightmare," which only the news registers as sensation. "If you get rich too fast, we will stop you now and forever."

What sells faster than the Kardashians giving birth on national television? The answer is anything bad relating to night clubs, to strip joints, to presidents' gaffs, or assassinations. Washington's District of Columbia had no real industry. The income was mostly generated from parking tickets, property taxes and from club sales and taxes. The three billion dollar budget of the city (in 2001) was 90% subsidized by Federal Government. The agencies created to monitor business activities were DCRA (District of Columbia Regulatory Administration) and ABRA (Alcohol and Beverage Regulatory Administration). There were other agencies like zoning, taxation, taxi cab Commission, etc. The money was mostly generated from issuing licenses and renewal of licenses, also from permits for construction. The clubs were easy targets to scrutinize. Police were never happy with anyone who was having fun while they were, "working." Their work was mostly to observe the beautiful women, watching them with Casanova eyes and expecting to flirt. The racial bias was obvious. When the Zoro club was promoting Goth events the young white ladies, twenty-something of age were asked different questions than the black attractive twenty-something ladies, during the Go Go events!

Officer Dwayne: "Hey, what is your name?" he asked a young white lady. She was dressed like a punk rocker, revealing long perfect legs with long black boots and short black leather skirt, slightly disclosing a nice pair of pink panties.

Punk Lady: "My name is Sheila!"

Officer Dwayne: "Are you going to college?" he was scanning her up and down at a too close for comfort distance.

Sheila: "Yes. I am in my second year at Georgetown University."

Officer Dwayne: "Great! Enjoy yourself." He wanted more attention, but she disappeared inside the Zoro entrance.

A day later the Addison Band was performing. The same officer couldn't hide his long, disappointed face. He was the one with his group of Police comrades, who were wishing to "bulldoze the club down to the ground," a few months before.

Officer Dwayne: "Hey, lady. Where did you park?" he was addressing the young black lady entering the club.

Takisha: "Yes, sir! I parked by the wall." She pointed towards her car.

Officer Dwayne: "Ok, thanks!" He observed her going towards the end of the line and he headed towards her car. He wrote a parking ticket and slapped it on the window under the windshield wiper. The group of women and men observed that action with disgust, but, they just swallowed their anger like the last 400 years their black predecessors did. The injustice was served up to them, right in front of their eyes, at the same parking spot the day before Sheila, (the white girl), had her car parked. The Police Officer could have said something and shown the, "No parking 10 pm to 5 am," warning sign that was posted hidden behind the light poll, but, he chose to show force, no mercy! Jim would warn the promoters to place signs by the line and by the ticket office not to park by the Wall, which belonged to the US Capitol Power Plant. Most of the time, they wouldn't do anything about that, saying most of the regulars knew about the Police and the signs.

Officer Dwayne: "What is your story Mr. Walker? You have two clubs, one with hooker patrons, and the other with cop killers? What will the third one be like?"

Jim: "I hope you will justify your pay check one day, but don't count on my help!"

Officer Dwayne: "What do you mean?" he was appalled. He wanted to be feared or liked, but he wouldn't accept being ignored, which exactly is what Jim was doing to him...

Jim: "I can't understand the Government and especially the Police in DC? When I do call you for assistance (911), you show up two hours later and the criminals are gone! When I don't ask for anything, then you are all over me, telling me you are performing a public service?"

Officer Dwayne: "We are public servants and unless you hire someone from the uniform police to personably protect the club; we are picking and choosing who to assist!"

Jim: "What is the going rate?" he was shocked. He had paid taxes already? So why should he pay more?

Officer Dwayne: "You should talk to the lieutenant. What I have heard is that it is 45 dollars per hour, four hours minimum per officer. Also, it is two officers minimum."

Jim: "That is extortion! That is $360 a night to pay! I have to cut short my own club security!" He was surprised.

Officer Dwayne: "If you think you could do it with your own security, great!"

Jim knew that Mr. Dodson was paying $250,000 a year to his own chosen cop friends, but that did not stop IRS from shutting him down at Ballers night club, later on January 22nd, 2010! So, Officer Dwayne, your suggestion to hire extra police wouldn't improve the business or prevent the events from occurring. Jim's style of keeping Police guessing worked at Randevu the previous four years. Why shouldn't it work here? His conclusion was formed especially after he observed the 1st District Police working his bar customers in a negative way; after the episode of the parking ticket at the Wall and after the conversations with White Mike and with Big Greg. That intuition would help him pull through the next six years like President Clinton through near an Impeachment by the US Congress concerning his affair with Monica Lewinsky. Was it intuition or connecting the dots, to the higher awareness?

God: "Yes, Officer Dwayne, keep your underpaid, greedy, incompetent, make-your-no money-ass away from Jim! Ok!" The Invisible Hand would direct away not only Officer Dwayne, but all the wolf pack of nobodies wearing blue uniforms of MPD, undercover vice, ABC Board investigators, wrong hours harassers, "shady entrance," old Miss Ziegler acting alike and all twenty-three pointers, trying to suffocate any business.

The tidal wave was rising towards and against Jim, (Fa octave), so was Jim's creative stubbornness (Mi octave). The gladiator at the arena (Jim) was not fighting the best representative of the opposition; he was fighting all of them at the same time. It was the beginning of the biggest Mind Game of one against The Minds of all. The analogy was of the Bruce Lee in the ring against 100 martial artists and he wins! Wining has a price, and the price is to write this manuscript, so that others, who come to the USA don't have to fight or even to think they will be better off; or they do not have to come to USA at all! Remember!

Once a foreigner, you are always a foreigner! Congress rewriting the immigration laws will not stop the bias; it will just modify it.

Jim always compared himself with Bible persons, like Jesus, or with David, who fought Goliath (the Philistines' 9 ft. giant), or Delilah and Samson, who she seduced for the Philistines, and with Noah's Ark and the flood. In life "staying in the game," means gaining knowledge and experience. Anything which happens quickly and big involves unusual suspects --Big money, crime characters, or just luck! Most achievers are looking for recognition through social media exposure or being on TV and with some rewards. Jim did not want to be in the spotlight, he did not wanted awards for achievement. He was just in a race with himself and he wanted to make a profit, hopefully to invest in real estate and eventually live on his investments at a later age.

Nikias: "Jim, what is your new idea? I see Zoro is making enough money for you to move to the next venture!" He was excited, but not surprised.

Jim: "I am trying to move the crowd from Zoro to a one floor huge space at The Zone. I have problems renting my second floor now."

Nikias: "If I did not know you better, I would think you are getting a bit greedy! That is the downfall of many club owners. You are stretching yourself too thin and losing track."

Jim: "I am not trying to get rich quick here. I am trying to be practical. Once the Zone takes off (and it rents for 1/4 of Zoro), I will sublease Zoro Club or sell the business."

Nikias: "I know you are pragmatic person. Want me to help you get a liquor license? I suggest you get a CT license, tavern license with no food sales!"

Jim: "Go ahead, "uncle!"

Nikias: "Let me warn you, young man. Do not stay in this town too long in the same business, or open too many businesses at the same time. The government is not your friend. They will target you and you will lose everything, especially, if your businesses are of the same kind. Greeks tell "do not put all of your eggs in one basket."

Jim: "I think they produce only olives?" he said it with a cocky frown…

Nikias: "I am not your father. I am your lawyer. I am representing some people like you and they are being raided, money seized in millions, house taken, business closed!"

Jim: "That is why we hire lawyers, I guess?" Wondering who is he talking about. Would that be someone he knew?

Nikias: "I can't disclose who they are, because of attorney-client privilege." He smiled uncomfortably…. "But I will tell you that I represent two of you and I don't represent Mr. Dodson, who doesn't have money anyway." He basically revealed that the 3rd person was Mr. Rogbin, without naming him.

Jim: "I can figure out whom you are talking about, but what are their reasons?"

Nikias: "Please pay your taxes! I am only a lawyer, not an accountant. It does simplify my work, when you are current and honest with your taxes, federal and state. I know your bar Randevu has the element Police do not approve, but that is your choice of income, or your business. They should not discriminate by clients, but they do. Second District Commander's agenda is to close every possible club in DC, Jeremy something...."

Jim: "I am expecting no opposition at the hearing. We are working with the same would-be protestors from the ANC."

Nikias: "You are something else; I have never had a client like you! Let's see what will happen?"

Jim: "See if I can have the new club dancing with bikinis and small bras for ladies." He remembered the liar mediator Mr. Baldwin who died on the surgeon table protesting his substantial change to that….

Nikias: "Now you are pushing it! You operate a whore bar at Randevu, you allow Go Go bands in Zoro, now you ask for a stripper type permit at The Zone. That is why you are so unique. I really think everything is doable, but don't forget to pay your taxes, ok!"

Jim: "Ok, "uncle" Nikias!" Both of the men shook hands, and split in separate ways.

Jim: "Am I greedy, God?"

TIH: "No, you are living the Life. Remember what Contessa told you before she died?"

TIH was the invisible hand, his sub consciousness, the Higher Self, God!

Chapter 6

While the Club Zoro was getting up to speed the Zone needed work. Jim needed a 30 amp outlet for big bands like Addison Band. He made some phone calls to some referenced electrical and plumber services.

Johns C. Flood: "Good morning! This is your plumber service. What seems to be the problem?" A nice female voice answered the phone.

Jim: "I am the owner of a new club at 1812 Half Street, SW. I need two bathrooms checked. One of them overflows." He found her voice to be phony but friendly. Just like many 6 dollars an hour minimum wage receptionist voices in Washington, DC in year of 2002, sounded.

John C. Flood: "We will send you the first available technician. The caveat is that your billing starts at the moment you accept and approve our service call."

Jim: "I am paying for the traveling time? That is unjust." He was appalled.

John C Flood: "That is our policy. You are free to call other services. We have the best guarantees for our work." The 6 dollars an hour female voice sounded more and more robotic.

Jim: "You should run for a mayor or senator! You sound very convincing. Ok, take my number and tell them to call me."

John C. Flood: "Thank you!" She was happy to start a new account. She was (assuming) pleasing her boss in more ways than one, just like many sweet sounding financially disadvantaged young ladies in USA and around the world... Jim had a motto, "If you want to control them, keep them guessing."

Not a bad approach, if it worked for him, or if the result was what he wanted? The adaptation of being in New York with rich people and being in DC with average government workers worked in both ways favorably for him. "The result always justifies the means." He wanted to satisfy his basic needs; money, sex and fame.

Having three night clubs was achievable, but it was time consuming. He needed a strong crew to support him and most people in DC were 100 dollars a day/night "whores." He would "up" their expectations. He was a good and fair boss. He would give them 150 dollars per shift guaranteed.

Jim: "Exceeding someone's expectations creates loyalty and self satisfaction. It prevents theft." Assuming that the third club would be geared toward exotic entertainment he started to advertise in the City Paper.

He also advertised on Craig's List. He placed an ad in the Washington Post. He even registered an account with My space.com a social network, equal to today's Tweeter and Face book.

The calls were coming from everywhere at Zoro. On Wednesdays he booked Queen's Ball nights with Mother Barbara from Baltimore. On Thursday's with WPGC, on Friday with Big Duke, on Saturday with Addison Band and on Sundays were Caribbean nights. Yes, he was getting there. At the Zone he needed a sound system and to create a terrace type railing. The two story wooden house, was supposed to be used as DJ booth facing toward the rear wall. The metal rail mezzanine was to elevate the crowd and increase capacity of people by 200. Every club had its own configuration. The idea of successful club is how to move the crowd without being bored immediately. Most club owners borrow ideas from other thriving businesses. Jim wanted the new club to look industrial, appealing to younger crowd 18 of age and over.

The Quantum Mind came to his assistance again. As he was working on the electrical system upgrade at The Zone, a U haul truck full of speakers pulled over. One 40 plus year old Italian guy came and opened the rear roll up door.

Luciano: "Hey, I heard you are promoting your new club. I got equipment for you." He had this slightly friendly salesman attitude.

Jim: "I can use some sound. Show me what you got?"

Luciano: "I brought that from Vibe club."

Jim: "You brought those speakers? They look beaten up and like they are homemade…." He got suspicious.

Luciano: "Give me $10,000 and you can have them all." He pointed inside the truck, which contained about 40 speakers.

Jim: "I will give you $5,000 for 20 speakers. I will write you a check."

Luciano: "Mr. Rogbin gave me this on consignment. I am just a consignee. He wouldn't take checks. He wants cash."

Jim: "Ok. Here is 5,000 cash. Tell Rogbin, "hello" from me. We have the same lawyer. Ok?" both were happy about the deal. Jim was able to equip both clubs with Rogbin's speakers.

Jim: "Losing of one is the gain for someone else. Thank you Mr. Rogbin!" He thought and smiled. Ten minutes after Luciano departed he was on the phone with his sound man.

Eric: "Hey man! What is new?"

Jim: "You would not believe what just happened!" He paused….

Eric: "Something to do with DC Ramble Band, or with the Gay guys?" He laughed curiously…

Jim: "Club Vibe, went out if business and I bought most of their good speakers, a lot of good stuff. Can you come and see what works and what needs repair?"

Eric: "I will. When are you opening your next club?"

Jim: "After the sound is in place, probably next week we can do a non alcoholic event?"

Eric: "That is about your style!"

+++* Eric will be the sound man for president Obama in 2011 *+++

Marcel: "Hey Jim, I want to sign up for Memorial Day Sunday event." He sounded gay.

Jim: "This day is contracted with Bonnie Heit, who is with WFL (women for life).

Marcel: "I will buy her Sunday day only." He sounded anxious.

Jim: "I have an idea. I will give you every Sunday including Memorial Day at Zoro. You will pay me $1,000 a day to hold the door. I will deal with Sheila."

Marcel: "You are a good businessman, Jim. What are you going to do with the Caribbean nights, on Sunday?"

Jim: "I will move them to the second floor for now or to the new club the Zone?

Jim was "interviewing" exotic female bartenders for The Zone. He was also looking for dancers. The line up for the positions for the next club included many strange responders. He met hookers, strippers; want to be pole dancers and promoters with many promises. He videotaped many of the want to be dancers and exotic bartenders at his office. He was surprised of their eagerness to get these jobs. They would do everything, including real sex to jump to the top of the list. Some of their escorts were waiting in the lobby. Some of the boyfriends were waiting in the car outside. Most of the candidates were of African American descent. Some of them were Spanish. Only one of them was white. That was very discouraging.

Most of the busy nights required six bartenders. So what Jim did?

He paired the bartender ladies who he had sex with, with the gay or straight men or with ladies who he couldn't trust with the sales. That created superior methods of inventory and minimum waste.

The progress at The Zone club was with a price tag of 20,000 dollars. He brought the promoters from club W in Bladensburg, and some 18 and over Party promoters from, Nation. John C. Flood technicians came and said the bathrooms were fine, but after ten people used them they got flooded again. Jim just opened the side door of Zoro and they were able to easily use the bathrooms on second floor. Jim had separated 1st floor from 2nd floor via a framed door. At this time, there was Go Go event going on and it was curious to see the Ravers mixing with them. It was a bit standoffish and funny. The Ravers also had a pick at the first floor to hear the sound and see the performance. They were shocked; to say the least....

Jim estimated his expenses at about $60,000 dollars a month. He was paying for six phone lines three of them at the Zoro club, one at the Zone, one at his house, and one was his cell phone. His rent was around $20,000, utilities were around $3,000, and the liquor cost was high. Nikias was charging high also. The lowest in the expenses was the payroll. He was paying everyone with cash, but he used the 1099 system.

To stop stealing he would ask every bartender what they made in tips?

Jim: "Alexia, how did you do tonight?" She was one of his spy-lovers.

Alexia: "$85 boss!" she was acting disappointed.

Jim: "I will make the difference to $150! Here is extra 65 dollars. Please sign here!" Both they were laughing. The crowd gathered and approved. They acted like children.

Jim: "James, how did you do?" He was Alexia's partner at the double bar.

James: "$90!" He grabbed the $60 Jim gave him, he signed and was about to leave.

Jim: "Make sure you clean up the bars and everyone to help with taking their trash bags out. The bar runner will clean the dance floor and outside the building now."

James: "Ok, boss!" He took a huge trash bag full with bottles and left the building.

Jim always checked amount of trash first. "Plenty of trash, plenty of money in the registers," that was his slogan. Also, he would think "bartenders can hide the money, but they can't hide the trash."

The party at the Zone was not productive. The non alcoholic drinks were mostly energy drinks and they were not producing much profit! Jim started having second thoughts. The only way to profit was either to increase the charge at the door or alcohol sales, or both!

He observed the Crucibles club next to him charging 25 dollars nonmembers and 20 dollars for members of that S&M s club. And even with money not everyone was allowed there. Usually, they would ask to fill out some personal information and verification through an ID before admittance. Jim was able to enter a couple of times to observe the weirdest things he's ever seen in his life. The owner was Frazier and he was in his mid-40s very well built Caucasian; true American man. They had special bus outside with no windows. It looked like military prisoners moving vehicle. The space inside the club was similar to the Zone, with tall 24 foot high ceilings and 5,000 square foot floor. The loading dock was blocked with brick wall. On the inside the space was greatly utilized with different sections of themes. One of them was admission room, then was the torture room, then was the judge chambers room and then was the jail room with real cage. The judge would send a "bad guy or woman" to jail and sometimes together. They would have sex in the cage. That would be the judge's order! At the torture room Jim observed a lady being hoisted with fishing-like hooks passed through her clitoris, nipples and her thigh's skin. It was weird to watch her naked body hanging facing the ceiling and her lover moving around and inserting his penis in her mouth first, then in her vagina. She was not screaming. She was enjoying it!

Jim: "That is "living the Life to the extremes." Contessa would add, if she were alive? Now Jim started to understand why the police were jealous, especially, when they could not enter a private sex club. "No alcohol, no jurisdiction."

Chapter 7

May 2nd, 2002. Three days before the GHM event Jim went to the supermarket to get soda and some beer for Randevu bar. The clerk was anxious to help.

Clerk: "Let me help you with the loading. I know how to do it."

Jim: "Go ahead!" He was surprised and he liked the offer.

Clerk: "Here you are" he handed the loaded flight attendant type cart with bungee cord holding the bottom and the top. On the way out the door the half cases started falling. Jim leaned down to stop the beer from hitting the ground. The metal hook was not properly secured and it released itself. Like the sling shot with which David hit Goliath, the hook hit Jim in the left eye; directly in the pupil/center of eye. He fell by the door in pain. The pain was excruciating. The burst of light was like a thousand stars exploded inside his head. There was no blood but it felt like a knife sliced his head. He would find out nine years later that the trauma to the eye pushed the lens inside and being loose, he would not see anything till the corrective surgery, (at a cost 250,000 dollars). The surgery would replace the lens and stop the pain in 2011!

****The irony of writing this manuscript is that it is written on a broken screen I phone 4, with broken left thumb finger, with a leaking left recovering eye, from the surgery, in a broken 4th language - English. If this is not TIH/GOD, then what is? ****

As of this May 2, 2002 everything would spiral downward! Jim was at exact age of forty-five. The creativity stopped at this fatal day. From here on he would only stay in a destructive mode. Time paradox, antithesis of everything he built was kicking in reverse as of 05/02/2002.

Mi octave met Fa octave. Creativity, (Mi = light) reversed to Destruction (Fa = darkness).

What communist's society in Bulgaria, Mafia, Federal Government, God Neptune, Al Qaeda, ANC, and KGB couldn't do to damage him was accomplished by a clerk at a supermarket? Was the TIH/God sending him a messenger, to slow down, to pull out of the game? Maybe that eye injury, saved him like Jesus on the cross to come back to the next life? The next ten years he had to fight and to win against the two thieves from the Bible like Mr. Dodson and Mr. Rogbin and against everyone and he would win with the help of his higher power TIH/ GOD/ his own sub consciousness...

While he was doing badly his two rival club owners were doing worse. We will look at these facts later. They will end up in bankruptcies, jail and deportation.

Jim drove to the emergency room. They couldn't help him and they said he had to see a specialist. The appointment was on Saturday, May 5, at 10 pm.

Meanwhile, the Randevu bar and the Zoro needed attention; liquor, beer, ice, etc. Jim tried to forget the stolen diamond turntables cartridges for Technics. He left all his stack of amplifiers and speakers at The Zoro and DJ mixers and CD players. He did drive with one eye patched to the wandering eyes of the liquor supplier and his help at both places. His manager just quit a day before because of salary dispute. Most of the profit was diverted toward opening of, the Zone. His Bar manager at Zoro thought he deserved more money, jealous of the money drained at the other club.

Jim: "Lora, I need Benson to go to Zoro. He is licensed for ABC manager and I want him to watch my money and contractors."

Jim and Benson hardly ever talked. Benson had no interest in Jim's expansion ideas. Benson was Lora's son.

Lora: "This is not a whore bar!" She would talk to the commander of 1st MPD.

Commander: "Actually I do like Mercedes," ignoring her remark. She was a snow white Philippine, pleasing plump twenty-four year old lady, who was very smart and she could hold great conversations. She had the strangest story to tell.... later on....

The Georgetown university eye doctor team seemed weak. It was assembled probably from some new. residency assignment? While Jim was strapped in the doctor's chair, the two young doctors were doing their experiments on his left eye. They were trying to reduce the infection by putting drops in his eye, then measuring the pulse every thirty minutes.

Jim: "How long will this take? I have a club to run...."

Doctor: "You have your choice. Save the club or lose the eye?" She was a no nonsense doctor.

Jim: "I prefer to keep both, but I can't text or call anybody in my condition."

Thomas from Evolve: "Hey, Jim. They are trashing your club. "The call came at 3.15 am on Sunday morning. Jim jumped out of the doctor's chair and headed toward the Zoro. The diesel Benz flew through many yellow to red lights. At 3.30 am he pulled over.

Jim: "Benson, what happened? What did you do?"

Benson: "Closing hours at 3 am. I told them to stop according to the ABC Law!"

Jim: "You are an idiot! Those are Ravers. They play music till 6 am. You can stop them from drinking, but not from playing music. Idiot! They have 8 DJs lined up. You did not know?"

Benson: "No. I did not know about that. Why wouldn't your staff know about it? I don't work here. You told me to watch your money. That's what I did. Your crew, here are the ones that started unplugging things around here! Here is the money." He handed a money bag and Z report.

Jim: "Where are my turntables, Dj mixers, and amplifiers and my Speakers?"

Benson: "I am not aware of what equipment you do have? Your crew here should have known, what was going on!"

Thomas from Evolve: "I know where your equipment was. They were trying to steal more stuff. I stopped them from entering your office. It could have been worse."

Jim: "I will call the police. I have almost nothing left here, except one stack of speakers and an amplifier rack."

Police officer: "Did you see anybody taking your equipment? Can you prove it is yours?" saying it very sarcastically, but not very helpful.

Jim: "Thomas saw them and he contacted me. I had to leave my treatment to save what is left." He was still wearing the pirate-like fresh eye patch. When he was talking the pain was increasing in his eye.

Police: "I can't search those trucks if you can't show me who stole your equipment?" He was just totally uncooperative!

Jim: "You see them on display with pictures. This is the lineup of DJs all night." He pointed toward the wall with a poster of the event.

Police Officer: "We can't open the trucks and unload them unless you show me a specific person?" Why were the Police acting this way? Acting like Jim was the thief and was telling them lies. Somehow, the Officer had put two questions in one. Meanwhile, Mr. Tucker from GHM made his own call to the police about Jim holding his trucks from leaving. More police cruises arrived to the empty club.

Jim: "Assholes!" he thought. "I guess because my ABC manager was trying to stop them from partying after 3 am?" He replied.

Police Officer: "They can dance after 3 am, they can't drink." Finally they agreed on something.

Jim: "I told my ABC Manager that, but he was just too concerned about the liquor license."

Police Officer: "We never stopped a license because of dancing; we stopped it because of violence and drugs usage".

Jim: "Just like the Friday's "the Buzz" at Nations?"

Police Officer: "You be careful with Go Go. Otherwise, your days are numbered here." He drove away...

Jim was disappointed at the whole situation and entered the club and shut the doors closed. He was looking around at his tornado like passed floors. The missing equipment was not the only issue. He was surprised of his loyal bartenders. How come nobody called him and warned him of GHM trashing the club?

Jim was glad to have sound and speakers spread between Zoro and Zone clubs. The next day he pulled all equipment from the Zone and he placed it in Zoro. Then he drove to the Guitar Center in Rockville. He spent all the money, Zoro and Randevu, made on buying new equipment. He got new 1210 MK2 dual voltage black Technics turntables and amplifiers at amount of 5,000.00 dollars.

In the evening he contacted Mr. Bender, his landlord.

Jim: "Hey Mr. Bender!"

Mr. Bender: "Hey Jim! You are calling on Sunday! Better be good news?" He always started with positive attitude.

Jim: "Sorry to tell you, but I have bad news." He paused.

Mr. Bender: "Something burned down?" he was still trying to laugh, but half way this time.

Jim: "Three things. First, I had bad eye injury four days ago. I may lose the eye? Second, last night, while I was at the hospital they robbed all my equipment at Zoro. Now I am trying to replace it at cost about $5,000. Third thing is I am in excruciating pain and I can't handle the Zone, the new club."

Mr. Bender: "I am sorry to hear that too. What do you want to do now? You know you owe me rent!" He was a bit agitated.

Jim: "I am thinking of letting go the Zone. I have to recover my eye before I lose it. Too much stress." He sounded like he was in pain, not common for him at all.

Mr. Bender: "Before you give up, why don't you find good help?"

Jim: "I tried and tried. Most of them are thieves or not responsible. I left my old club on weekend and they make half of my previous sales."

Mr. Bender: "Ok, talk to Eddie at the Bottoms Club and give him the keys Monday. Hope everything there is in good shape?" His voice was really the opposite of when he started.

Jim: "Hey Mr. Bender! I have invested 20,000 dollars last two months in there. You have better electrical and plumbing there and back walls are plugged with bricks, no more birds flying in and out." He was trying to be cheerful, but the more he was talking the more pain was building in his left eye.

May 8th was spent hooking the newly bought equipment and testing the extra speakers.

Eric: "The new sound system is not better than the old one. Just looks more modern." Eric was sound tech for many Go-Go bands.

Jim hired the new bar manager who looked like Denzel Washington, the famous Hollywood actor. He was unfortunately gay.

Walter: "Hey boss. I see you are hurt. Let me run the business, you just relax. Make sure your eye gets better, ok!"

Jim: "First, I need a full inventory and I want to keep track on the bottles of Remy and Champagne. We have around $60,000 in inventory. I have some of the old bartenders from the beginning. If you feel you need more help for Memorial Day you can bring them in?"

Walter: "May I tell you something? Most of my bartenders wouldn't work on Go-Go events, but they are ok with Big Duke on Fridays."

Jim: "Look mister, this is not a game. I can accommodate some of your gay friends, but sometimes I am short of help and I need requests for leave in advance. DC Ramble Band followers buy mostly bottles. How difficult would it be to serve them?" He was in pain. This eye needed less talk and more rest.

Walter: "Addison Band folks are wild and aggressive," he was capricious.

Jim: "Let's pull through the Gay Pride Memorial Day then we will decide who will stay and who will go? I need honest people first, emotions we will sort out later. Now let me rest for an hour!" He retrieved to his office. He used some eye drops and slept on the couch in pain on and off for an hour... Even in this condition he was supplying the remaining two clubs with everything they needed. The big Ford E350 was very useful vehicle.

White Gina: "Wow, you look great with the pirate patch!" She was 6 feet tall blonde with deep scars across her eyebrow and her lips. She was from Chicago. A knife fight left her with twenty-two cuts all over her body and face.

Jim: "You are as bad as me." Both of them were laughing. The bar Randevu was where Jim felt at home. It was his creation. It was his beginning four years before. He knew his neighbor restaurants were getting weak and losing business. While the happy hour at Normandy was busy with a young group of professionals, but the Starlight, had low attendance.

Jim's price changes worked. "Change the price, change the clientele" was his slogan.

The similar pub down the street, O'Harrah's, was struggling too. They had sales of beer corona all day and night for 3 dollars and their bar was still mostly empty. O'Harrah's was popular with the gambling and afterhours cocaine sales and use of it. It was a hangout for the stripper ladies working at Arthur's who wouldn't hesitate doing a line of white powder and occasionally, selling some sexual favors to johns they took with them after work to this after hours pub. The gambling was in the form of poker card games. One of the players was Sym, a manager at Arthur's restaurant, which was sharing same building with Zealots. The owner was Ronnie, who was also the owner of three more establishments called "Billards R us." They were mixed use restaurants that had most of the revenue coming from pool tables/billiards. The rumors had it that Ronnie's son was a cocaine addict and no wonder Ronnie's obsession was to find a manager to solve all his business and family problems. Ronnie was infamous with his cameras installed everywhere in his establishments and with intrusive voyeurism he was able to control his employees and his patrons also. Legally, cameras cannot be pointed toward the seating patrons, but, when they tip, they would walk to dancers to hand them the cash or insert the bills in their garter belt. Ronnie would kick out customers who would pass business cards to dancers, but dollars spending was accepted. His voice would be ghostly sounding on the PA.

Ronnie: "Tell Sky to keep her legs closed when on stage. Twisting, bending is ok. This is not a porno stage."

Mr. Cole: "Yes, sir!" He was his floor manager. He was in charge of "arthur'sdancers.com" with 40 registered escorts. Was Arthur's some front for a Catholic College, or nuns gone wild? Most of them will be invited to the fourth residential floor at club Cloud. One of them was Giselle, their number one mixed race beauty. There the host Mr. Dodson will bring his clients for wild cocaine parties and for the dancers to practice their true profession, charging thousands for sex. Later on a major cocaine dealer would be caught in Arthur's. Amazingly, with all his cameras Ronnie couldn't catch the white powder sales, but the FBI did.

Every restaurant and club in DC had a story to tell. From 1,500 liquor establishments in the area 35 had some kind of dancing promotions. Just during 2002, five major clubs were shutdown.

1. Element: Techno club with 4 floors. Infighting between partners, law suits, bad promotions attracting army crowds and three fights in one night.
2. Coco loco: Financial mismanagement, the owner's nephew on cocaine, taxes owed. "Panorama" promoters hang out.
3. Diversite: Spanish hang out. Tango dancing classes, stabbing and closed after years of legal battles.
4. Vibe: Tax evasion, work without permits, and closed.
5. 11th hour: Teswa, Ethiopian investor, tax evasion, closed.

The conspiracy to close restaurants and clubs in DC was very obvious. The ABRA was trying to move the players around, to close the Mom and Pop old establishments, to clear out the clubs for the Baseball Stadium in SE. They used the federal legislation of "eminent domain," to squeeze the undesirable business owners. ABRA decided to work against liquor license holders to prevent landlords from buying their tenants leases or to pay them for construction cost which is a clause in any legal lease ("demolition clause").

Bethesda developer wanted to invest in SE in and around the future Nationals Stadium. His name was Theodore N. Lerner and his group. At this time, they were dealing with Mayor Fenty. Most of the developers agreed on building condominiums, but the 41,000 seat Stadium needed 9,000 cars parking space.

The first targets were the sex clubs in SE area, next to the Navy Yard.

When a male dancer ejaculated from the stage on a US Senator at Bottoms, their liquor license days were numbered. One has to wander about the disclosing of the social status of this patron? Ziegfeld's, Follies, Secrets, Nation and all the other nightclubs would be closed by end of 2006. Bottoms, Sodom and Club 55 would be next to close in 2007. The developers would start demolition within a week of their closing. There was nothing coincidental here. It proves the conspiracy between government and developers, and the same applies to landlords against tenants, who were desperately trying to hold on to their investments and their liquor licenses.

That's where the destruction wave started. Once the government sees outside money arriving in billions, the loyalty stops toward the lease holders and towards the long built business or personal relationships. Jim's slogan was "Money is a divider, not a uniter." In his decades of doing business he found out once people see cash of any amount their normal everyday consciousness blocks out and the old greed symptoms kicks in. It is always related to vulnerability of the human psyche, "what could this amount of money do for me?"

There is a difference between "need" and "greed." When a person or government is poor and the money suddenly appears the need is real and the greed is hidden.

When a person is well off, and DC government was well off in 2002, then there is no need, but only greed. Mayor Barry used to brag about his ability to manage DC's 3 billion dollar budget (in 2002, but 8 billion in 2012), not a small amount for a population of 800,000 people spread, on some 50 square miles of mostly federal and some residential land.

The bartenders were lining up for the big Memorial Weekend Called "Gay Pride," by Big Duke promoters. Walter brought any kind of bartenders. One of them was Kurt, who was an undercover ABC investigator. He had seen when one of the bartenders was fired over stealing $10 from the first order of serving his three drinks. He, Kurt, had a terrible attitude. Jim was still wearing dark shades when they met, (the eye patch was removed a week before).

Kurt: "So, you are the owner?"

Jim: "Yes, I am? Seems like someone told you about me?"

Kurt: "I did not expect you to be this age? You are kind of young. I heard you have other clubs too?"

Jim: "Yes, they come and go! But only history will judge what stays? Now, I have only one requirement."

Kurt: "I have the experience. What do you need?" He was trying to be a smart ass.

Jim: "I do not tolerate cheaters. I do expect 100% of the sales to enter the register. I can understand mistakes as long they are written as soon as they occur. It gets busy at times, but never too busy to write a note."

Kurt: "I saw what you did to "the three drinks" bartender. I do not approve of what you did, but you are the boss here!" He was really an extreme asshole.

Jim: "Let's see what the Memorial weekend will bring? Then we will select a great permanent crew. Again, depends on you guys' performance!"

Jim was making sure there was enough liquor for the week of Memorial weekend. He had a Go-Go night on Tuesday, three days before the Big Event. He was hoping that no accident would occur and Addison Band crowd could be contained. He observed a bunch of slashed tires of women's rival cars.

Jim: "Want me to call the police?" He acted concerned.

The Go-Go ladies: "Nah, we know who did it. We will take care of them ourselves. It is Go-Go justice. Police would just interfere, we are not calling the Police, and we don't like Police." They were "hood," serious. The police did not like them either. They, the Police, were not too far. Matter of fact, they were busy stopping and searching cars and harassing their drivers and passengers at the exit of Half Street and P Street, SW. They really were looking for anything illegal, guns, drugs or simply intoxication! And if one with a Police badge could search for something they would always find it. The Police reports were piling up without Jim's knowledge. Some of the patrons would complain to Big Greg and he sequentially would tell Jim.

Big Greg: "Man, what is wrong with the Police around your club? They keep harassing and arresting my people. They really don't like your club, I heard." Things were getting extremely tense with him.

Jim: "I heard they don't like Nation's crowd, or anybody hanging in sex clubs. I really don't know what they approve of at night time?" saying it with a little nervousness.

Big Greg: "My people are looking for other clubs. I wish I could promote in your club every Saturday, but we have to calm down the cops."

Jim: "I will go to 1st MPD Monday. I don't want to stir up anything before Memorial Day."

Big Greg: "I told my people to stop fighting, but the problem is the outsiders waiting in cars and drinking in them. They tend to start trouble."

Jim: "Maybe we can stop them from parking nearby the club? And I have issues with your people giving me fake money."

Big Greg: "I get burned once in a while too, but my cashier got counterfeit detector pen and they stopped trying to pass fake bills."

Jim: "Great idea, you should have your own club!"

The May 28th, 2002 Friday night arrived finally and the crowd entering was building up. Many of them had tickets bought on line. Some were anxious to pay at the door and to enter. Walter was right. Big Duke was right. This was the event of the year. It was the first and last major event in Jim's business life. It was the Mount Everest pick of his career. The crowd grew larger and larger. The door count was near 3,000. The crowd outside trying to enter was approximately another 1,000 people. Jim asked the security to place barriers to keep the crowd at a 25 yard distance from the door. The six bars inside were well stacked and even they opened an extra bar upstairs where a new lady bartender was working. She was chubby unattractive thirty something.

Jim: "Martha, one thing I want from you. Be honest and you will be here the next ten years! Ok?"

Martha: "I heard of you. Yes sir!" The place was filling up. It was 95 percent gay men, some women were there, but they were from Bonnie Heit's promotion. They were happy and contained crowd. They were good spenders.

Jim was proud of himself. His ideas were finally materializing.

4,000 people were at his place spending money. Studio 54 was not here, but he could imagine the similarity then and now. Only twenty-six years ago his conceived and aspiring dream and ideas were coming to fruition. He even imagined if he had that amount of people every weekend then, "we are good."

The desire to achieve was an emotion compressed into energy and at specific wave length of his brain work he was able to send the light beam and with speed of light the electromagnetic wave, was in motion to create the gravitational wave (WeZon = Matter) and therefore that event in this club. The happiness was on his face; that radiation of success, which was his third club! The frequency, the success!

If anything was to be linked in this enigma algorithm, it was the link of 101 years of research, starting with:

1. Max Planck in year 1900, E = hv
2. Wheeler's magnetism to energy and reverse
3. Einstein/Bohr theory E = MC square
4. Alan Turing machine in 1937, breaking the Enigma code
5. Edward Teller's research in "Manhattan project" (hydrogen bomb... it should be called the helium bomb)
6. Let us not forget Tesla, the father of AC electricity!
7. Jim's "Quantum mind of creativity", The QMC Law!

Where would Jim's name be in history?

What does it take to outsmart the most powerful capitalist machine in the world to convert 100 dollars to millions in four years? No, no brand names like Michael Jordan, Kobe Bryant, Bill Gates, Warren Buffet, Kardashians, Marilyn Monroe, Kennedy, and Lindsay Lohan. ...was Jim to compare himself with? Those are "basement gurus, entertainment gurus, and financial gurus" of the decade.

A thousand years from now nobody would even know who they were? History does not remember Waldorfs, Vanderrbilts, Rockefellers, and Carnegies except for their substantial money's worth. Not one of them wrote any formulas for their success.

Rockefeller said, "God gave me Money."

Jim Walker said, "God gave me knowledge," and writing this manuscript in the 4th language he would say," God writes this book, not me." Was he the 1%? Yes, or in a lesser percentage. They are maybe twenty human beings of his category, or like his lawyer Nikias will say in his "league." Everything he touched would turn to success.

All those thoughts were interrupted suddenly by fire command sirens and police following the fire trucks. Jim was surprised to see them and he stepped forward to inquire why they were here.

Fire chief: "We heard a complaint about parking problems. Many boat owners cannot get out of their parking spaces and they are boxed in."

Jim: "I will send a message to the DJ to announce that and we can solve the problem ASAP!"

Police officer: "What is the crowd tonight, Go-Go again? I will make sure this building will be demolished!" He was biased and hysterical.

Jim: "Calm down, Officer! It is Gay Pride night. I think between the Fire Department, Police and "demolition" and this Gay Event, I am in a tough position to help you whatever side I have to take? But we have to pay the bills, and taxes. So I would appreciate your assistance more than your interference!"

Police officer: "No Go-Go? I will see what I can do, ok!" he disappeared toward the marina 200 yards away making way through a crowd of a 1,000 people, splitting them in two as they were reeds in the water. Jim entered the club through a side door. The only way to get to the registers was to jump over the bar.

Jim: "Would you scoot over? I need to get inside."

Gay men: "Sure!" unlocking hands and laughing watching Jim jumping over the bar. He made sure he never walked empty handed. He would bring ice and cash for change and on the way out he would take the "drops," (small amounts of hundreds of dollars, he would write a receipt for).

The ice was disappearing as soon the bins were filled up. The trash was piling up (Jim's "measurement of success"). The 1,000 dollars back up in singles was going fast. Jim had a system. When the bartenders would have enough singles in their tips bucket, they would convert them into larger 20 dollar bills, and then the 20 dollar bills would be converted to 100 dollar bills. That way there would be constant change in the circulation of small bills. He considered the tip bucket as back up bank.

The first shock came soon after he tried to convert some singles to large bills at the tip buckets. Walter and Kurt were working at the main bar. Melissa and Tanya were bartending on the other side of the DJ's booth. Troy and Victor were on the second floor and at a separate corner Martha was working at the 7th, make shift bar. When Jim approached those two characters, Walter and Kurt, they became defensive. They kept asking for more single bills for change. Jim gave them 200 dollars and was surprised within thirty minutes they were asking for more single bills. Jim pointed toward the tips buckets. He even started to count singles from their tips to convert into larger bills. They were very agitated.

Walter: "Please, do not touch our tips?" he screamed.

Jim: "What is your story? You do not trust me?" he observed many 50s and 20s mixed with the singles. He couldn't believe their resistance. Seemed some of the big bills never entered the register!

Kurt: "If you touch my money, I will quit right now!" he was threatening.

Jim: "I wish I had substitute bartenders. I would replace those two thieves right away." He walked away to see the other five bartenders.

They were busy too. He decided to drop the rest of the single dollar bills and wait and see. He instructed bartenders to use credit card machine. That way they wouldn't need any change. The jumping over bars and entering through side doors and through rear emergency stairway connecting the first and second floor became like a roller coaster routine for the next three hours. At times some bartenders would complain that they were short of change.

Jim: "Just use your own tips." He observed Charles and Kurt just taking the money from customers and circumventing the register they were throwing the 20s, 50s, 100s strait in the huge tip bucket.

Jim: "That's plain wrong!" he thought, but then he decided to gamble and wait for the reports.

He was looking at that human sea of people dancing, drinking men and he was both excited and disappointed. His mind was wondering if all of this was worth it. Was his drive toward expansion too soon?

He needed help; a second floor manager. When he asked Lora and Benson they declined. Maybe after the GHM (rave party/robbery) they chickened out? Or, maybe, they saw the chaos that was to come and didn't want any particular part of it…? He found himself running those two clubs by himself. The huge Ford van was busy moving 40 to 50 cases of liquor, beer, wine, soda and huge bins of ice. His eye was still injured and he had to remove the dark sunglasses at night time, so he could see. He probably needed night vision infrared goggles, because the crowd preferred minimum light. They were using rotating beam lights and huge fog machine on the first floor. It was amazing to see this club owner walking through the 100% black crowd. He was like a white dot in a sea of darkness. He was using a flash light to cut through.

He would drop money taken from the registers at the huge safe behind the double bar where Walter and Kurt were stealing and serving drinks at same time. At 3 am the music stopped. Trash bins were full. Jim took the Zee reports from each register. He decided to count the money later on. He brought two huge plastic bags. They could hold thirty pounds of leafs. Now they were holding sixty pounds of dollar bills total! He brought the money to his Mercedes Benz. He instructed the bartenders to clean in and around the club. They all left around 3.30 am. Jim decided to stay till day light in the office to make sure he would not be ambushed and to check for any stowaways in the club. He had a good cigar in the office, and relaxed on the couch with his favorite and loyal bartender lady Tanya. They had sex and she was pretending that she was concerned about his wounded eye.

Tanya: "Hey Boss, how did we do tonight?" She was trying to look at the total amount Jim was calculating. Her naked body was in perfect shape. She was one of the exotic bartenders he interviewed a month before for The Zone club. She was the only one on this Friday he could trust. Later on her and Melissa's Zee report were the most accurate compared to all the thieves, Walter recommended.

Jim: "Hey baby! You are not my wife yet! You can make your estimate judging your numbers, but I saw a lot of theft tonight. How much? I will figure that out?" he hid the report in the small office safe. "Go take a shower" he slapped her shapely tight ass.

Tanya: "I may marry you but this club business is not what I want to do for the next ten years, especially with Go-Go bands around!" she disappeared in the Jacuzzi room.

Jim: "Go-Go is bringing twice more than Big Duke. Show me who we can substitute for Go-Go?"

Tanya: "Hey, no more business. Come in the Jacuzzi. I need you to soap my back. Relax now!" Her shiny body was fully submerged and looking even sexier and inviting. Jim quickly looked at the numbers. It was about 14,200 dollars total. With the deposit $5,000 and two more days to go Saturday and Sunday he was optimistic. He put the account books away and joined Tanya in the Jacuzzi. Now he understood what Mr. Bender was saying "if the couch could talk…?"

Jim: "I think my landlord was wrong? He should of said "if that Jacuzzi could talk?" and then he grabbed the soap to do Tanya's sexy back.

Tanya: "I don't like the all gay crew Walter is bringing to the club, especially this guy Kurt." She was soaping Jim's back now.

Jim: "He gave me some lip earlier and he will be gone soon after the Memorial Weekend, trust me baby!"

Jim had three bartender ladies he treated like wives. Tanya was his favorite because she was not complaining about too much. And even if she did, she would still come to work. The other two were finicky like cats. They would find any excuse or just didn't show at all.

Tanya: "I want to go home now. Just walk me to my car." She dried herself up and put her dress on.

Jim: "I hope you make good money this weekend? Here is a small bonus for your company." He knew "thank you" was just not enough. She took the money and kissed him on the cheek.

Jim: "All women are the same… But not all have time for a Jacuzzi." He shook his head, but he was happy.

Tanya: "You are a great boss, Jim! Most people underestimate you, for real! Oh, here is your bonus!" she lifted her skirt to expose the great shaped flower like vagina. She trimmed it to nice black triangle and the big pink clitoris was sticking out like a small nose between those young and tight long and pink vagina lips.

Jim: "Keep doing that and I will never let you go! Go now, bye." He closed the car door like a gentleman and an officer.

Tanya: "Bye, Jim!""

Jim went back to his office. He waited two more hours until daylight. He had seen a cross dresser walking around many times. He never talked to him. He never knew what his intentions were? After he checked all the exit doors, under the floor two foot high stage, windows and roof sky light hatch, Jim turned off all the lights and he activated the alarm system. He locked the door. His diesel Benz drove him to his home. Nobody followed him. He heard horrible stories about club owners been robbed while driving home. Once in the parking garage at his apartment complex he was relieved to be home. He opened a blanket at his apartment and shook off the trash bags with the different denomination of dollar bills and he observed the two feet high small mountain of cash. It took him thirty minutes to sort them out in 5, 10, 20, 50, 100s denominations. He decided to count them later. He needed to go to sleep.

About 1.00 pm he woke up. He counted the money. It was around $10,500, he was puzzled. The report at the office was $14,290, he recalled. He remembered the careless behavior of Walter and Kurt.

Jim: "Those crooks!" ...He said. "I will do something about that!" He remembered the liquor was almost half gone, especially the top shelf brand. He had to sustain the rest of the weekend. He ordered ten more cases of Remy, Gray Goose vodka, Patron. The price tag was $4,100!

Jim: "I have low profit here. If they were honest I should have at least $10,000 net. My small bar Randevu gives me more profit for less inventory.

I will see how much they have stolen per register when I get there?" He stopped by Randevu, first. He dropped some of the liquor and beer, and then he checked the cash in the register.

When Jim checked the individual reports at Zoro, he found the discrepancies right away. Only Melissa's and Tanya's reports were close to the report adding the "drops." So, the other five crooks stole nearly $850 each! Marta's report was short 700 dollars, Kurt around $900, Walter around $820, Troy around $750, Victor around $630.

The meeting was outside the club. All bartenders were read their errors.

Jim: "I know what happened, two things. First, you rang the right amount, and then you stole the money. Second, you stole the money then you rang the assumed amount. Either way, you stole money from me. You also wasted liquor, by over pouring or by giving it free to benefit your tip jar!"

Walter: "The report is added to the report of the Go-Go on Tuesday!"

Kurt: "You are just accusing us without proof." He was the same asshole.

Jim: "I changed the registers. I brought extra registers. They all were zeroed at my other club. Five registers can't be all wrong?"

Walter: "Mistakes happen, we did not have change and we were running tabs to some customers."

Jim: "I need a Police Officer next to every register and you would still be lying. I saw many times you take money and you did not ring the drinks at the register. You just put them in the tip bucket!"

Kurt: "You need cameras. Then everything you say would be on video."

Jim: "That is going to be in the new club, in due time I will have everything. Right now what I do need is honest bartenders."

Walter: "If you had me as General Manager you would not have any discrepancies, I guarantee that."

Jim: "Do not tell me managers don't steal."

Walter: "They do not, if you pay them right?" he was a smart ass.

Jim: "Listen guys! Nobody pays anybody. The business pays for everything.

Unfortunately, there must be proper accounting. Don't think you should pay yourselves, without my knowledge? That is where our concepts differ. You decided to pay yourselves $700 to $900 dollars extra, circumventing the owner, me! I have to buy almost everything again today because of what you wasted yesterday, or gave it up free."

All of them got quiet. Tanya and Melissa were shaking their heads. They knew about the gay crew's conspiracy and they were secure in their jobs.

Jim: "It is funny how the guilty always argues first. Tonight I will decide who will stay and who will go?" he disappeared in his office.

He pulled out a Panasonic camera and ran a wire to the first floor bar where Kurt and Walter were to work their last shift. Not surprisingly the numbers at the end of the shift matched perfect and the liquor was not given away without accounting for it. That night was almost a repeat of the previous night, but there was no overcrowding, no Fire Department and no Police this time. The total was around $12,700 that Saturday night. After everyone made their reports Jim fired all the gay crew.

Walter: "You will not last long here!" He cursed Jim on the way out, throwing the club keys at him.

Jim: "If I kept you here too long, you are right, I would definitely, not last here! Go away before I call the Police." Both Kurt and Walter left the club, cursing, slamming the huge metal door.

Jim: "I hope they will not mess up my car?" he followed them outside.

"Go steal $1,000 dollars from the next club! This is not your first time, obviously! Bye." He returned to the club.

He kept Tanya and Melissa and he called some of his loyal female bartenders and one Spanish barman, Oscar. He brought a Spanish bar back. Everything seemed in order on Sunday.

Marcel: "Hey, Jim! I paid Bonnie Heit to buy this event. After all we have a contract with you to do every Sunday, DL Sunday's.

Jim guessed DL means Down Low, or Gay.

Jim: "Well, since you paid her then you do not have to pay me the usual $1,000 dollars fee today, ok!"

Marcel: "You are great businessman, Jim." He thought he had made a deal? The crowd was very small and it was a bunch of lesbians, probably from the initial Bonnie Heit advertisements? Some gay guys showed up too, but no line at the door. The drinking was minimal and Jim was hardly waiting to end the event. Was the curse of firing Walter and Kurt working already?

Marcel was walking around quietly disappointed. Jim felt kind of sorry for him, but that is the "nature of the beast." One day, "hell breaks loose," next day nothing happens.

Jim: "Welcome to the "club business," Marcel! It only looks good on outside and on some nights. That's what the advertisers use and to create an illusion that every night is great club night. They use the television commercials and websites to help spread the false feeling of this happy great crowd. But, they don't show the slow nights like this. I have to pay my bartenders regardless. Sorry brother!"

Jim was putting philosophy in something most young entrepreneurs were not seeing behind the scenes. Glamour, fancy cars, beautiful women, people with star status, drugs, champagne bottles, a lot of cash! Was that too extreme? Yes, it was a fantasy and nightmare at the same time. You have to include the positive and negative, the creativity and the destruction. The honest student trying to put himself through college next to the ten years, seasoned thief, alcoholic, drug dealer camouflaged as bartender, like Walter was, devils and angels, the antagonistic characters inside, the good cop and bad cop outside. The federal government fighting the DC government but at the end they were working together against club owners! It was like a marriage in hell, yet the couple would have a child. The end of the deal is "Mr. Cash?"

Whole USA and the world are obsessed with getting someone's money. They call it "free enterprise system?"

The definition is: Free enterprise is an economic system that provides individuals the opportunity to make their own economic decisions, free of government constraints, and as private profit-potential businesses.

The reader should remember the part..., "free of government constrains."

For some reason and somewhere in the translation the government did not like the paragraph, "free of government constraint." So, they invent "taxes."

If this is not a constraint, then what is? But not only do they invent taxes, they created "regulations." Using the regulations the "beautiful" mighty government now tells you how to do business with the public and it's suppose to be "safe." When they talked about safety, they also talk about "equality." When the equality kicks in they talk about "level the pay," no prejudice towards age, sex, pregnancy, alternative life style and nationality. And towards the end of the government constraint of business they would add "benefits." Now the business is not only regulated, but the benefits must include "insurance," "sick leave," "vacation paid for, pregnant woman up to 60 days and a guaranteed job when she returns." What happens to the "free enterprise system?" And then enter the unions with their similar demands, which are a carbon copy of most federal regulations!

Great economies rise when government assist businesses with building highways, bridges, help with aviation, and assure cheap energy. Jim categorized economies in next categories.

1. Capitalism: True capitalism will have minimal regulations, somewhat chaotic, but everyone makes money.
2. Socialism: Mixed regulations of different factions, where the government controls most of the large businesses, but will allow individual and small mom and pop businesses to flourish. People are 50 percent taxed, but they have free education, free health, and paid vacations.
3. Communist: Everything is centrally controlled; taxes are 90 percent, or just work for equal and minimal pay. Free education and free health, paid vacation.
4. Monarchies: Dictatorship. Almost no pay, people work on allowances, free education and nothing else.

When the government is intrusive, it taxes everything and pretends it is democratic, something is wrong with the whole picture!

Essentially, capitalism is a free market system of trade, governed exclusively on the economic principle of supply and demand and maintained through competition. Consumers and businesses form a relationship that ultimately determines the cost of a good or service and the health of the market.

The father of capitalism is 18th-century Scottish political economist Adam Smith. Smith pointed to built-in checks and balances of the capitalist system that are meant to prevent abuse. For example, higher wages mean a laborer can afford to properly feed him or her. In Smith's words, "a plentiful subsistence increases the bodily strength of the laborer." So a company that pays more than average wages will create a stronger workforce and increase its productivity, giving it a competitive edge in the marketplace. When Smith's capitalist theory was put into practice in the developing United States, these natural checks and balances didn't always emerge. As a result, the federal government has enacted forced checks and balances to counteract the weight produced by unfettered competition. What has emerged is a hybridized version of a free market. Essentially, each act limited markets by granting the federal government the power to regulate business. As a result, the United States no longer has a free market system. Instead, the United States now has a managed economy -- by definition, a nonmarket economy since it doesn't exist solely on supply and demand.

Robert Heilbroner and Lester Thurow, *Economics Explained* (1982)
"Capitalism works better than it sounds, while socialism sounds better than it works."

Rockefeller: ....once said, "God gave me money."
Jim: .... said, "God gave me knowledge."
Churchill: ....said, "I wrote the history."
Jim: .... said, "I explain the history."

One who tries to explain history without any personal experience in it is a philosopher or professor at school. One who explains the history through his own achievements and failures is a history creator. The slogan is not accurate, "Winner takes all." If it is once in a century or it is in world history that slogan may apply. But, in human history the competition creates instant and constant winners and losers. Every military battle is to create an antithesis, unless both withdrew and a peace treaty is signed. The victor will take what he wants and the loser will suffer. Victory always has a price and time limit. Unless he maintains his army and borders he may lose eventually to someone new and a more ambitious adversary.

In the business the rules of engagement are the same as in war. The thirty-five businesses with entertainment in 2002 were battling each other for share of the market. Three of them were dominating the night club scene. Jim Walker, Mr. Dodson and Mr. Rogbin had the combination of oldest, biggest and most advertised clubs.

1. Zoro, oldest USA Club, since 1971, capacity 3,000 people
2. Phantom, most advertised on radio WKYS FM 93.9, capacity 1,000 people.
3. Cloud, biggest capacity 4,000 people, advertised on the radio WPGC FM 95.5.

When the government targets clubs they go first through compliances, occupancy permits, zoning allowances, age restrictions, use of license, and percentage of food sales. That is the legal part of it. Then they move to accounting. They will look at the "books," the state and federal taxes, the net worth (bank accounts, stocks, real estate, luxury items, and insurance). If any outrageous events like funny accounting, major fights and killings, drug sales, they will raid the business and the home of the owners.

At the end of May, Jim received a phone call from his lawyer Nikias.

Nikias: "I have everything ready for you to get your liquor license at The Zone. He pushed toward Jim a huge file with pictures, articles of incorporation, DMZ625 certificate to be signed.

Jim: "Nikias, I already turned down the lease and pulled out from the Zone. I had serious eye injury and because of that the party at the Zoro, the Ravers robbed me."

Nikias: "Welcome to the club business. Sorry to hear that you were injured and robbed. Others have had it worse than you."

Jim: "What do you mean?" he got curious.

Nikias: "I can not disclose my client's name, but he was raided in his Potomac house and assets were seized, because he had "fuzzy accounting, cooking the books."

Jim: "I heard Mr. Rogbin is driving a Rolls Royce and bought a 5 million dollar house in the Potomac area. It must be him?"

Nikias: "I can't confirm that, but you can assume anything you want? You may be next, to be targeted?"

Jim: "I already noticed the Police resentment when I called them. They will not recover my equipment from the trucks where thieves were hiding my stuff. Also instead of supporting me, they were threatening me that they would bulldoze my club one day."

Nikias: "Don't worry. I hear you have Go Go bands there. If something happens (like a killing), they will take your license for a week." He was trying to accommodate more than to advise.

Jim: "That is all, a week? Thanks!" He was told a lie, but he did not know that, at the moment. Maybe that lie triggered the next event?

Jim thought, "If he continued with Go Go and something happened being closed for one week wouldn't be a financial disaster."

Jim kept reinvesting in his original lounge, Randevu. He built up the back of the private room. He installed frames in the windows, because of a burglary, early in June of 2002.

Mansur: "Let's expand Mike's and Randevu.Starlight is closing soon," Mansur was Jim's partner.

Jim: "I am not ready yet. My hands are full with what I have now."

The story of Sally's to Starlight was turbulent and amazing.

When Jim started Randevu bar, he was against two establishments with 60 and 40 years of experience to the left and to the right of him. Being on a secluded second floor, with a hard to find entrance, small 8 chair bar, he was supposed to have lasted only, "one week."

Sally's was established in the mid fifties and was occupying the space of a divided old house. At the time of the Korean War and Vietnam War, the press from the Washington Post newspaper would go to Normandy and the pimps, hookers and johns would go to Sally's. The normal crowd would go to Philadelphia Mike's, now shared with Randevu. Sally's would be famous with long lines of any kind of bohemian, outcast crowd. The first floor was the legal side of business, a normal happy crowd dancing on 45 rpm juke box vinyl records. The second floor was where the kitchen was supposed to be, and it was. The kitchen was fully equipped but it never cooked a burger or fish or anything. The main attraction on the second floor was the bathrooms. They were a unisex style and where the sex was happening when no one was around. To upgrade the game there was a third floor. The steps between second and third floor were rotten and anyone going up or down risked serious bodily injury. Some regulars figured out where to step and how to make it safe. One needed a flash light to choose the right steps. It was great deterrent for the Policemen from quickly climbing to the penthouse.

That's where the drugs were used, pimps had meetings with their "stables" to collect their money, or "break-in" new recruits. Police were aware of the second and third floor activities, but, because of the War and the sexual revolution the drug use and sex were tolerated to a great extent. Later on the owner Sally retired and basically relinquished her license and lease to her bar manager Jessica. They both agreed on the name change to Starlight and how Jessica would make monthly payments to the retired owner.

The Starlight, Lounge was open for lunch and dinner. Because of their CT (Tavern license), there was no requirement for food sales. Jessica was famous with her, shrimp cold sandwich (lettuce, mayonnaise, shrimp and her secret dressing), at ten dollars. Cheap beer (Heineken and Miller Lite only promotion drafts) and the place of ten bar chairs looked busy. Small dance floor by the juke box and a table by the stairway, three small bar round chairs by the window was all that was producing legal revenue. The second floor was for extra revenue from the johns, paying for sex. The third floor revenue was from pimps and drug dealers. Many times the Police would come to Randevu and ask, "where is your 3rd floor, we hear it is busy place?"

Jim: "We don't have a 3rd floor, but Starlight has!" laughing at the overzealous underpaid and greedy government nobodies. He remembered the movie "Scar face," with Al Pacino who said, "Cockroaches," looking at the TV screen. Here they were in front of Jim. What a coincidence... The next five years he would be fighting them and win.

Jim thought: "Winning is a euphoria of comparing yourself to others who will lose."

The next week was quiet. Wednesday the Queen's Ball was fun to watch (at Zoro), but not much sales at the bar.

Mother Barbara: "I need free drinks and to keep the show going!" he/she, was a promoter for the event.

Jim: "Sure, but I will give you two drinks allowance," he was trying to be nice, but not stupid. The floor was full of people cheering the contestants, who were cross-dressing men who looked like women. Some of them were really confusingly attractive. Jim was not concerned with how they look but how they behaved? He found used condoms behind the couches. He asked the bartender and Mother Barbara to watch for any sexual activities, because that was not allowed in the liquor license.

That show actually gave him the idea to start the exotic dancing next week with real ladies. He brought a promoter Sugar who had ten dancers and the flyers went to all stripper clubs. Unfortunately, at Sodom, Rob Howard was upset and he tried to stop Jim from stealing his customers. He even came to look at the next show to see what the dancers looked like and who they were, and of course who the customers were? The ladies were not local, seemed like they were from out of town and most likely from Maryland? Some of them were really good and they were masters on the pole. They were not nude, they had same outfit the strippers at clubs would wear, but without the nudity.

The next two months Big Duke kept his contract on Fridays and Big Greg accelerated his promotions to every Saturday.

Big Greg: "Beware of the police. They may shut you down if we promote every Saturday," he was concerned.

Jim: "I am looking for someone to come out here strong, but Panorama and other companies do not like the location!" he realized that getting the license does not mean the guaranteed success. Then he was missing Randevu bar, where he really felt at home.

July 28th started normally and the crowd was gathering as usual, being checked and processed inside the club. The second floor was closed for business with huge fortress of sliding doors. Everything was normal until closing time. About 3 am the Police sirens got louder and louder…

Jim: "What happened?"

Andy Sherman: "Something happened five blocks away on Q Street." He was the newly appointed GM. Jim hired him after the gay crew was fired on Memorial Day. He caught him stealing, many times, bottles of champagne and cash, but he still kept him on to work. Within fifteen minutes a commander from 2nd District showed up. When on weekend duty he had the power of the Chief of Police. That was a lot of power.

Commander Jeremy: "Are you the owner?"

Jim: "Yes." He was trying to ignore him.

Commander: "There is a murder down the street. I am here to investigate the case."

Jim: "Where did this happen?" he acted like he cared, but he really did not.

Commander: "On Q street and Half, SW" he was angry. He was determined to make his point. Jim stuck his head out. He saw TV crews pointing cameras toward his entrance and the yellow ribbon around the Zoro entrance.

Jim: "Q Street? That is out of my jurisdiction!" he was right.

Commander: "The victim came out of here, prior to being murdered."

Jim: "I do not have anything to do with that case and you cannot enter my club without probable cause and a warrant! Let me tell you something. When I call 911, the Police come in two hours. When I don't call you, you bring the TV crews and you are harassing me. If you are so concerned about my safety and my business' survival you need to check the patrons before they come here, not when they leave. I see you do stop everyone on the way out."

Commander: "You have Go Go and killers here and Hip Hop and hookers at Randevu. When are you going to be normal?" he was still talking outside the club door. Jim was trying to avoid the TV cameras.

Jim: "What is normal for the Police? Show me one club you like that is normal and bring me their crowd here, please! I guess you feel I am getting rich here? I got robbed two months ago here and at Randevu. You let the thieves go. I can't help you here, no crime was committed here. We have security and we check everyone. Bye Commander. From here on talk to my lawyer!" he slammed the door closed in front of the angry fake chief of police.

Chapter 8

That's where the government of DC started their own downfall, the Fa octave of the government vs. Mi octave of the Club Zoro. The destruction by the government started with words initially and now ending with the TV crews and guns pointing toward Jim's mind creation, the Club Zoro. This was not a hot dog stand, nor deli or coffee shop. This was the Godfather of all Clubs in the USA.

The gravitational wave of creation was meeting the Government hate, envy, bias wave of destruction. The perfect storm of emotions (magnetism theory of Wheeler), will create the swirl of neutrons with negative matter, (quantas are moving in direction toward the center, almost sucking the energy like in a miniature black hole, similar to implosion of a star and creating super nova). Astrophysics is a mirror of human emotions. The next example shows the creation of new time dimensions.

Can we produce micro black holes? Yes…

In a familiar three-dimensional gravity, the minimum energy of a microscopic black hole is 1019GeV, which would have to be condensed into a region on the order of the Planck length. This is far beyond the limits of any current technology. It is estimated that to collide two particles to within a distance of a Planck length with currently achievable magnetic field strengths would require a ring accelerator about 1000 light years in diameter to keep the particles on track. Stephen Hawking also said in chapter six of his Brief History of Time that physicist John Archibald Wheeler once calculated that a very powerful hydrogen bomb using all the deuterium in all the water on earth could also generate such a black hole, but Hawking does not provide this calculation or any reference to it to support this assertion.

However, in some scenarios involving extra dimensions of space, the Planck mass can be as low as the TeV range. The Large Hadron Collider (LHC) has a designed energy of 14 TeV for proton-proton collisions and 1150 TeV for Pb-Pb collisions. It was argued in 2001 that in these circumstances black hole production could be an important and observable effect at the LHC or future higher-energy colliders. Such quantum black holes should decay emitting sprays of particles that could be seen by detectors at these facilities. A paper by Choptuik and Pretorius, published on March 17, 2010 in Physical Review Letters, presented a computer-generated proof that micro black holes must form from two colliding particles with sufficient energy, which might be allowable at the energies of the LHC if additional dimensions are present other than the customary four (three space, one time).

After thirty minutes of taking pictures and making TV statements in front of the Club, the Evil crowd disappeared. Jim was warned from Nikias about this 2nd MPD Commander that he wanted to close all the clubs, and now he finally met him. He had heard about him having TV crews following him everywhere he goes, waiting for the accident to happen? Just minutes before those cameras were facing, videotaping and taking pictures of his own club, he observed Andy Sherman chatting a very long time with the commander just before they left.

Jim: "Why are you talking to these idiots? When I call them they never come in time? Or when they come they take the opposite side. The MPD in DC is useless for businesses."

Andy Sherman: "Nothing about you, just a conversation," he lied.

Jim: "They are investigating and definitely they are not, "just having a conversation!" They have a hidden agenda, mister! Do not talk to them. That is what the lawyers are for, ok!"

Andy Sherman: "Boss, I do not like Go Go, or the Police!" he had a smirking face and a dubious smile.

Jim: "Everyone talks, nobody delivers! What do you suggest?"

Andy Sherman: "I can buy your business and you can just collect a percentage, without putting your foot at the door" he was bluffing.

Jim: "You see, I had three clubs, now I am down to two and they help each other. Who will pay the rent, buy the supplies, pay the employees, pay taxes and make enough profit to give me a cut that I want?"

Andy Sherman: "That can be a gay club only; no Go Go and the Police will not bother you?"

Jim: "The history of gay clubs is not great. Look what happened to Tracks, to Bottoms nearby; to this club we are in now, The Pier 9 twenty-three years ago. Gay is as bad as straight, maybe the Police have a different approach, but at the end they are against everyone... See Nation with Buzz, see Vibe with urban ethnic, and see Diversite with a Spanish crowd. They are against everyone. I really do not know who they approve of? They are against Third Edition, Champions, students were escorted after hours of drinking to Key Bridge and were ordered to leave DC and to go to Virginia. Otherwise they would have been arrested."

Andy Sherman: "I have a rich investor and he may come and talk to you, ok?"

Jim called his lawyer immediately at 10 am.

Nikias: "Hey, Jim. You are famous now! I see your club on TV."

Jim: "Yes, for all the wrong reasons. Someone got killed five blocks away, out of the 500 ft range."

Nikias: "There will be a hearing soon. Maybe they will close you for a week? Did they take your license?" he was a bit sympathetic.

Jim: "Not yet," wondering…

Nikias: "They will. Just let me know, when? Relax. We will get through this eventually. Are the Go Go bands still there?"

Jim: "That guy was nineteen years old; he did not consume any alcohol. Yes, it was Go Go."

Nikias: "I know the commander and I know Chief Naylor's slogan is, "one murder, one license." This Commander you met, takes that slogan seriously and beyond. He wants to close clubs even if there is no murder. He is after the Element, 1223, Coco Loco and others, I heard."

Jim: "That maybe a challenge for me and you now?"

Nikias: "I will see what I can do, but I can't talk too much. I had surgery recently." Jim: "If you can't handle it, send someone else to the hearing, please!"

The license was taken away by Police on Thursday night. They came with guns drawn and they wanted to "meet and greet?"

Jim: "Meet and greet? Why are the EMS/Fire department here, why the guns and pump action rifles drawn to talk to me? I guess people like me would put up a good fight for a reason."

Commander 1st district: "We were sent by the Chief to take the license, not to arrest you. We heard you did not allow the Commander into the club, last time. We're just playing it safe."

Jim: "My license can't be taken without a hearing at the ABC board. There was no crime here. You have no reason to be here. Seems you take action before judgment. It is like justice in reverse?"

Commander: "Now you know why we bring guns! Evictions and license removals cause anger and who knows how you guys would react?" he was serious.

Jim: "You should go after the criminals. Taking away licenses is much easier work to do for you!"

Commander: "Go to the hearing. We are not shutting you down. You can sell soda and non alcoholic beverages."

Jim: "Why did you take my liquor license? The guy was nineteen years old and he never touched alcohol. Not because you are right, but because you can!" He was right.

When a creative person meets the destructive person there is no justification for the outcome. The justice would have been better served if the both parties had an equal weapons system. Then the battle would have been like in Biblical proportion. But since the regulation is through one side of the equitation (Fa octave, destruction - government), the (Mi octave, the Club Zoro - creation) needed to start a stronger opposition than all the weapons and regulations Jim was up against. The Energy does not ever get lost, it transforms to another form. The battle of survival of his dream club was not over. He needed to go to a hearing with ABC board. His lawyer sounded weak on the phone. Was that the beginning of the end? Most of the time, the presence of this great lawyer at the hearings would guarantee a successful outcome. When a lawyer can't talk, then his presence itself wouldn't suffice.

Jim: "I will try to convince them at the hearing that this guy was not innocent and he happened to be in my club, but he did not drink any alcohol."

Nikias: "Those people are mostly lawyers and they do not like the club owners to testify. They prefer talking to legal counsels."

Jim: "Hope you are going to be able to impress them, even with less talking?"

Nikias: "I will try," he was basically gambling by not sending a replacement at the hearing.

The Wednesday hearing at ABC board was a strange gathering. Six women and one man were presiding. They were mostly lawyers who needed extra exposure on TV and self motivated for their own reasons. The TV Crew was kicked out. There were two stories with different contents. One was written by the, Washington Post, (Democratic writers) which was very biased and ill informed. The newspaper was writing about changing the venue, they were totally against Go Go, they were looking for a new owner. The other was written by Washington Times, (Republican writers), which was correct and honest about the facts.

The presiding Chairwoman was Maria Laban. She was the one who would introduce the charge against the club and let the lawyers for the club argue in defense. Then after the witnesses from both sides, show their case the Board will make a decision. The board was allowed to twice a year to have emergency meetings. This was one of them.

Jim was prepared to fight for his club to stay in business. He had copies made of the newspapers to show the discrepancies. He had Big Mac security manager to defend him. Big Greg, the promoter was also attending on his behalf. Nikias was there also but he couldn't talk. What amazed him was to see Andy Sherman, his club GM, seating next to the Government Attorney, Walter Adams. That was like the Bible's presently, reconstructing the story of Judas betraying Jesus for thirty pieces of gold? Seems DC's government copied the Roman/Jewish priests' model some 2,000 years ago of manager against the owner, brother against brother, partner against partner.

Maria Laban: "Are all parties present?" she began the court like hearing.

Nikias: "Yes, Madam Chair! I am here as the club's legal counsel."

Attorney Walter Adams: "I am here for the people of District of Columbia."

Maria Laban: "On July 28, 2002 a patron of Zoro club was shot and killed after leaving the club. He was to be assigned as a fire fighter soon. We are investigating the club's license now. After the hearing we will decide how to solve the issue. We have a dead person here. We need to find out what we can do to prevent this from reoccurring in the future. What are the questions to the club management?" She looked around. Everyone of the board was asking the basic questions. What are the operating hours, does the club sell food, any previous violations, what the security was on the night of the shooting?

Nikias: "Club has a buffet food for patrons, it is CN class, and it requires minimum food sales."

Jim: "The patron, if he was a patron, was nineteen, therefore we did not serve him alcohol. I do not see the reason why my liquor license has been removed from the premises? The patron had ties to gang activities and was in trouble in a shoot out in early March 2002. He survived, but in May he was stabbed with a knife.

He brought his trouble to the neighborhood, but here he was himself intercepted before he got to his own Tec9. Was he in the club or not, we have no witnesses. We can't just blame everything that happens in the area on an open for business venue."

Commander: "Yes, there are no witnesses but based on the event, which was a Go Go promotion and the prior reports, we can build a profile for the club."

Jim: "What prior reports?"

Commander: "June 5th, almost two months before a patron was thrown out by the security. He informed us about silver gun with a black holder was brandished on the dance floor. He was thrown out after he complained to the security."

Jim: "That is not a fact. I am always there and the security checks everything, bags, hair, shoes, they also tap down the patrons for weapons and knives. This is not a credible witness."

Commander: "We are taking everything into account. We had a situation where a Police Officer was attacked that night by a mob of ladies."

Jim: "I was there and I stopped them, basically helping the Police Officer. They were fighting each other, when police interfered. Then they turned against her. That is why there was not an accident and no Police report at that time."

Maria Laban: "I can see you are actively involved in promoting the Go Go and also you are trying to assist the Police, but we have a dead person here. We have to make our own conclusions."

Jim: "I am sure without witnesses one can come out of anywhere; Staples, 711, any deli, but if my club is targeted, I can't stop you from taking my license? Here are copies from the Washington Times. Hopefully, that will explain the history of this guy?" He turned around toward Nikias, but, he was speechless, sick and afraid to defend him. Then he looked at Andy Sherman, who was whispering something to Walter Adams, the attorney for the ABRA equaling to the scene of Judas to the Pharisees.

Maria Laban: "We have a witness who will testify for ABRA. Can Andy Sherman step forward?"

Andy Sherman: "Yes. Present." He stopped chatting with Walter Adams and took the stand. Jim reminisced about Elba five years before who was taking a wrong side to protect her roommate/boyfriend…. and her own ass.

Andy Sherman: "I was the manager at the club but with very minimal input who the promoters were. Jim was making decisions on all bookings. I just joined as GM the last two months."

Jim: "I hired Andy because he supposed to help me with diversification of the club. He represents alternative life style and I asked him to invite any kind of promoters including gays and lesbians."

Andy Sherman: "I have never approved of Go Go and I witnessed underage customers given hand bands, not to drink."

Maria Laban: "So, if they cut their bands off and they could drink?" She was getting angry for no reason.

Jim: "Dear Chair Madam! Here shows the GM not being aware of the door policy and the bar rules of enforcement! The hand bands are given to drinking age patrons. They can show the bands and they can drink. Nobody would cut his band off and would get alcohol. You see your witness is incompetent and clueless as to what, hand band, means."

Nikias: "Do not talk to them. They will think you are hostile and they will punish you more." The ABC board dismissed to a back room. Jim felt like the reality was changing to opposite of everything he worked for in his life. He recovered his eye, but he was losing his dream. The anti reality was gradually building up as anti gravitational field, where the Fa octave was in destruction mode? He remembered the blind District Attorney who sent him to jail in 1997 for 180 days. The similarity was astonishing.

1. False witnesses and reports from the Police, anti Go Go.
2. The correct newspaper was ignored. Nobody was concerned with the Victim and his true criminal background?
3. Lawyer who can't talk and can't defend him, sick or inadequate.
4. His own GM conspiring against him, just like Elba turned against him.
5. The Big Greg promoter and his Big Mac Security were not Big at all.
6. The license removed even the alleged customer never touched alcohol.
7. Biased ABC Board because Jim was a foreigner (in the shadow of 09/11/2001) and because the Victim was allegedly to be a "fire fighter," in the future even though he was nothing but a criminal.

The perfect storm of Jim achievements and the anti reality of those seven factors to shut the club down, to clear space for the Stadium! Why was his GM against him? Andy never liked Go Go, but he was paid a goof salary. He was a thief, but he was never fired? Even he was trying to get an investor or a buyer for the club! So, what was his motive in testifying against Jim weighed against the license? The answer came sooner, than later (the Police promised him the club ownership in exchange for his false testimony).

The ABC board returned and announced their decision!

Maria Laban: "After careful evaluation of the facts and the witnesses' testimonies we, the seven members of the ABC Board, arrived at our decision. We have a dead person here. That is why the license was removed. The club lacks proper security and proper management. We are suspending the liquor license for 80 days, counting the day of its removal from the premises. We will review the situation with the license on the next hearing in October. We suggest the owner to create a plan on how to promote a better and safer operation to the public. If his lawyer can assist him with any recommendations, we will consider them in returning the license."

Jim looked around. No one stood up in his defense! No one from the thousand advisors on how to promote, how to improve his business, to partner, to share, to donate his wealth, all beggars and freeloaders, and the "23 pointers."

In 1995 the CERN laboratory created antimatter.

"Atoms of anti-hydrogen, which consist of a positron orbiting an antiproton"

"Antimatter is also produced in some radioactive decays. When 14C decays, a neutron decays to a proton plus an electron and an electron antineutrino"

14C --> 14N + e- +

Was the DC government in decay? Were they trying to self destruct themselves by destroying the businesses around them? Is the antiproton in the middle with positron (businesses), spinning around them? While in the normal Nature assumes that atom is a proton with positive charge (Jim/club), and the regulators/detractors are spinning around him with negative charge (electrons are positrons with negative charge), why did the ABC board act like the world/businesses/turns around them? Like the old planetary false theory of Aristotle and Ptolemy and Church, they thought they were the Godfathers, and they were above the law of business!

Copernicus (1543) published Revolutions of the Celestial Orbs,

("De Revolutionibus Orbium Coelestium"), a treatise that put forth his revolutionary idea that the Sun was at the center of the universe and that the Earth--rotating on an axis--orbited around the sun once a year. Copernicus' theory was a challenge to the accepted notion contained in the natural philosophy of Aristotle, the astronomy of Ptolemy and the teachings of the Church that the sun and all the stars revolved around a stationary Earth.

Here the DC government was accusing Jim of existing as entrepreneur, as club owner, as an existing Entity/matter!

On the morning of June 22, 1633, Galileo, dressed in the white shirt of penitence, entered the large hall of the Inquisition building. At age of seventy he was coerced by the Pope Urban VIII to reject all his writings supporting the Copernican Theory and they gave him three years suspended sentence. Nine years later this scientist and astronomer would die blind at his home humiliated and disappointed.

The analogy was too obvious to ignore. The whole operation here to open the new Stadium would go beyond the "one week punishment," Nikias was talking about. A week, no, eleven weeks yes.

Would the QMBC law (quantum mind business creativity) invented and described by Jim be accepted by the others or he would he be having Galileo's faith? Jim was born in 1957, Galileo in 1564, almost 400 years apart.

In 1609 Galileo discovered the telescope and observed the earth moon and Jupiter and the four small moons spinning around like a small planetary system. He observed the Milky Way Galaxy from his garden. He thanked God and he wrote in a 1597 letter to Johannes Kepler, a German mathematician confirming his theory. The sentence of Galileo Galilei ended and era of the Italian Renaissance. The sentence of Jim was the end of a business system in USA as we know it. The next six years would explain and confirm that. What happens in DC even in that club would create the biggest recession in years. It would put the biggest capitalist machine to a halting stop.

Jim was applying the QMBC law, based on his research and personal experiences. While the Catholic Church Inquisition was able to crash the 70 year old man Galileo, for his achievements, the DC self-governing body ABRA agency was not able to eliminate Jim as entrepreneur. He still had the original source of income from Randevu lounge and bar. Leaving the hearing he felt betrayed by his GM, who supposed to be supporting him, by the security, by the commander, by the press judging him out even before the hearing.

Mr. Bender: "Hey Jim! How are you?" He sounded cheerful and hungry.

Jim: "Hey Mr. Bender! I maybe not be able to pay the rent for a while, sorry!" he paused.

Mr. Bender: "Why? What is going on?"

Jim: "My license was suspended for eighty days. Someone was killed in the neighborhood. They blame the Go Go promotion. I am not sure if this guy was ever in the club, but even if he was he wouldn't be served alcohol, because he was nineteen. So police coerced my manager to testify against me. I don't understand what the conspiracy all about is?"

Mr. Bender: "I will make you a proposal:

1. You need to pay your rent, no matter the circumstances.
2. If you cannot pay the rent I need you to vacate the club. I will inspect the premises and review the license situation and if it is of any value I may even give you some of the construction money back?"

Jim: "I will talk to my lawyer Nikias and hopefully we can come to a mutual agreement."

Jim made a quick assessment. He had about 20,000 dollars inventory, in unopened alcohol beverages. He had a security deposit of one month. He had thousands of dollars in his sound system. He decided to liquidate.

Nikias: "I will try to transfer your liquor license to the landlord. I will get your security deposit back without penalty," he sounded old, tired and disappointed on the phone.

Jim: "I am disappointed too. I wish you were more convincing to the ABC Board. I am not sure if this guy was ever in the club? Then I passed copies of the Washington Times to each of the seven members and they never looked at them, nor took it into account."

Nikias: "I've known these characters for twenty years. If they have an agenda, they just cover it up and look for a leaf to drop from a tree and will blame it on a club owner. Killing is a great reason to make their point."

Jim: "I feel I am targeted for Go Go, but in truth their agenda is to clear clubs for the Stadium they're building up and parking spaces. This is like the Roman Inquisition in 1633. They coerced Galileo to reject all his discoveries and threatened him with jail and torture. Nobody argued with them then, nobody came to my defense now!"

Nikias: "I was sick, young man!"

Jim: "Then why am I paying you $250.00 dollars an hour? Send someone else who could talk to ABRA. Just being present is not enough! See what you can do with recovering my money back, please!"

Nikias: "I would expect a letter from him with a check. From now on we will chat less."

Jim: "Sorry about your health. Wish you well." He was wearily disappointed. He clicked the cell phone off.

The same day Jim started moving liquor and electronic equipment. He felt like leaving a sick child behind to Foster Care. He grew attached to this big club. That was the oldest club in the USA. This should be a museum. From here Studio 54, Palladium, and Tracks club was modeled after. Same lighting, same style, same DJs exchange network, same patrons. The liquor was returned to the distributors and he got cash back 18,500 dollars, the rest of the money come back from the security deposit, exactly 12,000 dollars.

Is the Stadium that anti reality, that great conspiracy, the reason for the ABRA to pick and choose? The change of venues to gay does not guarantee success. Especially, with someone who does not have financial back up like Andy Sherman. The hearing in October did not produce the results the landlord Mr. Bender planned. The ABC Board refused to transfer the license at the hearing. The idea was the lying GM to sublease the license from Mr. Bender. They recommended that Andy Sherman apply for his own license. He eventually got the license, he lasted two months and according to Mr. Bender he couldn't bring any promotions and therefore he couldn't pay the rent and he was kicked out in February 2003, exactly six months after that fatal ABC hearing.

The next decade there would be a lot of events which would end with number Six. The slogan in life is always "you will make it or not in six months." That's what the coupon Lady Alice, told him about his business in San Diego. Because of the reverse in his fate the next decade would end up in many destructive cycles. Many people who came across him with wrong intentions would lose their businesses and end up in bankruptcies. Some of them would lose their lives. There would be floods, hurricanes, earthquakes, tsunamis, Wall Street would collapse; the whole US economy will collapse. The major states would go bankrupt, wars with no end, Arab countries in unrest. European economy would be in chaos, the wrong President would rise to power, and the US national debt would double to 16 trillion dollars. All that over a fake case of liquor license removal? Common, evil government! The resilience of the world would be tested. The winner would be you know who? Jim! Why did he win when everybody else lost?

Reader, remember that "Number six is an incomplete spiral! Only four layers of incomplete quantum spirals (4x6) create Cosmic Matter."

"Why is the single day measured by 24 hours?" Jim thought.

God: "Genious, my identical thinker! I will prove you right in many ways.

That is the simplest example for the 4th dimensional, earth people, The Time."

Jim: "Maybe Cornell U should save their 3 billion dollars and CERN should save their 10 billion dollar proton/antiproton collider and buy my manuscript here?"

The quantum mind cannot be destroyed. The light beam he used to start creativity now was reversing to create destruction. He was the reflection of the society; Democratic, prosperous, greedy, mischievous but somewhat attractive until this fatal hearing in August 2002. Most people around the world believed in America, in its power, in its constitution and its justice! They would risk their lives to come to USA, to prosper! None of those border-crossers from Mexico, stowaways, container smuggled refugees from China, fake married immigrants from Nigeria, boats arriving from Haiti and Cuba, or even legally obtained work visa, no one was expecting to be a failure.

Jim was not a failure. The Bulgarians with their indestructible Nazi type communist society in 1980 could not stop him from escaping. Why does the US government seek to destroy him with its better structured society? The prison population is 2% of US population. At 6 million strong one should wonder, is this, a free country, free speech, the right to bear arms, the right of trial by a court of law; all those rights on paper and the library of congress' book. But are they implemented?

How can some loose end agency in the District of Columbia, like ABRA change the world history? City of Washington, the Capital of USA was established in 1791. The city is run by the US Congress. It is not a state. There are three power players here: The Congress, the President, and the Supreme Court. In 1973 the District of Columbia was granted limited power of self government. The city was run by a Mayor and thirteen council members since. DCRA was an agency who had the power to regulate business licenses, zoning changes, liquor licensing, building electrical and plumbing permits, occupancy and capacity, fire safety compliance and historic preservation certificates, etc. ABRA was the offspring of DCRA, which specializes in alcohol and beverage regulation, basically in issuing and suspending liquor licenses.

Instead of Jim reflecting on the wealth of the society, the false Democracy, the 400 years of constitutional law designed to withstand the wars, revolutions and the clash of ideologies, Jim reversed the game. Everything we just mentioned was a reflection of Jim's mood. The USA business cycle was similar to his achievements or failures.

Jim has a slogan "When I win, everyone wins! When I lose everyone loses, but 100 fold!" That applies not only in Quantum mind thinking. It relates to motivation speeches in business strategist. In Adam Smith's theory, in capitalist society unfortunately wining is related to money gain. In military battles the winner is the one with better strategy.

Jimmy Carter will say on April 29, 2011, "If Everyone 'Wins,' Everyone Loses. Not everyone can win." Here is the antithesis to Quantum thinking. Why? The business will prosper; the country will prosper because of more money in circulation. The army will win, the land will expand or there would be some kind of benefits; social, financial or just a safer environment. The winning is usually related to competing factions in earth dimensions, at Adam Smith's theory, similar to Jimmy Carter's thinking. Believe me Jimmy and Adam were on the right track in the physical world, but they were not thinking out of the box, where the QMBC law applies. For convenience we will call it only this way, to avoid confusion we will not call it QMBD (Quantum mind business destruction), just like we will not call the "positron, which is electron with positive charge" (1930, Paul Dirac's discovery). On March 10, 2012 the Pentagon would reveal the "Active Denial heat ray weapon." It would be a high frequency microwave heated gun crowd control cannon. It gives you an instant buzz and small non lethal shock. The first to buy it is Los Angeles Police chief. We are not dealing with small heat rays here; it is too small a subject in Quantum Minds. It is like taking an aspirin comparing it to a heart implant surgery. We are describing the facts after this fatal hearing in August 2002. Precisely six years later the 4th largest player in the Wall Street casino "The Lehman Brothers" (LEH on NYSE) will file for Chapter 11 bankruptcy protection. The other three "too big to fail" are Goldman Sachs, Morgan Stanley and Merrill Lynch….

Like in business before a big recession the business cycle is upward and great. So was the business at Randevu bar. Relieved of not running the excessive burden of the three and later the two clubs, Jim was focused on developing the original lounge Randevu. He had $30,000.00 extra dollars now. He decided to develop his Walker's Media and go with the future of all digital production. His first camera came from his IT guy. It was JVC 700 D9 series... It will take him ten years to complete his 250,000 dollars set up including 4 JVC D9 and 2 Panasonic digital MiniDV all in 3 chip TV format cameras, 2 multimedia computers and 8 tracks video/sound mixer. He would be ready by 2012. How many people would invest a decade of their lives in building up, while the whole economy goes into 16 trillion spiral nose dive?

Chapter 9

The April 2, 2003 arrived as usual. It was a boring Sunday in Georgetown. Jim was walking around and was just enjoying life. He knew many of the shop owners by face, some of them by name. Recently, he purchased a nice all gold watch Mark Echo, for a good price and the owner of the Signature store was happy to see him again. He was a smart salesman. He would engage in conversations with ease and he would sell and sell.

Jim was known to pay cash and always to carry large amount with him.

Jim had a thought about it; he called it "just in case." He always was wondering how people would open their eyes in excitement (greed is what he called it), when he showed the stack of hundreds dollar bills.

DC was a very wealthy town, but the money was hidden. All Hollywood movies show the secret service, the presidential limousine, Capitol Hill Building, the Monument, the Jefferson and Lincoln memorial, the Vietnam War memorial. One would believe that, that was common seen here, but, it was not. The President's limousine was observed by Jim maybe no more than five times in twenty-six years. One of secret service chiefs used to come to Randevu lounge and he would chat about everything, but about his job. He came to visit the night before, the April 1st.

Secret Service: "Hey Jim, you are back! I heard about you and what happened to your club."

Jim: "Yeah, some businesses last more than the others" with an agonizing face. "Where were you, when I needed you?" he would add.

Secret Agent: "I was at work, protecting the President!" He was cocky, a tall mid-thirties Irish man.

Jim: "I know the Secret Service was established on July 5, 1865 to prevent the US currency from counterfeiters. I get bad currency here from time to time, but nobody ever gets caught."

Secrets Service: "I think you need one of us to protect your stable of women? I will work for beer here. Do you know how to detect when the president is truly escorted?" He was trying to get some attention.

Jim: "I do not really care, but how?"

Secret Service: "There is always an ambulance at the end."

Jim just smoked a bit of his cigar and moved away. "Ok!"

Jim was strolling down Wisconsin Avenue when he was stopped by Waleed, the owner of the Signature boutique shop. The store had high end Dolce Gabbana, Christian Dior sunglasses and watches, and fur coats. Just as Waleed was trying to sell the next luxury item to Jim a tall lady appeared at the door. She was 6 feet tall and she was a mixed race beauty. Jim acted like he knew her and moved toward her secretly holding a business card.

Jim: "Hey. Where have you been? Listen, act like you know me and get me out of here, ok?" he was whispering...

Tall beauty: "Sure. How are you?"

Jim: "Let's get out of here! Are you hungry?" He grabbed her by the hand and both slipped out of the shop.

Jim: "There will be plenty of time to shop. What is your name?"

Tall beauty: "Kiana. I can't impress you much. I am just a student. You can impress me if you want? You seem established. Was that your friend in the shop? He seemed like he knew you?" she was checking Jim and she acted like she was interested in him.

Jim: "You have my number. I don't ask for numbers. You can come to my bar and have a drink when you have free time. Can you drink? Are you 21?" She seemed young yet acted mature.

Kiana: "I have school to study. I go to Howard University. I will think about it. For your information, I just turned 21 a month ago" she grabbed the sandwich he bought her and she disappeared.

Jim: "I hope she calls. She seemed proud, but hungry." He thought.

He went to the Randevu lounge where he felt at home. The regular customers received him like a hero returning home.

Tyra: "Hey Jim, we missed you. You were better off here with us. That club out there has passed it's "heyday." That Go-Go is being cursed anywhere they promote. Police don't like it. It is like renegade movement."

Jim: "Police don't like anything, but young white ladies and even then they are after the Buzz at Nation for drugs sales."

Tyra: "They have more tolerance towards the gay community because half of the council members are gay or women. Police women always hit on me." She had a point.

Jim: "I know firsthand here at Randevu how they threat my customers. They don't like people to dance, to drink, to use drugs, to have sex in general, while they are "working." The Police just make noise with their sirens and drive fast through streets. I have never seen a Police shootout except a robbery went wrong in California Bank, by some Romanian guy and an accomplice in February, 1997."

Tyra: "Are you afraid here? You maybe robbed, too?" She sipped on cosmopolitan, acting concerned.

Jim: "I had many instances of shady characters staying here late or harassing my lady customers, but I deal with them like in Vegas. We don't call police, what happens here doesn't go to Police reports."

Tyra: "Really? It looks so peaceful here and well structured?"

Jim: "It is a one man operation. I do the drinks, the sound and video, I bring the supplies, and clean the place and I deal with rowdy crowds solo." He did not go in details about his recent fight with MS 13 gang of four, its 3 members ended up flying down the stairs like arrows with heads down and legs up. What saved them was the 400 pound man blocking the first floor entrance, absorbing their bodies' impacts.

Tyra: "You know I am starting my health Spa! I will also teach Martial arts there," she was her usual sardonic cocky.

Jim: "How much you are investing? I may need an investor here to expand my place? My business is getting better here every night." He was smoking an average cigar and drinking diet coke."

Tamara: "Nah, I don't know anything about the liquor business, but I may talk to some of my rich clients?"

May 2003, the long standing Sally's/Starlight, closed. Jessica stopped paying the rent, because of insufficient business and deteriorating health.

Mansur: "I want to take over the Starlight but it needs too much work.

Jim: "Then let someone else fix it. They will go out of business too. That is my corner. Nobody will move me from here business wise."

Mansur: "You have the guts and perseverance! I wish my sons could be like you one day, but I doubt that."

Jim: "Nikias may not be the healthiest lawyer, but he can get the hours extended. We have to pay him a visit soon."

Mansur: "I agree." He always acted like he had a hidden agenda.

The first date with Kiana was in early May. She was smart. She was exactly every man's dream; tall, smart, zero fat. First time sex was great and memorable. Her legs were comforting this young club owner in any position. The untouched pubic hair was extended almost up to her navel like a tiny mountain pick. When she was wearing her low cut jeans the stomach was a perfect six pack shaped. The small cup like great breasts made her look like a model with the long slim legs. When she was wearing high heels she was turning heads automatically with that amazing affect on single and married men alike. She was not beautiful, but when she talked and smiled her maturity and personality exuded the radiation of a genius person. Yes, Jim was hooked.

Kiana: "Jim, are you going to take care of me?" She asked with her deep sexy voice coming out of the shower. She told him earlier that her father died in car crash when she was sixteen years old.

Jim: "I can't be your father, but a lover with potential to be a husband one day, is that a deal?" The conversation seemed to be turning into a serious negotiation. Whatever, the description Jim enjoyed the challenge. It was the beginning of a life time friendship. So he thought. Until this time Jim never felt anything like this. Maybe just having sex was taken for granted. Going beyond that was never on his mind. He thought of it many times how to fall in love as something that "would be nice." But nobody came close to Kiana. She knew how to talk, she was not experienced in sex, but she was the best at that.

Kiana: "You would not believe it maybe, but you are my second lover and the first one did not know much of what he was doing. I am almost a virgin!"

Jim: "Interesting. You are either pregnant or not, virgin or not! But I will take your version..."

Kiana: "I am leaving to go to Georgia soon. Can you wait for me a couple of months?"

Jim: "You mean not to find someone else to take care of and not to have sex with? Sure!"

Kiana: "We will see, hmm!" She acted doubtful, but flirtatious.

Jim: "I will miss you," smiling.

Kiana: "I will miss you too." The voice was amazing. Her happiness was mesmerizing. The glow of her youth and mature mind made her unique.

Jim gave her some vacation money and he felt she deserved much more. The faces of his estranged lovers flew through his mind -- Contessa, Frida, Amanda but nothing was more important than this new discovery. Yes, she will be missed, he thought.

In June, 2003 a new tenant signed the lease at the address 1428 X Street. He was the nephew of infamous cocaine head Mr. Dodson. While Mr. Rogbin bought a 5 million dollar house in Potomac with 2 million down and he was under the microscope of the police for undeclared cash, Mr. Dodson was not doing much better. An underage drunk twenty year old lady patron killed a state trooper while on Interstate 295 and Mr. Dodson was also under scrutiny of everyone possible. Jim met the lawyer representing the prosecution and the victim's family attorney Jerry Maloney. The family was suing the club, Cloud for 50 million dollars. What would save the club was the Mayor, Sony Wagner, who would use his own attorney to save the club from closing. The recommendation was to change the name to Ballers, while keeping the same players in the game. Mr. Dodson was still the GM, not an owner (but he pretended to be the owner any way). The true owners were the Ethiopian crew of ten who would put out 20 percent down (one million dollars) and Michael Jordan who would cover the rest 80% (four million dollars).

Mr. Dodson had the power of attorney (he could write and sign checks, but he cannot withdraw money from the bank). He would eventually settle for 20 million dollars to pay to the victim's family. Of course he would not pay himself, but his LLC cohorts he was hiding, would.

That new leaser of the old Sally's/Starlight, was an ambitious late 20s short man. He had his own construction company and he was quickly restoring the ruined club. His partner in crime was Louise, fifteen years his senior and a heavy smoker. She was a professor of Art at Howard University. She had bad yellow teeth and tried to look young, always wearing tight pants or miniskirts. They opened in October, 2003 after the hearing with ABC Board under the name Prosperity. If it was that, time would only tell?

August came and around the 20th Jim received a call from Kiana.

Jim: "Hey, gorgeous! Where are you?" he jumped in ecstasy.

Kiana: "Meet me at the airport! Then we will talk." Jim drove to Reagan National Airport and picked her up. She looked even slimmer wearing two piece blue jean set. Her hair was pulled back and it gave her the even younger look.

Kiana: "Hey Daddy!" it was an intimate way of being closer to someone.

Jim: "Missed me?" He gave a hug and a kiss.

Kiana: "A little bit." She was honest.

Jim: "You left me for more than two months, now I will leave you."

Kiana: "Why? Where are you going?" she was curious.

Jim: "I am leaving for three weeks. I am going to Bulgaria. My brother is celebrating his 50th birthday. I haven't seen them for twenty-three years."

Kiana: "Great. They will love to see you."

They went to eat at Annie's Steak House and then Jim invited her to his apartment. She took a shower and came out wet and jumped in the bed, laying down her towel first. Jim was sitting in the rolling chair, enjoying her presence.

Jim: "Last time you were here you were almost virgin. Now can you do me a favor? Touch yourself like I am not in the room. They call it masturbation."

Kiana: "You have to show me how? I heard of dildos, but I never touched myself that way except in the shower." She sounded honest.

Jim: "I admire your body and your mind, but I don't want to lose you because of some sex games." He went to a small drawer and pulled out a vibrator. It was something he bought expecting a visitor, but she stood him up in the past.

Kiana: "Put a condom on it. I don't know who has used it before?"

Jim: "Nobody. It supposed to be a surprise for someone."

Kiana: "Ok. What do you want me to do with this thing?" She was looking at a 9 inch small tower with fresh black tuxedo life style condom slid on it.

Jim: "Here is the speed changer. You may turn it on or off. Open your beautiful lips and move this up and down and if you like it you may insert it inside the vagina?" She looked confused like dear in front of car head lights.

Jim: "I will be seating watching you while I smoke my cigar. Tell me how it feels?" he returned to his black leather rocking chair. The Cohiba was smooth and the view at his bed was tempting and inviting.

Kiana: "That feels strange, but I prefer the real deal" she pointed toward Jim's aroused 8 inch live tower. "This is like going to gynecologist, take the vibrator away." Not rushing, gently he approached the stage like bed. He had an extra mattress on top, making it firm and comfortable three leveled bed. He was looking at her like she was a trophy, like a rare Faberge egg. He couldn't believe his luck. He wiped the slate comet clean of all the other ladies that he had encountered and any other prior sexual conquests. This lady was a keeper. Jim agreed with her and soon he was on top and between her long legs. The unshaven vagina was squeezing him and letting him go in natural rhythm.

Jim: "You should teach sex education "live." He told her to turn around.

Kiana: "You prefer doggy style?" She was laughing and enjoying it.

Jim: "How do you know it is doggy style, if you are new in the game?" he was trying to be smart.

Kiana: "I heard of it. I have never done it except with you last time."

Jim: "She knows how to lie very quickly" he thought, doubting that she was really honest?

Jim: "Nobody ever asked you for sex for the last three months? Are they blind, or gay or more likely nonexistent? Unbelievable!"

Kiana: "I don't think of sex like you or most men or women do!" She was telling she was working for her uncle and going to church.

Jim: "Oh, oh baby! I am cumming. We will talk later." He accelerated the pumping and she responded with convulsions and contractions. "Are you ok? I just came!"

Kiana: "Me too. Thank you, Daddy!" She ran to the bathroom to wash.

Jim: "You have secret weapon," pointing toward her wet and bushy vagina. "What can I do to keep you around and nobody else to have you?" he laughed but meant it.

Kiana: "I will never ask you for things you can't afford, so you surprise me. Give me things you can spare or you may think I need?"

Jim: "Want a car, cash?"

Kiana: "Bye, Jim. When you are ready to give don't ask the woman, just give. I don't like to negotiate." She was heading toward the front door. On the way out she spotted a lot of loose change on the kitchen counter. She swiped it clean from all quarters and dimes.

Jim: "Wait, I have an extra laptop here. Take it. And here is some change for now." He handed her a bundle of hundreds he always carried with him "for just in cases" like this.

Kiana: "Got extra car to spare?" she was serious; she picked 200 dollars from the bundle of close to $1,000.

Jim: "I have three cars. You pick one." He showed her the keys for diesel Benz Mercedes, BMW, Chrysler Van.

Kiana: "I will take the BMW. Thank you." She was not negotiating; she was taking whatever she wanted.

Jim: "Hope for Christmas you will take fewer gifts?" he was laughing of her attitude of entitlement.

Jim: "You must be a Democrat," giving her the keys, but not the title.

Kiana: "I am anarchist!" testing the car engine. "This car looks fast!"

Jim: "True, but drive careful and no parking tickets please! I still have to pay all fines."

Kiana: "Now we can meet more often!" She lied.

Jim: "We will see." He was happy to help but he was skeptical… somewhat. He just threw away around $15,000 in one hour. The BMW was older model, but it was all fixed up and passed inspection. The laptop was latest model "Dell Latitude." The cash would have been more, but Kiana said "I am not greedy, I just need some stuff." She drove away…

Jim would spend nearly a quarter million on her demands, off and on for the next five years, so at that moment that was just initiation, a down payment.

Jim was happy. God was working miracles. He discovered the physical laws of giving are different than quantum laws of giving. When one gives with love he gets returns in tenfold, when one gives with agenda, he loses tenfold. God (subconscious mind is quantum mind) while the normal conscious mind (active) mind is the working everyday 4% to 10% percent mind. Einstein was supposedly using the full 10% mind (active). The absurd of the returning wealth is in the "funny math." In the quantum reality the gravitational curves are returning and bending backwards toward the giver, while in the normal reality the linear world tends to get weaker or bends downwards for the receiver.

Jim came to the conclusion:

"The more you take (material things, money), the more you lose (light, ambition)" in the physical world. You live in 4 dimensions: x y and z and real time. "The more you give (light, energy), the more you receive." In Quantum world everything you wish becomes possible. The hidden Cosmic 6th dimension becomes visible, Cosmic Intelligence, God. The same principle works in reverse: "The less you give, the less you will receive in Quantum reality." You will reduce yourself to 4th, Earth dimensions; to Nature with plus (+) x y z t, 4 dimensions, or to minus (-) x y z t zombie like state, like the Underworld, where Death rules…

So who are the rich people? Those are anybody who thinks out of the box, anybody who gives without second thoughts. Rich is not defined as such in quantum world. Saints are not rich, but they solve problems, give life, split oceans, fly to distant galaxies with no money exchanges …Matter of fact they think money is a an obstruction of creativity. One who lives on his wealth will stop creating. One who is giving, creating new inventions is the one who some consider rich in physical world, but saint in the Quantum world.

Note: Healers, who charge money for improving your health, are not true healers. Only a saint is a true healer, because he only asks for respect, not for money. Basically one who enriches himself of the pain of others is a charlatan and ungodly creature.

Jim was able to cure many people, experimenting with his God given powers to channel his energy (Chi, He4) in 6th dimension to the earth people, living in the 4th dimension. He would do it for free. He cured brain tumors, back pain, gallbladder, knees pain, swollen ankles, etc...

Evil crowd/Government: "You think you are better than us?"

Jim: "I am more aware than you. My teaching is for everyone to be Aware, like me. Then we can compare who is better than the other? You can have regulations and jails and handcuffs and best weapons on earth. If you are not aware of the all dimensions, if you can't use the dark energy and the dark matter, then yes, you are inferior to me."

Evil crowd/Government: "Ok. Teach us. We want to be like you. We want the Awareness too. We want to be God-like. We want to be you."

Jim: "Really? Ok. It extends to a three to four year education. In my case it took me 11 months to achieve levitation. My discovery came through how the pyramids were built.

1st. Double reversing of polarity. The quantum, dark energy is induced, between the cycles of reversing.

2nd. Have you seen in the Bible or in drawings by famous painters "angels with wings?" Those are people, who can levitate themselves, mixed with quantum Saints. They also helped move the giant stone blocks and put them in precise positions."

3rd. The base of each pyramid has granite in it. Once compressed, the granite has piezo crystal effect and creates sparks, energy. With the light beams from the Sun, that cosmic alternator in the pyramid creates constant current. Because of the dark matter and energy, that current is not visible, but it can be felt in time zero."

Evil crowd/Government: "How did you come to these conclusions, without going to MIT or Cornell University? Why are you not at CERN now?"

Jim: “One, who is aware, does not need the top University or some CERN (Super proton synchrotron) with a 10 billion dollar grant behind them. All of you need to elevate yourselves to the 5th (galaxy) dimension, then to 6th (cosmic) dimension.”

When a person gives he emanates, and he radiates. The Wheeler theory applies; the magnetic gravitational fields compress and emit energy, quanta. When he dies the black hole creates a vacuum and from there the interest in him as a Saint.

Unfortunately there are no living saints on earth, who are recognized while they contribute to the world, except in Bulgaria…They have to be dead to be recognized. That is the irony and one absurd reality. The earth people can’t figure out why one rich man gives and why a poor person takes?

The slogan; “Rich people get richer, poor people get poorer” it is true, but the government blames it on regulations via tax laws. If one is smart, progressive, giving quantum thinker (out of the box of the physical world), then he should be awarded (not like Giordano Bruno, who the Inquisition killed in Feb., 1600 for heresy, spreading the Copernicus theory of the planetary system). Galileo was more fortunate in 1633. He was just convinced to reject his writings about his telescope discoveries (in 1609) and anything to do with Copernicus theory. Were they rich? No. They died spreading the knowledge. Were they thinking out of the box? Yes. Were they Saints? Yes, but postmortem.

The three week vacation was a test for Kiana’s and Jim’s relationship. Kiana asked for Jim’s apartment keys just before he was to leave. Jim was afraid to leave all that expensive equipment there to a lady he just met. Kiana had strange friends. She loved to smoke marijuana. She said it made her horny.

Jim: “I am not afraid of you. I do not want your friends to hang out here.” They just had sex.

Kiana: “I want to study here, no friends are coming here.”

Jim: "Let me think!" he wanted to please her, but he was not ready for a live-in girlfriend. He wrote her a check for 500 dollars.

Kiana: "That is ok. I may need more when you come back? Thank you for the car! Call me when you come back, please!" she sounded genuine….

Chapter 10

Jim was excited and cautious flying to his mother land, Bulgaria. He was a US citizen and of course had a US passport. He had heard all kinds of stories about his old country. He heard of the assassination of Georgi Markov in 1978 using the umbrella-like-rifle, with poison covered bullet. He heard of Bulgarians trained in Turkey attempted to assassinate Pop John Paul II, he heard of currency devaluation and new currency being printed, he heard of electrical shortages, due to undependable soviet made nuclear power plants, and the droughts that were affecting the hydroelectric power plants. The political turmoil was prevented when James Baker, who was a Department of State Secretary, handpicked the next Bulgarian President Mladenov. After the assassination of the Romanian President Nicolae Ceausescu in December 1989 the next to be followed was Zhivkov, the Bulgarian President. He was sent to house arrest by Mladenov, one of the better choices than standing trial.

Jim changed flights at Zurich and the smaller plane with dual language speaking flight attendants brought him to Sofia. The view from the sky showed a lot of agricultural parcels patched like a poor man's tailor. When the small airplane approached the capital the smoke of the bad emissions mixed with some left over factories of a failed policy of heavy industry in the past, showed some similarity with the big cities of USA, but only on outside.

The first impressions of the customs were the young 20ish officers with reddish cheek bones, more related to malnutrition than better health. Jim was reminiscing himself, at the Naval Academy with the similar looks, but he was always working out, so there was the better difference. He was then conditioning himself to escape. Those people were nothing but small thieves, living on almost a minimal salary, but greatly rewarded from confiscating anything possible undeclared or allegedly illegal to be carried on airplanes, or just from stealing luggage. Their chiefs were stealing even more, but they were more sophisticated. They would steal containers from trains passing through. The exercise would confirm that the cargo is insured.

Did they know anything about hedge funds, nobody knew? They knew if one who loaded the cargo would buy insurance, by law of Hedge funds. The speculators would bet on the price of seller and the price of the buyer, who normally would not ever meet or communicate directly with the hedge managers, would pocket the difference, but they would not ever invest without insurance. Sometimes, the price for speculators would greatly increase, if there is shortage of commodity, (the cargo). In that case the stealing is even more justified. Once the shortage is noticed and insurance covers the loss, then insurance fees increase for the speculators (and from there the hedge stocks managers' income also). Most likely the custom officers were not aware they were helping someone to get rich, but in the money world the only time one loses is when there is no game to play, otherwise said, one just watches, but does not participate.

The wise men theory is: "The one who knows does not talk, the one who talks, does not know."

In the physical world a lot of politicians or economist or dictators will apply themselves in something, they do not know and that is worst of all situations. Wars, recessions, depressions, terrorism and just poor management are obvious. That is why people start revolutions or in Democratic society they vote.

Jim theory was in quantum dimensions. The one who is thinking out of the box and knows and applies his knowledge is worth millions compared to who knows and doesn't apply it, or he is worth billions compared to who is plain ignorant. Here is basically the rule of how one acquires wealth. Advance knowledge creates wealth, while copied knowledge creates competition, when the regulators appear. Then the stagnation appears and therefore the benefits and the theft, and poverty, the more wealth, the more unions, the more taxes, the more benefits. The result is the business cycle of the recession, (not only because of saturation of product or "supply vs. demand" but the need of self adjustment). What made Jim successful was minimum reliability on other people to help him in the business. He was imagining, "how about if they ask me here for business advice or to become a mayor, maybe a President?" The thoughts were rushing in his head, but the thing that had priority at this time, was to check his luggage's out and to meet his family. He already met his sister in law Rebecca, when she visited Disney World in Orlando, Florida. Now it was time to meet the rest of the family and renew acquaintances again.

Adrian: "Hello brother!" he approached him and the hug was long and sincere. He looked shorter and all gray, but he retained the same youthful reddish cheeks the young custom officers had, at the receiving gate.

His father was right behind and he was speechless. He walked toward Jim almost in tears, hardly recognizing his son, he hadn't seen for a quarter century.

Father Michael: "Son, son, I do not believe it is you?" he was holding this tall handsome, westernized, mid-forties man. They hugged each other even longer, until Adrian tapped them on the shoulder. "Let's go." They each grabbed some luggage and headed toward the exit gate. Jim looked around; "No KGB (Bulgarian Secret Police had a similar name), nobody is following us." They entered a small compact car Renault which had enough space for one luggage, the other one they had to push across the back seat with father Michael and his nephew Paolo holding it on their lap.

Jim: "I could have taken a taxi, but looks like we managed!" The starter of the old Renault turned a couple of times before the car started. The main streets were congested with mopeds, old electrical trolley cars and chaotic fast drivers.

Jim: "Driving here through circles is an adventure." He was in the front seat. Adrian: "We have to catch up for the last twenty-three years. How are you brother?" He was driving like a maniac to keep up with the other maniacs in traffic. He kept a huge smile on his face like a mask. One had to wonder, if that was a sign of true happiness, or just a hidden pain behind the mask? Bulgarians are the type of people who do not show much emotion, something implanted in them to survive many of occupying conquerors in the past: Romans, Greeks, Attila the Hun, Turks and of course, the Russians.

Jim: "Finally we are together! You look the same, just a bit older."

Adrian: "How come you don't have any gray hair? What is the secret? Looks like America have been good to you!" He spoke in Bulgarian, which Jim understood but it was difficult to answer in Bulgarian without mixing it with some English words.

Jim: "Brother, life is what one makes it! I made the decision to risk and to attempt to escape, I did succeed, but if I didn't, I was to be executed on the spot. Remember the early 80's?" he was proud of himself, but he was trying not to show it too much. The car pulled over in some dirty road behind a gray quickly built high-rise in the 90's. The ready panels of cement and metal bars were assembled on site and the only thing was to install was doors and windows. The pipes and electrical wires were run quickly through the buildings and the rest was left to the buyer. All amenities like refrigerators, ovens and kitchen sinks, bathrooms tubs and toilets and showers were to be added by the homeowners. Phones (12 years wait) were a luxury and Cable TV was just coming in the year 2000.

Adrian: "We were lucky to get in that rusty building. We had a small business nearby but the business was vandalized by a gang which demanded protection money. We did not have money to give them, because business was hardly breaking even. They kept breaking the windows and stealing our stuff. After two years we gave up, especially after Paolo was born."

Jim: "What kind of business was it?" They were climbing up the stairway. Elevators were shut closed, after so many electrical outages and people getting stuck in them. On two occasions the breaks were not holding because of overloading and some six people plunged to their deaths.

Adrian: "I was selling imported electronics and home appliances from Saudi Arabia, where they use the same AC current like ours, 220 volts."

Jim: "Who are the manufacturers?" he was interested.

Adrian: "Oh, the Chinese produce a lot and cheaper, but they are not of the quality of Europeans or US products."

They entered the two room apartment. The kitchen area was like an extra room with a couch and table seating for four people.

Adrian: "No computer here. You know we keep devises like that away from young children. He can't watch porn." Speaking seriously like a father.

Jim: "Ok. Where are we going to eat tonight?" He was getting sleepy; the long night of traveling and different time zone was getting him off track.

Father Michael: "We are going to my house. Ophelia has cooked a big dinner for us." (Ophelia was his stepmother).

Jim: "How is she?" He remembered her to be beautiful, but cold and always with migraine headaches.

Michael: "Same." He paused and exhaled slowly, in pain.

Rebecca smiled at the door. She just arrived from work. She had just started her own company, something to do with selling health products. Everyone squeezed in the Renault and soon they were at Michael's apartment, some five streets south in a complex Lulin, the supposedly modern in 80s and 90s development. Here the elevator worked, but Jim preferred to climb up the steps, "just in case." When the door opened he saw around twenty people seated around a long table with plates ready to serve in the middle. They all stood up like the president of another country just entered. Jim liked the attention, but dismissed it at once.

Jim: "Hey, good evening my friends!" he recognized maybe two faces, who were his brother's friends and who knew, but who the other eighteen were? He assumed they were some neighbors, just being curious and some just hungry. A lot of wine and cognac was in the middle of the table. The tradition was to bring a good alcohol to social gatherings; that way no one feels like they have come empty handed. They would drink and eat for the same or more value; it was a form of gift/cover charge.

Father Michael: "Let me make a toast. We were patient enough to wait that long to meet again. We went through many changes, but the only thing we could never change is our love and respect for each other." He sounded like a general, at end of a battle.

Ophelia pushed him slightly from behind. "Ok, general, time to eat!"

Jim laughed at the odd couple. "Some things never changed here."

He really wished his real mother was here. Maybe if she was alive, he would have never defected in 1980? He always knew his success was because of the "guardian angel," a reincarnation of his mother Loretta, when he was a six month old baby.

He witnessed her death and he couldn't speak a word until the age of three.

The food was good. A lot of "skara," (skewered meat and long rolled ground beef and spices); also "kiftes," small burgers and meatballs hybrids with bread and spices mixed, rolled cauliflower with rice and ground beef, called "sirma." The wine and brandy was pouring freely and the noise of glasses and china and loud voices were in strange mix of fake happiness.

Michael: "What is going on with Bush and the war?" he had his own opinions, but he was still curious.

Jim: "You should never take the news at face value. They are targeting certain people and they have an agenda. Everything in USA has political points. The further one stays from politics, the better!"

Michael: "We always hear about floods, earthquakes, tornadoes, the wars USA gets involved in. We wonder what is true or not?" He was ready for politics.

Jim: "I am not a politician, but I know how to find answers. There are public records in USA where for a couple of dollars anyone can get the information of corporation standing, or one has to just follow the stocks rising or falling. Basically follow the paper trail (the money). Then one can see the trends in tax codes. That will give you an idea where to invest or to sell assets."

Michael: "You see; you are in a society opposite of what you left here in 80's. We never learned anything like that during the communist central managed economy. Now we sent our King in exile Simeon Borisov to study economics in London, in 2001. Hopefully he can help us when he returns?"

Jim: "I am glad you understand why I defected? I would have waited twenty-three years for someone to graduate in London to tell me how the economy works?"

Michael: "Jim, I knew you were the smartest of us. I just never imagined how you would get all that knowledge. We could have never been able to afford sending you to any major university to like King Simeon."

Jim: "Father, most of successful people on Wall Street did not graduate from any major university; they were just risk takers, entrepreneurs."

Michael: "Are you applying what you know to life? If not, you are just a demagogue." He spoke like a knowledgeable man, choosing proper words.

Jim: "I had a couple of businesses. I have two now. Also, I am thinking to start investing in real estate." He was not waiting for applause. Everyone around the table was listening; even they acted like talking and drinking.

Jim: "I had three clubs, but because of an eye injury I had to let go of one, and at the other one they falsely made a case against the club. The government in the USA is not different than the government in Bulgaria."

Michael: "I hear they are trying to use the US Constitution as a model for newly established Eastern Democracies."

Jim: "The only thing about the Western Democracy is one can start business and compete with others, everything else is just camouflage. The US Constitution meant well in the beginning, but if it is so great, why does it have to be constantly amended."

Michael: "So, the West is not what they promote in movies or in the news?" He was acting disappointed.

Adrian: "I know my brother! I think he makes his own decisions and I trust his judgment! Cheers!" He stopped the conversation.

Jim: "Cheers to everyone who makes his own rules, who believes in himself first, talks to God through inspiration and when down! Don't forget God starts from within and then he is all around us. God will not manifest itself unless you believe in yourself first and him second." Everyone agreed and tossed up.

Michael: "In my church they say believe in God first! Then he will answer anything you wish!" he was curious if the Western Church was different?

Jim: "My father, you all may be right? I do not go to church to listen to two hours of Bible stories. I may not agree with them and I may make a scene? What I believe is that no matter what religion one chooses there is always a holy man representing God, Jesus, Mohamed, Allah, and Buddha. No matter in what sequences one takes God first, human second or in a reverse order, the sub consciousness must be activated. It is like one living in the attic and never goes to the lower level to enjoy his big house of many floors. On the outside one will say, "It's a great house that person owns," but he or she will never guess that even the lights are on, the occupant never walks around the rooms and to the garden of the house, but only the attic. So when two humans talk they see each other houses guessing that they both are using all the rooms, but they don't.

When two religious people talk they may have walked through all the rooms, but to get to the best room, they need to work through a higher level of scrutiny, not just walk, but to solve problems, (solvitur ambulando). And to get the answer/result, they have to do yoga, true praying, fasting, and initiation. Then that secret room will open, the sub consciousness will communicate with God (the seven octaves will sing, the seven planets will communicate, the chakras will open, the kundalini will raise, the quantum mind will work to a human's benefit)."

Everyone in the room got quiet. They were listening to something no one ever talked in that way.

Peter: "Where did you come up with all those strange ideas?" He was one of the smart ones, with the only computer in the building.

Jim: "Nothing is strange if it happened and it can be explained."

Peter: "Something like reverse engineering?" he was almost right.

Jim: "Miracles can't be explained through engineering or reverse engineering. No miracles ever repeat. That is why they are unpredictable. In science we apply logic, predictable outcome. In miracles we expect all possibilities. To be a saint one will use all possibilities to get the right result. The scientist will use one device to achieve one result."

Peter: "You sound like you are in a different dimension than all of us. I talk to Michael everyday and he is very religious, but he never comes close to you. Can you show me examples of something in your life that is considered miracles?" He was smoking a cigar, which, Jim gave to most of the smokers in the room. Seems he was enjoying it and the cognac and the conversation about miracles. He was one of the men who had some connections with the CIA and he was a go-in-between for the Bulgarian government.

Jim: "Miracles happen every day, we just ignore them. One who sees miracles may not be able to comprehend them and go insane. One who sees miracles and accepts them is initiated or open minded. One who creates miracles is a Saint."

Peter: "Then what are you?"

Jim: "I do research, I see the miracles, and I create miracles. You decide!" He laughed smoking cigar and biting on a small dessert cake.

Peter: "Saints don't smoke!"

Jim: "I don't claim any status. I am a mix of everything!"

Peter: "Like Jesus!" He paused.

Jim: "You said it. I did not! But I feel the parallel faith that we have. It was amazing how my defection was predicted and then happened on the exact date it was supposed to - Oct. 28th, 1980. The miracle here it is not so much in the process of thinking and doing it, but in the precision of the prediction."

Peter: "And you never knew the person? Don't you think it could have been staged?" he was suspicious.

Jim: "The Medium did not hear me. I never asked in sound. I thought she was planted by the Police. But once I got the answers in silence I did not care what she was. Matter of fact, we made love and she was laughing at my paranoia. She never asked what I asked and what the answers were. Her dead grandfather was channeling the information through his spirit, and the book."

Michael: "You wrote me once about that, but I thought you were joking, or trying to play the KGB?"

Adrian: "What else is so unusual in your adventures, my brother?" He knew something about the risk taker young brother, but he did not know any details.

Jim: "I had a lover with 300 million dollars, I was living on billionaire's yacht, I reopened the oldest USA club, and I was the owner of the oldest restaurant in DC, about 140 years old."

Peter:" That sounds like a James Bond movie or Casanova!"

Jim: "No, gentlemen! That's what any opportunist with a high intelligence can do; who uses all possible ways, the esoteric world gives him."

Michael: "I believe in God, but what you tell us sounds like a fairy tale. If you were not my son, I wouldn't believe you. Now I think you are more than I thought of you. I think you are equal to a miracle worker, a Saint! I believe in you son. Whatever they did to you in the Naval Academy, or in New York, or in Washington, DC, I know you are on the winning side. I did not make a loser, I started a person, and you made yourself a phenomenon."

Jim: "I did research on all secrets of the pyramids, the Bible codes, the modern physics, and the metaphysics. I read a lot of science fiction in the past, yoga theories, everything; but the secret societies. I know one who knows too much, may stumble upon the future and the past of undesired characters. You know there is gossip that President Bush was initiated by free masons. Watching him, it is probably true?"

Adrian: "Where do you live now?"

Jim: "Oh, my lounge is in the White House security perimeter, some three blocks away, but my apartment is about six blocks from it."

Adrian: "That must be dangerously close!" He puffed a cigar and sipped cognac. "That is a good cigar and thanks for the gifts for everyone."

Jim gave every man in his family a nice expensive looking watch and a leather jacket, nice necklace for his Sister-in-law Rebecca, great French perfume for his still gorgeous step mother Ophelia.

Ophelia: "Thanks for the assistance after 9/11. Those characters would never ask you, but also will never say thanks either." She pointed toward Michael, Adrian, Paolo and Rebecca.

Peter: "Your father is doing yoga also, but is not that advanced like you.

I wonder about the miracles you do and are you aware of always the good?"

Jim: "I do not want to scare you off, but anyone who stood up against me got punished. That applies to everyone who has stolen money from me, lied to me, or simply hurt my feelings emotion-wise, work-wise or who challenged me on education."

Peter: "Education wise? That must be a long list!" He disbelieved.

Jim: "I will try to be brief for now but please check my Naval Academy records. I was one of the top three in the class, but they kicked me out for political reasons. After my defection, I was the first one to become a ship's Master/Captain of Ocean Going ship at age of twenty-six!"

Peter: "You did it without diploma?"

Jim: "One, who knows, does not need diploma. I got my 3rd, 2nd and Chief Officer's Licenses through examinations in English, not a multiple choice exam. Since I was not US Citizen I was licensed by Liberian Maritime and Panamanian Registry as Officer and a Captain."

Peter: "All that in four short years? Most of your class mates are just now getting close to positions as Masters, usually after twenty years. We need to check your DNA?" He laughed at the quickness and in awe, in which Jim had reached such a level.

Jim: "My DNA will not be different than my relatives but maybe the difference is the way I perceive reality? I will write my book on my research and discoveries, so everyone who wishes can move to my level!"

Peter: "The way you talk, you make people feel small." He was serious.

Jim: "I am trying to spread the knowledge, not to hide it or to make people inferior. If someone is a teacher, he should advance his students to his level. They should continue and improve from there."

Peter: "Most people prefer simple life. They get one or two skills and that pull them through life. I would say that they are lazy or just afraid to get out of the box. Getting a second job or starting a new business takes more than just an idea or money."

Jim: "The fear of losing is the same like the fear of pain. If you ignore the pain, then you can go through a rock, water, fire! I learned to ignore pain or minimize it when I was getting my degrees in Judo and Karate. When one does Yoga the body becomes more weightless, liquid, gas like. The hydrogen converts to helium when in meditation."

Peter: "That sounds like a chemistry class! Great cigar!" he smiled.

Jim: "No, my friend! It is a mixture of everything, chemistry, biology and applied physics to get to the Quantum State of Mind."

Peter: "Then you must know the formulas and how everything works?" he was still skeptical.

Jim: "Ok, I am not a nuclear physicist, nor bio chemist, nor dedicated Swami Yoga, nor black belt Bruce Lee in Jeet Kune Do (the art of fighting without fighting). I am a researcher and apply all of them in my everyday life. One will discover the link between them like a spider who makes a net and connects all the invisible dots to make his home, or a builder who builds a house gets all the ingredients the way I build my theory. I have everything proven by formulas. Matter of fact, we the researchers, we feed from each other, but we don't communicate with each other. I never met single physicist. I just read diversified literature."

That was in November, 2003.

Later on in 2013 this conversation would of have finished like this: "I arrived earlier than Team Higgs about the antimatter and the neutrally charged mass, they call it "God's particle, boson." It should be called "WeZon." I had e mailed that on June 13th, 2012, chatting with Andrea Roberson. Higgs announced it to the world on July 04th, 2012. I had never seen the Feynman diagrams, describing the Boson versions till Dec., 2012. That was in the book, I ordered on line, by Frank Klose "Infinity puzzle, Quantum field theory."Wezon/Boson" was proven to exist at CERN in March, 2013."

Adrian: "I see that you are always ahead of the curve. Let finish this conversation, some other time. Now it is time to sleep." He was right. Almost everyone looked drunk and tired. All those artificial smiles were fading away. After all they were all terrestrials, including Jim, who, even, in many strange mental ways, was still one of them. Or was he a Demi God?

Michael: "Can you spend the night here at my home? I deserve that after twenty-three years, my son."

Jim: "Sure, Dad! Do you have a TV here?" he needed to keep up with the world.

Michael: "No TV, but plenty of books, magazines, photo albums to look at."

He pulled some of Jim's old high school pictures, and then moved to the Naval Academy picture when he, Adrian and Jim took a picture with all of them, wearing his uniform. That would have been a great communist propaganda in 70's, but in 2003 it was a laughable idea.

Jim: "You must be very nostalgic when you look at those pictures?"

Michael: "God is the judge, if I was a good father? Only God will decide who was right and wrong after you defected? As a father I will still love you, no matter what your decisions were. You hurt us a lot when you left suddenly, but we understand now why you did it. We may be a family, but everyone makes his individual choices. If that's what you have chosen make you more accomplished and happy then our opinion is just an opinion."

Jim: "Happiness is a selfish thing. It promotes consumption and triggers the lowest instinct in humans. When someone is accomplished everyone notices. It brings confidence and certain glow about the person. Happiness can be induced by material things, drugs, alcohol, sex, massage and awards. Artificial confidence is character flaw and usually involves something criminal and evil. True confidence does not need to advertise. Everyone will see it and for some reason it will create envy, between the insecure, and loyalty by the want to-be followers."

Michael: "It is amazing that we never had this type of conversations before?" He was yawning.

Jim: "That was a different era, when you would repeat everything the newspaper says. Now you are all into God, which is amazing, but a right direction, father!" he was yawning too. The make shift sofa bed was uncomfortable, but he promised to "spend the night."

Father: "Good night, Son!"

Jim: "Good night, father!"

In the Bible the Jesus quotes "The Parable of the Lost Son." Here everything was in reverse, but the love of the father to his returning son Jim was the same. The story of Prodigal was that he spent his inheritance from his father's wealth traveling around the world. Wasting his wealth he ended up feeding pigs and sometimes eating their food. When he returns, he is welcomed by his father and rejected by his brother. Jim here was welcomed by everyone. He was prosperous, he brought gifts and tremendous knowledge King Simeon, couldn't show yet. There is no parable/comparison here. He was not getting an award, a medal, a Nobel Laureate prize here, but plenty of respect and love.

"One, who can bring people to their highest dimensions is better, than one who begs for mercy and love on his knees. Awareness makes one independent," Jim thought.

The morning after Adrian called. It was about 11 am.

Jim: "Hey, it is early! What are you doing?" He woke up to see around twenty empty bottles still around the table from "the Dionysus" night before. His father peeked his head through the door. "Are you awake?"

Jim: "You guys are early birds. I sleep till 2 pm usually." He was also feeling the jet lag. "I will get up now."

Michael: "Gods don't need much sleep."

Jim: "I am not a God, Demi God maybe?" both of them laughed.

Jim: "What is on the agenda today?" he was hungry.

Adrian: "Uncle Radi wants to meet us. We will take a train to meet him."

Jim: "Train?" I haven't ridden a train in the last twenty years. I always have two to three cars." He was appalled.

Adrian: "My car wouldn't make it with four people inside."

Jim: "I will think of something for your birthday as a gift." He paused.

Adrian: "Just being here is good enough for my big 50." He was smiling, but the phone couldn't show it, but Jim heard it in his voice.

Jim: "Come drive me to the rental car place." He was devouring some eggs and bacon and French toast. Ten minutes after Adrian was driving him and Rebecca toward the rental car place some ten blocks away eastward toward Sofia's center. Rebecca was heading toward her business, something to do with selling health products. They pulled over at a rental car place. Jim looked at small shiny gray 190i Mercedes. It looked like new, but with some major mileage on it.

Jim: "Do you like that car?" he looked at his brother.

Adrian: "Yes, but it is not for sale."

Jim: "My brother, in this world you don't ask, you take! But be civil first and try to negotiate."

Adrian: "Are you implying that this car is already mine?" he was amazed how Jim was approaching the reality.

Jim: "Negotiation shows intent and wisdom. Stupidity is when one just flashes money down the drain and try to impress wrong people, like the salesman here." Thirty minutes later Adrian was driving his first Mercedes. Rebecca was confused.

Rebecca: "I am going to be late for work, but for a good reason." She was puzzled on how easy was to change reality. Now they were in a better car and Adrian couldn't believe he was getting a car of his dreams.

Rebecca: "I am driving the Renault to work. You two enjoy your new ride."

Adrian: "Ok. See you later at the house." The two brothers jumped in the Mercedes. It was fast, manual shift transmission. Adrian was happy. Soon they pulled by his office, an affiliate to US AIG, but under German company name "Allianz."

Adrian was the chief instructor there, teaching new agents about how to sell insurance and the insurance policies. The irony would be that President Obama would sign the stimulus of nearly a trillion dollars to help AIG in 2009; therefore he helped also his brother to retain his job in Bulgaria. At the office they were waiting for his brother's arrival and the usual birthday cake and champagne was served. There were a couple of beautiful women there but they were married and not the right type for flirting with Jim. He gave some of them his business cards with shiny Randevu bar and lounge address, even a map showing the proximity of the White House. He could have had a better response in the cemetery. The women were either too conservative or plain damn dumb? They had never offered any business cards or even a small chat in return.

Jim felt like the Bulgarian society did not progress like the Western Europe or even more socially oriented like the USA. That was his first observation, but it did not change much with the next encounters with other ladies, while he was staying next two weeks. But he would understand why the Bulgarian society survived for centuries. They would be more of a thinking type, talking with words with subliminal messages, making friends and enemies alike wonder? You hardly see Bulgarian people sincerely laughing, unless they are in the family friendly circle and mostly drunk. Jim classified them as people, "with a chip on their shoulders," not the RFID (remote frequency identification, approved by US in 2004). Jim called them the people from the dark ages, smart but staying in groups, brilliant but not recognized, never rich, because of the closed society which does not tolerate local success. One has to leave the country to be recognized abroad and if same decides to return to Bulgaria he usually gets mistreated or simply killed. Jim had heard of stories of mayors lasting just a year and getting killed, or mafia wars announced by TV anchorwoman.

Adrian: "Everything you hear is true. The harsh times we went through after the Berlin Wall was dismounted did not bring us the Western Democracy type, but the Eastern Russian mafia expansion. One of the emigrants returned with 3 million dollars. He settled near Varna and they killed him. The President of "MG"

(Multigroup; employing 10,000 people), a billionaire Iliya Pavlov was killed in July 2003. He testified about the assassination of Adrian Lukanov in 1996, the first Bulgarian Prime Minister after the fall of the Berlin Wall."

Jim: "Ok, let's go see the rest of the family. Politics gets you nowhere." Both excused themselves, thanked them for the cake and the champagne and they left the office with socially handicapped ladies.

Adrian: "You can work with them, but you can't fuck them. Even you with business cards, money and Mercedes gift can't impress them."

Both brothers agreed.

The evening was more exciting. At the hotel Sheraton Jim met with his old girlfriend Alexandra. They had been in contact on and off for nearly thirty-five years. His brother was next to him and he was wondering to see Jim and Alexandra hugging and crying at the same time. They decided to have a nice dinner in the restaurant on first floor, which was not as fancy as the location and the name brand hotel they were in. It was an Irish theme cuisine. The interesting thing was that Alexandra's lover kept driving around in circles angry and jealous. She was laughing at his calls and insecurity.

Alexandra: "That what happens when you date fifteen years younger than your age!" she was tall and slim. Her age did not affect her and the dark long hair was replaced with thick blonde hair, retaining her glamour Hollywood movie star look; a very close resemblance of Catherine Zeta Jones.

Jim: "Mine is twenty-eight years younger!" he was talking about Kiana.

They were great friends. She was the one to send him letters to the Naval Academy with red lipstick imprints on the back. It made everyone envious and he was proud of her friendship. Unfortunately, it also attracted the attention of the Naval Intelligence.

Alexandra: "You look the same, handsome and mature!" she was holding his hand. Adrian was acting like Security. He was watching the door, also scanning the other tables, especially the new arrivals seated nearby. Jim was not a target but one never knows who is friend or foe in this new and confused Democracy.

Jim: "You look like a model and a movie star. You lost weight. And Hollywood would be glad to accept you as a star. You know I have my own video and film production company, Walker's Media."

Alexandra: "You know the slogan: "Better be first in a small town, than second in big town." She crossed her long legs and had a sip of some Jameson on ice.

Jim: "I have similar slogan, but it is coming at different angles "if first in New York and DC, one can be first anywhere." I was one of youngest captains in the world at age, twenty-six; licensed in New York by Panamanian Consulate. I am probably the youngest owner of Harvey's Restaurant at the age of thirty-three, that restaurant was 133 years old. I reopened the oldest club in the world, The Pier 9, the predecessor of Studio 54, closed for 22 years. I own a very successful lounge near the White House."

Alexandra: "How that happens to certain people, but not to any of our classmates?" she was chopping some salad with her fine long fingers and perfect nails and pale hands.

Jim: "It is partially myself upbringing. I did many sports, I got into yoga and science fiction books and I was living out of the box. You know me from before.

I never relied on anyone, not to my family, not to any connections in Bulgarian government. I passed many subjects in the Naval Academy without examination.

I was detained, and coming out after ten days I passed the final exam of my last semester with flying colors."

Alexandra: "I remember you always had extra days for vacation because of your great scores, my Jim!"

Jim: "Everything in life has, "cause and effect." To become a successful person it takes some education, no fear of losing, utilizing the opportunity, physical conditioning to perfection, never regret what you have done."

Alexandra: "Why the physical condition?" she was drinking a nice glass of Syrah and following that with bites of pepper steak with brandy sauce.

Jim: "I was discovered by one of Shri Lankan crews on the Greek ship when I was trying to move to a cabin to hide. They conducted a search of the whole ship. Thanks to my training I was able to hide in various places. First I hid in the quarantine room. I left the door open and the captain did not search inside. I was behind that door. I run to steward's cabin. When I heard the captain approaching the room, I hid under the sailor's bunk bed. The height was very low and only one side of the sliding door could open. I stayed under the bed and waited for the conversation with the cook to be over. I was suffocating. I was trying to open the door on the back side of the bed. I had to twist my body in a number 8 almost breaking my back. All my yoga and martial arts came into play. When I returned to the first and only sliding door I opened it and breathed like a new born baby. The captain and the cook were still talking, but I survived. That's where my physical flexibility helped the most. The Turkish pilot did not call the authorities to search the ship. He said to the captain to worry about that in the next port of arrival. Next day I reported to the bridge and asked for political asylum. The Greek FBI advised me to proceed to USA, where it would have been safer for me. The Bulgarian ship, Buzludga attempted to intercept the Greek ship after Gibraltar to take me back. Captain refused and I ended in USA."

Adrian: "We heard all kinds of stories about you, but look who was talking? Now we know the true story."

Jim: "The motivation was higher than life. I had no fear. I had nothing to lose and so much to win."

Alexandra: "We believed in you. Things are not getting better here, but the best of us will make it."

Adrian: "Why don't you try to open a club here? I will run it for you."

Alexandra: "I heard you lost your business because you couldn't pay the mafia?" she addressed Adrian.

Adrian: "I was hardly paying my rent. I also had a child. I decided not to pay them. They kept breaking my windows and stealing my stuff. I would drive to Dubai, I would buy inexpensive electronics, when I come back here they would rob the store. I used my house storage in the basement. I had to bring every day the important stuff back and forth. They started breaking into my basement. I was afraid they may kidnap my son. I talked to the Police. They looked the other way. Finally I decided to get some another job, Rebecca, also." He paused as if remembering the trouble…..

Jim: "What is the guarantee they will not do the same if I get you a new club here?" He lit a cigar.

Alexandra: "If the location is in Downtown Sofia, where the police are more present, they may be less aggressive?" She was looking at the desert menu.

Jim: "I think if a guy like me opens a business here, which holds US passport, they may think twice to bother me or you." He was confident.

Alexandra: "True. They don't bother foreigners the way they deal with locals. May I have cappuccino, please?" she addressed the waiter, who spoke English. Jim was talking to him in English and they got better service than other tables. And the tip was adequately 20 percent! The waiter was puzzled, but then he assumed that Jim was not Bulgarian, which was ok. The credit card was showing Bank of America, that was the proof for him.

Adrian: "Ok then, let's start looking for a club space here. That way Jim can come and visit more often!"

Jim: "I do not mind that as long everything turns out to be profitable?"

Alexandra: "You were always different than the others, I never seen you as capitalist minded before, but now you sound better than our King Simeon II." She was laughing.

Jim: "We heard about capitalism from Marxist theory that it will collapse. I see that it is expanding to Russia, China and India. I guess Adams Smith's theory, the father of capitalism, works. He says that capitalism needs some regulation, but the communist don't want just regulation, they want to control the money flow, by diverting it to workers. Their power is in unions and the unions are the ones to choose government officials and therefore they dictate federal and state laws. Sometime the federal and union regulations copy each other. The US labor unions used to be everywhere, but now they are only 17 percent, the more regulations, the more outsourcing to India or China."

Alexandra: "So how the workers feel? No "revolutions?" she quoted Marx laughing.

Jim: "The difference between India and China is that USA and Western Europe have welfare programs, with cash assistance and medical insurance."

Adrian: "That is what I sell here, insurance!" He felt proud. The cigar was good and the Amaretto he was holding in his hand.

Alexandra: "Ok, enough of politics and economics. Cheers for meeting after so many years and for good health."

Jim: "Happy Birthday, Brother!"

Adrian: "Thanks! I thought about this many years and finally we are together again!"

Jim: "Same here, I thought of coming back here eventually but I was just not ready. Now I am with my best friends! Cheers!"

Adrian: "I am going to leave you alone for now. Brother, I will see you later at home" he started the Mercedes and took off.

Alexandra: "Let see where my son is and we can go to some quiet place?" She made a couple of calls and she found out her son was with his girlfriend. Her boyfriend kept texting and she answered to him she would see him next day.

Alexandra: "I love him, but he is a dreamer. He is an opera singer and he keeps talking about going to Rome and singing there. They are supposed to pay 30,000 dollars for thirty minutes of singing?"

Jim: "That is great. Everyone follows his star, his mind path in the future. I did.

I am thinking of buying an island in the Caribbean."

Alexandra: "I know Capricorn Zodiac sign. You talk a lot, but you take a lot of effort to achieve it and not everyone can wait that long. Look at my situation. While you were away I had a son, bought two condominiums. Now I am buying a third one." The valet guy brought a brand new SUV Isuzu Diesel. She gave him a small tip and Jim joined her aboard.

Jim: "Finally we are alone" she was driving manual transmission SUV. She stopped briefly and gave Jim a nice and long kiss.

Alexandra: "I like you and love you in special way, Jim! Time is a cruel thing if wasted. I appreciate your coming here but things don't change instantly. Hope you open a club here also, but that will not make me drop my friends and future plans. I suggest you help your brother and family, but don't leave USA. And go ahead and buy your island. I will come and visit. Maybe more?" she quickly grabbed his hand.

Jim: "People in the whole world think I am just another club owner. I don't want to be remembered as such. My legacy should live for millenniums how I think and archive my goals. That is why I am writing my book. Knowledge is more valuable than today's dollars or any money and wealth. Michelangelo's artwork, Da Vinci's inventions, Nostradamus' predictions, Galileo's telescope and celestial theory, Newton's gravity, Churchill-the historian, Einstein's theory of relativity or any theoretical physicist they are not rich, but have left a great legacy behind."

She drove her SUV to a small lounge on second floor on boulevard Vitosha across The Palace of Culture. There were playing some music videos with Donna Sumner and Marry J. Blige and some European artists. Jim was trying to get her to open up a bit. They had some cappuccino and small chat. She was smart and playful, but not seductive. Jim invited her to big birthday party for his brother and to meet his closest friends Vladimir and Milen. She declined. She agreed to meet with his father Michael and Igor, a classmate.

After an hour she dropped Jim at Lulin Complex. The small room was enough to stretch to a bed and a small night stand and it was cold. Jim slept covered with two blankets and on top he used his fur coat. When he woke up he made a call to Kiana in USA. She was surprised to hear his voice. She wished him well, but something was missing. Then Jim was concerned about his lounge. He asked Lora to deposit some money in his bank account. He told her he bought his brother a Mercedes.

Lora: "Very nice, but be careful." She sounded concerned.

At this time of 2003 the on line banking was new for him. He just signed for Bank of America on line, before departing USA, and he asked his brother if any computers nearby were? The only places one can get Internet was at internet cafes for a fee per hour. They were similar to pay phones at USA. The more quarters one uses, the more time one can stay on line. It was basically a hangout for kids and adults alike. They had some kind of ID cards, so the Big brother was watching who is in and out in those establishments. Paolo, Adrian's son was very familiar with the locations of those cafes and he was acting as tour guide. Jim gave him a video camcorder and Paolo became an overnight producer, following him around. The next day they decided to pay a visit to his uncle Radi in Sliven, one of the major cities in southern Bulgaria.

His uncle was holding the family together. He was the new and true businessman. They were only two of a kind in the city, Radi and Leskov.

They both owned gas stations and hotels. The first was Jim's uncle; the second was the Mayor of the town, who became an instant success after he scored against Germany during the World Cup soccer tournament in 1994. The signs all over the town were telling "If Leskov can beat the Germans, he deserves the Mayorship." Radi even drove them to the hotel and club Leskov owned. Then he drove by three of his own hotels. They were not big and with clubs, but they were profitable.

Jim: "You and I are alike. I owned three clubs, you own three hotels. And you own gas stations and real estate. The capitalism has been good to you, I guess?" both of them were laughing.

Radi: "Everything has a price."

Jim: "I know. Hard work and higher purpose in life shows results."

They had a gathering at Radi's house where there was showing international soccer team battle between Turkey and Bulgaria. After two hours of drinking, shouting and eating, the score was 2:1 in favor of Turkey. Even they were very upset, they managed to accept the loss with more drinking and more eating. If Hollywood could have recorded the remarks and the emotions of soccer fans a movie made of that could be a best seller.

Same evening they traveled to meet Jim's cousin Dino at nearby small town Mladovo. There were no real roads to it. The dirt roads were made by travelers who had relatives or business with Sliven. There were no signs to and from the town. One can follow the electrical and phone wires stretched atop old wooden posts sometime 50 years before by some overly ambitious communist program, but as usual they would neglect or forget to create the infrastructure to travel.

Dino: "Hey cousin. We haven't seen each other for thirty years. You look the same, but a bit heavier, mature!"

Jim: "I heard many things about you. Seems like you are doing everything I should be doing?"

Dino: "I am watching the gas station. I am breeding cattle. I am doing some agriculture. We need to catch up." He showed him inside the house. It was remodeled. It had a shower and inside toilet.

Jim: "I see you driving a Volkswagen. You are moving up with the times!" he approved.

Dino: "I see you are driving a Mercedes. My father Radi owns one too," he got even.

Jim: "Let's have a good cigar first. Here is nice watch for you."

Dino: "That is a nice watch, and it looks expensive. I rather have time with my favorite cousin than get any watch on earth." Meanwhile, a small kitten was following him around. He called him Misha. The little kitten was a fighter and full of life. In the evening he was spending time in the house, but day time he was out hunting. All night, Misha would spend curled up on a comfortable chair.

Dino: "Hey Misha, want a cigar, my friend?" He was getting drunk.

Jim: "What is amusing here? I wouldn't make it here one day."

Dino: "I have a shot gun here which I use for hunting. I scare the hell out of gypsies trying to steal my gas."

Jim: "Don't you feel lonely here?"

Dino: "If you need company, there is a club in Sliven we can go check it out now. Do you want to go? I am ok. My wife comes here every weekend."

Jim: "Sure, but you are intoxicated?" he was hesitant.

Dino: "Bulgarians hardly stay sober night time. Drinking is not the problem. We are very social people and staying home alone is the worst choice," he started the Volkswagen. He did not want to get too much attention driving the Mercedes.

Jim: "I am curious, but not desperate. Let's go!" They drove around thirty minutes to the club. Seems Dino knew the manager. That was one of Leskov's clubs. They entered through a private entrance like VIPs. They got a nice table on the mezzanine and it was overlooking the dance floor below. They also were able to see other smaller balconies which had velvet curtains for privacy designed like in an opera house.

Jim: "This Leskov has style and class," he remembered the face of the short slim man with a bald top who made the 2nd and winning goal in 1994. Bulgarian team supposed to fight for second or first place against Brazil, according to the world famous blind Oracle of Petrich Vanga Dimitrova (1911-1996). For some unknown reason the French referees of the match between Italy vs. Bulgaria were bias and they did not award many penalty kicks or faults in favor of Bulgarians. As a result Italy qualified for the final match. The best scorer in that 15th World Cup was Hristo Stoichkov, who earned the Golden Boot with 6 goals, but Bulgaria took the 4th place, unfortunately. So even Oracle Vanga could not be accurate, or maybe knowing her prediction the evil forces (referees) proved her wrong?

That is why the orthodox followers very often miss their opportunities at the last minute.

For example the Russian Tsar in 1904, Nikolaus II announced that the Trans Siberian express was accomplished with five miles to go, just to be destroyed by Japanese sabotage. Then they lost Port Arthur against Japanese. The whole economy was destroyed over building a useless railroad! To build this giant venture the Tsar sold Alaska to USA for 14 kilograms of gold! The returning naval ships to Russia started the revolution.

Dino: "If you see any girls you like I will help you chat with them ...I know you need some sex!"

Jim: "Sure. It is has been awhile for me to meet a Bulgarian lady."

Dino: "I will leave you alone for ten minutes. I will scout the place for an attractive lady." He grabbed a cigar and disappeared. Jim was observing the floor with mostly mixed couples of men and women and some of them were just women. The single malt was great balance for a great Cohiba cigar, but a little female company wouldn't hurt.

Dino: "You are in luck. I found nice young lady for you. She has been observing you for a while. She wants something in advance, unfortunately."

Jim: "What does she want?"

Dino: "She wants 150 euro, sorry."

Jim: "Hey, that's just like in the USA. I guess that is the price of Democracy?"

both of them laughed.

Jim: "Let me look around, I maybe able to find someone else, cheaper or free? What happened the last fourteen years? We never had prostitution before?"

Dino: "You look foreign and too mature here" he was getting drunk.

Jim: "Are you implying I am old?"

Dino: "Personally, I wouldn't mess with those young ladies. They think about money more than any generation before. You got the money and the right car, but they fall for young, gangster type guys."

Jim: "I get young ladies all the time in USA. Age is never a factor there. I guess my new country is more advanced and more open minded?" He puffed the great cigar.

Dino: "You are going to Varna. There you will feel more at home, I guess?"

Jim was getting tired. He drove the car on the way back to the house of his grandparents, with the gas station, cattle and Misha, the fighter cat.

Next day his brother and father went to the cemetery. They paid their respects to, the deceased grandparents Dino and Mita. Michael couldn't stop chatting. Jim just hushed him to stop. Michael was surprised, but he understood. He had a weakness and respect toward his younger and smarter son, Jim. Next day they visited Danka and Denka in a small town near Sliven. They were in good health, just with gray hair. One of Jim's cousins George had died in a car accident. His favorite cousin Yonka was killed at work, while cleaning some offices in Sofia. Police claimed she fell while drunk, but probably was attempted rape gone wrong?

Varna was a great city, the pearl of the Black Sea. In 2005 the archeologist would uncover a series of pits used for rituals as well as parts of a gate. Carbon analysis will date them to the Chalcolithic age to between 4,700 and 4,200 B.C., more than a millennium before the start of the ancient Greek civilization. That would make it the oldest town in Europe. Was Jim incarnated spirit of some old Demi God? Here, where he was born, and here where his young mother Loretta would die in a car accident leaving him without a mother's love at the tender age of six months, exactly forty-six years before. Michael, Paolo, Rebecca and Adrian headed back to Sofia, while, Jim decided to stay a couple of days. He kept the Mercedes. He drove around trying to recognize old places. Everything had changed. The only things that did not change were the Naval Academy and his favorite hotel where he used to hang out near, the Black Sea. He checked in for a couple of days. The luxury was there, but something was amiss. He enjoyed the view. The roof top restaurant was overlooking east toward the Naval Academy. The truth was that the merchant marine division was moved to a civilian college.

Jim: "Those military cockroaches, could not handle more defections, like mine!" He ordered double single malt and requested huge ashtray for his cigar. The front desk Concierge shift was about to finish at midnight, so he expected by then to enjoy the view, the drink and good smoke.

Svetlana was a blonde Russian with the longest legs and smallest upper body he had ever seen in Eastern Europe. She saw his US passport when he was checking in and the Mercedes the valet parked, still with German license plates remaining attached on it. She was speaking perfect Bulgarian, English and Russian and she was complimenting her income with a part time escort service. When she would get into garage level she would not get into her car immediately, but she would meet a date either in the hotel or she would drive away in someone else's fancy car.

Svetlana: "I got this job with contingency that I have to pay 50 dollars a shift. I feel like a stripper/dancer. I feel like I am on stage. The mafia assumes that women are hookers anyway, so why not cash on men's weakness? You see we work in couples. The man next to me is my body guard. He also provides some of our known clients with small arms, if they need them. They cannot bring them on airplane, so they rent them and then return them before they leave. Sometime we act as a couple, when we attend dinners with big shots, but basically we are drivers, escorts and security at same time."

Jim: "Sounds like a Hollywood movie. So what does it take to spend an evening/night with you?"

Svetlana: "One night is 200, two nights is 300 euro." She was laughing. "And that is because you are Bulgarian and you do speak Russian. Arabs pay three times more."

Jim: "I am amazed of the whole picture. I can rent a gun and a "wife" for two days? What is nice gun rental?" he was curios.

Svetlana: "Same as my rates. The difference is if you use the gun we charge you for the ammunition and cleaning." She was making sense.

Jim: "What happens if one loses the gun? Do you take insurance?"

Svetlana: "Then you lose your rental rates. You will pay in full the value of the weapon and next time you will be buying it, not renting it. The good thing is that if you return the weapon, we will deduct the rental rate, but refund the balance." She was robotic, but still cute.

Jim: "Do you like playing casino?" he needed more entertainment than just plain sex.

Svetlana: "You are paying for my time all night. Why not? I know a nice casino at Golden Sands, but you need an ID."

Jim: "I have an US passport."

Svetlana: "I have Russian passport." She grabbed Jim's aroused 8 inch "tower." And after we win, we will play in your room. I have spare clothes in my locker."

Jim: "I can buy you new clothes, my rental wife. I do not rent or buy weapons. I am black belt in Judo and Karate."

He was enjoying the blue neon lighted front of the Naval Academy. He was imagining to go to the reception kiosk and to announce himself. He wanted to make a tour through the class rooms, which he hated some thirty years prior. He wanted to attend the martial arts school, (where there were only ten cadets allowed to enroll a year). He wanted to meet his old favorite "rota" commander Captain Ganev, to meet and argue with Commissar Kostadinov, to thank Admiral Danev for kicking him out, therefore, motivating him to escape and become ship's Captain at age twenty-six! The phone text woke him up from the semi induced dream.

Svetlana: "I am in the garage. Come and let's go to the Casino. Bring your passport, please." She was demanding more than just asking.

Jim: "Yes, madam. I am coming." They easily entered the Golden Sands Resort. They followed the traffic to Casino city. That was the home of Greek, Macedonia and Russian investors. Names like Black Sea, Palm, Havana and Grand were too familiar.

Jim: "I used to hang out here when I was a cadet in the Naval Academy. I came here to practice my English. One time I was late, returning to school. The officer on duty reported me and I was detained a week in jail."

Svetlana: "I come here to practice my escort skills. English I don't need to master."

She pulled her mini skirt down coming out of the Mercedes, angering the curious eyed eighteen year old valet.

Svetlana: "Sorry, no freebees, but we tip well."

Jim: "You do speak great English. He thinks you are British!"

Svetlana: "I know him from before. He is horny little devil. He knows I am Russian. When I speak English, I get more respect. He thinks you are British."

Jim: "You must be popular here?"

Svetlana: "Yes, but between wrong people. I get harassed mostly by the Macedonians and some Greeks. Russians are too drunk to notice me. That is why I never come here by myself."

The registry desk was taking pictures, checking IDs, passing the rules to read before entering. Jim was puzzled. In US casinos nobody was asking for IDs or taking pictures. Seemed the Big Brother in Bulgaria was more intrusive than his counterpart. Svetlana had already a casino card and she was anxious to have a drink and play. Jim waited five minutes and he joined her at the cashier's office. They bought tokens with 500 euro and they headed toward the roulette tables.

Jim: "I have better luck with black jack." He grabbed Svetlana's ass, while entering to deflect any Casanova want to be.

Svetlana: "I am better in roulette. If I win I keep half ok?" she grabbed Jim's crotch. She started with 300 and soon she won about 1,000. She took her cut and they moved to black jack tables.

Jim: "Always play on less crowded tables. Then you can psych the Croupier. The more you get to know him the more you win. Usually the floor manager tries to change the Croupier to more experienced one, when the casino losing gets too obvious." Svetlana was busy drinking and she was getting hungry.

Jim: "Hello Sir! I will play two hands. This way I will be quicker."

Croupier: "Welcome!" He was playing against two more players. The tokens were at 50 euro minimum to bet. Jim started betting with 100 euro per hand. Soon he lost some and gained more. Totaling towards 500 he walked away. The profit was 300.

Svetlana: "Hey, we should come here more often. We made total of 1,500. I keep 350 from the roulette. We started with 500. After my cut you kept the 650.00 profit, and of course your initial 500.00, nothing like free sex!" She finished her "cosmopolitan" drink. "I am hungry."

Jim: "There is no free sex, nor free money. There is risk taking and because of this there is smart money." He looked at his net gain. On the way out something out of the old times books happened. They were stopped by armed Police at check point.

Police: "IDs, please!" They were young and serious and spoke good English.

Jim: "Sure!" he stretched his US passport out.

Police: "Did you enjoy your games?" That question was out of context and probably was more likely to be asked by the restaurant host, than someone with a gun in your face?

Svetlana: "Of course! We will be back next week." She showed her Russian passport. Police was puzzled a bit.

Police: "Friend of yours?" they addressed Svetlana.

Jim: "Client! Can we go now?"

Police: "Yes, sir! America is our friend now. Have a nice night." Police officer couldn't comprehend the Bulgarian name, the US passport, the Russian citizen and just shook his head. He saluted. Jim stepped on the gas. The Mercedes took off fast and they both laughed.

Jim: "I feel they would have kept us longer if we'd won more money. I bet big winners don't leave alive with their money. They must get radio communications from the casino owners, who are mafia related any way."

Svetlana: "I try to stay away from the casino world. It is too complicated and not very well regulated. I know the hotel is safer than the "Big Money." They pulled over at small restaurant which was three miles down the road. It was owned by some Greek guy and the food was similar to Bulgarian, simple and with a great taste. Soon after, they were naked in the Jacuzzi.

Jim: "It was good I did not possess any guns in the car. Who knows what they would of done if they searched and discovered any arms?" He was soaping that beauty's ass, who was trying to turn on the radio and showing the perfect pear looking ass and small waist and back, bent in inviting doggy style position in front of Jim eye level.

Svetlana: "Music/noise is necessary here. One never knows who is listening?" She was right.

Jim: "In USA everything is videotaped, hallways, elevators, entrances, garages and roof tops, everything, except bathrooms and showers." He was getting aroused.

Svetlana: "If you want me for two days we have to play it secret and smart. I am not sure if I am protected in the Casino world?"

Jim: "Maybe you should come to USA and stay with me forever?"

Svetlana: "You cannot afford me there. I will demand much more than 150 dollars a night."

Jim: "My girlfriend cost me six to eight thousand a month. That is almost double than I am paying you here." He stopped the soaping and inserted his 8 inch torpedo in her perfect vagina. She moved away from him and pushed the volume of the radio up. Jim just followed her, she pushed back to him making a reversed wave and the slapping sound almost synchronized with the R&B sound coming from the radio. For some reason Marry J. Blige was more popular in Bulgaria than in the USA.

Jim: "That is a casino sex and is good. Do you like it baby?" He was breathing fast and talking in bursts of air.

Svetlana: "Yes, daddy! Why do you fuck like a black man? It feels really big inside!" she even turned slightly in disbelief. "I do enjoy your rhythm."

Jim: "Hey. How do you know how black men fuck?" he was playfully curious, but continued pumping in and out.

Svetlana: "It is slippery here. Let's move to bed. My knees are going to be swollen tomorrow." Jim followed her to the bed almost not pulling out. She was laughing at his determination not to miss any stroke and momentum.

Svetlana: "Vasily, you are as stubborn as a drunken Russian, greedy like Arab, rhythmic as black man and great as Bulgarian, keep it going, Vasily!"

She wrapped her long legs around Jim back and started lifting herself up and down while squeezing the swollen to the maximum penis.

Jim: "I feel like Vasily Grigoryevich Zaytsev with the sniper rifle but you are not German! Call me Daddy, I like that better, please."

Svetlana: "Shut up. Vasily is my idol. But I will call you anything you want. After all you are my, client."

Svetlana started swinging back and forth while the knot of great long legs was staying in one place. She looked like a horse rider under the belly of a horse instead the normal position on top.

Jim: "I guess that is the way top models fuck? I guess it is a knee saving position." He gently dropped her on her back slowing her down. He wanted to prolong the pleasure. She seemed a bit in a hurry. She smelled like a mixture of shampoo, sexual sweat and four "cosmopolitan" drinks, with a bit of Greek food. Jim smelled like a great cigar. Both were in the mist of sexual encounter only a rich man and high society courtesan can enjoy. It was a perfect sexual storm without love and commitment. They would not even kiss; they were enjoying the sex and the money benefits.

Jim: "I am happy for the two days marriage. I know I am not going to the casino tomorrow." He slowly directed her to turn her great buttocks toward him for the final thrust in doggy style. She was observing her Gwen Stefani look-alike image in the pink mirrored head board, like she was putting on a lipstick. Jim was riding the pear shaped ass with the vigor of the winning jockey about to cross the finish line.

Svetlana: "Oh, Daddy! Ya zakonchila Vasily" she was contracting and screaming with low voice.

Jim: "You came? I am cumming too… Oh, oh, oh baby." He collapsed beside her. She was still convulsing in final slower pace.

Svetlana: "The last client was an Arab who wanted to do lesbian scenes with two of his wives and they were so boring I couldn't even get turned on. So you were a real Gem lately."

At around 9.30 am room service delivered a champagne breakfast. Jim paid the room service guy who was trying to look over his shoulder.

Jim: "Looking for something you lost?" He laughed and gave him a small tip. "Here is a little baksheesh. Try to be less curious."

Svetlana: "They all act like they have never seen a naked woman before. The valet, the room service, the bartender! Everyone is the same except my security guard at the front desk. He is gay." She laughed.

Jim: "Russian men are gay? I never heard or seen one yet. That is first for me." They had a champagne toast. The pancakes were emitting the sweet and wet flavor which was asking to be smothered with syrup.

Svetlana: "That is better than McDonalds across the street!"

Jim: "I really was surprised to see the worse American food chain in such a great location? This is for kids and poor people in USA."

Svetlana: "They are packed all the time. I really enjoy the Bulgarian cuisine. It taste better, but it can make you fat. But in moderate portions it is world's best."

Jim: "I call it God's food." That is what I really miss when I think of my old country besides my family." Soon after the breakfast they made love again but with less intensity.

Svetlana: "We have one more night. Don't be greedy!" She jumped in the shower and changed to her day time stylish, but not glamorous look. Her dirty blonde hair was not loose and down to her shoulders. She lifted it up in a small knot behind and with glasses on she looked more like a teacher, than a mixed professional concierge/escort.

Jim: "Ok, Gwen Stefani! I can see the Arab man missing you even with his four wives!"

Svetlana: "And I charged him much more than you. I wonder does he pay his wives. I asked them but they did not talk much." She finally pulled up her pantyhose and headed toward the door to work. "I will see you tonight.

I am leaving my extra clothes here, ok!" She kissed Jim who was walking around with long white hotel robe, puffing a Cohiba.

Jim: "I need to do some yoga to recharge for the next round." His lungs were slightly hurting. He transferred three times "Chi" energy from his solar plexus area to each lung. The pain disappeared immediately and his penis also felt filling up from the energy emanating from the tight and vigorous testicles, even one was long time been damaged from karate fights. He thought of Kiana and her juicy pussy, but there was no comparison of a professional courtesan and a new girlfriend at this moment. For a moment he felt like he was in USA. He was in his old country with all the amenities of USA could offer him. It was an illusion he did not want to lose, the sex, the casino, the Mercedes, the location candidly observing his old Naval Academy. Was the God of his success playing with him? Basically he was reminded again and again of his own slogan, "Beware of what you wish; it will happen! But then can you handle it?"

The time zone difference between Svetlana and Kiana was (-) 7 hours and he decided to drive around and to call around 3 pm Eastern Time in USA, but 10 pm in Bulgaria. He reminisced about his beautiful girlfriend Christina, who wanted to marry him in the second year of his studying in Naval Academy. He consulted with his father in 1977.

Michael: "You have to wait! We have to marry your brother first." He was rude and disconcerned. Jim told his Cleopatra looking girlfriend that and she moved on. She started dating a civilian who did not waste any time to make her pregnant. One day (in 1978) he saw Christina pushing a baby cart walking down the avenue Prince Boris the 1st. He invited her to come to his apartment. She declined.

Jim: "Do you love him?" he asked even he knew the answer.

Christina: "You see this baby? This baby could have been yours, Jim!" She pulled out the little cute guy who had the same green cat eyes like hers.

Jim: "I know the answer now, but why couldn't you wait just another year or two till my graduation?"

Christina: "My parents got married young. They were pushing me real hard, especially when I got pregnant by this loser!" She started crying.

Jim: "Are you going to marry him?" He held the baby. He couldn't stop admiring those beautiful innocent cat eyes. A month later he was walking down the steps toward the famous Sea Garden. He was just enjoying the sunny weather and even he invited with him Kiro, the unattractive, bird face class mate. The only reason they were friends was because he needed his apartment to change to civilian clothes. That way he got more options to move around. Suddenly he saw a beautiful bride with familiar curves and smile.

Christina: "What are you doing here? Did someone tell you where my wedding is?" she was confused.

Jim: "God sent me here! I was walking down without invitation obviously. I see you are enjoying the ceremony?" The exchange was fast like two wild cats would strike each other, but it was just verbal duel. Her husband to be was late and her mother and father did not recognize Jim, because he was wearing a wig. Jim was tempted to grab her and both of them jump in a car and run away, like in the movies, but, the cry of the little baby brought him to reality.

Christina: "You know I named him after you, Jim. That way even though he is not your son, at least he will remind me of you anytime I look at him!" She shed a tear, but quickly brushed it away. Her mother approached them and she was wondering who Christina was talking to? Jim just moved down the steps without turning around. He wished that it was his wedding, not the other guy's. Kiro was smoking cigarette acting like he was not interested. He also was wearing a wig. They looked like two Hollywood actors, who were in some mischievous situation.

Kiro: "Who was that? Your ex, I guess?"

He acted concerned now, while following Jim. He always envied this superman-looking, unusually intellectual man. He felt sorry for him but with mixed feelings that Jim deserved to lose that beautiful lady. The answer actually came from Jim himself.

Jim: "One can't have them all; sometimes we lose even a lady like this."

He turned slightly to see Christina waving to him good bye, entering a black limousine... He waved back, but she couldn't see him. Her husband pushed her inside the back seat and he was intentionally blocking her. Seems the mother sensed Jim's presence more through her instincts, than visually.

Jim: "Kiro, I think the mother told Christina's husband I was around. That is why he shoved her in the limousine that way. He seems very insecure person, even with a baby? Now I really feel sorry for her. It would be one hell of a marriage!" Both decided they needed a drink.

Jim was trying to contact Ivailo, who was fifty at the time, and who was his first cousin. He used to work as chief at employment headquarters for Masters and Mates in Varna in 1980. After many attempts he answered the phone.

Ivailo: "Who is this?" He sounded the same, with a harsher voice.

Jim: "I am in Varna. This is Jim, your cousin!"

Ivailo: "Who? I have one cousin Jim, but he defected to United States!"

Jim: "Yes, that is me. I am back in Bulgaria for a couple of weeks."

Ivailo: "Oh, it is you, Jim! It has been quarter century since you left. Where you have been?" He was not an excitable person. He was always conservative in his chat and emotions.

Jim: "I was pursuing my maritime career for a while. I traveled around the world for four years and I became ship's Captain on ocean going ship. I was twenty-six years old when I accomplished all of that." He paused, as his memory took him back to that time.

Ivailo: "That is amazing! I haven't seen a captain in Bulgaria or any merchant marine achieving that at this age on unlimited tonnage and any ocean going vessels. And I was in charge of personnel placement!"

Jim: "You should know me by now! The choices we make are somewhat triggered by situations we are in, and then they are assisted by our sub consciousness and God!"

Ivailo: "Are you talking about God? You were never religious, when I knew you, quite the opposite." He was curious.

Jim: "It is a long story. I am not religious still. I just find God easier to relate to people who are not in Quantum State of awareness."

Ivailo: "Are you now into this magic, occult, witchcraft or into science?"

Jim: "One answer is not enough, but my book is coming soon about how I do accomplish my thoughts. Just to be brief the yoga made me aware, the occult made me more of risk taker; the research in pyramids, Bible, metaphysics made me explain the secrets of many things the general deterministic science can't explain or can't touch it or they do not want to dig in."

Ivailo: "Great. You were top of your class, why should you not be on top of your research either? Meanwhile, we got a second child in our family a decade ago," he sounded like he was a proud parent.

Jim: "While I am busy openings three clubs in Washington, DC you guys are doing my job, increasing the population!" He said it like he was disappointed and happy at the same time.

Jim: "Can you find me a nice space for a club here in Varna? Maybe I can expand here?"

Ivailo: "I am not into commercial real estate, but they're plenty of real estate agencies on Boulevard Primorsky."

Jim: "Can you come to the hotel and we can decide where to go for dinner?" he suggested.

Ivailo: "Sorry, I work nightly and sleep day time. I work as ship's captain on the channel leading ships to Varna West, where you defected from. We do dredging, to make it acceptable for supertankers and deeper draft ships. Now I am heading to work. Keep in touch."

Jim: "Ok, maybe in the future we can meet?" He was a little disappointed, but he understood.

He drove the car toward the now Navy War College and he was puzzled to see the inactivity inside. With a few cadets in and out of the main gate he was wondering where the vibrancy of the past thirty years had gone to? Was the war ready society in 70's turned pro western to become one sleepy institution in the 21st century? Was his risk taken defection worth it? Was everything he thought he achieved driven by a selfish ambition? He would assume that was God, who guided him, triggered by his subconscious thoughts (commands), or was his theory just kind of combination of convenient excuses and coincidences?

God: "What coincidences are you talking about? Everything you want you have achieved. And the way you have achieved it is unique and it is for the history books and for your own legacy! Nobody will repeat what you have done."

Jim: "Right! And now I am in my old country and waiting for Svetlana to get off of work, while I am driving the 190i Mercedes. Ok, you win. I should never criticize myself for not trying! So, let me go check some clubs for sale or rent?"

He parked nearby Stefan Karadzha Street. He quickly discovered a real estate company with a shiny entrance. He entered and he was greeted in English by a tall brunette with a pale face; she reminded him of Elvira Princess of Darkness in USA.

Vera: "May I help you?" she was drinking a nice cappuccino and puffing a long tiny cigarette.

Jim: "Why do think I am a foreigner? Your English is great!"

Vera: "Well, the attitude is foreign, and then the clothes are unusual. You got a fur coat witch even the Russians don't wear. It looks western." She puffed the tiny cigarette almost to the filter, followed with the sip from the coffee cup. Her long legs were full of inviting curves and she was not afraid to cross them left and right, with the rolling chair pulled close enough to the desk, not to reveal too much, but just where the male attention should be triggered.

Jim: "I am here to check on some clubs. I wonder what the market is." He pulled out a Cohiba cigar and approached the desk.

Vera: "You need to see my boss. He is in a meeting now. He will be done next ten minutes." She walked around the desk and invited Jim to a huge brown leather couch. She brought a huge photo album with pictures of hotels, lounges and clubs.

Vera: "Please look at those while you wait. The prices are negotiable. We don't rent out, we only sell them." She set next to him, flirting and chatting at same time.

Jim: "I like some of them but I need numbers." He was again reassured that most women are hookers, but not all of them are real estate agents.

Just before Vera was to get any closer, the big sound proofed door opened and a tall, slim blonde man at his early thirties appeared, followed by two fat Arab men one of them holding a briefcase. They walked toward the exit and they shook hands good bye.

Igor: "Hello. Have you been here long? Sorry. It is business." He spoke great English.

Jim: "Vera showed me your properties for sale." He offered a Cohiba to Igor. He accepted.

Igor: "I just declined the sale of three casinos-hotels. We charge Arabs much more than Europeans. They did not have enough money."

Jim: "I own a restaurant and three clubs in USA. I am trying to expand here." He was puffing the cigar, being aware that was truth, but in the past.

Igor: "I think we need a good drink. I like black label." He pulled a bottle of "Johnny Walker" and poured it in two glasses.

Jim: "I know the prices are negotiable. I like those two: the open space two story lounge and the hotel casino."

Igor: "Lounge is 300,000 euro. The hotel is 500,000. The hotel is cheap, because after the earthquake nobody wanted to fix it?"

Jim: "I was just inquiring here. If the deal was good I could sell my business in USA and move my operation here?" He took a sip of the golden liquor.

Igor: "We work with cash up front and no partial payments or financing."

Jim: "I may return with all money required next year? Like I said I am just gathering information."

Igor: "Great? Here is my business card." He called Vera in his office. Jim was finishing the drink.

Igor: "What kind of idiots are you keeping in my office? Next time you don't flirt with them, screen them!" He spoke in perfect Bulgarian.

Jim: "I am heading to my hotel. Thanks for the drink and the information!" he peeked his head in the main office. There was a huge map with a logo in the corner Aramex (Russian Arms dealers). Underneath was a huge bank volt like safe.

Vera: "I am coming, sir!" She excused herself to Igor and walked Jim to the exit. He laughed.

Jim: "Igor walked out the Arabs, but he could not say good bye?"

Vera: "He is on important call from big client in Germany. They call here every day." She lied quick.

Jim: "They lost the war, but not the money!" he exited the door. Vera made a sorry face. She wanted to flirt, but she had to work.

Jim: "I will be in touch. I will be back next year" he lied.

Jim strolled up and down the avenue. He found a nice Bulgarian restaurant and he was amazed to see the variety of great tasting food. He was missing that in the States. It was getting dark. He was looking to chat with someone normal, who would not charge him 300 dollars for two nights? He made a small chat with few ladies, even they took his business cards, but he did not get much of desired response. Seemed in the States accepting someone's business cards were more of a ritual of beginning of reciprocal interest! The conversation would lead to information exchange and if a lady gives a man a business card that almost seals the deal in future relationship. Sex in the states was easier than most European countries, but it was always in contingency of instant or future benefits. In general, older ladies were more generous in many ways, while the younger ones were takers and always looking for Sugar Daddys or a husband. The love was false, in fact there was no love, just transactions but the benefits were real. Guys with nothing to offer were rarely chosen and they were in natural law of survival of the fittest, which they were not, unless they were in the same group of destitute ladies….

Jim went to his room to take a shower and to recharge with some yoga breathing and stretching. He watched the local news on TV. The amazing thing was they were all talking in positive ways. They were showing models of new complexes with mixed commercial use, or new bridges and new highways. The yoga uplifted him and he thought of calling Kiana.

He almost visualized her disappointed face at his return, if he ignored her. To his surprise nobody answered? He calculated the time. It was 3 pm at USA. The international code to use was (01) plus the personal phone number... She should have been out of any classes? He dialed a few times in five minutes intervals. Still no answer! That was a bit unusual, but his mind was distracted by the phone ringing at the night stand next to him.

Svetlana: "What are you doing, Casanova?" She sounded upbeat.

Jim: "I just finish meditating. You must be missing me?"

Svetlana: "I want you to buy me a gift from the duty free shop in the hotel. They close it at 11 pm."

Jim: "Sure. I am coming downstairs in ten minutes." He was happy for the attention. At the shop were all kinds of clothes, fancy watches, jewelry.

Svetlana: "The necklace or the watch?" She was wearing them both like a mannequin or a Model.

Jim: "When in doubt, take both." It is my slogan. "You look great and they fit your image and performance" he whispered toward the end.

Svetlana: "After the wining in the casino that is basically free!" she was laughing, and she was right.

Jim: "You sound like a true wife, like you are entitled? I like the game, but by tomorrow morning it will be over. I wish I could take you back to the States!" He held her waist, but he did not kiss her. She was still on the clock.

Jim: "Wrap those items up, please," as he directed the chubby 40 year old woman that had a great personality, but nothing else. "I guess they can't hire hookers everywhere with gay bodyguards?" he thought.

Jim: "I will see you after the shift."

Svetlana: "You are right. I can't be seen bringing boxes of Bulova and Cartier to front desk right now. See you in an hour, Daddy."

Jim: "I will be at The Roof Lounge for now. Just call me."

Svetlana: "Be careful with my gifts there. Don't show those to anybody, ok!" she was playfully disappearing through the exit door. The high heels and the lifted up stylish dirty blonde hair was giving her extra 8 inches, giving her the Top Model and Gwen Stefani mixed look. She almost brushed the upper frame of the door with her hair. She laughed while she tilted slightly her beautiful head sideways and waved to Jim and to the puzzled clerk.

Clerk: "I wish I was twenty years younger. You are very generous man" she spoke in a weird voice.

Jim: "Thank you, madam!" He gave her a twenty euro tip and walked away, thinking; "Just being younger does not mean you will be getting same gifts, damn lady."

The escort ladies are a special breed. It is not just wishful thinking of just being a young woman to rise to Svetlana's level. Also it is a process which starts to build up at an early age of ten, when Society shows its greed. Young boys turn to their idols to become Superman, Rocky, Darth Vader. Then everyone will decide his profession in the future, not exactly as his movie idol, but somewhat parallel to it. The same applies to young ladies. The society seems favoring the beautiful, athletic, bright young women. Their idols are usually what they see in the environment they live in family, church, mass media. They are usually coached by their mothers or older sisters or closest friends. If they can not relate to any of that close circle for advice, they turn to second layer of cousins, aunties, step brothers, uncles. The third layer is amazingly interesting and controversial. Here are father, step father, boyfriend, pimp, lesbians, gangs and mafia. To graduate to third layer one need to ignore the first two layers. That takes somewhat intrusive action like rape, kidnapping, and death in the family, or runaway because of some disagreement.

The psychology of growing to prostitution is usually based on material benefits or emotional and physical freedom. It is basically coaching someone to turn off everything the school or church or politicians would talk about. Being a high end escort seems that one achieved all; car, money, gifts, nice living accommodations, visibility in competitive style. The top models are constantly in spot light, in mass media, in movies, and eating in great restaurants. The motivation for young women driven to being look alike or in style like Marilyn Monroe, Brigitte Bardot, Tyra Banks, Gwen Stefani, Beyonce, and Jay Lo manifests in the way they talk, dress and interact. The sexual part is subliminal for the masses of young women, but is not hidden for high end socialites, who may choose the category to be courtesan, escort, or wife. At the end ninety five percent of sexually active women will desire something of a benefit. The stretch now from age of ten to age of forty five is huge, but the legal aspect of age starting at age of eighteen gives a period of eight years to coach, brainwash, and rape the runaway and kidnapped women.

A good family is not guarantee they have great offsprings. Statistically, seventy five percent of families in US are in good standing financially, in physical health, optimistic. Then where are the rest standing? We will call them "the transitional people." They could be the great motivators or destructors in life. Those are the 14 million court cases a year in good economy. Six million will go to trial by jury, 2 million will get probation, and 6 million will be detained. That is pretty huge for "land of the free" of 320 million people (twice the amount of China's prison population)!

The view at the rooftop was great again, but it was like living the final moments of something irreversible, and feeling like at a funeral. People try to enjoy the few moments in life, but even they may come back, Jim was trained to think that every moment in his life is not to be repeated and it is final. Basically, because of not fearing death, he was able to enjoy the gift of life to the fullest....

Jim thoughts were: "Live your life like you own it. Walk in places like you are in charge. Eat the food like is your last supper. Have sex as much as you want. Travel the world like you can see the end of it (we know it is circular)." Jim was not into drugs or drunkardness, but into yoga and higher thinking. That was his gift and his escape from the earth's reality.

He called Kiana again and again, no answer. The waitress was circling around trying to be charming and to maintain a small conversation. She looked at the wrapped up gifts and she intuitively guessed they were expensive. The cigar and single malt scotch were shrinking and the blue light beams, pointing upward at the near distance of the renamed Naval War College were becoming less and less significant. If it was not for the waiting of the contract wife, Svetlana, he would have just taken off for the capital Sofia. Seemed his family clan was not in any better shape than before, just multiplied and aged. Was that the meaning of life? To have sex, eat, work and die, hopefully leaving someone's legacy? If the reading of someone's name on the wall of a monument, in history books, or in a jail directory makes the legacy, so be it. The worst is to fly through life with wings at half speed. The leaders and last in the birds V formation are easier to distinguish. The gray middle is just a cloud with no meaning. Do you ever ask yourself where is your position in society, in that strange formation of life? You can be delusional that you are a leader, even you if have the upper hand on only one person! That person can be your brother, your sister, your mother, your father, a hooker, a drug user, a not too intelligent classmate, a slower paced athlete, a not that popular singer. To get to the number one position one need to create a brand. That is when others are paying for it. Svetlana was a brand and she was getting paid. The ones who are not a brand usually are envious, and they would try to exploit the brand people by becoming their friends, managers/pimps, or their copy-cats. The ones who cannot create or befriend a brand become their opposition, by trying to regulate it by so called judges, politicians, tax clerks, fathers, mothers, relatives.

Selena, a Tex Mex super star singer was killed by her best friend, when she couldn't control her. Society would impose different age restrictions to the general population so they can work and drive after sixteen, vote and have sex after eighteen and drink after twenty-one. If this is not regulation of the brands then what is? By giving any restrictions it is preventing someone from becoming quickly aware of his capabilities. The deviations are many. We see everyday ten year old working the register, twelve year olds helping in the kitchen of family business, early sex between same age fifteen year olds, ten years old driving cars, under age eighteen year old geniuses or killers. Nobody went to jail for being beautiful, underage athlete champions in Olympics, for political views or homosexual tendencies. If society approves certain behavior we will see rising brands like Justin Bieber, Miley Cyrus, and MaCaulay Culkin. If they don't approve you, the anti heroes will be the homosexual teenage sniper killer, Lee Boyd Malvo, or Joseph Lyle Menendez and Erik Galen Menendez, who killed their parents. The only way one can brand himself is to think out of the ordinary at the moment. You can be the next Galileo, Leonardo da Vinci, Einstein, Tesla, Hitler, and Napoleon. They were self made brands. No one can force the brand to evolve to their highest or lowest levels. That is driven by the subconscious mind and it is recognized or punished by the society and it is judged by history.

The cigar was nearing its end and with single malt almost gone, suddenly he was awakened of his thoughts by simple text.

Svetlana: "I am in the garage. I am coming your way. Meet me in your room." It was more like an order than a playful message.

Jim: "Great! See you in three minutes." He threw the 20 dollar bill on the table and headed toward the elevators. He was well dressed and foreign looking and the curious pairs of eyes of many seated couples were naturally following him until he disappeared into elevator.

Jim: "If I was more concerned about my safety, I probably would be paranoid" he thought. He noticed some men leaving the lounge at same time he got up, but they did not follow him to the room. He was more concerned about the old fears when he was in Sofia, but not here. He was born here, he knew how they behaved and thought here. He did outsmart them many times. He was more protected now with the US Passport than twenty-two years prior. He had foreign currency. He had a nice courtesan meeting him in his room. He was driving a

Mercedes. Was that supposed to be a dream he pursued from early age now becoming reality? Yes, yes.

He entered the nice suite overlooking the Varna sea shore line, traced by Highway 9, from here to Zlatny Piasatzy (Golden sands) resorts. Just as the door closed behind him a knock on the door sounded. He checked through the spy hole.

Svetlana: "That was the longest shift I had today. My knees were shaking and I needed to rest. The only thing made me uplifted was your generosity, Daddy!" She jumped on his waist like a child. Fortunately the couch was behind him so both fell on it in a knot like position.

Jim: "Watch your gifts." He pushed the boxes on side.

Svetlana: "I don't care about boxes. You need to be rewarded and I need a drink!" They started stripping like in a crazy dance. Svetlana was undressing Jim, he was undressing Svetlana. The naked bodies were reflected by a huge mirror which was installed in front of a mini bar. As both were to engage in some kind of intercourse Svetlana stretched her long legs and kicked the swing door of mini bar. The rotation disclosed a bunch of miniature bottles ranging from J&B, Johnny Walker Black, Amaretto, Ouzo, Absolute vodka, and Remy Marten Cognac.

Svetlana: "Wrong damn door!" she was almost ready to enjoy sex but something was disturbing her. She kicked the second door. This side had mini bottles of wine. She quickly scanned the selection of wines. Some of them were chilled, but nothing got her attention.

Svetlana: "Vasily, we need good champagne! I want Crystal, daddy!" Her voice was not demanding, but with sexual power of seduction, where "No" was not an option.

Jim: "I will call the butler, baby!" He grabbed the phone and dialed the room service while he commenced pumping in and out of her juicy and young vagina. He was surprised to see how both were performing something the hotel service couldn't hear and see. The voice on the other side said "Yes, sir! We will be there in ten minutes!"

Svetlana: "Ten minutes? Hurry "she starred to squeeze him and to move up and down on Jim 8 inch tower, using the corner of the couch as tripod.

Jim: "Did you go to yoga school?" He was wondering how she was able to twist her long legs around him, one on the floor the other on the couch and her two hands supporting her body backward in the corner.

Five minutes passed in some dancing, twisting and screaming ritual. Jim was enjoying himself and his company. Svetlana was in her own world. They were interacting with different intentions. The rewards were guaranteed. There was no time to negotiate. The gifts were bought, the casino was won, and sex was not a challenge. Was that the beginning of the end? When the money can deliver you everything you want, then what would be the next challenge? Some people desire to explore the universe. Some people just stop trying and just waiting to die like parasites. The overly ambitious nobodies become politicians, judges, police officers; something with the exercising of power over successful or destitute alike..

Toward the eight minute the sex intensified. Jim commanded her to face the back of the couch. She positioned her small torso atop the back of the couch. Her long legs were up in the air and her perfect buttocks were forming that pear seductive shape where the sex becomes confused art. One could debate to stop and enjoy the view or just keep thrusting into that worm and comfortable hole, feeling home and in somewhat ecstasy. They both contracted their muscles on the 9th minute. They felt like in a contest with the butler. Will he be on time to deliver the Crystal, or they would be interrupted? The challenge worked. Both came at the same time and both ran to the bathroom. Exactly on the tenth minute the door bell rang.

The Butler: "Hello sir! Here is your Champagne. Want me to open it for you?" He was not the same guy from this morning, but he acted almost in similar way. "The Crystal is a different account. It comes from the restaurant. Can you pay now, please? It is 250 euro in cash or charge?" Seemed he wanted his tip right away?

Jim: "Here is, 280 with baksheesh" he laughed and closed the door, showing the bottle to wet Svetlana, who was hiding in the bathroom.

She grabbed the bottle "I know how to open that thing!" She grabbed a small fork and quickly found the eye of the metal wire under the aluminum foil. She was like a kid in Disney World.

Jim: "You will catch cold!" He threw a nice white hotel bathrobe on her. She walked around him with a bottle in her hand. Jim was wondering where she was headed, definitely not toward the exit door!

Svetlana: "If I catch cold I want to catch it with my "Cartier" and "Bulova" on, ok?" She handed him the bottle with precious liquid. She grabbed the boxed gifts and ran toward the bedroom. Jim followed her with the Crystal champagne, filling up two glasses half way. She started unwrapping boxes with a childish frenzy.

Svetlana: "Am I beautiful?" finally she calmed down. The Cartier necklace was made of fashionable white gold and it was perfect match for her dirty blonde hair. The Bulova watch was in dark platinum frame with diamonds at hour points. She pulled Jim toward the huge king size welcoming bed. He grabbed the champagne glasses and placed them on the night stand. Svetlana was definitely at the top of her brand. She was working to make Jim happy. It took her less than five minutes to see her results accomplished. Jim erupted again and she had one smiling face. Both of them ran to the shower and were enjoying the hot water and the gift of life.

Svetlana: "Where did you get that prowess? If I did not know any better, I would think you are the reincarnated Rasputin, dear Jim?" She had all the right words to say…all courtesans did.

Jim: "Baby, have you ever heard of yoga and meditation? Besides I am black belt in martial arts and also I am proven healer." He was proud.

Svetlana: "I don't know who you are and where you came from? I just treat you as a two day client, but you make women fall in love with you..."

Jim: "You can come to the States, but you said I cannot afford you!"

Svetlana: "It is complicated. You have to release me from my "sponsors," The Mafia. They will ask you for a million dollars. And they may take the money and still kill you? So, enjoy your moment now."

Jim: "You are right. I thought only in the West or in Middle East women are commodity, but seems like that happen everywhere now; Taiwan, Russia, Japan, North Korea…"

Svetlana: "Have you heard of "white slavery?" She was less excited now.

Jim: "Yes, but I never came across any victims of that."

Svetlana: "Now you are. If you tell my secrets they will kill both of us. That I can tell you here in the bathroom, but in bed I can't. It maybe bugged?"

Jim: "Ok. No more secrets. No more talk. When I come back here hopefully, we will meet again?" The morning arrived as one cruel saboteur of life. He went through his briefcase and pulled out 350 euro. The bonus was 50.

Jim: "I wish I did not know everything about you, but I still enjoyed every minute with you. Here is a little bonus." They were still in the bathroom.

Svetlana: "If they heard something from us it was just sex!" she packed everything and she ordered breakfast. Suddenly she got quiet.

The "good bye" mood, Jim guessed. He felt like he was in some scripted James Bond movie with the difference that here nobody died. He enjoyed the game. After all "living every moment to the fullest" usually involves unusual logistics and characters, but always money. The history of the world may involve any kind of poor bright men and women, but they end up always interacting with kings, rich men or women, they will always leave certain legacy by building a church, writing bibles or becoming scientists, healers or philosophers.

At about 11 am the departure was without drama and tears. She suddenly looked more businesslike than last two days contract wife. Her hair was back up and the high heels made her look like an Amazon Queen.

Svetlana: "Good bye, Jim Walker! Here is my business card. Hope to see you again soon!" she shed a tear, which she quickly wiped out. She grabbed the gym bag and disappeared toward the elevators. Jim packed his suitcase and looked around not to leave anything behind. He sat down on the balcony overlooking the beautiful Black Sea shore and in the corner to the left was his old Naval Academy. He relit the half Cohiba and enjoyed every breath with it. Jim was really a bad yoga example. He reminded his friends, "It is better to smoke, than to overeat." It was said by some Japanese gymnast.

Jim's slogan was: "It is better to think yoga (meditate) than twist yourself to oblivion, thinking that you do yoga."

Around 11.30 am he pushed down the left over cigar, he put on his fur coat and grabbed the suitcase. At the lobby he stopped by the gift shop. He picked something for Kiana, but not Cartier this time. She was not answering his phone calls. Not a good sign for new relationship. He paid the two days stay in the Hotel at the front desk. He looked around to see Svetlana, but she was not around. He did not ask for her, but for his Mercedes car. The valet service was quick and soon he was on the road to Sofia.

The two brothers Jim and Adrian went to Mezdra, a small town famous more for changing trains than anything else. What was only important there was that they inherited the house from their grandfather. The cemetery where all of their family members were buried was there also. Jim reminisced about the circumstances of how he escaped from Bulgaria. It was the invitation from his father to visit Sofia, where he met an occult lady, who represented herself as his stepmother niece and who channeled her dead grandfather spirit to tell him when he would escape (65 days in advance). After the Séance, he traveled to Mezdra where he went by himself to the grave of his grandparents and his mother. He lit two candles and asked his grandfather's spirit, "to give him his business mind." Then he asked his mother Loretta's spirit, "Give me your blessing to escape, Mom." He promised them to sacrifice his first monthly salary to sea God Neptune. That was twenty-three years before. The prediction was 100% accurate and he officially escaped on 65th day, his father Michael's 50th birthday!

They went to city planning and zoning. The house needed to pay back taxes of 500 euro for seven years. Jim gave them the money.

Adrian: "Jim, you are the savior here, but when I needed promotion the army declined me because of your defection!"

Jim: "Life is parallel universe. Good and evil coexist. The change of balance is where one becomes more of good or more of a bad character. Think if I never came and you still had to pay the property taxes, after you lost your job's promotion? Then I would be the bad guy, right? Think the other way. I stayed here all my life. I had low paying job and I couldn't help you. You would have had your promotion, but I wouldn't ever have my three night clubs. And I would have been married by now and I would have been a captain of a ship and maybe been ok, but not great?"

Adrian: "Having successes in business is great, but you need family!"

Jim: "I live in a spiritual world, you live in physical dimensions. When I come to show my creativity most people are puzzled. The unconventional ways I manifest my power angers many, and benefits some of earth people. If my 8 chair bar can create a million a year, with lowest overhead possible, then Rockefeller and I are on the same page. "God gives me money!"

Adrian: "It is unfortunate that we are born poor and we try to measure ourselves with the established societies and with old wealth."

Jim: "I think the economies are created unbalanced for a reason. This way they ensure that hungry people supply is enough to create the work force." He continued, while Adrian kept wondering "who is this man?"

Jim: "Half of the Fortune 500 companies on Wall Street are owned by non college graduates. The wealth usually is related to intelligence and opportunity, a lot of money and some luck. I changed that algorithm and now I am writing a book about it. The trick in my algorithm is to eliminate the money factor. I would replace money with personality and quantum thinking. It is more similar to creativity by God. When there is no money or barter system (weapons/tempting women/drugs), then The Quantum law applies (QMCL).

$e + p = n + 2Q$

"Matter meets antimatter, which results in annihilation and it releases two quanta," that where creativity or destruction starts. The interesting part is how we determine of the outcome? The result is usually related to the human state of mind (Yin and Yang). We can call it "White magic" or "Black magic." When one is in neutral state (after the big desire/command is send to spiritual world/the sub consciousness and it is annihilated), then the compressed magnetic fields release the energy in quantum bursts to create electromagnetic fields which move with the speed of light or higher to create gravitational fields and therefore, the Matter, the visual event."

Adrian: "Hey brother. When we grew up I noticed you like to read, but I see you moved beyond that. When you left Bulgaria you were just a refugee, looking for freedom. Now you are a scientist, teaching me things I will probably never comprehend?"

Jim: "Nothing in life is given or taken without asking for it, and without personal sacrifice or personal ignorance. We blame the rich, because we cannot be like them. Once we become rich we blame the poor, because we don't want to be like them. So, there is a fine line, who we would like to be and there is a constant struggle between both realities.

In Europe or in the old societies it is impossible to cross the line, but in USA the opportunities are still available to cross that line from poor to rich and in reverse. The game is which side are you the most comfortable being on? Here is the algorithm in quantum physics where Richard P. Feynman diagrams are used. (He was a teacher at Cornell U). He calculates the terms for the perturbation theory solution of interactions between particles. I am not sure if he uses Black or White magic but the interaction are between time and wave function and uses The Quantum Field theory. The interaction picture of quantum mechanics is somewhere between the Schrodinger and Heisenberg theories. Schrodinger theory (1935) is about the experiment with a cat in chamber with low radiation is that the cat is dead or alive based on observer's thinking."

Adrian: "I am a good brother, but a bad student. Hopefully, your discoveries can help the world and many confused souls, who are searching for answers?"

Jim: "Schrodinger says that the person's thinking in the experiment of observing of the cat effects the outcome ...dead or alive! That turns mankind to God like! Here the consciousness and subconscious communicate actively (fear of death, reward of life). Man turns to Saint (life), to Satan (death). The quantum reality kicks in without inducing drugs, initiating techniques of free masons, yoga meditation, animal sacrificing, astro projection, voodoo shamanism, crystals crushing, mass prayer, occult rituals. The mind reacts to the possibility of death in much higher speeds than in any other emotion compressions. We can introduce here the John A. Wheeler's magnetism-energy conversion and reverse theory. It opens instantly the dormant 95% of human mind (the sub consciousness). We become aware of the invisible, spiritual world and we become God like, all that is while we are awake. The religion will tell you that 99 percent of their communication with the spiritual world was in a dream state, why? They are too unwilling to hit the books and look for the formulas. They are explaining everything with planets, spirits, Gods. It is like to explaining everything is ruled from outside and mankind is to follow. Then the religion will make a human a Saint or living Saint. I will agree to the point, but if I write the formulas how all the miracles work I will become a teaching Saint, not just a living Saint."

Adrian: "Is being a Saint a good thing? I hear any kind of stories."

Jim: "I am the only teaching Saint so far. I am like an educated judge.

I mean well as standard. I will reward the progressive, I will try to correct the unaware or uneducated, and I will punish the people who are intentionally mean to me."

Adrian: "How do you punish anybody? That doesn't qualify you as Saint!"

Jim: "An electron is with negative charge and mass. But positron is electron with positive charge with same mass and opposite magnetic curvature. The hydrogen atom (matter) is one positive proton in nucleus, one negative electron spinning around, but the anti hydrogen (anti matter) is a negative proton p- (antiproton) with positive charged position e+ in orbit. Basically, I am Saint and anti Saint simultaneously, depend of which side you show to me, I will react. I don't react through my physical means (hands on, weapons, words). The quantum gravitational wave/field creates matter and destroys it at Biblical dimensions, God like.

Note…Colliding proton and antiproton creates the Top #6 quark, the rest mass/Matter is heavy and equal to the Gold atom nucleus at 160,000 MeV. (See Paul Dirac, the father of Anti Matter).

1. Creativity: My discovery of yoga and healing. I fought sickness and death since age of 13. In the process I tapped into the occult, antimatter, predictions. I reversed sickness to well being since. Entering the naval Academy was predicted to be on 5th of September in 1975. My defection was predicted 65 days in advance. I was ship's captain at age 26 on Wall Street, Meeting Contessa, working on billionaire Mr. Smith's yacht, owner of 133 years old restaurant Bellini's without any money down, an owner of the Pier 9, the oldest US club, with 1,000.00 dollars on hand, owner of the Randevu Lounge with 100 dollars to start and owner of Walker's Media last 25 years.

2. Destruction: After I got mad at Amanda six months later the World Trade Center collapsed on 9/11/2001. Many of my enemies in

the Naval Academy were kicked out of school. I used to write their names in a special book. They were laughing at me, but all of them were expelled. A class mate damaged my left eye; his name was Orlin, now dead. I was not paid by my partners in Bellini's. They lost both restaurants. Someone stole 13 dollars from me at Doral Hotel. He lost $1,300 the same day (cash and VCR robbery at his house). Some lady took a gift from me then she ignored me. Two days after she was in car crash. Her VW car was totaled."

Note: Next 10 years (2003-2013) the destructions will manifest themselves in Biblical dimensions.... The biggest earthquake in Indian Ocean in 2004, the biggest recession in 80 years (2008-2012), his club rivals in bankruptcies and deportation, the biggest El Nino/El Ninya 2009/2010 three feet snow fall on East Coast of Canada and USA, lasting 3 months, his theory of 666+6 will be proven with his rival Prosperity, with the death of DP the Don, with lowest possible NYSE readings at 6626 in 2009 ... and many more like hurricanes Irene, Isac, Debby and Sandy.

Adrian: "How the destruction works?" He was curios.

Jim: "Usually I do my best to gain someone's respect and I am very generous with my time and gifts. If I don't get the desired attention I would warn them about the sequences, that God will give them what they deserve. If they ignore me I just get quiet. Then I usually let my sub consciousness do the job, the God at work. My sub consciousness creates the anti mater and within days or months I will see results of destruction. If you know about the light; it can move through wormholes and around black holes. Everyone on earth creates mini black holes, which don't last too much and may pass as undetected, unless the Quantum Laws apply. Fortunately there is no charge that mind can destroy reality, which leaves me out of court."

Adrian: "I heard of witchcraft, heresy during Inquisition times by The Catholic Church. Are you not afraid?" He was concerned...

Jim: "Police around the world looks for evidence to present to judge. No court case was made for quantum thinking yet! Maybe after I write that book, they will? You know Tesla has 700 inventions, but he was only arrested for creating a resonance earthquake machine."

Adrian: "Ok, be careful. Most scientists are restricted and punished. After that lecture I need a drink." They poured wine in their glasses.

Jim: "I am above science, I am a teaching, living Saint, and anti Saint!" He was happy to spill out not just his stories but his theories backed with formulas.

Adrian: "Ok, what is Satan then?"

Jim: "The Satan is a person who is disguised as good person, but he achieved everything in life with negative means. He was smart, but he cheated to get good scores. He would steal someone's trophy of achievement and pretends it is his. He will inherit his money and maybe he kills family members to get their house or business. He will forge a diploma to show an education he never graduated from, he will become a government chief to extort money and perks, he will be a casino addict or alcoholic, he will be a false prophet, and anti Christ!"

Adrian: "That is true. So everything is based on intention. Sometime the results are very similar. We see rich man who everyone loves until some horrible story reveals."

Jim: "Wealth and honesty is tested every day, poor people are not. In the States the biggest financial crime is not paying IRS. The tax public records show how rich men or women are doing?"

Adrian: "So one who pays taxes is not a Satan?" he laughed.

Jim: "Paying taxes shows responsibility. If you are not fiscally responsible, probably you have other vices? So paying the taxes makes one half Satan."

Adrian: "I understand more how you do think. Can we eat now?" They headed to a small restaurant nearby.

The going away night in Sofia was in a night club Miracle, located underground across the Ministry of Interior. Jim was in a bad mood. He was missing Kiana. He tried to call her a few times, but she did not answer. He expressed that to his brother. He just answered, "You will see her tomorrow. Don't worry. I will show you a nice bar with great show."

Jim heard of many things about Bulgarian night life but what he saw was beyond his wild expectations.

Doorman: "If you have any weapons leave them here." His robotic voice could have asked if they had umbrellas with no excitement whatsoever.

Adrian: "No, we don't. We called earlier. We have reservations. It is my birthday." He could have said nothing. The doorman just said "three, no weapons" on his microphone, hidden in his sleeve.

Doorman: "Proceed, please!" He pointed toward the lower level. At the dark entrance Jim noticed two more guys who were checking-in a group of five guys. One of them was in his mid-fifties short chubby man, who was submitting his gun. The other four were in early twenties athletic built men with black turtle neck outfits, which were also dropping their weapons, small 38 caliber Berettas.

Adrian: "Welcome to the new Democracy!" he whispered.

Jim: "It is amazing, the wild, wild East!" He heard about assassinations. He just has never seen live assassins/bodyguards next to him. He tried not to stare toward the coat check which had mixed use of arsenal also.

Jim: "Want a good cigar?"

Cigar lady: "20 euro for any selection." She was built and with strong mannish features, brunette, mid 30's, probably with kids? Jim was missing Svetlana, but he brushed that thought away.

Jim: "Two Monte Christo, please."

Rossi: "We want a good table next to the stage." The night club manager personally assisted them. He probably observed the foreign behavior and the expensive cigars Jim purchased? Soon they were seated in the middle of room, next to the stage. The group of five they encountered earlier was seated above them in an elevated table. They had their table ready with Absolute Vodka on ice table service.

Jim: "Taittinger bottle, please! Comtes the Champagne, Blanc de Blancs 2000" he requested. The bottle was well priced at 150 euro for year of 2003. His brother was puzzled at the cigar and great champagne they were to enjoy.

Rebecca: "That show is amazing!" She acted like she had never seen a Cabaret before. Soon the mood changed. The alcohol was pouring and cigars, and false mood of not thinking of tomorrow was all mixed up. There was not really food there, but they would give some "mezze" (cold appetizers, kifte, lukanka, cheeses and olives). The manager stopped by and hoped that they "enjoyed the show, appetizers are on me." He probably was trying to befriend the customers and to find out who they were? Within ten minutes the Taittinger and the "mezze" were served, the shiny blue curtain opened and the show began. The stage was streaming with beautiful young women were like a Victoria Secrets but with a sexual twist. They were like Playboy centerfold rejects. Very attractive of any size, from brunettes to blondes, even there were red hair ladies. The true surprise came when a Cuban music Cha Cha Cha erupted. Soon a tall black man showed up followed with two Spanish colorful dressed ladies. They were dancing and singing many styles of music. The rumba music was performed by additional drummers and singers. Toward the end they slowed down to more romantic style of Bolero. There was no announcer, so the attention was a necessary fluid. People were drinking and walking around and watching the show.

Jim: "This reminds me of Miami style show, except this is too outdated for USA. Seems like someone has reenacted the 60's in Cuba before the Fulgencio Batista was overthrown?"

Adrian was happy, Rebecca was silly. Jim enjoyed the show, but he felt that behind the alcohol vapors was another reality. He was missing the new country USA, the Lounge he established, the new girlfriend Kiana.

Bulgaria was not what he expected. He was grateful for the education, for his family surviving the transition to new Democracy and that his family was still missing him, but he did feel emotionally out of place. Svetlana was just copy cat of the Western influence, but the hooker in Sliven and the conservative behavior of his long lady friend Alexandra was definitely a turn off. Bulgaria had her modern heroes, Vanga of Petrich, Hristo Stoichkov the soccer player, but that was their legacy. Jim needed to continue his own legacy elsewhere.

He observed the population in general was ignorant to words, but not to action. They wanted to see manifestation of events, not just to dream and talk. The great leaders in the world would promise anything, but they have to back their actions up. Most Demi gods were predicting events or able to use their minds to make wine from water at an instance, to split and open Red Sea on command, to change the earth's axis inclination to continue the battle for two hours day light and win it. Jim realized that he couldn't rise to the top in Bulgaria in one human life time, but to be recognized he was lucky to be in USA, and after he writes his legacy, he would be recognized everywhere. It is like to live 10 lives in one or to solve the life algorithm where the answer is predicted based on expectation/the input of the observer.

The show was over in thirty minutes and dancers were mingling with the crowd for their own reasons. Some of the regular customers were chosen first. The black turtle neck security, were fending off the ladies, which were most likely prostitutes. The Taittinger was replaced with a second bottle. The brothers were smoking great cigars, watching a Cuban show, surrounded with assassins, observing the show girls working the crowd of drunken men. Adrian was wearing the nice watch Jim gave him as a gift and he was happy as a kid.

Adrian: "Jim, you are the best brother I ever had!" He squeezed Jim's shoulder. Bulgarians don't usually show affection. "I am sorry to confess, but maybe because of our long separation or just of age and feeling the mortality near, I am a bit sentimental." He shed a quick tear, hopefully nobody noticed.

Jim: "Hey, we made it through a quarter century. We will see each other more often from now. I was trying to be strong in USA. Everything I have achieved was in some dream state, but not with real help. Sometimes I wanted just to let go everything and just to return to the original Jim, but I couldn't picture him as a successful and going anywhere in Bulgaria. The fate of him was meant to be; "The underdog to become a leader, but only after he passes all the tests in the real and spiritual world."

Adrian: "Ok, my brother Saint! What was the scariest moment in your life? That must be close to spiritual experience?" the cigar was enjoyable and the great semi dry champagne was a superb mediator.

Jim: "First, my teacher in martial arts thought me not to think about pain; the factor fear will stop you from moving forward. I never thought in judo or karate that pain is anything but a state of matter, something like a steam, fog, bad air and paper. Once you think it is rock solid wall, you will retreat. With that as a background I defected successfully. I have seen death many times when I was defecting on the Greek ship, like my ship was sinking in Bay of Biscay, or at the bay of Tijuana Tepic, or near Cape Town."

Adrian: "I have heard many stories about ships sinking, but I never thought it would happen to you, brother!" he squeezed him again.

Jim: "That's where we are different. You don't think about it, because it is convenient for your state of mind. I think about it as possibility to happen but to be accepted when happen without fear. You live in your reality Earth's world, trying not to be spiritual; I live in spiritual world trying not to be real earthy."

Adrian: "That is why you achieve more in the material world; when you solve problems and it looks easy."

Jim: "I represent the few live saints in the world, matter of fact I never met another one like me. Hopefully my book will open the door to mass entrance into my way of thinking and the world would be a better place. Imagine seven billion saints on earth, the new spiritual normal!"

The morning was like a funeral. Alexandra escorted Jim to the Airport. Michael and Adrian tagged along with unhappy faces. Michael said he knew the chief of the airport and in case of any complications; he may call him to the rescue. And there was a complication.

Customs officer: "You needed entry information stating the address of where you are staying. Not filing the information is penalty of 2,500 euro."

Jim: "I was not aware of that, nobody advised me about it?"

Customs officer: "Next time you arrive please follow required procedures. Ok! Here is your Passport and ticket. Bon voyage!"

Jim: "Thanks." He turned around. Alexandra, his brother and father were at the gate waving, "Good bye."

The airplane took off toward Zurich and toward USA, the words, the ideas, the action, and memories. It was like a holiday chapter with strange players involved. He was not impressed. Even he would be away 200 years those characters would not change much. The few strong famous Bulgarians were sport or religious figures. Where Jim legacy would be is to be determined soon.

At Zurich the airplanes needed to change from smaller to transoceanic range. Jim needed to pick a nice hotel, to spend the night. The first surprise was the fare to the city. At the airport he was approached by a Greek taxi driver.

Taxi driver: "Hey young man! I will take you to the city. It is about ten kilometers."

Jim: "I will need to find a hotel. How much do you charge?" he was not damned.

Taxi driver: "50 franks (equal to 53 US dollars)."

Jim: "Give me a minute. I will be back with you." He walked toward the subway terminal and he saw the price; 5 francs to center of the city. He didn't look for the greedy taxi driver to apologize. He just boarded the train. Zurich was a nice structured city. One thing obviously was the highest prices. Jim was looking for a reasonably priced hotel room in the center. They were at 400 francs. Two blocks away they were 300 francs, and two extra blocks they were at 200 francs. Jim got a bright idea. He flagged a taxi driver and asked him to drive him to "Red light district." The taxi driver smiled and helped him load his luggage. At the red light district the prices were at 65 francs per night, including airport shuttle service. Jim checked in and soon he hit the streets. He was looking at expensive Swiss made watches Omega, Rolex, and Cartier walking down a tiny street. They were near 5,000 francs price. Then he wandered in a nice decorated lounge Tropix. That was very similar to Randevu, his own bar and a nice blonde hostess approached him and sat next to him on the bar chair.

Jim: "I will have a beer, something local." He said to the bartender, a tall 6.5 feet Russian looking chubby man. His guess was confirmed within a minute.

Hostess: "My name is Nataly! What is your name?" she was beautiful and aggressive.

Jim: "I am Jim. I am not looking for friendship now. I am here changing flights to USA." He observed with the corner of his eyes the big bartender and Nataly interacting. "What was the game here?" he asked himself.

Nataly: "I need a drink, could you choose one for me." She handed him a long list of drinks choices. "Ladies here drink only champagne, ok!" She moved her body very close to his, her perfect breast with perfect lingerie under long red kimono like dress.

Nataly: "We can start here. I will dance for you at the pole. After the dance we can go to private room on the back. Ok, Jim?"

Jim: "I will get you a splitter champagne to start, baby!" She reminded him of Svetlana, but the game was in a public place.

Nataly: "Sergey, davai malenkoe shampansko!" She spoke in Russian unaware Jim was fluent in her native tongue. He was feeling the entrapment, but he liked the game. It was so similar to the business he was doing at his own lounge Randevu in DC. "I may learn something new here?" He thought and just smiled toward Nataly, acting like he did not understand a word they were saying. The pole was occupied at this time with a tall brunette, who was nearly undressed. The beer was good and the company was very entertaining.

Jim was curious of the prices there?

Jim: "Do you have just a champagne list?" he addressed the friendly bartender. Nataly became even more flirtatious. She started rubbing Jim's thigh and almost kissed him. She was obviously trying to distract him from getting the true information.

Jim: "That is pretty extensive menu! …And I may use your prices for reference in my lounge?" He saw the starting prices at 50 francs for a champagne splitter to 3,000 francs for top brand Taittinger. The owner showed up sensing the commotion. He was speaking perfect English.

Edward: "Hello! How is everything? Are you enjoying the show and your company?" he seemed sincere, but that was just a front.

Jim: "Hello, Sir! Everything is great. I am owner of similar establishment in Washington, DC in the USA."

Edward: "Nice! What do you think about our establishment?" he acted curious, slightly angry at Nataly and the bartender.

Jim: "I like everything, but the prices are outrageous, ten times more expensive than in the USA."

Edward: "The competition in the USA and the high volume of people there drives the prices down. We don't have competition here and we make our own prices. Most of our clients are regular and they agree with the prices. Please, enjoy our show!"

Jim: "My lounge is similar in size; only 15 seated no high volume, regular crowd." He stopped short of price discussion. He started to pull away from Nataly. She was getting agitated.

Jim: "I am ready to leave. May I have the bill?" He stood up with 100 euro in his hand.

Natalie: "Jim, I am to dance now on the pole, and then we can go to private room in the back."

Jim: "... And how much would that cost," he was not surprised of anything here, he was learning.

Sergei: "For private room you need to order 1,500 franks champagne bottle minimum." Sergei thought he was a better salesman than the sexy Nataly?

Jim: "No, thanks!" He took the change, tipped the bartender and headed toward the door.

Nataly: "Come back later. I will be waiting for you!" She was acting according to the lounge rules.

Jim: "Pimps" he said to himself leaving the building. "For the 1,500 francs I am not guaranteed anything, but to go behind a curtain and hold hands, no thanks!"

He headed to see the real Red light district. Soon he was in front of blue, neon lighted windows. It was a show where the women went about the business of sex. It was a parade of beautiful Brazilian tall young women, then some Eastern European, and then some local really repulsive, red haired 300 pound women. They were usually seated behind windows in couples, smoking and drinking. They would negotiate prices with customers before they entered the establishment. At this time they required 100 francs for ten minutes. Jim declined any offers and he went to a normal bar. He picked a nice mixed race lady. They had a couple of beers and soon they headed toward her house. Jim was happy. Maybe she really liked him? Jim remembered the French ladies in Roanne and in Calais. They were free twenty years before.

Moroccan lady: "Do you like me?" she started kissing him. He grabbed her firm ass. Her breasts were small but very firm and inviting. Her hair was thick and well styled, like a model. She was athletic, at medium height.

Jim: "I am leaving tomorrow to USA. Maybe you can come and visit?"

Moroccan lady: "That depends? My rent is very high here. Can you help me now?" she started undressing.

Jim: "I can, but how much? Maybe I can help if we become good friends?" he was undressing too. Her body was impressive with zero fat at age twenty-five!

Moroccan lady: "You can spend an hour here with me. I need 250 francs."

Jim: "I thought you were different than the ladies in the red light district?" He started putting his clothes back on.

Moroccan lady: "Prostitution is not allowed in bars, that is why I am not charging you 700 francs an hour. Please don't tell the police!"

Jim: "I am heading to the hotel." He left the small apartment, thinking about Svetlana, but then his mind shifted towards Kiana's company.

Next day the airport shuttle picked him up and he was happy to board the plane. He was leaving behind the old continent with his family, Svetlana, Nataly, ignorant cousin Ivailo; he had no nostalgic feelings here. He was happier landing in his new country. He knew how his stepmother disrespected him; he knew not to expect any difference from the new step country. He felt the dynamics were better here, in the new country. In small country you may change two big towns and then get stuck. In USA one can reinvent himself ten times and at many places. The idea to start a business was the best thing that ever happened to him. And that is what the USA was driven by, the entrepreneurs! How the others would play along is the story in this manuscript. This is not a reason to foreigners to flee to USA. If one has no plan, no physical and mental and emotional strength, Jim's advice is: "Do not come to the USA."

It is like the chance to be a Super Model and how many are walking the Cat Walk during Victoria Secrets doing The Angels show? Your chances to get a job as skillful worker are more likely than to become overnight success unless you are with a fake British accent and are sporting James Bond's looks. Hollywood is starving for new faces with the billion dollar pull in the movie box. Why continue to watch Mission Impossible, Rocky, and Die Hard, with the same characters? Actors, become directors, CIA operatives become writers, transformation is required by competition. Jim was returning to USA with a different mission. He had to change the history and explain it.

Chapter 11

He called and called Kiana arriving in USA. She did not answer. Passing through the gates he observed Kiana wasn't there, and he was disappointed. He caught a cab to his apartment. When Jim got home he observed his BMW in the garage. That was the same BMW he gave to Kiana before he headed out a month ago. One of the tires was blown. He was wondering where she was? He called her again. No answer. The expectation to see her was getting mixed with the building anger toward her, similar to the one he had against Amanda in New York. (That was in March, in the year 2001. The Word Center Towers imploded six months later.) Jim was aware of his powers, some creative and some destructive. He left a couple of messages on her machine, then more and more.

It was the fatal day of November the third, 2003! Jim decided to go to work. He was hoping that work would deter his irritated mind from Kiana. The bar looked normal on the outside. Some customers greeted him and even said they missed him. Jim was a bit skeptical, but he lied also that he missed them too.

Jim: "They did not miss me, personally. They just missed my style of business, and then probably they missed me too" he thought. Jim had unique way of interaction with his customers. He would select his customers, who would respect him for life, and they would get awarded with free drinks and cigars and they would be allowed to stay and drink after hours. The ones he did not like he would charge extra, or he would bar them out from the establishment. The newly opened three story bar next to him was called Prosperity, was managed and owned by the nephew of his biggest rival in town Mr. Dodson, the cocaine head.

Jim slogan was, "I do not mind competition as long I am winning!" And he always did. This is not just am empty statement. The proof is in the facts, not just in the words. Jim noticed the loud noise coming to the street from both floors. He did not mind the first floor noise, but the second floor he did. Randevu bar was basically a second floor bar with balcony sound on third open floor. The sound coming from behind the second floor dry walks on Prosperity side was so loud that nobody around Randevu bar could even chat or hear themselves. The bottles were shaking on the shelves and Jim had to install tiny rubber mats to stop them from falling. The Saint needed to switch to anti Saint. Jim sent some of his customers next door to scout the source of the noise? Soon he found out that the 2nd floor behind the wall was empty! The only things there were four huge sound speakers surrounding a small dance floor. What the next door owners were doing were cranking up the speakers and sending people from downstairs to check them out.

Jim: "What the Hell? I have to do something about it!" He quickly ran a wire from second floor to the first floor right behind the bar of the Prosperity.

Jim: "Now your bottles will shake too, assholes!" he thought. Yes, he was not always a good saint. It worked like magic. Gods rewarded him again. At about 1 am when Sally's/Starlight usually would run out of steam and customers, so was also Prosperity.

Jim: "Losing business is a bitch, isn't it?" he mentioned that to Lora, who was his bartender. He went downstairs to check on traffic. Usually, Randevu lounge would get packed around 1 am. Not to his surprise he met outside his door the angry owners of Prosperity.

Owner of Prosperity: "Hey, what is with the speakers behind my bar walls? My bottles are falling, my customers are pissed off!" he was getting closer and closer, almost touching chin. He was a short, African American twenty-eight years old athletically built.

Jim: "What? You are doing the same thing upstairs and there is nobody drinking or dancing there!"

Owner of Prosperity: "You are fucking up my business! We are going to have problems here." He was getting a bit out of control. His girlfriend Louise was watching the conversation.

Jim: "Listen, piece of shit! I have been here six years; you won't last here six months!" He shouted at his braided, unshaven face, without fear whatsoever.

Louise: "Do not fight him, ok?" She cut in between two fearless men.

Jim: "You do not know who are you really up against? This is my street!" he shouted leaving the scene.

Jim retrieved his speaker to his second floor knowing that he taught the ignorant little man a lesson. Also, he knew that this man, who can't keep his cool from the beginning of his business, would not quite make it here or anywhere. The bar Randevu, filled up to maximum capacity in next thirty minutes and turned to profitable night after all.

Jim: "Can I help you with something?" He was enjoying a good cigar, when he observed the bartender giggling. "It must be a set up." He assumed.

Tall man: "Your bartender made a bet that I would lose in arms wrestling against you. You know, I won against Darrell Green, one of the fastest men in NFL." He was around 300 pounds of steel.

Jim: "I don't know anything about NFL, but I will see how good you are?" He put down his cigar and took a deep breath. Four seconds later the opponent hand touched the table first. Jim picked his cigar and continued smoking. "Tell the bartender, I am buying you a drink for being brave. You decide to pay her or not for losing the bet." The tall man confusedly left. He was one of the 200,000 men to join him in the "Losers fight Club" through the club's existence. Jim lost only five fights in arms wrestling. The majority of his opponents were half his age.

Toward closing time one of his best customers showed up.

Nathan: "Hey Stranger!" He was an IT guy who was into late bar hoping and women chasing. He was not a regular, but he was one of the smartest guys that Jim could keep up with in a conversation with.

Jim: "Hey Nathan!" He was smoking a great cigar but he was in a bad mood.

Nathan: "You are too quiet tonight. Can I join you?" Jim was seated by the window watching the street traffic. When he was at the bar he had a rule not to drink alcohol.

Jim: "Sure, but I do not feel like talking. Ok?" he paused.

Nathan: "I will buy you a drink, boss!"

Jim: "Ok! I will take bourbon, strait up." Lora delivered the drinks. Nathan was at early thirties and he reminded him of his brother Adrian, but at an earlier age. He was average height, healthily built Caucasian, with kind of Tom Cruise look. He liked all kinds of women, a man of variety, which made him close to Jim.

Nathan: "You look worried! Hope you had a good vacation?" they had a toast. Jim paused, wondering should he give in to his emotions and tell, this total stranger how he feels, at this very moment.

Jim: "I met a lady who I am involved with sexually earlier this summer. I helped her here and there, but now she is ignoring me" he said with heavy breathing. Nathan: "Hey brother. Your bar is full of women who are willing and able to give you everything you want!"

Jim: "That what makes it even more complicated. I treat people who are at the bar at a distance, like customers but not like friends. In the case with Kiana it is just the opposite. I feel I am giving her everything, but I am getting nothing in return."

Nathan: "You got bitten by the love bug, buddy! Is she that good?" he tried to seem concerned.

Jim: "I have feelings toward someone I never had before. If is beyond sexual experience. I had sex with Kiana and it threw me in another dimension. I had plenty of sex and this one was different."

Nathan: "You, the biggest player and pimp I have seen in the world, fell for one lady? I can't believe it, Jim!"

Jim: "I wouldn't mind getting married soon to the right person. Now I am not sure she is that right, one? And, I am not a pimp, ok?"

Nathan: "Give yourself time to digest. Maybe it is just an obsession, more than likely infatuation?"

Jim: "Even you maybe right, I never had pain in my heart and enjoyed sex like that at same time!"

Nathan: "I do think you are obsessed and in infatuation at the same time!"

Jim: "I feel stupid when I am in love. She basically controls me. The antagonistic feeling between the rational/business and the creative mind is in a quiet war with the emotional/destructive heart."

Nathan: "That is a bit too heavy even for IT guy like me."

Jim: "Nathan, life itself is difficult to explain, but stupidly in love is less likely to explain. If a woman loves you are taken for granted like some kind of entitlement. Some people consider it being lucky, or they found the perfect match. Think the opposite. How about if one never finds his or her perfect match? The world may be the way it is because of missing true love? Or people not knowing what it truly and really means and Wars, ignorance, theft, cheating, any kind of greed and crimes, because of search for love!"

Nathan: "True! The only love is from your own mother. No matter what, she will be supporting you. You are her product, she gave you life!"

Jim: "In my case I never found what mother's love is? She died in car crash when I was six months old. The rest in my life is self built, a lot of books reading, a lot of risk taking with failures and successes!"

Nathan: "So you say that one can build himself up without love?"

Jim: "One can achieve more when thinking of love, but not really having it. Love/lust/money search pulls you back to 98% population! I am the two per center."

Nathan: "So, because you are there you are better achiever? Does your category prefer fake love then?"

Jim: "Unfortunately my category is targeted by the some elements of the 98% who only see dollar signs! I think that is where Kiana is coming from?"

Nathan: "Well, if you have to pay for your happiness, then go for it."

Jim: "I need someone to love me for my intelligence and my contributions to the world."

Nathan: "Good luck! Hope you will find your match eventually? Thanks for the conversation. I see you hardly talk to anyone here, except for business!"

Jim finished his cigar and he headed home. The travel, the Kiana's ignorance toward him, and the verbal altercation with the new owners of Prosperity bar next door, the conversation with Nathan ...all that was settling into his worry soul and it was creating the next Quantum Gravitational wave, the next destruction. He reminisced 9.11, 2001. Did he really do it? Did his curse at Amanda toppled the same building he climbed 120 floors to have drinks at the Windows of the World with Contessa (in 1984), just six months after he left New York in March, 2001? Was his mind the creative or destructive kind, or both? To answer he needed to see a pattern, theory to move to law, the QMCL. It did not happen right away, but his fears were to be confirmed soon.

A week later Jim's love was tested…

Samantha: "Hey Jim! I need new pictures for Eros.Com" … Remember, she was looking like short version of Marilyn Monroe. The pictures were taken in the small room. They closed the gate and she was like a playful cat. The camera loved her at any angle. She was very proportionate at 5'2" and her fake blonde hair was a perfect match for her pale beautiful face.

Jim: "I am tempted to take advantage of this situation, but I have a girlfriend now?" he was fully aroused and she almost grabbed his 8 inch tower, bulging inside his pants.

Samantha: "You think you have a girlfriend! Usually men would act different when they are secure and in love. They would not even look at me."

Her perfect ass was in Jim's face and the young twenty-one year old pink clitoris was more inviting to smell like a flower than to enter as pleasure box of sex. Jim was close to enjoy the secret of her juicy inviting body orifice, but he stopped short. He wished Kiana was here and not this pin up lady of the streets. Jim took about a whole film on his 35 mm camera and he called the photo session out. They had sex previously in 2001, during their first encounter, followed by the photo shoot.

Jim: "I am done here. Come tomorrow night and get your pictures. No charge! Please put your clothes on!" He turned off the camera.

Samantha: "Yes, you are either in love or very stupid! Nobody turns me down, nobody!" She was laughing and disappointed at the same time.

Jim: "I maybe both?" he was laughing too, watching his 8 inch tower imploding inside his pants. When they opened the gate the whole bar got quiet. The eight chair bar was full of regulars with no real life. Everyone thought there was wild sex inside the enclosed room with two couches.

Lora: "I hope you had a good time with Samantha?"

Jim: "Give her a Long Island Ice Tea drink, ok?"

Lora: "I am not sure she is of age to drink? I did ask her many times to show me an ID, but the one she showed me I think is a fake?"

Weseln: "I will be watching the door. She will be quick."

Samantha was quick. She drank the strongest mixed drink in the world "like a fish." The drink was gone in thirty seconds.

Lily: "Candy, Candy!" she was running fast toward Samantha.

Lily was an old acquaintance of Jim and a neighbor. He knew her ever since she was eighteen and they used to be intimate to the point. Lily, was lesbian 100 % and a virgin. She was built more mannish with no fat, superb tits and ass. She was the total opposite of Samantha/ Candy. She had short hair, dark skinned, wearing a hat backward like from the hood and wearing pants like a boy. Jim remembered her once they had threesome in the past two years with another lady when Lily used a huge 15 inch strap on dildo to have intercourse with one of Jim's lady friends. The show was amazing. Jim had never seen bi sexual lesbian having sex with a straight man and a lesbian at the same time. WOW!

Jim: "Friend of yours?" He addressed Samantha/Candy.

Samantha: "Lily is my body guard!" They hugged each other." She calls me Candy" they both were laughing.

Jim: "Candy is my super model, ha ha! Tomorrow you will see her pictures."

Jim: "Lora, give Lily soda or juice." He knew Lily was twenty and she couldn't drink.

Lora: "Ok" she was looking confused watching those three characters interact with each other. Jim had many interesting acquaintances in DC who would cross roads eventually and at times they would appear at the lounge Randevu also.

Lora: "Phew! You guys are something else!"

Jim: "If I remember correctly you were the one talking to the cops that you will change that bordello to something better? Those people have been around before us and they will be here after we leave. Why not take advantage of their presence? Men are looking for these kinds of women like Samantha, so are the lesbians!"

Lora: "You do live in different dimension. You may lose your business with those characters?"

Jim: "Live for the moment, live to the fullest" that is my slogan, Lora." He laughed.

Lora: "You may lose the business harboring everyone?" She was concerned mostly. She enjoyed occasionally a margarita drink.

Jim: "Look who is talking?"

Lora: "For being such a genius, you tend not to use just plain old logic in what you do and where you do it. And I wonder about you and how you think?"

Jim: "I have been with you ten years. You have seen me working in my field of video productions Walker's Media, graduating from

Lincoln Tech, working for Mercedes Benz dealership, banquet captain at McLean Hilton, went to jail and opened three clubs in the last five years. Who am I? God will judge, and no human being can!" He talked with passion.

Lora: "Jim!" she grabbed his hand, "you don't even know what you are about, you are a puzzle even to yourself, maybe you will figure it all out before it's too late!"

Kiana was still hiding. Early November, she called Jim. It was Saturday night around 10 pm.

Kiana: "Hey Jim! How are you?" She had that deep playful voice of the seductress.

Jim: "What? I don't believe you are alive?" That would be his standard repartee with this one for the next five or more years.

Kiana: "Why are talking like that?" that would be her answer for the next five or more years.

Jim: "Are you playing with me? I am coming to pick you up now!"

Kiana: "I am studying! Maybe I will be done around 1 am. I have a test on Monday" she lied. Howard University usually had tests Tuesdays and Thursdays.

Jim: "Ok, call me around this time" he played along.

He waited till 1.30 am Sunday morning. No call. He was to leave the bar and to go and check on her. Lora, was wondering why he was so depressed, but she was about to find out soon. At about 2.30 am after numerous calls Kiana answered.

Jim: "Wow, what is the hold up?"

Kiana: "I am studying, plus my drunken mother keeps bothering me, so I kind of ignored all phone calls."

Jim: "I am not to be ignored. You could of called me to avoid the avalanche of phone calls, baby!"

Kiana: "I am not your baby, ok! Come pick me up in an hour." She sounded angry.

Jim: "I will, but please answer your phone, ok?" He was angry too, but he calmed down toward the end of the sentence. "After the bar closes I will be on the way." He hung up.

The bar crowd unwillingly left around 3.20 am, pushed out by Jim and Lora. The regulars were used to hang out an extra hour, after regular alcohol serving was legally allowed. Jim emptied the register and rushed out the establishment. Within ten minutes he pulled over at 650 Edgewood Terrace.

Kiana: "I will be out in a few. I am almost finished!" She lied.

Jim: "Ok," he was tinkering with the FM radio stations, but they seemed dull. Thirty minutes passed.

Jim: "Hey, where are you! It is cold out here," he texted. No answer for another ten minutes.

Kiana: "I am coming now!" she screamed at 4.15 am.

Jim: "Wow! Ok!" he was beyond upset. He was about to explode like a grenade. Another 15 minutes passed. Finally Kiana appeared wearing blue jeans jacket and blue jeans pants shivering.

Jim: "What the fuck is wrong with you? I have been calling you for five hours!" He got out of the car mad; Kiana had a pale face like she had been smoking something. She did not say anything in her defense. She stopped at the door, going backwards, acting like she wanted to go back.

Jim: "Now where are you going?" he spat in her face.

Kiana: "Whaaaat?" She ran into the building, hiding.

Jim: "Come out, bitch!" he spat again at the glass door twice. He couldn't believe he was doing that to a woman he loved?

Did he really have any idea what love is? The evil powers got the worst of him. That spit will cost him 250,000 dollars for next five years relationship and it will change the world's history to the worst in last 100 years.

Jim: "God have mercy on you." He texted her after thirty calls he made to her without an answer.

Kiana: "I rebuke you, evil man!"...

Jim: "I am not evil, but you make me what I am! Who is been nice to you, gave you a car, cash, and took you to nice restaurants, shopping?"...

Kiana: "Anybody can do all that! You spat in my face!" That was her last text and phone went to disconnected mode. Any phone calls after just went to her voice mail.

Jim: "Oh, my God! Is that what love is?" He felt betrayed by his emotions/heart/destructive wave. He felt like ripping off his shirt and cutting that little engine of life, and just throw it in the sewer. The pain was a pain of betrayal. He knew how Menelaus felt when Paris stole his wife Helen to deliver her to the city of Troy. Helen loved Paris very much. At this time, he was not aware of who the Paris was, or was there any Paris in the picture? He would find out later that the Gods were playing games with him in parallel universe like Hera and Athena were enjoying the blood battle between Achaeans and Trojans. Here Paris will be DP the Don, Jim will be Menelaus, Trojans would be the Georgia mafia of marihuana distributors, but amazingly no Achaeans on Jim's side! That elevated him to God like position! One against many! One who will win all battles by himself in next ten years. When he loses his night clubs, he may lose the opportunity of becoming rich in conventional, earth way. Creating the legacy of survival against DC government, Georgia Mafia, Lebanese Mafia, US Federal Government, Bulgarian government, against any adversaries and to create a legacy and to teach others, that is a God-like deity!

As in every situation he crossed, Jim needed answers. To reaffirm his saint like behavior, (at this situation with Kiana he maybe anti Saint from her point of view) he needed to explain to himself and to the world that he was?

People judge from the position of observer C, while the initiator A (Jim) and reaction of B (Kiana) and counter reaction on A, (Jim) is ignored or over exaggerated. We think good and evil are judged by C without looking at speeds of events, or some called it "time line." We assume that the A and B move with same Earth speed! Wrong, judge C, wrong! When A, B are not moving in the same direction or even opposite direction, how can one judge those two characters? They should not be even in the same court room. The next diagram will explain the quantum conclusion, which it starts with the physical, (Euclidean, to Maxwell), to quantum (Einstein to Max Planck), to Jim's laws.

Jim moved between both worlds, one is physical (earth) and galaxy (space) reality… from 4th to 5th Dimension and beyond; that would be the Cosmic, the 6th Dimension.

The positive curative will move two parallel geodesic (space-time) lines closer (on sphere), while the same starting lines will separate in negative curvature (horse saddle). Material moves in world lines, while photons (light) move in curvature (cones, wave like). From there it is Jim's "cone theory." The wave-particle theory by Einstein will explain the special relativity, where Newton's gravity and Hermann Minkowsky's zero gravity combine. Maxwell will discover the Electromagnetic fields, Wheeler will explain the energy creating in compressing magnetic field or in destroying matter, Einstein will write the formula, Max Plank will explore the quantum characteristics of bursts of light and write that electromagnetic fields when move with speed of light will create gravitational field and create or destroy matter! When we observe the Earth it moves around the Sun in cork screw line.

Is that the theory of ancient scientists that our life is related to the Sun? But there are seven planets that also rotate around the Sun. They have different speeds of rotation and different vibrations frequencies of sound, (tone - octaves) and mass. The octaves in musical scales are related to those spheres (planets) by mass. To create we need Mi octave, to destroy we need Fa octave.

We will talk about entropy, thermodynamic laws, but in simple terms Energy in entropy will diminish, unless a new energy is fed. Business will slow down unless new money keeps coming. The temperature in entropy will move from hotter to colder, the energy will disappear. Love and entropy are similar in behavior. When one who moves with higher speed like Jim cannot meet the equal reciprocal love, something had to give. Kiana decided to drag her feet (Fa octave). Later on Jim will discover that she was talking for hours to her boyfriend DP the Don; she would bear ten pregnancies by him.

She was calling DP the Don and they were speaking on the phone for 5 hours that night, while Jim was waiting for months and years to hear from her. Was the spitting justified then? Yes, if he knew her true manipulative nature. Yes, he guessed right she was ignoring him for evil reasons. He needed to know why?

Galileo had it right. If a body falls free without resistance of air, it will fall with the same speed any body with any mass would fall. So let's reverse the game. Jim postulate will be: "If no resistance in upward direction (after all it is the same air, or no air at all) the person or his business will achieve his goal with the same speed!"

That maybe true in the physical universe. Where is government and regulations with the zero resistance? Or where is the "Free enterprise?"

For someone to create excessive capital, to win a battle, to create or to destroy, the trick is to work on curved line, not on strait line. To make a prediction what will be the outcome, and to be different than to others, the creator has to move with speeds where the curve taps into the future or into the past.

If an event is to be seen in the future before it happens the creator has to move with the speed so fast that the others to be seen as moving backward. The paradox of time is that the higher the speed the less time becomes significant. Matter of fact in the energy formulas of Einstein or Max Plank the time is not even mentioned! The creator seems that he is not concerned with that, nor it is the destroyer. Once he created the universe he just needed to maintain it. The earth people are the ones concerned with time and wars and creativity.

Jim was looking at the world events as an interactive game. He was like in Sigourney Weaver's movie "Alien." He felt instead the world to control him, he was controlling the world. He was in a negative curvature now.

Kiana was hurting his feelings, next door were not welcome neighbors. The police was pressuring him to change his hours of operation according some "agreement," he never agreed or complied with. They were envious of his style of running businesses and definitely they did not like his clientele (at least on the surface). His partner Mansur was pressuring him for more money for rent and bills. The only place he felt comfortable was at the bar, where he have, at least temporary control.

Thanksgiving came and went - Kiana was not calling. To find some way to think of something positive Jim decided to invest in his video production Walker's Media. Eventually it would grow into a quarter million dollar investment in a decade.

Jim: "If I do not invest in me (my production) those characters are going to take all my money." He was thinking of Kiana and Mansur.

Kiana called just before Christmas. He picked her up. They went to a small restaurant. The date was not moving very well.

Kiana: "What? You don't talk now, but you blow my phone up!" she was eating and talking. She was kind of irritated.

Jim: "I just want to watch you. I am not here to eat." He was sipping on coffee.

Kiana: "I am going home for Christmas. Are you going to help me? I need some clothes." Her deep voice sounded sexy for her age of twenty-one.

Jim: "While you were ignoring me the last two months I did expand my investment in my video production."

Kiana: "So, you don't have money to give me?" She stopped eating.

Jim: "I have money, but my priorities have changed with time. I had a lot of money for you, but I can't wait for you to date me? Let me ask you a question."

Kiana: "Go ahead." She was chopping the steak and acted interested.

Jim: "If I did not give you money, would you ever see me?"

Kiana: "Sure, but much less!"

Jim: "Much less? You hardly see me now. It has been two months!"

Kiana: "I can also disappear and you would never see me again" she was serious.

Yes. When she would have her frequent abortions, she would demand money, and then she would hide. Jim figured out some nine years later her strange behavior, but at what emotional and financial cost to him and to the planet Earth? Writing this manuscript is like rewinding or forwarding the VCR, or some time machine device, only God knew how, then Jim. Figure this Cornell University!

Jim: "So, how we can make this work?" He tried to be soft with her.

Kiana: "First, dating now is not my priority. We had sex but we are not in a relationship. You want more than I can give you now. I like you the way you are. Don't change for me. And don't ever spit in my face again. Be patient with me, please! Let me grow and live my life while I am young."

Jim: "I don't have much choice here!" he was confused…

Kiana: "You can enjoy my company, but you can't control me, ok!"

Jim: "You know that I like you. Do not take advantage of that. Now what do you want?"

Kiana: "I need my phone bill paid, because you left too many messages there and too many voice mails. Ok? Then I need to do some shopping."

Jim was surprised to see how her behavior changed when she was shopping? She was happy like a child! She was beautiful when she was happy. They both forgot their grievances and she enjoyed the secret of rich man, poor lady sex… She was great in bed with long legs and tight nice, juicy and hairy vagina. Jim wanted to remember the view; he was trying to hold as long as he possibly could the moment of pleasure. He was to dismiss all previous encounters if this beautiful twenty-one year old agreed to love him?

Jim: "You have a secret weapon!" He collapsed next to her. The eruption was not just sexual; it was from a different time and space dimension. Were Gods making love like that? When space, earth and time are linked through love, the sex becomes expression of highest love.

Kiana: "What are you implying?"

Jim: "When you talk, you sound 40ish. When you are naked you look like a statue. When you make love, you are the best!" He shouted in a hurry, breathing heavily...

Kiana: "That is just sex, not love!"

Jim: "Whatever else could this be called when I feel like I am on cloud 9?" He kissed her vagina and started licking her clitoris up and down and he moved down to her long tight lips and his long tongue probed deep into her juicy opening. Then he stuck his middle finger in her equality juicy asshole. She started to moan in rhythm of his licking and fingering.

Jim: "Touch your clitoris, baby!"

Kiana: "I have never done that before. I only do that in the shower." She said that, but Jim did not want to argue with her. He put her own hand on her clitoris and she continued massaging her vagina. Jim pushed his pointed nose inside her vagina and started licking her asshole. She got into frenzy shivering and she started to come. It was a long subdued scream and she busted in long orgasm.

Jim: "Are you happy!" He mumbled with a suffocating voice still licking and probing inside her vagina and asshole.

Kiana: "Beyond happy! You should teach what you do at Howard University, or any university, ha ha!"

Jim: "Sex college education! Great!" Both of them were laughing.

She never asked for money.

Kiana: "Are you going to take care of me!" That was her question she asked in that turbulent spring of 2003 when they met. It was imprinted in Jim's psyche and he felt obligated to do everything possible to please her. Sometimes he felt like a father substitute, sometimes he felt like the lover she needed. Little he knew about her mystery world he would get entangled into later. At that time he was where he wanted to be. It reminded him of the Russian Lady Svetlana, but she called the numbers ahead and she was a contract wife. This one was in an unknown category.

Jim threw at her a bundle of 1,000 dollars. That was in 10 tiers of folded 100 dollar bills.

Kiana: "Don't ever throw money at me, ok!" She was acting angry but once she saw the bundle of 100's she softened up. "Can I have two?" She looked with a childish expectation of approval. It was amazing.

Jim: "Sure, take as much as you want!" he felt light headed and happy and careless about money matters.

Kiana: "Can I have three?" She never had held thousands of dollars cash and given that choice. That was not singles, fives or twenties! That was 100's she could have!

Kiana: "I am not greedy, I will keep 300 dollars, ok? I am not after your money, Jim! Before I met you I was almost a virgin. What is the most disappointing is that we started with sex, before we developed a true relationship?"

Jim: "You keep disappearing on me. If I see you more often, then it could be the way you wanted it. I am at an age when I am looking for someone to invest everything in so I could have a woman like you."

Kiana: "I am now at age twenty-one. I really needed you two years ago, when I was freshman in HU. I was really starving. One day I was so hungry and I asked a friend to buy me lunch. He said, "I can give you a bag of chips." I couldn't believe it! He was giving me 50 cents for some chips. I turned him down."

Jim: "So, how did you manage to survive?" He was washing his penis in the bathroom. She followed him.

Kiana: "How? I met some marijuana dealers. I was selling drugs for them and they would give me a cut. That way I was able to eat."

Jim: "That is pretty dangerous. If you were to get caught you lose not only your education, but you will lose also your freedom and you will have a record for years."

Kiana: "One of my suppliers, a guy, he got caught. He did not snitch about me, or anyone who was selling for him in HU. That is why I was not reprimanded. I had to seize my whole operation. Then you showed up. God is watching over me!" She jumped in the shower. Her wet, soapy body was similar to Svetlana, the beautiful courtesan, but this was not a two day contract wife!

Jim: "God is good to me and you! I have the proven theory that we are the champions and victims of our own thoughts. You needed me and that is why you responded to my advances. I needed you and that is why we are together today!"

Kiana: "Cool off, buddy! I am still young and I need to live my life! Don't suffocate me, ok!" she was drying her long legs with the towel and headed to living room.

Jim: "I believe in predestination. If everything works well we can get married one day?" he was serious. That Mother Nature was calling on him. The big biological clock was ticking.

Kiana: "This guy is nice, but I think we are definitely on opposite planets in many ways. I have to deal with him differently" she thought. "Good he has money, but his business is something that I need to research before I commit myself to any serious friendship. Sex is good, but my emotions are still in Georgia. My best friend is in jail and he needs my emotional support, also he needs money. Maybe I can channel the money to him from Jim? Maybe I can reactivate my old gang and they can provide me with marijuana and I can sell it to my old HU customers, but this time I will not be dealing directly with them. So, I need this white man's money for sure."

Kiana: "Thank you, Jim!" she reminded him of Frida from New York or Mandy from Hamburg; sexy but stubborn and proud.

Jim was happy, he did not think of the expenses or the two months of Kiana ignoring him. The emotions he developed toward that slim African American (Einstein smart, Model like) young and mysterious lady, those emotions were so strong he could cut them with a knife! The love in any shape or form is self inflicted wound. People will love or hate someone for no apparent reason. Nathan called it "Love Bug" or an "obsession." Jim called it a "hunger for similar emotions." Since his mother died and left him at the age of six months to fend for himself, he felt the burden to prove himself to the others that he could survive. Jim needed respect and love. He felt disrespected in Bulgaria and he escaped! He felt more respected now in Washington, DC, but not by the Federal or DC authorities.

Jim: "I will give you a ride home. Are you ready?" She was leaving the bathroom.

Kiana: "Can I come to your bar now? I want to see it!" She was excited.

Jim: "Really? Ok! There is a caveat. My bartender Lora is strange."

Kiana: "I was in a gang. I can handle anyone!" Both were laughing.

Jim: "Hmm. There are two ways to get initiated in a gang. Which one was yours (murder someone or get raped)." He was pensive.

Kiana: "That is my secret. I will tell you in due time." She got serious too.

Jim: "Oh, my God! I have a secretive gangster lady, I am in love with." He was ready for surprises.

Lora: "Hey Jim. What is up?"

Kiana: "High. I am Kiana." She stretched her hand with a smile.

Lora: "I don't shake hands with anyone. I am from New York." She was drinking a margarita and she generally never approved of any of Jim's lady friends.

Kiana: "What is her problem? Is she your girlfriend or something?"

Jim: "She is kind of territorial. She thinks this bar is hers. Can I fix you a drink?" he offered her.

Kiana: "No thanks. I don't like her attitude. Can you drive me home?"

She started walking down the stairway.

Jim: "I will be back in thirty minutes."

Lora: "Enjoy yourselves!"

Jim: "Fuck you! Leave us alone. I can't bring anyone here."

Kiana: "What is going on here? You have a situation here. I have my own problems. I do not want yours!" she was running toward the car.

Jim: "Lora is my bartender, nothing else."

Kiana: "She seems very unwelcoming." She had a point.

Jim: "Do you want to come and work? She just starts the bar between 9 pm and 11 pm. I take over after that. Then I make most of my money (from 11pm to 2 am - 3 am)."

Kiana: "I am a student and you promised to take care of me, didn't you?" She got some kind of attitude entering the Benz. "In general I do like your lounge. Maybe we can do some promotions here?" She was smiling with some Mona Lisa expression. Her long legs needed extra space. She pulled the passenger seat back and inclined the seat in "gangsta" style.

Kiana: "It has been a long day, but you seem nice today and you came correct."

Jim: "This can be everyday thing, but you are generally unavailable."

Kiana: "We may have a problem with Lora around?" she was comfortable in the sunken seat.

Jim: "I have known her for ten years and she seems loyal, but I agree she is also an obstacle" he grabbed Kiana's hand that was falling asleep. Then he slid his hand between her legs and she did not respond at all. He wanted to keep her around. The moment was like for the centuries to remember. Why? The next decade his mood would almost destroy the physical world and himself along with it.

December 26th, 2003 was a great day for Jim for two reasons.

Kiana: "Happy Birthday to you, Happy Birthday to you." She was singing on the phone, her voice was deep, playful and arousing.

Jim: "Ok, thank you Marilyn Monroe!" he wanted to kiss her, but the phone line wouldn't allow it. He just paused in disbelief she remembered his birthday? On second thought he enjoyed the attention.

Kiana: "I am no Marilyn, I am black and you should say thank you. Ok?" She was getting attitude and that was sexy in some mysterious way also.

Jim: "Why are you always trying to correct me or teach me something? Thank you Kiana!"

Kiana: "That is more like it," she started laughing. The up and down of the conversation had the dynamics of the two totally opposite worlds interacting.

"I don't like white people and you are the exception in my rule" she exhaled on the other side of the phone line…

Jim: "I do not want you to like anybody but me. I agree on your exception!"

Kiana: "Want me to come sooner rather than later back to DC? I supposed to come back mid January. I can come back a week earlier."

Jim: "What do you want me to do?" he felt somewhat uncomfortable.

Kiana: "I am in need of cash."

Jim: "Listen, sending you money is not a problem. Can you guarantee me that when you come here you will spend time with me?" He was in a down slope spiraling mood.

Kiana: "Jim, nothing in life is guaranteed! Remember that." She hung up the phone…

Jim: "What was that?" it was like a hurricane passed through the room. The silence after the greeting and abrupt ending was unbearable.

Jim called and called back to no avail. The New Year evening came and gone and three weeks into the month of January, with no calls from Kiana.

Jim: "I know her mother's number." He dialed it with hesitance.

Kiana's mother/ Magdalena: "Hello?" It was 10 pm and she took her time to answer, being closer to the bottle of liquor than to any phone.

Jim: "I am looking for Kiana. I am calling from Washington, DC."

Magdalena: "If you are looking for Kiana, she is never home. She is on the streets with her up-to-no good friends most of the time."

Jim: "I am helping her here and there, but she seems evasive."

Magdalena: "When you do that, she is never grateful. She beats me up if I try to correct her behavior." The drunken voice lowered in pain. "She thinks she is the boss, like the mafia. Do not give anything."

Chapter 12

One day two Moroccan guys came to the bar... They were kind of regulars. Samantha and Lily were also there. Samantha was happy with the photo shoot.

Jim: "Did you receive some good business from ErosDC.com?"

Samantha: "Your pictures were amazing! Customers kept asking who took the pictures. Some of them recognized your famous white leather half love chair!"

Jim: "Really? I hope you did not tell them the pictures were taken here at the lounge?" After half an hour of drinking and small talk one of the Moroccans disappeared, so did Samantha. The bar was busy and no one even noticed. It would have remained unnoticed until some screams from the bathrooms were overheard and the Moroccan playboy was running down the steps holding his neck.

Moroccan: "She cut me up!" pointing upward to the balcony. Samantha was coming down like Miss America.

Samantha: "He is crazy!" she was trying to leave the bar area.

Jim: "Let me see what happened first?" he stopped her.

The police were called. They took too long as usual and by the time they arrived (sometime thirty minutes after the call) both Moroccans were gone.

Samantha: "This man is keeping me hostage here" she pointed to Jim. That was one angry cat.

Jim: "She cut up someone with a knife. Please search her."

Police: "Where is the complainant?" She was short muscular built mid 30s blonde, somewhat attractive even being mean.

Samantha: "I don't have a knife. This guy is imagining stuff. Please check my purse." She opened the Louis Vuitton handbag. It was full of jewelry and stolen credit cards. Police went through her purse but they couldn't find anything looking like a knife or anything sharp like it.

Samantha: "You see. He is lying" she headed toward the door.

Police: "We can't charge her with anything. No complaint, no weapon."

Jim: "She probably hid it somewhere. Can you wait? I will check the trash."

Police: "We don't have time for trash checking." They left to another call.

Jim pulled out the big black trash bag. He emptied in a new bag. He found a bunch of condoms and a Swiss Army knife. He opened it slowly. There was fresh blood on it.

Jim: "Damn police. They could have caught her. First; they came late, second; they did not do their job, acting like I am disturbing their work, third; they left in a hurry?" He decided never to call them again. He dialed Samantha's number.

Jim: "I found the knife with blood on it. Please don't ever come to the lounge again." He was resolute with the matter.

Samantha: "Fuck you! I will shut your place down. I have friends in the police. They will raid you!" she clicked the phone off. Within thirty minutes the glass door at the lounge entrance was bending from the boots Lily was kicking it with. She couldn't break it but she bent it and shattered the middle of it. Jim thought of dialing the Police again, but he decided to wait and to take the matter in his own hands.

Jim: "God will help me out. Government here is useless." He spent the night in the lounge, sleeping on the couch. In the morning he called Leo Welding and they installed a whole metal door and even a small window in the middle to see who is coming?

The Gods were with Jim. The perfect storm was brewing from Kiana ignoring him, (a habitual thing with her), and then from situation developing in his rival next door club Prosperity. Samantha and Lily were barred from Randevu so; they went naturally to Prosperity (next door). They promised to bring Louise and her "I candy" boyfriend a big promotion. Lily was trying to be a singer. She had a meowing voice, but with some camouflage music as background anyone could have been a singer. They developed their cash flow from selling drugs (crack and cocaine) from their suppliers at Baltimore. The rumors were that one time Lily sold fake cocaine to a white person in the alley, who subsequently got sick from it. The money they made from those sales was invested in their CD production, where Lily was the main meowing singer. Her voice sounded like someone was cutting metal sheets with scissors, screeching. If one had never met Lily, he would laugh at her squeaky sound. The closest one can compare her to another artist (if she was an artist), is R&B singer Michel'le Toussaint.

The window facing the street on the first floor at Prosperity was always occupied with Louise and her friends. Jim was surprised to see Samantha and Lily's happy faces on the inside. They waved at him often. He was ignoring them in the beginning. One day in March he waved at them back and said "God will take care of you," and just smiled. They couldn't hear him, separated by the window, but they read his lips and translated it as something positive. That was the furthest from the truth. The quantum algorithm kicked in. That was open not to all possibilities, but to one, which was equal to destruction.

Meanwhile his relationship with Kiana had no particular destination, save nil. Valentine's Day came and went and so did her twenty-second birthday; everything was looking like in downhill roller coaster motion. Jim remembered the 9/11 disaster, which seemed similar to Amanda/Frida formula, which toppled "the Towers?" Would his prediction on Nov. 03rd, 2003 become true? He knew his powers. He was not quite sure how things were going to turn out in pushing these phony bologna characters out of business and to take over their space? God/his sub consciousness/TIH were working in mysterious ways. Losing his club the Zoro started the negative curve, and the down-spiral of Government self destruction. Jim had the power, now he needed results.

Einstein wrote in 1935 theory of Quantum entanglement if a particle is split into two parts, the two new particles remain linked to one another, even separated by vast distances. Here also kicks in the Feynman diagram in reverse. Wheeler energy/magnetism theory is also in the picture.

Jim's theory is combination of all theories above.

1. Business equals mass, creativity by the owner. Zoro Club.
2. Breaking the business by the government through license removal is outside force.
3. Two parts as result are the two quarks W+ and W-. Here will be the two rival establishments – Jim's and Prosperity. Those two quarks are the Energy in John Wheeler's theory.

Government/Force (collision with) + Business/Mass (Zoro) = 2 quarks (Jim's +, Prosperity-)

He was in trouble. He needed to change his Modus Operandi. He realized that part of Kiana's hesitation may be because of the nature of the operation he was into... with a bar full of hookers, pimps, Mansur squeezing him for money, incompetent lawyer Nikias, DC and Federal Government pressuring him to fix liquor hours of operation and harassing him and his customers, he wanted to get married, but it was an impossible mission working seven days a week and with Lora around.

Schrodinger equitation describes the deterministic time evolution of the wave function. The caveat is the wave function needs to be broken down to pure tones. To measure quantum effects, we magnify them to the classical level (like a giant microscope). The quantum amplitudes turn to classical probabilities.

Jim's theory in life is that one human to be in quantum state is to be blind, weightless, senseless, all bones removed. Only then can he be in plasma, helium, state of matter and he can move freely in the time dimensions with warp speeds in holographic images. Unfortunately, we need a spine/vertebrate to contain our soul and intelligence, or the spirit as whole. We can only live in molecular density in state of astroprojection, when in our state of sleep our spiritual body leaves in molecular state our physical body. The magnetic and intellectual fields are mixed, but that still contains the firmness of our physical body. It shows we can be at two places at one time, which is the paradox of highly developed living saints or during the sacrificing ritual, when masses witness the spirit becomes alive and firm.

We can also fake the molecular state by staying fully alert but in mediating state. We basically imitate the solar state of being, The Sun.

The implosion of hydrogen to helium is basically a chemical reaction where with the infusion of oxygen and the thought process the algorithm leads to emitting photons, but only with the creation of He (helium is with two positrons in nucleus and two electrons in orbit). What is the input here is the quantum mind (the Thought), which requires specific outcome (from quantum amplitude to classic probability in physical world), in form of perceivable results (negative or positive facts).

Jim and Kiana met briefly in Georgetown at end of March, 2004.

It happened in restaurant Pino's on M Street, NW, DC.

They had a heated conversation about Lora's involvement in the bar operation.

Kiana: "You have a choice! She is stealing from you."

Jim: "She is not. When I am at the bar the money is always good..."

Kiana: "If she is there I don't want to see you!" she was acting ("acting" operative word here), hysterical.

Jim: "You are stealing from me! The difference is you are taking 100,000 to 200,000 dollars; she is not even paid, except for her tips.

Kiana: "You are fucking me and you love me! I think I am worthy" she would deflect the straight answer as usual. Then to demonstrate her anger she zipped out the door.

Jim: "Hold on, Kiana!" He gave his credit card to Geof, the proprietor, and ran after her. He caught up with her a block away.

Jim: "Do not ever embarrass me like that in front of my friends, ok!"

Kiana: "I will come back and we can make up if you get rid of Lora!"

Jim: "I think you are just looking for any excuse not to see me." He signed his credit card and both calmed down.

Geof: "Hope everything is ok?" he was smiling as usual. Quarrels were not a strange thing to him, but he always liked the happy endings. "Jim, your friend is fierce, or a great actress, or mostly just young and temperamental!"

Jim: "We need the good, but we have to deal with the bad part also of their sides, unfortunately!" both men agreed.

April was a boring month. The next door bar/club Prosperity was promoting stripper dancers. Jim observed beautiful ladies with carry on cars (like flight attendants or lawyers would pull). That was not in their license and occupancy permit description. It was illegal and showed signs of desperation! Jim called his friend in ABC board Inspector Ceaser. He was chief enforcement investigator. He made a note, but nothing happened. They were operating as usual. For a moment Jim thought the Gods were against him, but it was not true.

May 9, 2004 was just another night at Randevu lounge. The crowd was happy and the drinks were pouring in. Cigars were passed around and in general it was business as usual. It was Saturday night and the next door Prosperity lounge was busy. Samantha and Lily had brought the rift rough crowd from Baltimore to debut their meowing, songs. Suddenly just before midnight huge thumping sound shook the walls between the adjusted buildings. The loud speakers sound next door was mixed with earthquake like commotion. Jim turned down the volume at Randevu. The screaming next door, mixed with the loud sounds and walls shaking at least four to five times was the indication of something going awfully wrong.

Then the crowd and the screams spilled to the street. Through the windows Jim observed Samantha running eastward on X Street toward Bank of America. Some people were following her with angry faces. Around 50 people scattered in different directions.

Within five minutes the police sirens filled up the air. Then the ambulance and fire department truck also blocked the street. To everyone's amazement six bloodied bodies were pulled out one after the other from the Prosperity lounge. The yellow caution tape line "police, do not cross," was wrapped around the tree toward the guiding polls for crowd control. The TV crew from channel 7 arrived also. They were looking for witnesses and of course to interview the owners.

Jim: "Do you mind moving your yellow tape away from my door entrance. You are scaring my customers away!" he advised the police.

Police: "Sure! Hopefully you don't have this type of crowd?" they cooperated reluctantly.

Jim: "I kicked them out two months ago; they broke down my glass door. Now they are destroying my competition!" He commented, but the police were more concerned with the wounded and the Prosperity's owners input, not with his opinion.

Jim understood later that Samantha was pushing fake cocaine sales and the buyer detected that. The fight had broken out to get his money refunded, in the amount of 500. The buyer had two swords and he went through the crowd slashing anyone in his way to chase Samantha who sold him the fake drugs. He was able to cut up six of her friends, who tried to shield her.

Again, was his prediction correct? Yes. On November 3rd, 2003 he told his neighbor "You would not last here six months!" Exactly six months later and six days, six people got stabbed! If this is not the 666 sequence, then what it is? This is to mathematicians to calculate and historians to analyze, but there is no mistake in the precision of events! The difference of Satan numbers and Demi God/anti Saint is in the process of the Thought. Jim was on top of his Quantum field. Through this and many future examples (read what happened on June 2nd, 2011 in this manuscript), he discovered the magic number of God sequence. It is 6666! Yes, God, or any creator/triggered thought need more speed and stronger coil/cone than the destructor/Satan (666).

Majority of population and the observer C/the judge, fall for the result and what the police and media say. They take the information and accept the information as real and they don't get into how the mind creates the events, they're deep into constitution, witnesses, and affidavits in interrogations to create a profile.

Most criminals fall into the trap of their own words/confessions.

The Miranda rights are recited for a reason by law enforcement! It is to protect your rights as a citizen and your lawyer's work. Once someone confesses the lawyer can't defend him. Words do not necessary represent the thinking process of a person, contrary to the popular belief. Words are used to represent someone in a way he/she wants to be perceived. If one believed every word a politician running for office would say then everyone should be elected! Unfortunately, for the Satan there is a time line, which represents his true actions in life. That where the Demi God/anti Satan and Satan/anti God differ. The time line represents education, work experience, religious and marital status. Let us not forget to include the tax record! There are many points where the achievers are similar, but what makes or breaks the end result, is the true thinking behind the scenes. Jim would win. He knew how to create the unbreakable enigma, the algorithm of his success!

He wouldn't fight his enemies in conventional, physical world. He learned from mixed Martial Arts that there is more damage to the enemy not from frontal punch, but from letting him fall and he will damage himself more in the process. The evil thinking of the opposition will bring him/her negative curve of bad karma, or the quantum density, will make him to deviate from his goals to achieve. Satan will start with good intentions but it will end like in a bad marriage. For example, Jim's partner Mansur cheated him out of his money. Mansur filed up a chapter seven in the year 2011, for personal bankruptcy, he lost twice Mike's restaurants in DC and at College Park, Maryland. The "buyer" of Randevu /Mike's Khalid will have a similar fate (chapter seven and losing the Rogue club), the next owner of the 1426 X Street will lose Zephyr within two months of opening in 2012.

Jim had the best business approach. He would start a small club business to grow to three clubs within three years, and then he will last near a decade. Then everything will implode, but not because he was not producing profit… Please, read why?

Can the classical/physical reality be explained through quantum mechanics? Yes. The whole Prosperity lounge was doomed from the beginning. It started with Marsha disrespecting Jim when it was Starlight, then Louise's boyfriend was threatening him. They did not know who they were up against? They thought Jim was just another foreigner with an accent, trying to make it in USA. They thought being born in USA or being natives of Washington, DC that gave them the upper hand, or some better leverage? Here the American nightmare of foreigner doing better than them manifests in its true colors. Jim was called any kind of name by Marsha and Louise: "Terrorist, drug dealer, pimp, KGB, arms dealer, mafia, and pornographer.".... Anything but, "hard working, seven days a week tax payer and good citizen!"

Wednesday, May 13, the license of Prosperity Lounge was revoked for good. The illegal sex parties with strippers and the six wounded bodies were hard to be ignored. Seemed the dream of Randevu and Mike's expansion was coming to fruition.

May 14th, 2004 Jim met with his lawyer Nikias.

Jim: Mike's needs to expand to next door. They had CT (tavern license). We may use their license, which does not require 45% food sales, but only 10 to 15%."

Nikias: "Great. I will make a couple of phone calls. I need zoning change to one address, occupancy permit and new lease signed by all parties."

Jim: "Ok. Give me some time to negotiate the lease. Then we will meet at your office. I will need also the liquor hours extended to the normal ABRA allows."

Nikias: "Wow. Fifteen years make a tremendous difference, doesn't it? You are on top of your business. I would never guess you are going through 4th venture and expansion again? You Bulgarians do not give up easy…..going and going, like the ever-ready bunny!"

Jim: "I am not your usual Bulgarian, sir! Bye." They were both laughing and shaking heads.

Meanwhile at the bar Tyra and Benny were flashing money, driving two identical Cadillacs, the latest model in 2004.

Jim: "You are doing well! What is your secret?" he was amused, but not impressed. New and flashy things were sometimes camouflage for some kind of scheme.

Benny: "You don't know, but I am a realtor and business is good. We get great commissions in selling houses or business." He was telling the truth somewhat. What he was not telling was that he and Tyra were extorting money from a deep well off businessmen. One client was paying Tyra $10,000 a month so she would not tell his wife about dating her. Beside the stolen credit card business and prostitution, things were believable.

Tyra: "…And I am fitness instructor. I have an investor, who will back me with 400,000 dollars to build my health spa. We will do yoga, martial arts, massage therapy."

Jim: "That sounds great. Why don't you invest in my club expansion next door? They just lost their lease twice in one year period!" He was referring to Starlight and Prosperity. They all laughed.

Benny: "1428 X Street has a bad omen. What is the guarantee we will not get shut down?" They were still laughing.

Jim: "Maybe I should get a real estate license too?" he was serious.

Benny: "It is not easy as is looks. You need to go to school, pass a national exam, then state exam. After that you have to get a broker and pay for services at the office. Then you need a MRIS access and a GCAAR access key to properties."

Jim: "Nothing is impossible as long there is motivation and possible result/creativity expressed in profit," he said. "Thanks Adams Smith," inside, but nobody heard him.

Tyra and Benny: "Good luck!" they screamed in one voice. Both of them were in good shape, fit, and Tyra was bragging about she could take anyone on in Karate. Jim laughed about it, remembering his matchmaking with his friend Rafael and her in 2001, and nobody can take down Rafael.

Next day he made a couple of phone calls to real estate schools. Within a month he was in real estate class. Long and Foster Real Estate Academy was near University Boulevard and on New Hampshire Avenue in Maryland. The course was one month and it was unusual the way Jim was studying! The school usually started at 8 am. Working at the bar till 3 am left him with three to four hours sleeping window.

Teacher: "Hey, Jim! How are you going to graduate this class if you keep sleeping every day the first two hours?" He sounded very concerned.

Jim: "Mr. Reynolds! How do you think I graduated from the Naval Academy? I used the same method. I did graduate with the first three in class" he bragged proudly.

Teacher: "That would be amazing. I don't want you to fail and to repeat the class and to pay again 225.00 dollars. Ok!" He smiled puzzled.

A month passed fast. From twelve students in class only three graduated. One was a banker, the other was a lawyer. The third was …you guessed right! It was Jim. Why the challenge was working always in his benefit? He felt the negativity of others was creating the positive in him. The perfect balance in the nature was creativity based on annihilation.

E + n = e + p, or in reverse!

The next step was to pass the National Real Estate exam. It was 8 hour, 400 questions exam. To pass one had to answer 80% of the questions correct or 320 questions, which was in multiple choice formats. That was the new challenge. Who is Jim? Is he a loser or a winner? The exam was like mixed bowl of mathematics, laws and regulations, and strange real estate terminology. It was hard, but not impossible to pass. Mid October Jim got licensed as realtor. He passed! Viva la cavessa! Jim joined Weichert Realty at their headquarters in Bethesda, MD. They sent him to their Weichert Academy in Northern Bethesda to be in full to the par mode. Now he was ready. He got his DC, VA, MD licenses.

But the clouds were still around him. His emotions were unanswered. He wanted to spend the Valentine Day with Kiana, but she was acting strange. She kept asking for money, but she kept avoiding him.

Jim: "I am puzzled! Why you are teasing me, then you make me fall in love, and then you are avoiding me?"

Kiana: "Many men love me and want to be with me? Why should I choose you?" she would answer sarcastically.

Jim: "Why? We made love. You liked me. I thought we clicked well. I have never felt like that in my life before. We can get married if you want? Business is great. Money is not an issue!" He was serious and almost hysterical on the phone.

Kiana: "I have five different men in my life. You are my best man friend, but you are not my boyfriend. The other is my uncle, the third one is my priest, and the other two are helping in different ways." She wouldn't confess she had a boyfriend DP the Don for next 2 years. She would not tell him next 8 years how many abortions she would have by him. She would not confess who the number five was? It took years for Jim to discover, that the 5th man was her final impregnator, her baby father, Mr. Julius. Yes, she was a beautiful manipulator and a liar. Even she would, if she told Jim the truth, he would still love her, but he would not support her financially ...and that was what she really needed him for, nothing else!

The whole mystery around Kiana was peeling off like an old onion. Every layer revealed more and more rotten content underneath.

Jim: "Crystal, can you tell me anything about my future?" he addressed his newfound psychic in Georgetown. The amazing thing was that her office was right above where he and Kiana met a year before and next to Signature store on Wisconsin Ave. NW.

Crystal: "I see you are looking for love. The tarot cards do not lie. There is someone in your life but she is not looking at your direction. There are other men around her, an older man and a younger man. Your business is good, but that is not where your heart is now. You want to travel, but something is holding you here. Something like investment or real estate venture. There is a partner of yours who is not sharing the same interests like yours."

Jim: "I have a question. Can you tell me if my girlfriend is seeing or emotionally involved with someone?"

Crystal: "I see someone who is homeless with nothing but a backpack on his shoulder. He seems obscured, like he is hiding or he is fugitive from the law! He is controlling her mind."

Jim: "Interesting! How about my partner? He seems a nice guy. He gave me the opportunity to develop my own concept, my business."

Crystal: "Remember! Who gives you the most, that is who takes the most! He is not your friend. You should stay away from him! He is the Satan" she somewhat repeated the words of his ex girlfriend Nina (the same lady who was dating the biggest 300 million a year drug dealer in the US history Rayful Edmonds III). Were they independently telling the truth? Was Mansur really using him with black thoughts in his mind? The Prosperity lounge out of business and the lease not signed yet Jim was wondering "what is the hold up." It has been 3 months and no progress and Kiana was hiding in Georgia.

Kiana: "I am going to study in Dorsey, California my graduate years for a doctor" she lied in August, 2004.

Jim: "That is no good! How can we meet and date?" he couldn't believe it.

Kiana: "Distance is not important. If I want to see you, I just jump on a plane." She was right, but she was doing that to see other people, not him.

Jim: "In California you need a car, maybe two to get around. Do you need one?" He blurred, entrapping himself in the question.

Kiana: "Sure, I need one now, my mom's car is falling apart" she lied again. In true she was driving a new Jaguar, but it was a loaner from her boyfriend to pick his 2 kids and him. She really needed her own car and here the damned Jim was coming to the rescue!

Jim: "I bought a smaller and sportier 2 door 300CE, all black. It is in the shop changing transmission and engine. I may give you the 560SL? You know it is all fixed (for $20,000)!"

Kiana: "Thanks! I thought you like the 560 Benz? Why are you so nice?" she was playing naive.

Jim: "When someone loves, he gives. The power is in the giving! I can replace material things. I can't replace you with no one else!"

Kiana: "You don't love me! You think you love me? I can't promise you reciprocity now!" she was telling the truth.

Jim: "My psychic told me you are with a boyfriend right now! Is that true?" he was curious.

Kiana: "That is not your business who I am with? If you play your cards right you can be with me every day, but your love is suffocating me now!" she was talking with low, unemotional voice. "Giving me money does help, car will help, but that is not the way to gain me, mister!" She knew the game. "Give a little, promise nothing, keep in suspense, lie"... (If there is college for that, where it is?)....and it worked for her. Jim was believing her and not believing the psychic, her mother, her roommate, the most important think he did not believed himself how the rational mind (God) will give in to his own loving, stupid heart (Satan)?

The real estate career was promising and something to look forward to. The club was making money. One day in early November Kiana called him.

Jim: "Nice to hear your voice, baby!" he was excited.

Kiana: "I am not your baby! I am your friend. Ok?" ...mean and cold.

Jim: "You are calling. It must be important. What can I do for you?" he was not happy with her voice.

Kiana: "First, congratulation on passing the real estate National Exam! I can see you one day as Walker Realty sign all over Los Angeles or Atlanta?" she was exaggerating as pre curser for next question, seemed like her gang and boyfriend have agreed on new scheme.

Jim: "Ok, what do you need?"

Kiana: "You offered me a car, right! I am coming to pick it up next week and I will stay with you 3 to 4 days. I have to go to Howard University to get some of my documents and reference letters from my professors. Hope your sport car will be ready by then?" she had a plan. For 22 years old she was far ahead in any game and she would have made a great politician!

Jim: "I am sure they will be ready if I pay them the money (it cost me $12,000 repair so far). They offered me another car to buy from them for $8,000, same model 300CE, but champagne color."

Kiana: "You see. God works in mysterious ways. I get the 560SL, you replace it with 300CE. You still will have 2 Benz cars. Bravo!"

Jim: "Kiana! You don't understand. Wealth is given to people who can handle it and multiply it. I do love you and money and cars mean nothing to me. I will be very disappointed if I find one day I wasted all my resources for nothing! I rather help my father and my brother, who is struggling and who love me more than any of you and your hidden boyfriends and uncles and drug dealers in USA. My purpose now is to create a family and to buy a house, not to be used and robbed in a day light!" he meant every word.

Kiana: "Do you know who robs you every day? Mansur. You volunteer to give me a car. I need money but nobody force you to give me any. If I don't get it from you, I have to get it from someone else. If you do not have it or you do not want to give me anything, I can always go to plan B."

Jim: "In your own world you make sense. I will give you anything you want, just stop seeing other people. Spend more time with me, ok!"

Kiana: "It is a process! Maybe one day I will be your wife and you can have me every day. Let us talk more when I come to DC! I am bringing a female friend with me, ok?"

Jim "Whatever makes you happy, Kiana!" he was confused. "She was coming with a friend? That was their time together?"

The emotions of spending time but with the price of one of the best cars Mercedes auto builder ever made and a female companion? If this is not a magnetic field compressed to create gravitational field and quantum energy, then what it is? Jim was about to call everything off, but he was afraid to lose the first love toward a woman he ever felt!

"The option of supporting a liar was better than have no option at all," that what his heart was telling, but his mind was moving in different direction.

"Leave her alone, the bitch is using you Mr. Businessman." His mind (God) was screaming.

From here Jim will refer to those both antagonistic forces, which were the two quarks, W+, W-. Or with those proton, anti-proton colliding. Those two were the Good and Evil, God and Satan, Light (Quantum) Gravitational field and Dark Matter, Destructive Energy.

When Kiana arrived he was happy to see her. He showered her with gifts and cash like it was a wedding preparation. He played along that she was going to California. He gave her the keys for the apartment and the 560SEL Benz. The room with the huge bed was occupied by the two ladies. Her companion was a chubby average height white twenty year old young lady.

Clarissa: "Wow. This is like in a movie "Pretty Woman." Kiana, you are living "the Dream!"

Kiana: "Julia Roberts was playing the hooker. Yes, she pushed the wife to be out, but she was selling her services."

Clarissa: "We are all hookers. We meet different men and we settle for different benefits. You are lucky to have this man." She was excited.

Kiana: "This man owes me. He spat in my face!" rolling her eyes.

Jim: "Hey, we are not discussing how women get stuff. Marriage is the ultimate contract. The women are less giving when they are with a contract. They work harder before marriage," he theorized.

Kiana: "I am only twenty-two. This man wants me to drop everything and be his wife! I am here to get my documents to further my education. He wants to keep me under his control," she was laughing with evil grim.

Jim: "I am here to facilitate your faster growth. The investment I am making is to thwart off any undesirables. The only think I want in exchange for my help is you, Kiana to be honest, ok! I do not have to call your mother, to pay psychics and to call you to oblivion until you say something to cover your actions."

Kiana: "We will talk later about all that. Just to remain you, we are moving with different speeds, Jim."

Jim: "I see that" shaking his head…

Two hours later she joined him in the next room, where he was sleeping in a make shift bed of roll up cushion.

Kiana: "I know you love me, Jim!" she undressed and her long legs wrapped around the sleeping man like the tentacles of the soft and warm octopus. Her vagina was always juicy and ready to enter.

Jim: "I am always ready for you." His 8 inch penis was hard like a rock. He gently kissed her clitoris. Then his long tongue slid between her long vagina lips.

Kiana: "Jim! You always knew how to please a lady! Oh. Oh" she closed her mouth. "We have to be quiet, not to wake up Clarissa. Shhhh!" she turned around and bent over her long body like Cheetah. Her perfect ass was up in the air, almost reaching Jim's chest. Love making was in its best possible. Jim has been waiting for more than nine months for this moment. Yes, he had other offers and encounters almost every day, but nothing like that! Kiana had the natural rhythm. She was better than Svetlana and Amanda and equal to Frida at times.

Jim: "Oh, my God! You can start a 100 years' war with that vagina, Kiana!"

Kiana: "Just fuck it and shut up! Faster!" she almost screamed.

Jim: "Oh, oh! Squeeze, squeeze. Ohhhhhhh!" he exploded. The contraction felt like a mini earthquake inside. Her perfect muscles wanted to hold longer, but after a couple of strong waves the 8 inch torpedo started to collapse.

Kiana: "Damn it! I came too, but you make me greedy. I need some more." She was trembling.

Jim: "I can do it again. You know I love you!" he kissed her on her pear shaped back.

Kiana: "Don't kiss me! Please me!" She turned around to expose her well trimmed hairy vagina. Jim dug in to it with a vengeance. He wanted her to complete her climax to the fullest. He wanted her to be happy. He liked and chewed her clitoris until she finally pushed him away.

Kiana: "Stop! Stop now." She collapsed with final contractions.

Jim: "I hope this is not the last time I am seeing you? You seem to stretch more and more our meeting lapses." .... And it was the last time they had real sex. ...

The day Kiana left was a day of false good bye and "I will see you soon." The white lady was surprised to see the day time interaction of Kiana with Jim.

Clarissa: "Kiana, you are killing this man! Why are you acting like he is nobody to you? He has been very hospitable and giving to you. I have never seen anyone in your life being even close to what he is doing here?"

Kiana: "Shut up! He spat in my face! He is not my boyfriend. He is what I call a "Special friend."

Clarissa: "I will take a spit from anyone who gives me a car, $3,000.00 dollars cash and gifts," she was envious and serious.

Jim just received a hug from Kiana, before the car and those two rotten squanderers took off for California. That was their version.

Next day Jim registered his newly repaired 300CE black Benz. He also registered the 300CE champagne color Benz. The owners at Malibu Cars in Kensington were so anxious to get rid of it they practically gave it to Jim on his word to buy it from them for 8,000 dollars. Again, it was his reputation which was preceding him. He had just spent $20,000 in rebuilding the 560SEL; he spent 13,000 on repairing the black 300CE. Yes, he needed to get rid of his 300SD turbo diesel Benz and to make room for the champagne 300CE. Probably, sounded a bit complicated but he also had 533i BMW and an old Ford E350 van parked on an abandoned parking lot nearby, where were about to build new condominiums on 10th and X Street, NW.

Nikias: "Hey Jim! How is your lease coming?" his lawyer was concerned.

Jim: "We are working on it. The zoning change is approved. The landlord will not bulge on reducing rent yet." He was more concerned with Kiana than expanding to some other buildings. That burning sensation called, "Love" he thought he felt, was consuming him entirely. He did not need more money, he needed more love interaction.

November 17th, 2004 the phone rang. It was Georgia (478) area code number.

Insurance: "This is Geico insurance. You had an accident on Nov. 15th at Macon County, Georgia. We need your phone statement." They sounded robotic.

Jim: "What accident?" He was surprised.

Insurance: "A Mercedes with tugs numbers DX 3256, issued by DC was in collision with a Honda on this day. The Benz was black color and had rear damage. The other car had front damage. The driver's name was Kiana Hines."

Jim: "Oh. That was my girlfriend? She drives my other car. She supposed to change tags and to get a new title on her name?"

Insurance: "If she drove it on weekend, we have different policy and we will not change your policy? If there are more than three days we need to impose penalties!" in a robotic voice.

Jim: "Oh, it was just for the weekend!" they knew he was lying.

Insurance: "We will cover the damage of the other car, Honda, but not on yours. You have "no fault" insurance, ok?"

Jim: "That is ok. Let me call her."

Insurance: "Next time put her in your insurance as co driver!"

Jim called and called Kiana. She wouldn't answer at all. Matter of fact her phone had a voice recorder, "the number you have called is disconnected." Wow! He felt used… The next thing crossed his mind was to call her mother. She would not answer her phone either. She was "drunk all the time" according to Kiana's information.

The car was supposed to unite them, the gifts, and the cash. It seemed that was working in the total opposite direction. The negative curvature (with two parallel geodesic space-time lines) was working from the beginning separating them and if it was not the material need, Kiana, would have left him alone the first week they had met. Jim should have been lucky she was still around a year and a half after their first encounter. He was naive to believe she could have been more serious with him. The assurance by the psychic was not enough. He thought of hiring a private investigator in Georgia.

Investigator: "Berman services! How can I help you?" the voice sounded like a police department dispatcher.

Jim: "I need information on someone in your area. I want to know what I need to do to retain your services."

Berman: "First, I need any information on the person you are searching for? That will be the name, social security, address, license plates of vehicle she drives? Then I will quote your cost!" robotic voice.

Jim: "Sure. I have all that." He quickly spelled out the details.

Berman: "This will be 500 dollars a week. We need you to transfer the funds to our Bank of America. Once the transaction is confirmed, we will start the investigation. Every Monday we will e mail you a report with our discoveries. If any further investigation is needed, we will ask you to send another 500 dollars a week, until your full satisfaction."

Jim: "Great. I may need you to check on my Benz and act like you are investigating the car damage. From there we can find where she lives and to trace her activities."

Berman: "Yes, sir! Here is the routing number to our account."

The report came a week later. Investigator Berman was good at his work. He was able to pull out a lot of private information which only the police officers can do or FBI agents.

Berman: "I was able to find her and interview her. She was apprehensive, but she gave me her driver's license and I took pictures of her car... nothing major in damage. That car is a beauty, my favorite at this vintage..."

Jim: "I know. I saw it in the movie "Coming to America" with Eddie Murphy and Arsenio Hall. I fell in love with those cars since."

Berman: "I did follow her around. She did not date any man. She went to the Billiards Room one time, but she was not socializing with anyone. She kept looking toward the door. She seemed paranoid."

Jim: "Thanks! I will call you again if I need your services."

Jim was disappointed in giving his car to a liar. He knew she was in Georgia. He just needed confirmation. Seemed like Kiana was buying time? What for? It will take years to find the reasons why, but at this time he was satisfied that she had no visible boyfriend and she was nearby. But why did she change her phone number? The confusion was creating a perfect storm. That was pleasure of being the giving living Saint, (quantum-light, matter) and the angry anti-Saint (quantum, black light, anti-matter). The quanta bursts of love were quickly imploding in mini black holes. The White Magic was converting to Black Magic. Something was brewing in this super brain and TIH was to start, from his refined use of his sub consciousness, the next Mega Destruction! It will last eight years (2004 to 2012).

Jim: "I know TIH (God... my sub consciousness) blew up the Towers. Now what is the next manifestation of my protector?"

The answer arrived soon…and it was not good.

At last week of November of 2004 a very aggressive Pimp arrived at Randevu lounge.

Vicky: "Hey, we heard about you in New York!" She was a mixed race, voluptuous and beautiful for any race. "This is my Daddy Candy man." She showed him a tall, evil and ugly looking man, mid 20s age.

Candy Man: "Yo, I am from New York. I like your joint. I see you have a diversified crowd here. We can make a lot of money here."

Jim: "I am ok. You make your money, I make mine. There is no "we," here, ok?" He sensed the bad vibe coming from him.

Vicky: "My man does not know much about DC. Someone has to show him around. He is a bit hard headed."

Jim: "So, am I. It took me a decade to figure out this city."

Vicky: "Do you like me?" she was the better part of the couple of strange characters.

Jim: "Sure, but are you implying sex?" He looked around for her Daddy. Candy Man disappeared going down the stairs, holding drink in his hand.

Jim: "I am a man. I should like you and desire you, but I am in emotional situation. I am not sure I want to talk about it now."

Vicky: "I hear that one has to go through your "Test," to work from here. That's what the ladies at the bar were talking to me earlier about."

Jim: "Do not listen to anyone. Some of them offered me, "the Test." That means they wanted to have sex with me. I used to accept that earlier, that was before I met my girlfriend. Now I have to decline you. Sorry!"

Vicky: "I also heard that "The test," verify that the lady is not a cop!"

Jim: "There are many ways to find out who is a cop or not? We get info from the pimps, from the interaction with johns, from sharing the beat with other hookers. The bar has much more limitations that the world outside. I can have sex with you, but that will not help my emotional situation. It will be only sex."

Vicky: "That is fine. I just want you to accept me at the bar. I am not the police!" she undressed and her young, perfect body was amazing.

Jim: "They should legalize the oldest profession. All beautiful women should never be married. The ugly ones may need to get married." Jim unzipped fast and vigorously torpedoed her with his long overdue erection. The sex was fast, there was not even kissing or talking. Both took it as a Randevu's initiation. It was any straight man's dream to have sex with young, willing and beautiful ladies without negotiation and relationship building up to sex.

Jim: "Viva la courtesan!" He exclaimed in a rhythmic motion. "One day I will build a monument dedicated to the beautiful Courtesan he mentioned as he was wiping off his cum splashed all over her fine and round ass. As he finished with her he headed toward the door below, where he overheard an argument.

Candy Man: "This cracker is insane."

White man: "He took money from me, saying it is cover charge to enter the club and for guaranteed sex with a lady. He says he is the owner of the joint."

Jim: "I am the owner. Can I help you?" he pushed away the Candy Man.

Jim: "What are you doing? Why do you ask for a cover charge? I never charge cover and I don't guarantee sex to anyone! You will bring the cops on me with this kind of bullshit talk! Take your lady and take a week off. Then come back and we will talk!"

Candy man: "Yo, my girl needs that spot. I will come back in a week, but you are embarrassing me. After all, my chick gave you some ass for free!"

Jim: "I never pay for sex. It was her idea. She can stay if she wants, but you take a week off now, ok?"

Candy Man: "Cool! I have other businesses. I am not pressed for your raggedy joint. Let me think about it." He walked away with bad attitude. Vicky followed him reluctantly.

Jim: "What an odd couple?" He was angry about the owner/imposter, but he was happy to initiate his girlfriend/hooker to be! That was the nature of the bar business. Always up and down. For some who observe the club life, it seems glamorous and enticing.

We see great looking women and fancy cars and the paparazzi taking pictures, then the rich men, the champagne bottles, the provocative dancing. Everything seems like a paradise for sex, drugs, and mafia faces.

Nothing in reality is even close. The small lounge was miniature representation of the bigger picture. There were some drug dealers, but nothing to catch the eye of the law. The girls were active in getting tricks, but that was no different than what was going in his rival clubs.

The biggest club Cloud, was infamous with their 4th floor, which was supposed to be residential. One could pick any girl at the club and spend the night there and use the 4th floor as a hotel room, where cocaine was easily available as soap and towels, around the Jacuzzi. At The Paparazzi, another popular club, the reserved tables (at $2,000 minimum) would include 250 dollars waitress/hookers. So, Mr. Dodson was not only club impresario, but also a pimp and cocaine dealer. He would invite all strippers from Arthur's, from Camelot, and from Fuego to entertain his clients.

The DC government was protecting the club Cloud. The Mayor then, Philip Gordin and his lawyer, both had personal interest in that club and they delayed and deflected any law suits against the club. One night, a twenty year old female patron ran over a MD trooper and she killed him on I-295. The plaintiff lawyer against the club was Joel Baum, who was also representing Sodom (Rob Howard's/Mr. Bender) club. He was suing the club for 50 million. Later on they would do an out of court settlement and the club would change name to club, Ballers. That would be a temporary remedy because they kept the same promoters, who were bringing the same suburban crowd.

The other rival at Fusion and Phantom would not be more fortunate. He would buy a five million dollar house with a two million down payment. The owner of the home would sue him for nonpayment of the promised three million dollars. That would attract the attention of IRS who would raid his Potomac home and his two clubs. Mr. Rogbin, a native from Ivory Coast, would be detained and never released and eventually deported to his native country. He would hire the same attorney for Wesley Snipes, Monica Lewinsky and Michael Wick. His name is Brut Maloney. Every case he would take would be lost.

Jim: "Why do people with money think that money will work for them to their benefit? Don't they know the algorithm includes personality and character, but excludes the factor money?"

God: "Yes, but only the quantum Turing machine would answer your question with positive answer."

Jim: "They live in physical reality. I don't. And that will give me the most suitable answer. I accept the punishment and the rewards equally. I believe in my survival (financial, physical, emotional, and mental). It is like jumping with a faulty parachute, but surviving to tell the story!

"Survival" is the answer in the quantum algorithm."

The week passed and Vicky was working the crowd of men at the bar, looking for conversation, confessions, role play, sex, or just to get drunk. She became as good as the regulars "veteran" hookers. The mix of normal drinking ladies and ladies of the night sometime was indistinguishable.

December 7th, was another day at the bar. Jim drove to work his newly registered two-door sport coupe 300CE Champagne Benz. The customers were happy. He was smoking a great cigar and he was fixing drinks from time to time.

Candy Man: "Hey Jim! I have an offer for you. I will come at the bar and we can be friends again! To show you my good intentions I will let you fuck my bitch Vicky again and it is free." He got the devilish look again.

Jim: "Hey Man! I don't make friends with any customers. I make good customers, only." He almost laughed.

Candy Man: "As you wish! Give me a drink, I am out!" He took a shot of Belvedere vodka and ran toward the street.

Jim: "Vicky, your man seems that he couldn't stay indoors much?"

Vicky: "Do you want to fuck or not? I feel here like a peace maker between the two of you!" She almost cried.

Jim: "You are the best looking ambassador I ever have met here!"

Vicky: "I made a lot of money at your bar last week! I owe you a big favor! And I kind of like you. If I did not have my boyfriend with me I would take you as permanent!"

Jim: "Really?" Both they were undressing in the private room.

Her young breasts were touching Jim's bear chest and she was kissing his neck, while she was unzipping his bulging pants and he was grabbing her zero fat ass, slipping her pink panties down; some Victoria Secrets latest invention.

Jim: "My love and pain is in Georgia. You really can make a great mistress, but I do love her, sorry!"

Vicky: "The police do not bother you here… You seem comfortable taking your pictures in the private room…"

Jim: "I have been here six years and nobody bothered me much. Actually they send me, "ladies from the street" to the bar. Go figure!"

Suddenly the "garage" style door shook violently. Lora was pounding on it.

Lora: "Hey Jim! Open up, now!" Jim stopped the great sex they started and both were putting their clothes on. "We will continue later, sorry!" He told the naked beauty.

Vicky: "No more freebees buddy!" She laughed a bit confused and disappointed to stop the great sex they couldn't finish.

Jim: "What it is now?"

Lora: "There is fight at the door the last 10 minutes. Candy Man is charging our regulars cover charge at the door and they called me on the phone. He would not let them in without paying 20 dollars."

Jim: "Again?" He waved at Scott, a short white athletic built great regular customer at the door.

Scott: "Thank you! Who is this guy? Is he your new partner? He is asking for money just to enter. He says there are ladies, here to provide sex. You know I am not here to have sex. You know I am married." He laughed and pointed at Candy man.

Jim: "I told you not to bother my customers, Candy Man! How many did you stop from coming? I see yours plan is a diversion. While I am with Vicky you work the door! Now, both of you must leave. Do not come back here again, ever!"

Candy Man: "Yo, I was security in New York. We do that there all the time. Why are you "sweating" me, man?" He got very close to Jim.

Vicky: "I told you not to play with this man's business, Daddy." She jumped between both men, who were ready to fight. "I am tired of your games."

Jim: "DC is small city and you cannot do that to our customers. You are lucky we don't have a door man here."

Candy Man: "I will punish you if you kick me out of your club again, man!" He screamed while walking away.

Jim: "That is jail talk! Been there, heard that! Bye" he pushed Scott inside the door. "Let's go, buddy." Both men walked up to second floor.

Lora: "I told you those two were bad news. Each of the guys paid him ten dollars. They negotiated it down." She pointed toward two Spanish guys, who were holding coronas beers in their hands.

Jim: "Amigos, esta servesa es gratis! Sorry!"

Two Spanish guys: "Si, si…" They all laughed.

At 1.45 am Jim received a phone call.

Angel: "Jim, someone is breaking the widows of your car. Hurry up!" She was one of his favorite customers. She never caused him any problems so far. Her story was that she was making 475,000 dollars a year! Wow. It was great for night job as a courtesan/hooker. And she was not paying any taxes! In a letter to US attorney Walter Adams later on Jim would ask "Why the gun buying in DC is legal, but not the prostitution?"

Jim: "Do you know what he looks like?" She immediately described Candy Man. He was not surprised.

Jim: "Thank you, Angel!"

Jim went to his car parked next to Washington Post newspaper building. All tires were slashed except one. Then the passenger door was dented and the door window was with marks of a brick. Mercedes windows are almost bullet proof. Brick is not the best tool to damage them. Jim called a tow truck. They were really surprised.

Tow truck driver: "Man, somebody did not like your ass," as he was continuing to hook up the front tires on flat bed truck. He was shaking his head.

Jim: "I am not calling the police. It is one of my supposed to be customers, who I threw out of the bar earlier."

Tow truck driver: "That is completely different approach than anybody I know. Most people would make a police report, and then the insurance would pay for the damages." He drove Jim to 4th street and Florida Ave, which was open 24 hours. Jim paid him and thirty minutes later he was driving back to the club with four almost new tires. He acutely laughed at this poor man. Then he thought of Vicky and he felt sorry for her. He was grateful for the distraction from cheating Kiana. Then he remembered Contessa's slogan "Live the Life, live the Life, Jim." Next two weeks he was busy with selling the Van, getting rid of the diesel Benz 300SD. He needed the parking space and he sold the 300SD for $150!

December 26, 2004 arrived as usual. The difference was that day was Jim's birthday. He waited for Kiana to call him. He felt really bad. He asked the bartender to give him seven Patron shots. He fell asleep on the couch. Toward 11 pm he decided to head on home. The apartment he was residing was three blocks away. He had a splitting headache. He took two Advil tablets and mechanically he turned the TV set. The news channel flashed the local bad news first.

Anchorwoman: "Tonight two people were shot to death in Forestville, MD. The couple, a man and a woman were found in black late model Toyota with New York license plates. Police found drugs paraphernalia and numerous condoms. The street names they used were Candy Man and Vicky, a 711 clerk testified to the police."

Jim: "What? This is the man who slashed my tires and who damaged my Champagne Benz 300CE! But why was Vicky killed, also?" He would learn later God does not recognize just individuals as targets, TIH would destroy everything and everyone associated with that person. To simplify the area of destruction on Earth they will be called "Zip Code targets."

His thoughts were replaced with new emotions from the viewing of the next images.

Anchorwoman: "Around the world news. Giant tsunami hit unexpectedly the Indonesia coast and Philippines coast. Approximately 300,000 people are affected and missing. The cause was the biggest earthquake in 40 years in Indian Ocean."

Jim sobered up. Wow and all of this happening on my birthday.

Jim: "Thank you, Kiana! If you made this call those people maybe still alive?" he couldn't agree with his mind powers. Why should other people in the world suffer from the cowardness of one and from the unreciprocated love of another?

The destruction was the inability to communicate in the wormhole between two controversial minds. The negative curvature was obvious, but the anti-gravitational wave was able to open the earth and to lift the oceans. Destruction is anti-mater, anti reality, black light. Not being prepared for it caused lost of everything, including life. The irony was that it hit one of the highest populated areas of Muslim followers. They were the ones cheering the 9/11 tragedy in USA, but now they needed help. Who helped them the most out of all countries in the world? It was the USA. Jim was aware that his sub consciousness could send messages with specific wave lengths to the end of the universe, and beyond to the Cosmos. He was not aware it can trigger earthquakes, hurricanes, tsunami and floods on the Indian or Pacific coasts at this fatal day and later on. He just remembered the Towers. Was he the one to trigger the last push and to succeed in their destruction after he got mad at Amanda?

He remembered his defection, the speechless séance which predicted it with 100% accuracy! Then the betrayal of Bellini's Restaurant partners, the death of Contessa, the mind games with the police and with ABC Board, with the next door, Prosperity, restaurant. He would have been great leader if he had some earth upbringing with real mother and father, with a happy home and normal earth friends. Seemed all the cards were stacked against him to lose, but he was doing the opposite, Jim was wining in a negative way.

The New Year 2005 was approaching and the year of 2004 was fading away. If anything positive to think about was that his neighbor's bar competition, since 1998, was gone twice in the past six years. He got his real estate license, but he lost his favorite 560SEL Benz to a liar. He had sporadic encounters with beautiful ladies like Samantha and Vicky but for some reason he couldn't hold on to them. They were like fast cheetahs, beautiful to watch, but impossible to hold on to and to possess. Both Samantha and Vicky were perfect and wild street ladies. Kiana was not, but she acted just like them - fast, great sex, disappearing.

Jim: "Do I make those people the way I want them to be and because it is a fantasy, they can't be held onto permanently," he thought.

"But why do 75 percent of them get married and stay married and they have children and they buy houses? Those people go to baby showers, to picnics, to wars, to each other funerals. It is like a huge social club where everything it is cozily arranged. Their kids would go to public or private schools. Some would become presidents, other prisoners ...in between it will be the rat race of too busy to read and think democrats and knowing too much and having too much money, republicans. The twist is when democrats become rich and republicans become poor. It becomes an antithesis of two societies. The democracy has many faces and colors, but the quantum reality and its antithesis have only two states of description, "Light" and "no-Light." One to outsmart the quantum mind needs to move with unpredictable speeds much higher than measurable light speed.

There are two states of invisibility, one which moves with speed too fast to be noticed, no matter of the size of the moving object (rocket, vehicle, energy). Second, the size is too small to be seen. The energy can be seen as a manifestation of results of it, but not seen visibly with the normal eye or with telescope. For example, we see the trees twist and waves rising but what make them do that? Yes, the air gas density, but in front of our eyes it is invisible. To detect the quantum wave and results we may compare it to imploding the magnetic fields into a black hole. We can't see the black hole but we can see the result of it in the form of radiation of X rays which when going through gas does create radiation and does create solar winds and increases the temperature of the body and then the person glows. This may be close to human or animal sacrificing visual effects. Fear of death creates radiating gas and the spirit becomes visible temporarily (no more than 40 days). Then if the ozone layer is intact, then the soul will reincarnate in newborn vertebrate (animal, human). Then the glow will stop once inside the newly found body or just it will wander as lost spirit forever between earth and ozone layer of atmosphere...in ghost's forms.

New Year day of 2005 at 1 am Kiana called.

Jim: "Hello! Who is this?" he checked on the private status of his incoming caller ID.

Kiana: "Happy New Year and belated birthday! You can't recognize me?" she acted upset.

Jim: "Happy New Year, Kiana! Why are you calling so late?"

Kiana: "Late? I could have not called you at all!" She sounded as always threatening. Jim remembered her mother's warning; "Kiana is a bad seed. She thinks she is mafia."

Jim: "Did you see the news on my birthday? 300,000 people perished because of you!"

Kiana: "Because of me? What did I do?" she was acting defensive.

Jim: "Kiana! You know I do love you like no one else! I got angry and got drunk for the first time on Dec. 26. 2004. When I went home I saw the news. Two people I threw out of my club and who slashed my champagne Benz tires were shot to death, and around Indian Ocean the poor people lost property and life because you did not call me!"

Kiana: "I heard of psychic powers, but I don't think a human can do that alone just by being angry!"

Jim: "I am wondering myself of too many events in my life which are related to similar incidents! I remember the World Trade Towers, my defection, working on a billionaire man's Yacht, owner of oldest Restaurant in DC, owner of oldest Club in DC, all that is not normal!"

Kiana: "Where do you see the link? That maybe just bunch of coincidences?"

Jim: "I see it in the similarity of horrible end of people who disrespected me!" he exhaled on the phone.

Kiana: "What happened to other people?" she was in disbelief.

Jim: "Mr. Smith died from AIDS, the owners of Bellini's lost their two restaurants, the ABRA had to relocate twice in last five years, downsizing."

Kiana: "I think you create and then you destroy anybody you meet!"

Jim: "I never destroyed Tavit and my family! Basically I never met anyone around the Indian Ocean, who did wrong things to me; and I navigated through it many times. The Invisible Hand/God/my sub consciousness do all that creation and destruction, ok!"

Kiana: "Sometimes I wonder what to think of you? You seem very unstable!" she sounded concerned.

Jim: "I am in a country where being a foreigner is not "chic" any more. One has to come up with a bunch of new tricks everyday to keep up with the government or to be ahead of the game! I am capable of doing that, but I need emotional exchange with someone."

Kiana: "You need love, buddy! I can't give you that. That is why I don't call you much."

Jim: "You are an enigma for me! Maybe one day you will appreciate my love to you?"

Kiana: "I think you are addicted to me, obsessed. People who love behave differently. They do not kill people." She laughed.

Jim: "I did not kill anyone. God follows the vibes of people who do not do right by him or who are mean to me! You do badly; you will be punished by God!"

Kiana: "You see why I am not calling you? You have always something good and something bad to say!" She hung up.

Jim: "Damn it!" he wanted to finish with some positive results. He wanted to ask her about the car accident, about California lies ...and more...

After New Year the business at Randevu lounge was booming. The landlords changed hands to new ones, who were more flexible and willing to negotiate. The new lease was signed on May 13th, 2005. It was an eight year lease till 2013. Finally the expansion which Mansur and Jim were looking for was coming to fruition!

Nikias: "Jim, you are doing it again! You are expanding! Salute!"

Jim: "Hey! You should know me by now. Time is my best friend. I am very patient and persistent."

Nikias: "God is on your side! Mr. Rogbin was not that fortunate. They raided his house in Potomac and they closed his clubs Fusion and Phantom. Mr. Dodson changed venues at Cloud" night club. Now it is Ballers club. A lot of weird stuff is going in DC and ABRA has a lot to do with it."

Jim: "We need to change the hours of operation to the full extent that the liquor law allows. We need entertainment license. The zoning now is changed to one address."

Nikias: "Are you keeping the same crowd? Police think you are running a whore house?" he would never change his mantra about the undesirable customers.

Jim: "I have been talking to the police. I did ask them to post a sign of restrictions at the liquor establishment? They are so afraid of law suits; they would never post something like that. If I call the police, they either do not show up, or when they show up they take the criminal side."

Nikias: "Take names, badge numbers, police reports numbers. I am your lawyer. You pay too much money in taxes and improvements not to be represented."

Jim: "True! I feel sometimes I am all alone on this damn street. Homeless people laugh at me when the police come. My only power is in the club."

Suddenly Kiana called.

Jim: "It had been 5 months this time. Do you remember me?" he was not happy.

Kiana: "I can also hang up. How are you, Jim Walker?" She sounded sarcastic.

Jim: "Hmmm! I want to tell you the good news, but you do not sound right!" he paused. The perfect storm was brewing in him. He was happy to hear her voice, but seemed she had an agenda, as always.

Kiana: "My transmission failed. I need either a new car or transmission?" She was not loving, kissing nor, missing him like lovers do.

Jim: "You can't find a similar car even with 25,000 cash in your pocket. I suggest you fix the transmission. I will drop 3,000 dollars in your Wachovia account. Give me thirty minutes to get there."

Kiana: "I know you are a good man. Now tell me some of your good news? Then I will tell you my good news."

Jim: "Oh ...We are expanding to the next building. It will take a lot of money, somewhere in quarter million."

Kiana: "Great! Sign a legal contract with Mansur, so he will not screw you out of your money."

Jim: "Ok. What is your good news?" they both softened up.

Kiana: "I am coming back to DC to grad school." She said it initiating another lie.

Jim: "When?" he was excited.

Kiana: "I will be there in August. I will need furniture, car, and cash."

Jim: "You know I love you. All your wishes will be granted. You have to change your attitude toward me. Ok?" He thought he was demanding positive answer.

Kiana: "You want answers I cannot give you. We have a whole life ahead. Don't pressure me!" The answers of that liar were almost predictable.

Kiana: "This man is asking me to tell him words he wants to hear? I am not in love with him. He basically is making me lie. He wants to live in some fantasy world. I will lie but it will cost him dearly." She thought.

Kiana: "I need two phones also. My mother's phone is dead and I need to talk to her." She was really bluffing. The second phone was for her boyfriend "DP, the Don."

A week after that call Mansur called Jim for a meeting.

Mansur: "We need to start construction soon. I don't have much money to spare now. Basically you will benefit much more by opening three floors with bar on each floor. I will just have more space on the first floor."

Jim: "I do not mind spending money on this project as long as we have been partners concerning this lease. Can you sign a contract with me?"

Mansur: "My brother! We are not from the USA. We don't need a contract. Trust my word. As long I am here you will be here. We are from the Mediterranean. Ok?"

Jim: "My lawyer would not approve with just a handshake agreement." He became quite skeptical.

Mansur: "If something happens that we have to go our separate ways, you can sell your part of the business, your bar investment! Ok?" He almost became aggressive. There was a streak of subliminal gangsterism in Mansur, which was well masqueraded.

Jim: "I will take your word, but we have to make arrangements on how to pay the contractors and the rent at the same time?" he sensed the entrapment, but he had no other options. The cash reserves in the bank were low (around 50,000 dollars). He decided to choose "pay as you go" method. Eventually he will either take over Mansur's business or he will sell his share in the three bars investment?

Jim: "I can give you $4,000 to fix the first floor, and $1,000 dollars to fix the electrical wiring between both buildings." This was the beginning of a 200,000 dollar investment. The ratio of investment between Mansur and Jim was 1/3rd to 2/3rd. The caveat was that Jim was giving his partner either cash or check. Mansur would deposit it to his bank account. Then he would use the total funds as his own. Later on he would say that Jim had not invested anything here, but that is later subject to talk about.

The walls were all torn down, so was the original stairway of Mike's which has been there for 150 years. They moved it to build a new stairway to the right at the new adjusted building/at the old Sally's/ Starlight/Prosperity 1428 X Street address. The amazing thing was that Prosperity owners demolished everything before they left (no bars, no kitchen, no toilets were left standing). Jim and Mansur found an empty shell when they opened the door to expand.

To prevent Mansur's customers to go to the third floor Jim built many gates sectioning the new building in some strange labyrinth, even architect Daedalus to king Minos of Crete would be puzzled by. He separated the food section from bar side by a huge metal gate. He built frames around the back entrance to second floor, that way his customers from the second floor could use the second floor bathrooms without going to Mansur's food section on first floor. Then he built gates on second floor preventing Mansur's customers from entering his bar area during day time hours.

Mansur: "How about if I want to use the second and third floors for food services?" he had a point but mostly was to challenge Jim, not because he really needed the space.

Jim: "This fucker is slowing my grand opening down" he thought.

Jim: "We are going to have gates on the second and third floors. That will allow the flow to all the floors without my liquor being stolen by the day crowd." He said to his weird and crooked partner.

Mansur: "I hope we can make that business profitable once we complete the renovation?" He sounded phony optimistic.

Jim: "Yes, with my money in construction?" He thought, but he envisioned more success than failure. "No one enters the battle field to lose."

A lot of construction was done the next few months. Mansur recommended his nephew's construction company Agile. The timing couldn't be worse for Jim. The nephew was a contractor who was collecting numbers from electricians, plumbers and carpenters. Then he would go to new and old business alike to promote his scheme. He would take money in thousands and he would not deliver the performance.

Jim: "I need this work done by November 1st, 2005." He approved the estimated numbers and they both signed the contract.

Nephew: "I need $3,000 in cash now, $5,000 in check within a week and before completion pay in full."

Jim: "No problem." He had $25,000 in each of his accounts, business and personal. That was at the beginning of August.

Kiana was awfully quiet. While the construction was moving ahead Jim emotions were mixed. She was hiding obviously.

Jim: "I need to find out what she is doing?" He was heading to Georgetown. He wanted to see his world famous psychic Crystal, but she moved. He strolled down the M street and he came across one of the old signs for Miss Zamora, the psychic. It was next door to Pino's Italian restaurant. He was frequent customer to that restaurant and he befriended the owner Geof.

Here, one time, in March 2004 Jim and Kiana had a heated conversation about Lora's involvement in the bar operation. That was a huge difference than in year 2003. That was when they were on same page, when they had the best sex, when they were traveling to Miami South Beach like going to next city of Baltimore. The mystery was to be revealed soon. It was like a giant puzzle which Kiana would never confess, but Jim would give his heart and soul to know. Who was behind that puzzle? Was his thirst for love that drove him to the extreme search of the truth? He felt at times like a dying man who wanted to hear what the answer was before closing his eyes for the last time!

In spiritual world Jim knew who the "soul puppeteers" were in play. He felt that Kiana was possessed by her dead father's spirit. He sensed no normal person in the world could be that emotionally cruel to him! Kiana was the devil in disguise. She was able to give him the best sex, but she was destroying his fortune, his finances, his emotional world, his health. The only opposing force to Kiana's evil wrath of destruction was Jim's spiritual protection.

Loretta, his mother was always with him in spirit. Her untimely death from the truck accident in 1958 was in some mysterious way helping him through her reincarnation in him. That was definitely unnecessary human sacrificing to advance the next life (Jim's) to deity dimensions. In a normal life the family should stick together, build a home, help each other till everyone prosper and dies in natural way. In Jim's and Kiana's case, the similarity was only that they both lost parents. The disadvantage for Kiana was that her father's spirit came to help her at very late age of sixteen! At this age the vertebrate/spine was inflexible and only the mental part is open to manipulate the reality and there was total a disconnection from the enjoying the emotional benefits of love, respect and basic human dignity. The result was that Kiana was one walking evil, who Jim unfortunately crossed roads with. He was emotional toward her, obviously. She accused him that it was "all about sex." Jim couldn't be spending 250,000 dollars on sex, if he got it only three times in five or more years! Common God, you can't be that cruel (shall we address it as subconscious mind/The Invisible Hand, this time acting as Satan…). Who was the one to really benefit from her "generosity sex"? The secret was to be disclosed within next three months, but with what price to pay?

After the hired private investigator and all calls to Kiana's mom, breaking Kiana's code for her voice messages and also the breaking of her boyfriend code later, Jim was still wondering what truly, Kiana doing?

Miss Zamora Jr.: "Hello, young man! You need an advice?" she seemed genuine and friendly, but that was so far from the truth. Jim needed someone to talk to. He could have chosen a shrink for much less cost.

Jim: "I am here to find the truth! I have seen your sign for years on M street. I hope you are a good psychic?" He exhaled finally.

Miss Zamora Jr.: "I am the best ever, but I am not cheap!" she smiled with confidence. Jim liked that.

Jim: "Maybe finally someone can help me, for real!" he shrugged and smiled. He felt the sales technique of being taken, but he thought he could afford any exaggerated comment as long the result he wishes is achieved. It was like some people want to get married, but leave themselves exposed to opportunists with complete different agendas...

Miss Zamora Jr.: "What is the problem? I am a Christian follower and I believe in helping everyone. Are you religious?" She was pointing towards a huge Bible in the middle of her office like desk. Jim felt like he was in some corporate office, where the flags were replaced with any kind of psychic paraphernalia. He also noticed a credit card terminal behind the desk. "It is not wireless, like mine, hmm..." passed through his mind…

Jim: "I see you are all equipped here" he pointed toward the credit card machine. "Any way… my question is about my lady friend. I cannot figure her out?" he almost cried. "And I have some other questions" he continued with a bit stronger voice.

Miss Zamora Jr.: "I have different ways to give you the answers. One is palm reading; the other is tarot cards reading." She was getting in position to make her move and her body language was showing it.

Jim: "I don't mind your ways of doing anything. I just want the truth." Now he was getting ready to negotiate.

Miss Zamora Jr.: "I will give you the best reading of your life! You will come to see me and to thank me after that again and again!" she was really confident. At age thirty-five she was all about business. She was good looking. A medium height, she would of been a great candidate for any man for a girlfriend or wife, but Jim did not put too much thought into her looks; he needed her knowledge in the spiritual world.

Jim: "I can handle any requests. Please, don't charge a million!" he was asking for "it." ….And she delivered "it."

Miss Zamora Jr.: "I require $5,000 down payment now. It depends on how long you will need my services; I will require 5,000.00 dollars more, later.

I can give you references of some of my satisfied clients, but not details, if you wish?"

Jim: "Everyone has great references. Reminds me of good doctors, who brag about the successful surgeries, but never talk about how many people died on the surgeon's table." He almost laughed at her price and confidence, but he kept that small talk thought for himself...

Jim: "Here is my credit card! Let's get down to business." Seemed they both agreed and they were both happy.

Miss Zamora Jr.: "I will read both your hands and the cards. I can't guarantee you instant results but I can rearrange some of the circumstances around you. I want to stop that emotional self destruction you both are doing to each other. Let see what your situation is?" She handed the tarot cards and ask Jim to split them three ways. Then she looked at his palm.

Miss Zamora Jr.: "Wow. We are in the same field! I wonder why you are even here?" she almost jumped up in her seat. "You are very high in spiritual world. You are probably stronger than anyone I have seen in my entire career! Let look at the cards also." She pulled the cut deck of cards and started to analyze them. She was similar to Crystal in reading them. Seemed they went to the same school, but, why she placed the bar so high, at such a price?

Jim: "Do you see any hope for me and Kiana?" He wanted something positive and he wanted it bad.

Miss Zamora Jr.: "Stop worrying. She is coming here soon. She is bringing some problems with her, something or somebody from her past is following her and she can't get rid of it. It is something like a bad spell." She pulled more cards out.

Jim: "I think her father's death affected her and she has poor judgment when it comes to who her friends are? What do you see?" puzzled of her body language and comments, surprised that she held his hand still.

Miss Zamora Jr.: "This guy controls her. It is not a spirit. It is a real person. He may be dangerous. She is the one who is choosing him over you. You did something wrong to her, did you?" it sounded like accusation.

Jim: "Yeah! I spat in her face once." He confessed.

Miss Zamora Jr.: "You know young ladies perceive reality different than experienced older men. You pushed her in some opportunist's hands."

Jim: "I wanted to teach her a lesson to respect me." He exhaled.

Miss Zamora Jr.: "You scared her away, mister!" She was right.

Jim: "Ok. She is coming back. Is she coming back to live with me?"

Miss Zamora Jr.: "Yes! There is only one condition. Once the airplane is over water I need to cast a spell, so she can be a different person this time, more to your liking, ok?" The reading was almost over.

Jim: "I have one more question. What about my business expansion and what about my partner? Do you see anything there?" He wanted to know more about his money now.

Miss Zamora Jr.: "Your partner is looking the other way. He does not have your interest at all. He is manipulating you."

Jim: "Ok. That is similar to what Crystal told me, the other psychic nearby." He mumbled.

Miss Zamora Jr.: "What? Why are you coming to me? I don't like someone else's clients! You should go back to her. Ok? Mixing psychics is bad luck for you and for us. We are not doctors who you ask for second opinions!" She almost walked him to the door.

Jim: "Oh that was a year ago. She moved and I needed an answer now. Then I came here." He almost saw the 5,000 dollars disappearing fast with no result.

Miss Zamora Jr.: "I will burn candles for you. I will go to church. We have to work together on this project. I will read the Bible, and then I pray for my clients. She is doing sinful things too. She is young. You, being much older than her, you should calm dawn and be patient. Young ladies like to be pampered, but not too much. Make her wonder. Come see me next week. Ok!" she closed the door behind him. Jim inhaled the dirty M street air from the nonstop traffic and felt somewhat relieved. "Hope this lady can help me get Kiana on the right track?"

He went to Pino's and made small talk with Geof. Mr. Rogbin was a customer and friend of his too. Mr. Rogbin told Geof in detail how the Feds stole two million of his dollars and how he was suing to recover the money from the raid in Potomac.

Geof: "Be careful. They may raid you too for any reason…."

Jim: "Police don't like club owners." Both men agreed.

Park Hyatt hotel located east of 24th street, NW between M and N Streets. He pulled over. He went through many floors and he ended up at presidential suites on the top floor. With near 50,000 dollars in his account everything seemed cheaply available. He blew up quickly

10,000 dollars and he bought the whole presidential suite. He got three love chairs, three couches turning into beds, ten black marble tables, 2 mobile coffee fold up bars, and 2 king sized beds, and one huge wall to wall gold framed mirror. He thought about furnishing his newly expanded club, to furnish his office, to furnish Kiana's new place.

Amazingly she called him the same day.

Kiana: "Hey Jim P. Walker! How are you?" she acted excited.

Jim: "You should have called this morning! I was worried sick about you. Where are you now?"

Kiana: "I am coming your way for real this time. Send me information on nice and safe apartment buildings near Howard University, please!"

Jim: "You cost me a lot of money again. I just went to psychic to tell me about us? I spent thousands of dollars to find answers you don't give me. You could have had this money for yourself!"

Kiana: "You are the weakest man I've ever met. No one of my friends goes to psychics to spend thousands. Just curious; what did she tell you about me?"

Jim: "She told me you have someone who controls you, a bad guy. She told me that Mansur is not good for my business. The good news is I bought furniture for your (hopefully our apartment), for my office, for my club. I blew up near $15,000 today."

Kiana: "Wow, Jim! You need a wife. You spend too much."

Jim: "I have you. What do I need a wife for?" He knew it was a silly answer. "You spend my money with the same speed a wife would." He was trying to justify his comment.

Kiana: "I am neither. You should help me with my tuition, not with spending on furniture and psychics readings."

Jim: "You should call more often, ok? Don't blame me for loving you. By the way, I hired your roommate Khloe as bartender."

Two days before her ex roommate Khloe asked to work in the bar. Weselin said "sure, why not!" He needed her connections from Howard University. His competitor at then Ballers Club, (Mr. Dodson, the cocaine head and pimp) built his promotions on Howard U's "delta sorority" after all. Rumors had it; he almost lived at HU!

Kiana: "Khloe is troublesome. Remember, her boyfriend threw a brick through her window? Then when she gets drunk, she talks too much."

She never liked Jim to talk to anybody about her (nor with her mother either). She was like a mystery, conspirator type, almost a spy type.

Jim: "She needs money." The other side of the line went silent.

Jim: "Hello….." He thought he lost the signal, the number was blocked, so, even if he wanted he couldn't call back.

Kiana: "Do what you like, bye!" She hung up.

Jim: "Wait!" he needed the flight schedule to "cast the spell," he felt he lost the magic and the money. The crying, happy and now unanswered and angry again ending day could make anyone blow up and go ballistic, but not him. He actually could not wait now to see Khloe drunk. It seemed the day had more than 24 hours this day. Too much was happening and then still no real result, at least till this moment.

Khloe arrived at about 9 pm. The bar got busy for awhile with some of her friends from HU. Jim allowed her to do "two for one" happy hour prices even the time had long passed for that.

Khloe: "I can fill this place up!"

Jim: "I see five people so far."

Khloe: "I can pass the word. It will take time, but it is doable." She was drinking already. Within two hours the bar was full. She was good, but when the pimps arrived her attitude changed.

Khloe: "Who are those people?"

Jim: "We cannot discriminate anyone here unless they are under age. And they are the ones who pay my bills here. We kick the bad ones out. Try to be nice. Ok!"

Khloe: "One thing about those characters is that they are great tippers." She laughed counting her money in the tips jar. "The bar made almost 3,000 dollars, wow!" She was really surprised. "You make all this from eight chair bar, two tables by window and a couch in the back?"

Jim: "You see how Kiana gets money, from a busy bar and man who loves her?" He shook his head.

Khloe: "My husband really liked her, but you and your money pushed him away. Then he married me for spite, to show her he could. I did not mind, because he is really good lover." She laughed, being really drunk.

Jim: "Kiana is a great lover too." He laughed also.

Khloe: "Is she? She is playing you, mister!" she was almost leaving out the door. Jim stopped her. He was puzzled to be addressed twice in one day as "mister,"

thinking of the appalled psychic earlier.

Khloe: "She's got a boyfriend in Georgia. He is in and out of jail. I don't understand why a man like you even talks to her? Even more, I am wondering why you are giving her that crazy money. You are a good looking guy and smart too. Just an opinion ..."

She slid down the stairs. That was the last Jim saw and heard from her. He could not believe his ears. The tarot card lady, Kiana's mother, the code breaking voice messages were all leading to betrayal. The next week appointment showed even more details. Now the puzzle got even more twisted!

Miss Zamora Jr.: "Let me do the cards again. Cut please!"

Jim: "I hope there are no more surprises?" He was not crying any more. He was prepared to hear just about anything.

Miss Zamora Jr: "There is a third person involved here; someone who has problems." She displayed the card.

Jim: "I know she helps her uncle and he is always talking to her, or that's what she is telling me!"

Miss Zamora Jr.: "He is not her family member. He looks more like a thief, burglar, and intruder."

Jim: "Maybe it is her boyfriend? He is in and out of jail!" He suggested.

Miss Zamora Jr.: "Jim, there are three of you around her, you, her boyfriend, who is like a drifter and a family man, who seems to have kids." She was expensive, but accurate. That was confirmed soon.

Jim: "I was not able to get the flight schedule when Kiana would be flying over water!" His eyes met the cold gazing eyes of the psychic.

Miss Zamora Jr.: "I needed that for my spell! Now this will cost you more.

I have to crash special crystals to make things happen in your favor. What can you give me today, Jim!" she pointed toward the credit card machine.

Jim: "I know how the crystals work. They have special frequencies. When pressed they release energies." He thought. "I can do most of the same stuff using my own power! Do I really need a psychic now? Besides the tarot cards interpretation I do not see much progress here, except she makes a great shrink. She is very good listener. Well, I am paying her near, 10,000 dollars to listen!"

Jim: "Let us make an agreement. I do not have a problem with giving you any money in the future, but I need results. I will give you now 3,000 dollars and 2,000 more when the spell materializes and she is in my room and all mine and all those men around her disappear!"

Miss Zamora Jr.: "If I was Gennie in a bottle I can grant you all your wishes, but I am a psychic, not a magician. Also I detect some internal resistance from you and she is resisting you also. I know you got similar psychic powers, if not better than mine. Kiana is protected by an army of men and it is like going to a battle to win her. That battle you may win or you may lose? It is not that you are not trying, the question is "does she want to be rescued and to come to your side and leave all those men behind?" Here is where your investment of money and my many years of dealing with similar situations will help you."

Jim looked how her credit card machine swallowed in seconds the next 3,000 dollars out of his account. He had second thoughts about the whole situation. Who is the married man? Why would Kiana need someone with kids? Was he also supporting her, or, they all were sucking on Jim's good fortune to have a successful bar and plenty of cash?

The Evil Crowd/Satan: "Yes, yes, yes! Now, finally we are happy. You damn man. You are in our field now. We have tried to pull you down for years."

Kiana showed up two weeks later. It was end of August. She demanded two phone lines and two mobile phones. She let her voice mail be inactivated for a whole week. Jim set up her voice mail and created secret pass word. With that he was able to get all her Georgia connections. He soon discovered who the married man was (Mr. Julius) and that he had two kids and supposedly dying wife from cancer.

He basically started to avoid her. He also stopped seeing Miss Zamora Jr., the greedy psychic. Meanwhile, he met a gorgeous light skin lady who was working as Human Resource Manager at "Charter Plan" in the building next to him. Her name was Shelley. The encounter was during her lunch break.

Shelley: "Who are you? You look like someone important!" She and her co worker were giggling, expecting some weird answer.

Jim: "I am in charge of the night life in DC." He was telling the truth. He, Mr. Rogbin and Mr. Dodson were the Kings of the biggest night clubs in DC.

Shelley: "I will believe you when I see it? Show me your club. Now!" she was beautiful and serious. She was exactly a copy cat of Carmen Electra, a model and actress, married to Dennis Rodman (a controversial basketball player).

Jim: "Here. Follow me, please!" he opened the door leading to the second floor of newly expanded Randevu lounge, soon to be renamed Zeus Lounge of DC. Her ass was moving like two small balloons trying to escape from under her skirt going up the stairway. She looked quickly around the second floor, and then she proceeded to the third floor.

Jim: "This floor is under construction." His hands stretching toward her tiny waist, he almost poked her ass with his erected penis. She turned around.

Shelley: "I am satisfied. What is this? Happy to see me, huh?" she almost rotated her body 180 degrees toward him and now his hands fell naturally around her buttocks. He grabbed her tightly.

Jim: "See what you did?" almost kissing her. She did not resist initially, but she slowly distanced herself from him in a playful fashion.

Shelley: "....To be continued some other time! I just came to see if you are telling the truth. Three kings, what is your number?"

Jim: "I may be not No. 1, but I will do better than the others. I am predestined to survive!" He was not smiling anymore and his erection was gone watching her walking down the steps. "Here is my business card."

Shelley: "Here is my number," she quickly dictated her number almost hitting the ground floor. The street welcomed those two newly found friends.

Jim: "I will be in touch." He would have thought that was a dream, but the number he just took was still lit on his phone, "probably, a fake number, anyway?" He was too busy to dwell on negative thoughts. Between the liar Kiana and crooked partner and desperate Khloe and the construction with missing foreman, (Mansur's nephew) he was just trying to have the place turned around to bigger, cleaner, profitable operation.

The call from Bulgaria couldn't be at the worse time in mid September '05.

Michael: "Son, I am turning 75! Come see me and celebrate my birthday."

Jim: "I am in the middle of construction now." He initially wanted to say no. "I do understand, I will come to see you, ok!" He promised against his will. "See you October 26th!" he stated it and almost regretted it. Mansur's nephew promised to complete the huge construction by November 1st, 2005! He made a quick assessment. He had to pay the rent to Mansur at amount of 6,000 dollars. Kiana was pressuring him for money also. Now a new star Shelley, was rising on the horizon. He decided to spy on Kiana. He resorted to the old technique of recording her activities. The car she was driving (one of his 300CEs) had a digital recording device placed in the trunk. Jim was not sure where she would move her stuff? She arrived one day with some angry movers who were looking more like an eviction crew of hired criminals.

Jim: "Where are you moving to?"

Crew supervisor: "We are instructed not to disclose her location. Sorry!"

Jim: "I will find out sooner or later. Nobody outsmarts me!" He said it to the departing crew with 1/3 of the furniture he bought at the presidential suites during Park Hyatt Hotel auction. The total value of new furniture would have easily been around 15,000 dollars.

The drama at the bar had its own dimension. Mid August, 2005 a drifter came to the bar. He was tall, fit, and age 40. He was carrying a huge military green bag. He would order a beer and he would lay on the couch semi asleep. A few times Jim had to shake him to wake up while he was closing the bar.

Jim: "Where are you from buddy?" He usually tried to stay away from men, but this one was different. He seemed clean and hip.

Larry: "I am from California." He sounded proud. He had his hair pulled back in pony tail style, which made him look like a samurai.

He was 6 feet tall, blonde and with blue eyes and with friendly demeanor.

Jim: "Do you need a job? I need security at the door" he asked.

Larry: "Hmm, I am not looking for a job, sir, but I do like your joint, why not?" He smiled.

Jim: "I will need you four hours or more? Most of my business is night time between 11 pm and closing at 2 am or 3 am."

Larry: "Sure, I can do that! Just find a place for my traveling bag. Maybe I can place it behind the couch, under the stairway?"

Jim: "Go ahead." He agreed.

The taking over of Sally's/Starlight/Prosperity, brought that same element to Zeus Lounge or the old Randevu. The pimps and drug users moved to Zeus Lounge. The business was booming. Unfortunately, with more crowds the problems increased also. Some ladies of the night would bring their clients/johns, from the street and they would use the bathrooms for sex. At the end they would slip $10 or $20 to Larry as a thank you note, without Jim's approval. Jim discovered used condom wraps in the trash can and soon the 2nd floor only bathroom was clogged with female tampons and the Roto-rooter plumbing service was called to assist.

Roto-rooter Man: "My God! I have never seen so many condoms and female stuff in any establishment pipes."

Jim: "Sir! I just opened the floor a week ago. What you see here is seventy years of sex leftovers. The full employment in World War II included the service of prostitutes and pimps and lose control of drugs. The war on drugs and sex escalated in mid nineties and Rayful Edmonds and Pablo Escobar paid for it, so have Mayflower Madam. Here in DC it is a game of cat and mouse, between cops and prostitutes. They squeeze the pimps and drug dealers of their cash and let them go in exchange of their freedom. The prostitutes serve the clients and the police alike and unless someone squeals on the police, everyone is happy. If you don't believe me come tonight and watch the game.

Roto-rooter Man: "Really, but business first. You owe my boss $200 for now."

Jim: "Sure!" he tore up the check with his signature. "See you tonight. Drinks on me!" they shook hands good bye.

The next two weeks were spent in talking to the lawyer, who was working on occupancy capacity increase, on entertainment license, on liquor hour extension. ANC were not helping with the hours, they needed to provide a letter of approval. The ABC board approved the hours, but without ANC approval the license couldn't be changed, go figure, how DC government works and its Mafia like agency ABRA operates?

At the Bar the ladies of the night were going wild. It got so busy that one night Jim called Larry and offered him a job as bartender.

Larry: "I never mixed drinks before, boss!" He liked being security, but he was hesitant to try something he was not familiar with.

Jim: "Bartending is a state of mind. It takes five minutes to show you and to copy the basic drinks and some of the more requested ones. It is all about proportions and speed. The rest is your personality. The more comfortable people feel around you, the more drinks they will order. From there your tips will grow."

Larry: "I am ready!" He jumped behind the bar. He was a quick learner. Within an hour he was up to speed and he was ready to go.

Jim: "I will give you a challenge! Try to beat my sales! I make 3,000 dollars a night or I get close to it. We need money for construction."

Larry: "Sure, Boss!" He accepted. "Just show me where things are?"

Seemed the crowd approved his presence behind the bar and he made the bar move into some drinking frenzy. He was helping with the DJ sound upgrade. Usually Jim, would play CDs, or radio on weekends from WPGC or WKYS FM stations remixes, and all day videos from BET (regular and uncut). Larry would select music from on line free songs (MP3) and he would make a great variety of popular dance music;

at times it was better than the music on the radio. He got many requests for selecting or repeating some songs.

Jim: "Charge them a dollar for any extra work or for any requests! You know I charge for anything they ask; using my phone, going to the bathroom, if they are not customers, even rubber bands are a dollar."

Larry: "Really?" he liked the power of manipulation already. Anytime someone pays for anything is because he submits to certain rules of the supplier, so the demander pays. If there is no demand, the supplier will reduce the price or he/she will create a new product to lure the interest of new customers.

Jim: "Here is my rule; "In business you do not have friends, and you do have good customers."

Larry: "I do like your sign: "Address the bartender for drinks only." It is a bit standoffish, but I understand that most drunks are just wasting someone's precious time."

Jim: "I usually tell them go play with the other customers. If I feel like it and I do have time I will listen to your story… Lora is worse than me. She would tell them, "I am from New York. You are wasting my time."

A week before he left to go to Bulgaria, Jim noticed one of his active bar beautiful hooker, Layla talking to a Vice squad officer. They chatted almost thirty minutes. Her friend Fiola arrived later on and she was very upset.

Fiola: "I don't believe that bitch!" she screamed getting a seat at the bar.

"Give me a Long Island Ice Tea."

Jim: "You must have some bad news to have that kind of drink?" He stated semi-laughing, but ended with a serious face, basically reflecting, Fiola's her own mood.

Fiola: "You know, this bitch Layla is snitching on you and your bar!"

Jim: "How so? I treated her like everyone else, if not better?"

Fiola: "Your bar manager allowed her to have sex in the bathroom and she was about to get arrested for something else, but she snitched on you and they let her go."

Jim: "I told Larry to be careful and stay away from the hookers. I will do something about it after I return from Bulgaria. Thank you very much." He drew on a good Cuban cigar and instructed Larry not to allow Layla on the premises.

Larry: "What happened?" he was puzzled a bit.

Jim: "Our lounge is under surveillance. Keep everything clean, bathrooms, every floor. I already kicked the drug dealers out. You know alcohol and drugs don't mix. It is a felony charge."

Larry: "Ok, boss!" he was confused. He really was closer emotionally to those street people, than to the upper level of management.

That week before Jim was to depart for Bulgaria he decided to open the 3rd floor. He hired an attractive mixed race (Spanish-black) bartender lady. She was good with the customers and the liquor and beer was selling quickly. Jim was happy. Even with construction moving slowly, with all problems from the ABC Board, with his never-stopping-to-ask-for money-Mansur, with his cheating "girlfriend" the things were moving forward.

Toward midnight a young and aggressive Spanish pimp arrived. He claimed that Layla and Fiola were his ladies. He ordered many drinks, assuming that would soften Jim and would change his mind.

Rico: "Hey man! I need my girl to come back and to get customers from here!"

Jim: "Fiola is here, but anyone talking to the cops and snitching is barred from here!" He reminisced about the pimp Candy Man and his lady Vicky just a year before. He was also begging for his return at the bar, after he screwed up with cover charges at the door. He ended up being dead (and his lady) even Jim granted his wishes. The similar situation will be here soon. Rico will be run over by Layla with H2 Hummer six months later and he would end up in a wheel chair in prison for underage human trafficking and labor, according to the same name law "RICO." He has used Layla for five years, starting at age of 13! Read why this happens, Cornell U?

Jim: "Bartender lady! I see you are spending too much time talking to Rico. What is the story? I have other customers for you to attend too."

Bartender Lady: "Oh, he is very entertaining and funny! He invited me to his hotel and he promised to give me extra tip-money!" she sounded drunk and happy.

Jim: "Let me advise you that he is a pimp. He will take your ID, he will take your money, and he will put you on the street with instruction to bring him 700 minimum to 1,000 dollars a night. He would work a split with you and he would promise you protection from other pimps. Is that what you want?" he told her in one breath. As soon he moved away from the bartender lady Rico approached him.

Rico: "Hey, slim! What are you telling that lady? Something about me?" he brought his face within an inch, typical in pimp style.

Jim: "Listen buddy! She works for me. I told her you are a pimp. Now, let her work. Stay away from her. Ok?" he did not bulge to this young Turk, intimidation.

Rico: "You are breaking my game, cracker!" he hardly finished his sentence and he swung quickly and unexpectedly toward Jim's face.

Jim ducked down the punch, and returned the punch. The guy was definitely strong. He was built like a light weight boxing champion. He was 5'8", but with body like spring coil and with zero fat. He was punching furiously and relentlessly. People started screaming and some of them went down to the second floor. They called Larry who arrived quickly to the scene. He and another tall guy tried to separate the fighting couple. Even holding his hands Rico was kicking with his feet like an uncontrollable child.

Larry: "Wow. What is wrong with this guy? He fights like a monster!"

Suddenly one of Rico's feet landed at Jim's face, bloodying his nose. Someone called the police and the fight continued but down on the street. Rico overheard the police sirens and he took off running. Police gave him a good chase and within two blocks he was apprehended. They brought him back for identification.

Jim: "Yes, that is him!" he pointed toward his assailant.

Rico: "I have never been here. I do not know this guy! I never met him before," he lied while he was being handcuffed and he was taken away in a paddy wagon (police van).

Police officers: "You need stitches. Go to hospital, now!" The ambulance took Jim to George Washington Hospital, against his will, but police insisted.

Police officers: "Hope he has good insurance?" they laughed watching the door closing and Jim disappearing down the street. Rico was processed and given a barring notice. Looks like the Police liked Layla as a whore and informant, but hated Rico as a pimp and as violent suspect. Go figure?

Jim spent the night at the hospital and in pain, waiting for some students to practice their profession on him on how to stitch a broken nose's skin. In actuality he needed his nose bone aligned first, but they skipped that. It took him two weeks more until he pushed the fine arrow like bone back in the nose slot, causing excruciating pain. He did that while he was in Bulgaria and then the swallowing started to subside.

The visit to Bulgaria was in the last week of October of 2005. Just before he was leaving Mansur was begging for money, asking for $8,000 dollars to pay Sarkisian, who placed mechanics lien against him.

Mansur: "If we don't pay you may return to a club without a liquor license, sir!"

Jim: "That statement is redundant! When can I save money for myself? Your nephew Agile took $40,000 from me and he did not accomplish anything he promised. I should have all bars on all three floors working by now?" He was getting frustrated.

Mansur: "You can always leave! And sell your part!" he was trying to seem convincing.

Jim: "Between you and Kiana I feel burned from both sides. If I don't give you the money, she will take it."

Mansur: "Select what is your priority now. Once you make the business successful there will be money for everyone. Tell her to wait!"

Jim: "It is easy to say! She is telling me to sign a contract with you. She does not trust you, Mansur!"...

Mansur: "You have been with me seven years and you still don't trust me? You are spoiling her too much. Save your money, young man!" He was considering Jim young, being ten years his junior. Jim was looking good with no gray hair and almost full head of hair. Seems they both were giving him good advice, but they were both self-centered and selfishly-motivated...

Jim enjoyed his father 75th birthday. When he gave him a hug he felt the bony body under the clothes of that one head turner in the past a Christopher Reeves look-alike.

Jim: "You are my Super-father, not a Superman from the movies, even you look similar.

Father Michael: "I heard he is dead!"

Jim: "Yes, even Superman can die, but let's celebrate life now. Cheers! And to many more years to come."

Uncle Radi: "Cheers, brother!" he addressed Michael, then he turned around "Cheers to my favorite nephew, Jim!" He looked around like a king who worshiped a champion gladiator as equal. He arrived to the capitol Sofia for medical checkup and to see Jim at the same time.

Uncle Radi: "We have many faults. We have big family. We never had anyone going to America and to do so well! We are proud of you Jim. You never complained about anything. You started businesses without our help. You actually helped us here in many ways. You were our motivation in dark days. We, the Walker family believed in you. You helped us financially, but you never asked us to help you. Yes, we are proud Bulgarians. We survive by association, but never individually. I wish I can know more about how such a young country in the world is able to become super military power? How in USA people can start business and succeed individually, the way you did it? Write that book soon, I may never have a chance to read it, because of my age, but let the world know about The Walker family. We are big, but unknown. I shake your hand and I congratulate you my general!"

In Bulgaria every man gets drafted at the age of seventeen to the army, navy and Air Force.

Jim: "Father, uncle, brother! We are here to say thanks to father Michael. He should be celebrated. I am not a general, but the things I get involved and the way I win my battles are unconventional and on a level unknown to present human kind. I tap in the knowledge of many generations before me and I do find new ways to accomplish many things in one life. In other words I do live the seven incarnations of the human soul in one earth life.

Father Michael: "You know I am a great church follower. I believe in Jesus. But no one in our congregation talks like you. Where is your knowledge coming from?"

Brother Adrian: "Hey, leave Jim alone. He is not like us. He maybe is our blood, but he is in another dimension mentally. The more he will explain to you, the more confused he will leave you. There is a reason the Bible is written the way it is. Imagine, if it was reversed and written in formulas? Who would read two pages of physics and mathematics without giving up? Not Jim. Let us leave him alone to write his book and hopefully, everyone then can ask questions... Cheers uncle, father, and brother!" Jim felt relieved that he did not have to play Jesus to the crowd.

The stay in Bulgaria was shorter this time. It was only a week. There was no Svetlana this time, and Alexandra was ignoring him as usual. She paid courtesy to him by escorting him to the Airport. While his brother and father were sitting on another table, Jim and Alexandra were holding hands, aging in some love to be dimension.

Jim: "You know I am expanding my business. I am spending nearly a quarter million in construction to connect two buildings, hopefully to create enough capital to move to better business!"

Alexandra: "What is your real dream my Jim?" she held his hand more like a nun than a girlfriend, or lover...

Jim: "I wish she was physically and emotionally available. Damn she looks great at that mid forties age" he thought, but he said something completely remote from what he wanted to say.

Jim: "I am thinking to buy me a hotel in the islands of the Caribbean." He blurred.

Alexandra: "I guess you will invite me then?" she paused. "Why don't you buy the island too?" now she was giggling.

Jim: "Why not? Let's get the island too. Nothing is impossible. It is the matter of thinking. Then it happens!" He followed her giggling lead.

Alexandra: "You know you Capricorns are always big dreamers. You talk a lot,.." she was suddenly serious. She seemed disappointed of her own thoughts. She did not like liars and fast talkers.

Jim: "Everything takes time and everything is possible. Just have patience. I like when people are doubtful. That motivates me more. I never met someone who immediately agreed with me on anything I said. Do you know that my discovery is that when in crowd people move slower and less? Only an individual can excel himself or herself. Not everyone can be a winner. The crowd is good for big projects like highways, Hoover Damn, the Great Wall of China, but they still need a leader. My projects are achieved without a big crowd, without money, without the External/Earth's help... Mostly of my achievements are because I pull the greatest strings from my sub consciousness and with the strange high speeds I create events, which only Gods can explain."

Alexandra: "Ok. I believe in you, but don't talk. Just do it and then you can show me, talking is a sign of covering up something."

Jim: "Yes. The Bible says that one who talks a lot is not a righteous person… I will find ways to own my island. I did everything I thought so far, except marrying you." Both were laughing.

Angelika: "This guy can have me if he wants, just I want to see it, not hear promises anymore," she thought.

Both: "Shhhhhhh," they kissed good bye. The airplane swallowed Jim the next three minutes. His father and brother were crying. Nobody was happy on departures. It was like check-in boxes. Yes, we met. No, we did not meet. The family was like a microcosm of the universe. Those Walker people were everything a society can produce... engineers, generals, merchant marine captains, businessmen, mayors, and basic civilians. Now they had a God like person, Jim. The puzzled souls on the ground were looking at the airplanes like bunch of thieves. Who stole their God? Will he be back again? There was a mystery with Jim's uncle too. Eight months later he would be dead from cancer, he had concealed from everyone. He told only his sister Dana, "I did not want to make you worry about me." What a person?

While on the plane Jim kept calling Kiana. She never answered. Dark thoughts were flowing into Jim's head, déjà vu again. Those twelve hours of traveling back to the States were mixed with emotions. At times he wanted that 30,000 feet high plane just to dive straight down to the ocean and finish his suffering. He did not feel like God emotionally. That always puzzled him in his life! How he can be business strong and emotionally so very weak? How would history judge him as? What would be his legacy? Soon he will restore his powers. It reminded him of the Bible story of Samson and Delilah. Government keeps cutting his hair or ambitions, but they keep forgetting that the hair will grow and he will push the "columns" down destroying everyone cheering his misfortunes. The difference is here he will survive and live longer and better than his opponents. The legacy is not in dying, being a victim, or being a loser. It is in the opposite.

The slogan "Survival of fittest" is outdated and wrong. "Survival of the Quantum thinker and most Aware" apply for Jim here and in the Quantum Time Machine.

The new country who adopted him was not welcoming him as a dignitary or deity type he was. They were too busy with selling digital toys and creating frivolous wealth. He was the rising star; he was the next Jesus, Buddha, Mohammed, Allah in spiritual and the Quantum World! He was in the league of Einstein, Tesla, Max Plank, Wheeler, and Edward Taylor in theoretic and applied physics and even better!

Jim was a notch above.... He was connecting the real and the metaphysical world with formulas and his own stories to prove them.

While flying above the sunken Titanic in 1912 he was thinking of the 1500 pour souls laying down in freezing water on that mid April fatal night. Were they thinking the same way he was thinking? Did most of them leave families behind on the Old Continent and did they dream of a better future? Similarity was astonishing. Did the modern gadget, the telegraph then, cause the ship to sink? It was one of the reason and their general ignorance. The lookouts did not have binoculars; the captain was overconfident of the unsinkable ship (after all that was his retirement voyage and those were "little, silly icebergs," he had dodged for many decades successfully).

The Newfoundland appeared on the horizon and the delta of the big St. Lawrence River connecting the Great Lakes all the way to Lake Superior.

The airplane was approaching the land of Google, Face book and Twitter fighting for their share of socially deficient souls. The name Google was taken of the number 1 followed by 100 zeros (Google), twitter was of birds communicating and Face book of people who were looking for known friends. That was the world of communications without real relations. Gadgets do help, but they do not create the emotion, the gravitational wave, the Quantum burst of energy and light, the God like creativity. The land was down below, full of intrigues, with successes and failures. Just 24 years before he was approaching the New York City wide eyed and full of expectations. Now he was approaching with two things in mind, to make that club profitable and to win finally Kiana's heart.

Detective O'Conner: "Hey, who is the ABC manager here?" He was investigating the place three days prior Jim's return. Layla was snitching seriously and the only way she was to gain her freedom was to trash talk the club. She was kicked out and she did not like it. Fiola was inside but she seemed to be not cooperating with the police.

Larry: "It is me, boss!" For him everyone with authority was "the boss." Are you the police?" he asked the plain clothed undercover officer.

Detective O'Conner: "Yes! Here is my badge" he pulled a necklace out hanging under his dark blue sweater.

Larry: "Cool. What can I help you with?" He had his ABC manager license current and he was ready to answer any kind of questions.

Detective O'Conner: "We are investigating a fight ten days ago and a pimp had been arrested here for an assault of the owner Jim" he lied. The truth was that they were scouting the place. Not only Layla was snitching, but now Rico was aboard too. He would say anything to get the club tainted and to get back his freedom. His situation was way more complicated, but the Police negotiators were crooked and they would promise anything to anybody to break the club code of silence. They knew nobody would say anything without intimidation. Government smart does not necessarily mean street smart. The club had too many layers of familiarity and built in network to get simple answers.

The federal investigation usually involves catching bigger fish. Larry was not able to distinguish between the regular Metropolitan Police detectives and the federal undercover agents.

Larry: "The owner is not here. He is out of the country" he was relieved that they were not trying to investigate him. He was a veteran with questionable past.

Detective O'Conner: "What?" he was expecting any answer but not, "out of the country." He almost kicked the bar chair with his boots. His partner Waldo pushed him on the side. "Chill, Ok! Just ask when he is coming back?"

Larry: "What is the problem? He will be here in three days!" he answered them even before they asked.

Detective O'Conner: "Ok. We were just checking on his condition. We heard he went to the hospital" he quickly lied heading toward the exit door. He tried to peek into the dark, semi private room where they were few people sitting on the white leather sofa. Nothing seemed out of ordinary and he was concerned how to penetrate this Secret Bastille on X Street, called "Zeus Lounge."

Waldo: "We can set him up, you know?" He was his partner in crime.

Detective O'Conner: "We can put all options on the table. We need to get a warrant to search the premises. Let see what HIPS can help us with?" HIPS were another layer of Police undercover operations. They would give jobs to ladies, recovering from prostitution. The pay was like seven dollars an hour, a far cry from what they used to pull a night for their pimps. Jim barred HIPS from the club for years, but gradually he allowed them back a few months before. Huge mistake.... They were passing free chocolates, condoms and crime stories updates related to prostitution. Jim liked the chocolates. He would sell the condoms to anyone for a dollar. He felt he was contributing to the safety of the hookers. Before he left to Bulgaria he warned Larry to stay away from the prostitutes and keep the bathrooms clean.

Arriving at DC was more intense than two years prior. This time he had invested hundreds of thousands of dollars and he had given a sport Mercedes coupe to Kiana. She was as usual, ignoring his calls. Seemed the psychic predictions were all manufactured to benefit the psychic, not Jim. Eight thousand dollars gone and nothing to show for it! Mansur and his nephew Agile were laughing after they had stolen nearly 50 thousand dollars from Jim.

Jim: "Where are my bars? I see only the second floor ready? Third floor is not touched and first floor bar is half done." He was upset.

Mansur: "Listen! I just recommended my nephew to you. You should have not given him all the money upfront until he had finished the project to your satisfaction!" he was right. Jim proceeded to the second floor where he crossed paths with the newly promoted Bar Manager Larry.

Jim: "Hey Larry! How are the things the week passed?" He tried to get something positive of this whole negative puzzle.

Larry: "Do you want to hear the good or the bad news first?" He was evading the straight answer.

Jim: "I can see the good news. We are still in the business. Now, what is the bad news?"

Jim: "After the ignorance of Kiana and Mansur cheated me of my savings, what could be worse?" he thought, pulling a good cigar from the humidifier nearby. He lit it up in a hurry and poured himself a shot of Courvoisier VSOP (his preference over Remy).

Larry: "The Police was here looking for you?" he blurted out.

Jim: "That is the bad news? Those cockroaches have been here a thousand times. That is the norm here for them to harass me!"

Larry: "Maybe they treat you differently, but they were really mean and viscous to me, like wild dogs."

Jim: "I have been dealing with those characters sergeant Morrey, his accomplice Tobias "the tits watcher," and Detective Olsur who hangs out at Skylark lounge, by the stage, with his mouth open."

Larry: "They have some grudge against you and they did not hide it at all. Maybe I see things you do not?"

Jim: "I know them very well, this guy may be new?" He sipped on the great cognac. "Usually DC police are more relaxed about clubs unless there is stabbing or murder. I lost my club Zoro over a shooting in the SW area and they blamed it on the club! My lawyer had throat cancer and he could not talk. I felt he was against me, not working for me. My club was punished with a suspension of 80 days by the ABC Board and I just let it go. Listen! Just stay away from the hookers and let's keep this place clean. We need to fix many problems here. You just got here. You can stay here till the end of lease in 2013! That is eight more years, buddy! Ok?" He felt he was a bit too optimistic, but the cigar and cognac were calming him down at this moment, a small resting stop in an ocean of intrigues DC constantly provided.

Larry: "Leave that club to me to manage. Shelley probably is missing you? You go and you two enjoy yourselves, ok!" he suggested while going through the liquor and beer inventory.

Jim: "Sure! If police comes and ask questions, just call me!" He dialed his new girlfriend's phone number. He really wanted to be with Kiana, but Shelley was a great distraction.

Jim: "Hey Carmen Electra! How are you?" he teased Shelley.

Shelley: "You are back, Jim! I am not Carmen. You will be punished comparing me with other ladies" she giggled. "Where are you now?" She sounded busy.

Jim: "Meet me at McCormick and Schmick" restaurant on K Street. We need to talk."

Shelley: "Sure, at happy hour, ok?"

Jim: "See you at 5 pm, after work." He really wanted to meet Kiana, but she was not answering her phone. As soon he hung up the call, Kiana was calling.

Jim: "Are you kidding me? I have been calling you for the last two weeks. Nice to know you know my phone number?" He bitterly answered the phone. "Do the women have intuition when man talks to their competition? Does the Einstein Quantum entanglement Law apply here? Yes. If a man interacts with two women at same time, those two women telepathically communicate with each other!" He thought and it was true.

Kiana: "I was at school. Wow. You want me not to talk to you?"

Jim: "You don't act like a girlfriend or a friend! You spend my money, sleep on my furniture and drive my cars! I am not Santa Claus."

Kiana: "Where are you? I want to see your face." She had a voice which wouldn't take excuses…

Jim: "I have a meeting with a client for real estate." He was half honest. He couldn't tell her Shelley was a date.

Kiana: "I am coming to see you. If what you say is true, your client will not mind my presence!" she acted jealous.

The meeting was weird. Shelley arrived first and she handed Jim a nice tie in box as a gift.

Shelley: "It has been a good week and I kind of missed you" she leaned toward Jim for a kiss.

Jim: "I missed you too, Shelley. Here is something from my old country" he gave her a necklace of white gold. Then he kissed her.

He was hoping that Kiana would not show up? The restaurant on K Street McCormick and Schmick, was popular with power lunch and fancy dinners for the people with corporate accounts and some dinner guests staying in the many major hotels nearby.

Shelley ordered mussels for dinner. They arrived quickly within ten minutes to the table. Seemed that happy hour was also fast hour.

The bar was full and there were no free tables and chairs at the lounge area. Many people were trying to borrow Kiana's reserved chair, but Jim thwarted them away.

Mr. Perkins: "Hey Jim! How is the club business?" It was the shoe shine man nearby the table. His stand was in the corner, some ten feet away.

Jim: "Great and expanding!" he answered to Indiana Jones like chatterer, with the same cowboy looking hat. Jim liked to be recognized at any place and he was secretly showing off with his new girlfriend Shelley.

Mr. Perkins: "I see you are busy. Enjoy your dinner and your company!" he waved his glance toward Shelley, kind of approving with smile.

Jim: "I will see you at the bar. Ok?" He did not want to chat with a third party, nervously checking the door. Meanwhile, he saw Mr. Perkins stuffing something like a small, one inch square bag in the long sock of a customer, nothing to do with shoe shining. "I guess the Moe's client for white powder was also a dealer at this fine restaurant. The shoe shine stand was just a cover for something more sinister than the public sees? Mr. Perkins was frequent walker through the alley next to Normandy (one of the longest surviving small Mom and Pop businesses in DC, almost seventy years). Jim had seen him sniffing cocaine with Zita out in the open, but now he had seen him selling it too! His thoughts were suddenly interrupted by the grand entrance of Kiana.

Kiana: "Hey Jim!" she quickly assessed the situation. She noticed the doll looking face of Shelley and she knew that that was not a business to sell real estate.

Jim: "This is my client Shelley. She is looking for a house to buy." Jim told the semi truth. In reality Shelley was really looking for a house, but not at this moment.

Kiana: "I hope you will "find" her a house!" She smiled with sarcastic thoughts, only lovers can detect. "What special drinks can I get here?" She turned to passing waitress.

Waitress: "Melon martini or apple martini are my favorite, they are very refreshing!" She blurted out...

Kiana: "I need an apple martini!" That drink was her life line to cover for the situation she provoked with her demands and curiosity.

Shelley: "Are you a fitness trainer?" she was naive to not see those two had a relationship. Kiana was wearing a jogging outfit which was not fitting at all with Shelley's business HR manager look.

Kiana: "I am doing my weekly 5 mile run." She lied and smiled.

Jim: "Kiana is going to be a doctor one day, she goes to Howard University." Jim tried to act neutral and he was somewhat surprised by Kiana's sudden curiosity.

Kiana: "Thanks for the drink! I have to run now," she stood up with her almost six foot tall perfect body.

Shelley: "Well, nice to meet you!" she was not aware of the tension and that was basically, "Change of the Guards," in the relationship. Her interaction with people was based on the rule "start always positive." It seemed naive, but it worked perfectly at that moment.

Jim: "It is complicated, but one day you will know more about Kiana. One thing about DC, here in this ten square mile area everything and everybody is interconnected." He sipped on the single malt slowly.

Shelley: "I have been here only one year and I already feel the drama, the intrigues, the success the Big City brings to everyone." She dipped into her cold then mussels.

Jim: "Want me to take you home? Larry is the manager now and he can deal with the business."

Shelley: "No, but you can follow me to where I live? Hope you are a good driver? I drive fast!"

Jim: "I have two fast Benz coupes. I will pick the champagne one, so you can see me easier. The black one is difficult to see at night time."

Shelley: "Ok, Mr. 2 Benz, Man!"

Jim did not disclose that one of the cars was driven by Kiana. Inside of him he wanted to be with the tall goddess Kiana vs. the short, doll like Shelley. On the other hand the only way to slow down on his self-destructive path was to find a new love… Shelley at thirty-seven wanted to get married. She wanted a house, children, and a husband. Kiana was her opposite and just twenty-three years old.

An hour later those two new lovers were in bed. Sex was great and rewarding. Shelley was in perfect shape.

Jim: "You look perfect and you will make one man happy! How come you are single?" He couldn't believe the new relationship was unfolding that easy?

Shelley: "When you have so many men looking at you but not producing anything and just talking a woman may choose to leave all of them alone." She spread her legs in inviting position and Jim did not wait much to insert himself in that perfect bushy and juicy vagina.

Jim: "It is happening again. I am getting a new girlfriend! Thank you, God!"

God: "I hear you. Try to forget that Kiana. Ok?" The Invisible Hand was telling him in imaginary conversation.

Jim: "I love her, God. I am not sure Shelley is the right one to replace her?" he continued the conversation. He felt in his mind that mentally God was giving him right advice, but his heart was in pain. Was the heart and his emotions guided by the anti-God/Satan? Was the fight between those two with opposite intentions annihilating the light (love) he felt for the first time in his life toward someone in Kiana's image? Why the best feelings in him had to he crashed? In Hollywood movies even the worse possible characters get together, make up, fall in love and live forever. Why not here?

Shelley: "Oh, oh, Jim! How are you doing that "vibe thing?" she woke him up of his dream like inner conversation.

Jim: "What is so amazing?" he found her suddenly in bent over position and he watching her from behind. Wow. Was he temporary in another time dimension not to remember the position change? Was his mind trying to survive Kiana's influence on him directing his love beam toward the heavens, where the annihilation would break the ionosphere and connect with the dark matter, with Anti-God? Once there the black mass would be his mind changer, the Anti–God, would pull him in this self-destructive relationship? Was his heart hurting because of that battle? Was the sex with Shelley an intended substitute, like being in some masquerade?

Shelley: "Wow. The wave through my spine and hitting my brain in some light burst fashion is not explainable. What is your story? Oh, I am cumming, oh, ohhh." She grabbed the pillow closer and started chewing it, seems that she was trying to muffle the moaning from the nosey neighbors.

Jim: "I am cumming too." They both collapsed. Both were sweaty and breathing heavily.

Shelley: "I think you are a keeper!" She was wondering still what just happened? Her sensation was too unique to explain in plain words. She thought she would be considered insane if she mentions the wave, the white light, the vibe tingling her spine and the pulses of light flashing in her head like a broken flashlight!

Jim: "Consider this as a gift." He stretched himself from her fine lower back toward the roots of her hair with long licking trace finished with a kiss. He was enjoying watching those pear shaped curves from behind and her buttocks trembling still from the last orgasm.

Shelley: "And gift it is! I needed that." She thought that everything was just some coincidence. She was wrong. The same experience will reoccur many times during next twelve months of their short term relationship.

Jim: "I cheated all this time, Shelley!" He would tell her after they would break up in December of 2006.

Shelley: "I knew it all the time, but I did enjoy it regardless!" She would confess also.

Jim: "You knew it? I always thought of Kiana when I was making love to you and you did not mind?" he would be amused.

Shelley: "Women are just selfish with their bodies as men are. Why do you think we allow you to watch porn now or in old times couples go to ballet, some 200 years ago? Why do men buy art in the form of paintings or sculptures of naked women? Women may not like it, but they like the affect of it on men, simply explained."

Shelley was very helpful to Jim. She seemed God sent. Like Contessa, Frida, Mr. Smith, Molly, Nikias, Nina and even Mansur; they all had reasons to cross Jim's path of life and help create his legacy, and now was Shelley's turn! The relationship had its up and downs. It was not easy to balance all at the same time; the saga of the cheating Kiana, crooked government, greedy Mansur, a club with wrong hours of operation, a sick lawyer, and a new girlfriend like Shelley. The next algorithm was a puzzle with all signs facing toward the exit; the last calculations were like in the Feynman diagram in QED (quantum electrodynamics). The anti-creation, the destruction:

E (Government, energy) attack + ne(business, mass) = Wzo (no mass, business out) + 2 W-/+ (Mansur - out of business, Jim + survivor)....

Jim had hired two more bartenders; both came from Victoria Secrets store on Connecticut Ave and X Street, NW. They were both African American ladies in their mid twenties. For some reason Jim trusted them equally to Larry, if not even more. Every one of the bartenders would have his/her own floor. Jim sensed the pressure coming from outside, he was connecting the dots!

To soften the impact he started going to Church at St. Mathews off Connecticut Ave on Rhode Island, NW. He met people with disabilities; he practiced his Creative Powers (QMCL) to cure them from back pain, knees pain, brain tumor, and gallbladder. One of the old ladies entered on crutches and after Jim cured her she walked out without them. The church filled with the smell of roses. Wow. Was his ability to create Quantum Energy able to suck some ions from the plasma in the ionosphere, make a hole in it and even bring black mass on earth? Was the mixture at this mini black matter (from the QMC) with the air of church able to create the odor of roses? Are the people just walking antennas and only those with higher awareness were able to tap into the void of the universe?

Dark matter does not emit or absorb light or electromagnetic radiation, but it affects the gravitational effects on the matter, radiation and the universe. It constitutes 84 percent of the matter in the universe. When EM (electromagnetic wave) hits plasma it creates OX conversion (fusion).

O (ordinary) EM converts to X (extraordinary) wave, now photons act like as if they have mass. That is basically similar to Jim's theory of Quantum Gravitational Wave, the Creation!

There are three types of plasma. First is the solar plasma; the second is in the ionosphere, the earth plasma. The third is a personal plasma/bioplasma. We can use either one of them for different projects. If a small task is needed, we use the personal plasma. We train, we meditate, we pray, to create that fusion in our body, so when we need it we use that extra invisible gear, to become champions or extraordinary citizens.

Jim describes "It" as the 4th Six in the Quantum spiral/cone, God's Number; the H2 (hydrogen) converts to He (helium) and releases photons. Helium is a stable element, has mass that is the plasma, also emits quanta. The whole reaction is a fusion, conversion of inhaled air (molecular state) into nervous impulses (bio electrical state) and emotions (magnetic state).

Temperature is the judge in the relation to the kinetic energy in molecules. The colder the molecule the denser, the more visible the matter is. When kinetic energy is zero, the object is motionless. The hidden symmetry is visible. That explains the smell of roses. Church is usually a cold place. When Jim was converting his thoughts to Quantum Energy to heal people, he was basically breathing and reducing the temperature of the plasma, he was creating (the conversion of H2 to, He). He was duplicating what Sun was doing to ionosphere. The light, via sun rays (photons) were entering the ionosphere, creating plasma and cooling it off. Plasma has density and radiates energy, quantum EM, the creativity. Energy has wave length and is related to the frequency, the lower the frequency, the longer the wave length radiation. Jim was aware of Raja Yoga. The purer the person who cures, the better the patient will feel. When one thinks of white or violet colors entering through 3rd eye (between the eyebrows) the frequency increases and the brain wave is shorter. The breathing is deeper and usually he will count in fives (breathing five seconds, holding the breath in five seconds, exhaling in five seconds). That process will bring the temperature down; it will increase the Quantum Energy at his solar plexus to create mini plasma and to transfer it to the patient. It always worked! Was he communicating with God? To connect the two person's plasmas at will it is like entering a wormhole, where two minds were communicating in time machine mode! The puzzle here will be confirmed with BEC (Bose-Einstein condensate), the super-atoms, the 5th state of matter, with creation of He4 (helium 4), the anti-plasma. He was not working with subzero temperatures here, but the results were somewhere in between plasma and antiplasma. No matter of the theories, the lady was cured. Hey Cornell U! Don't hide MIT…

Most of Jim surrounding was unfriendly. He was not fulfilled emotionally while dating Shelley. She was performing in 75 percent range of Kiana sexually and the need to see her was not in Jim's mind.

Both were living in separate apartments and he did not mind it. He was still hoping that Kiana would come to him. He started planting electronic devices in the Mercedes he would lend her to drive. To impress her classmates in Howard University she would alter driving the black or champagne color Benzes. Amazingly she would not ask for sex, but for anything else; money, cars, shopping.

One day Jim checked the recording device and after he passed it on an eight hour VHS videotape (he used the audio track only), he recognized Kiana was talking to a man for an hour. She really showed a lot of emotion! Her style was to speak deep and seductive when she was normal and to yell like a wounded wolverine when she was angry. At times she would calm down her lover with words like that.

"Hey, DP. I got you a car, I furnished my crib, and I got money, what else do you want?" Jim could not believe his ears. They were talking about his stuff and his money after all. She continued…

"Hey Man, my phone is on vibe and on mute when I study. You know this guy Jim calls all the time and I keep ignoring his calls, therefore, I do ignore yours also, sorry!"

Jim was about to smash the TV/VCR combo "What?" He forwarded the tape to the point where Kiana made a call to him.

Kiana: "Hey Buddy! What are you doing?" She was a great actress.

Jim: "I am heading to the club in an hour. Where are you?" It was around 3.30 pm. Even in his hate toward her his penis almost lifted his pants in the air, grown to full erection in less than two seconds in conversation.

Kiana: "I got out of class! Want some company?" She sounded like she came out of liquid nitrogen bottle.

Jim: "Of course! Come to 1200 N Street. I am home." He almost exploded, but he ran to the bathroom and just relieved himself. Kiana even to this present day of 2013 had the same influence at him, yes. She was his first and last infatuation.

Kiana called DP soon after. "I will see you in an hour, hope you are hungry?"

flirting.

DP: "Yeah, hungry and horny, baby. Hurry up!" He ordered her.

Kiana never told DP where the car, money and furniture came from. She wouldn't tell Jim about DP also. She wanted to keep her relationships separate from each other. But soon that was to be disclosed. Jim made an art of catching her lies. Now the tape was giving him the opportunity to place everything in real time sequence. Her arrival was around 3.45 this afternoon. He remembered the next time lapse on the tape, because she came to his house.

Kiana: "Missed me, Jim?"

Jim: "Don't ever call me buddy! I am everything a man can provide you with. I am like a gift given to you." He was trying to induce some gratitude in Kiana towards him. The opposite happened.

Kiana: "Hey. Don't rush me. We have four years ahead to spend together. Now chill!" she was the female emotional gangster toward him.

Jim: "Come here! It has been a year since we made love?" he pulled her toward him. She resisted.

Kiana: "You want that pussy bad, don't you?" she moved even further away. He threw himself on bed unzipping his pants. She stood up watching him in disgust.

Jim: "What is wrong? I thought we moved to next level!" He was getting frustrated of her inactivity.

Kiana: "Do you have $700?"

Jim: "What for?" He was puzzled. His erection was diminishing faster than he wanted it to.

Kiana: "You want sex. We are not boyfriend and girlfriend! Want something against my will you pay for it." She was an icicle.

Jim: "You know! I gave you almost 250,000 so far in cars, gifts, credit cards, cash and you would still want to charge me? Get out of here, now!" He could have shell out to her $300 dollars, as usual, but he was appalled of her demands to pay for sex. Why? As she was leaving the door he short stopped himself from screaming "give me back my Benz, too!" He wanted to know where she was heading from here. He wanted to know how long it would take her to get to her boyfriend's home or her own home.

The tape fast forwarded. He clocked her time at six minutes. He was wondering where she was hiding? To Howard University was approximately that time in traffic. But she took the furniture to another location. She was maybe with a boyfriend, but Howard University dorms do not accept co-eds and was tailor-made for first two years undergrads to live there. Jim knew her schedule of classes. He knew where she did park his Benz. He decided to take his car back.

On the next day he drove to Girard Street which was curving around from Georgia toward 6th street, both with opposite "one way" street signs. He was driving his lesser mileage 300CE champagne coupe. Soon he spotted his second 300CE Benz which was in black color. He parked the champagne car and quickly entered the black car. In the side pocket on the driver side he found an envelope with the current rent due, addressed to Kiana Hines.

Jim: "Eureka! Finally!" he sounded like Archimedes, solving the problem. "Now I know where she lives with her boyfriend!" He saw the address 3636 16th street, NW, apt. 934, DC. He drove the black Mercedes to the Woodner Apartments and saw a nice building with security, garage and restaurant inside. He remembered recommending that spot to her earlier in the year with four more others to choose from.

Jim: "I know her apartment, but the building has East and West Wing. The rental information did not disclose which side? Hmm…? I will figure it out." He blended with the constant traffic passing through the main door... it was mostly Spanish crowd and some blacks. He passed by the semi alert security and he ended up on the right floor. Then he moved curiously toward the apt 934 W. It was the top floor and at this time in the afternoon he did not observe any people, but the maintenance guy who was pushing the trash bin down toward freight elevator. Jim greeted him and acted like someone who would be living here. The maintenance answered with a courtesy smile without real meaning.

Jim suddenly saw himself standing in front of the door. He hesitated for a moment. He did not want to knock on the door. He knew she was not there. After all he just repossessed his own car from her. He wanted to verify that he got the right apartment.

Jim: "I know my furniture. I bought it from Park Hyatt hotel and it should be here." He layed down on the floor quick and he looked under the door. The opening was almost half an inch and one with difficulty can see inside the apartment.

Jim: "Damn it! That is my furniture!" He recognized the long sofa, the love chair, even the lower box of the mattress he gave her. There was another thing which grabbed his attention. There were big feet walking around the apartment.

Jim: "Who is this? Maybe it is her boyfriend?" The feet were walking back and forth. He saw big white socks only. "Please, sit down, damn it!" he wanted to see who this person was? "Make a phone call to Kiana" the voice inside commanded him. He did. The phone rang inside the room. Nobody answered. "Hmm... I need to find out who is inside, now!" He felt he was spending too much time lurking around this door. Occasionally, an apartment door would open or the elevator doors would open. He would jump away from the door, but after five minutes he got enough courage to face the door and to knock on it. He heard steps coming toward him. Someone looked at him through the peep hole.

Jim: "God, open the door!" he almost screamed. He felt the person behind the door heavy breathing. He almost kicked the door open. He would never get that close to the person who caused him so much pain and cost him $250,000 dollars and probably his clubs. It was DP "the Don," who was afraid to open the door. Suddenly his phone rang.

Kiana: "Where are you Jim?" she was yelling on the phone.

Jim: "I am in front of your door!"

Kiana: "What door? And where is the black Benz?" She was hysterical.

Jim: "First, who is the guy you are fucking in your apartment? Second, why does he have your phone?"

Kiana: "So, you took your car and you found my apartment? Great."

She was furious ...And suddenly she was speechless... It was the silence of a liar caught in the "house of cards," and everything was collapsing around her. She was thinking fast.

Kiana: "That is my cousin from Georgia," she blurted, lying as usual.

Jim: "But of course... Liar." He hung up on her. The steps behind the door were moving away. Seemed there was no carpet and the squeaking of the bad parquet floor was unavoidable.

Jim: "At least I have my second Benz back! And I still have Shelley."

He was lying to himself now. He really wanted to have it the opposite way.

"I really want nothing else but Kiana to be honest and to love me."

God: "Stop fantasizing! This woman would cut your throat and you would still not believe her that she does not give a damn about you?" It was rational mind talking to him.

Satan: "You love her, don't you? You should be nice to her and be patient. She will come to you sooner than later." His heart was pumping with love and anger and in pain.

Jim: "I am losing her, God!" he screamed in his mind.

God: "You never had her, son. …count your loses, forget about the money and gifts. You will find true love one day. Run as quick as you can away from her." His rational mind was wondering.

Satan: "Listen to your heart. Love is stronger than everything" the weakening heart was in agony.

Jim did not want to hear anyone of those antagonistic phantoms.

Jim: "Why love would cost me $250,000, and nothing to show for? No respect, no love, no home built, no family, no kids? The only true thing here is empty bank account, broken heart, nothingness, one big zero."

Satan: "You are better than some unfortunate souls, who died at birth, in horrible crashes, or from terrible deseases" he laughed.

Jim: "You both make me miserable, not happy. I wonder how the normal people feel and survive and get what they want."

God: "There are not normal people. Everything is one grand illusion. The normal is presented as things we agree on! We write the rules according to common comfort in the society. If the Bible and the Constitution were perfect, why is there so much crime and amendments to the Constitution? The imperfection is because the deviation from normal."

Jim: "We recognize people by their profession and legacy in history books, right? We think they are better or worse by the actions they chose to take under circumstances presented to them, right?"

God: "Wrong, wrong, wrong my Son! I and you agree on only one thing. You are writing your manuscript and listen not only to your mind and what people write and talk. The complete normal is when one is fully aware not only of his surroundings, but also of the universe and its influence on the person. All that knowledge has to activate the Awareness in the person. Awareness is connecting all of the cosmos, universe, earth and human body as one! Then the person is normal. Ok, Jim?"

Jim: "God, I guess I am not normal, if, I am in pain and I am suffering?" His mind was wondering, his heart in pain.

Jim: "Go away Satan! I need my heart back, ok? Your well wishes don't do me any good. See where my generosity and being in love got me!"

God: "Do not blame my adversary, the Satan! He initially means well, but he will put you in your deserving spot eventually!"

Jim: "What do you mean deserving spot?" Now he was getting mad at his Mind/God.

God: "You are following the mistake most people do in their relationship! They keep pouring water in bucket without checking the bottom. Sometime one can dedicate all his life to a woman or to a man, who do not care a second about the sacrifices of the giver. They will take everything one possesses like money, home, steal his cars and treasury, kidnap his children, forge his signature in the will, write themselves as beneficiary and eventually they may even kill him?"

Jim: "God, you are saying that Kiana is a bucket without a bottom, and I got what I deserved? Wow! That is a harsh judgment and horrible punishment! I do consider myself a nice guy."

Satan: "Nice guy," does not spy on his girlfriend. "Nice guy" does not give everything possible to someone who generally ignores them! "Nice Guy," does not take his car back and he does not spit in someone else's face! You needed to connect the dots, sir! She told you in many ways that you are not her boyfriend, but you demanded attention and love and respect regardless." He started to laugh (assuming here Satan is a male, but in cosmic terms the evil is without sex determination).

Jim: "You both God and Satan are working against me now? Great!" He was arguing now with his mind/God and with his heart/Satan.

Jim: "Why are you telling me now what is true and false after three years?" he stormed out of the cursed building 3636!

"Great, I am in the Devils 666 numerology again!" He jumped in the black 300CE Benz and drove it away. He felt everything inside that car was contaminated. He decided to get to the bottom of it.

Read this Cornell University and MIT.

The Good (We will assume it is creativity and it has positive sign or God) has multidimensional reading. We will assume that the six dimensions are the all possible circles and we will call them complete, perfect, stable Cones of the Abyss (01x, 02y, 03z, 04t, 05u, 06c). The Bad (We will assume it is the destruction and has a negative sign of Satan) has less visible dimensions and they are unstable and are delusional (-01x, -02y, -03z, -04t, -05u, -06c). They may represent the opposite of the Abyss. It is similar to the shadow of a person verses his or her real body. God works in Mi octave, while Satan works in Fa octave out of seven tones. Satan works with lower dimensions, where 99% of the people are busy with drinking, having sex, buying too much of unnecessary items, using drugs, involving in hideous crimes (lying, cheating, robbing, killing).

God is the programmer and the creator. He, being in +6th dimension appears only to the chosen ones, who are truly seeking his Awareness. Time in cosmic, God's space, does not exist.

Only Satan can measure time in lower dimensions. The earth real time is limitation to the imperfect humans. Only humans with the highest Awareness can cheat the earth time and Satan. They can do it through special meditating techniques and through tapping into their sub consciousness. Next steps would trigger communications with cosmic intelligence in the future or with deceased geniuses' minds in wormhole methods.

Vatican is fully knowledgeable of Cosmic Awareness. They were able to extract the knowledge, coming to us through Inquisition methods. They have not only the best knowledge of history, but the best scientists and telescopes, scanning the Cosmos. They do not appear and fade away, like funded/defunded NASSA program, or 10 billion CERN (Super Proton Synchrotron) program.

He was able to complete the construction of the bar on first floor also. He installed a great sound system. The Community base boxes and mids and high speakers sounded great. The narrow bar and small dance floor opening by the door needed just one stack of speakers. He was ready to open all floors by the mid December.

Anika: "Look at this beautiful bar, all in black granite and black marble." Jim caught her showing it to some friends of hers.

Jim: "Oh, my God! She acts like she put the money for it. My $50,000 means nothing to them?" he thought.

God: "If you cannot win someone's respect and trust all the money in the world you put in are worthless in that venture."

Jim: "I heard of vortex theory. I feel I am sucked in some whirlpool of liars, cheaters and crooks" he was appalled.

God: "Well, maybe that's what it is? You are in some kind of bottomless hole and you keeping fighting and resurfacing. You still have a chance to come on top. Just be honest and pay taxes."

Jim: "Yes! I know the competition and they are not paying taxes." He thought of Mr. Rogbin and Mr. Dodson, both were his rivals.

One Sunday mid December Jim went again to Kiana's apartment. It was early in the morning around 8 am. He overheard violent squeaking of the bed inside. Seemed they knew he was able to see under the door previously and they blocked the bottom 1/2 inch gap. The noise was mix of female groaning and a man screaming in pleasure.

Kiana: "No, that hurts. Pull it out. It is dry and you are too big, DP!"

DP: "I know you love me! Say it, bitch!" he was too selfish and he had too much pleasure in hurting her.

Kiana: "I don't like anal sex, but you are too crazy and you keep making me pregnant. If you want to do it there, be quick, ok!" she was begging him.

DP: "Bitch, I am almost done! Ohh, Ohh." The bed shaking continued for another two long minutes. Jim was listening in front of the door while monitoring the floor for any noises. He did not observe any cameras at the hallway and that was the only good thing in that bizarre situation.

DP: "I am coming, squeeze bitch!" he commanded her with deep voice.

Kiana: "I am trying, DP! I love you, baby!" She knew how to bring him to orgasm quicker by talking buzz words to him "love you, cum please."

It worked, he finally did it and she run quick to the bathroom to soak her swollen ass in hot water. He followed her to pee. Both voices mixed with the splashing water and Jim decided to leave the "crime scene." He knew they would head to church soon.

The Howard University Chapel would start the Sunday mass usually at 10 am. It was not real mass, it was just symbolic thing. Most students were either Muslims or quasi Christians, who equality hated the white establishment and rich people. One time in the past Jim went there to pick up Kiana. He entered the all black audience and he was looking for Kiana. Suddenly, he saw her leaving through the side exit door. He did not want to be obvious and he slowly followed her outside. He caught up with her a block away.

Jim: "What is wrong with you?" The correct question would have been "What is right with you?"

Kiana: "I couldn't be seen with a white man there" she replied.

Jim: "But you invited me there!"

Kiana: "Yes, but I did not ask you to follow me around" she sounded crazy.

Jim sat in the bushes freezing in the December cold weather until 9.30 am. Suddenly, they appeared at the bus stop. There was no bus and they took a taxi. Things were happening fast. Only a detective like Magnum PI, could trace that cheating character. Jim jumped in the black 300CE Benz, parked a block away and tried to follow the taxi, but it disappeared fast.

Jim assumed their destination was the Chapel and he drove straight toward Georgia Ave., while the taxi had chosen the 16th street route.

He turned on Girard Street then turned right on 6th street. The situation was familiar, just a week before he repossessed his own 2nd Benz here. He saw them getting off the taxi (probably they paid with his own money?), then he proceeded to follow them to the Chapel. He heard increasing noise of people screaming at him "wrong way," but he just ignored them. He wanted desperately to see DP's face and probably to confront him?

They (Kiana and DP) saw him at the last minute. They were almost turning toward the Chapel entrance. They were holding hands!

Jim: "Mother fucker" he rolled the window down and he screamed at DP.

Kiana: "Bye, Jim!" laughing.

Jim: "I will see you later, Kiana." He drove in a circle around them. He needed to get off the area before he would do something he might regret later.

Jim: "Now I know what the impregnator looks like!" He was disappointed. The guy was 6'3" tall and seemed fit, but that was all he could see in him. He did not look smart or rich. He seemed to be afraid to open the door before and now to do something about Jim being in his face?... Seemed that Kiana instilled some fear in him, which explained why he was so passive, or him being in jail on and off made him more cautious? That was the last time Jim and Kiana faced each other. A week before Christmas Kiana left town for good.

Jim tried not to think about her. He was just entertaining the new prospect in his love life, with Shelley. She was not aware of the drama behind the scenes. She assumed that Jim was just preoccupied with the reopening of the club.

Shelley: "Happy Birthday to you, Jim!" she was singing to him on the phone... Her voice was even better sounding through her braces she was wearing to straighten some of her front teeth.

Jim: "Thank you Miss Monroe!" referring to the famous Marilyn Monroe birthday singing to JF Kennedy dinner party.

Shelley: "Want your birthday present?" her soft childish voice always threw him off.

Jim: "How old are you young lady?" they role played.

Shelley: "I am twelve, but I look thirty!" She would play age games.

Jim: "You must be Amanda from the Chris's Hansen show; "To catch a predator?" both were laughing.

Jim: "Let me drive you from school to your home, Amanda!"

Shelley: "Yes, Daddy! I was a bad girl," both laughing again.

Jim: "I will let you surprise me! See you at your home at 8 pm!"

Jim: "Wow!" she opened the door and she was wearing the "Material Girl" outfit of the singer Madonna, who also tried to imitate Marilyn Monroe. "Where are we going like this? I may get arrested? Especially if you are "twelve?" they both kissed.

Shelley: "We are not going anywhere. You have been good to me. You helped me fix my Honda with the repair bill of $1,500. You bought me a TV/combo. You paid my rent the last two months. I owe you, Daddy."

She undressed and that perfect pin up type figure showed all oiled and bubbly.

Jim: "I do not deserve this! I love someone else" he thought.

"Come here, gorgeous lady!" He grabbed that perfect body close to him. She kept her red stilettos on. That gave her almost the extra 3 inches she needed to rise to 5'4" height. Jim was led to the bedroom where the big red candle lights on each side of the bed were lit with strawberry fragrance. She undressed him and just before his erected penis to penetrate her juicy, bushy vagina, she pushed him away.

Shelley: "Jacuzzi, now!" She pushed him toward the bathroom. She shampooed him like a baby from head to toe. "Sit!" she acted like dominatrix.

Jim: "Yes, Madam!" he allowed her to role play. He sunk under water.

Shelley: "Now, obey my command! I will blind fold you, ok!" She did not wait for his agreement. She placed some Mexican looking folded huge napkin around his eyes and she led him to the bedroom.

Jim: "I can't have sex with you. You are underage!" he acted like a guilty guy.

Shelley: "I will bring someone older for you. I do not want you to go to jail!" She kept role playing.

Jim: "I do not want ménage a trois either, ok?" He was acting like he was innocent visitor.

Shelley: "My substitute had legal proof of ID that she is over eighteen, relax!" she pushed him back on the huge bed.

Jim: "Ok, then! I am all yours!" He surrendered. He felt her moist mouth swallowing his fully erected 8 inch tower. Then her hands were magically touching his body like a spider web. She ordered him to move further up in the king size bed.

Shelley: "How do you like that, Jim?" She moved in the position 69. Her vagina lips were rubbing on his nose, wide open and ready to be licked. Her perfect round breasts were now embracing his abdomen area and with her moving up and down with her mouth on his ready to explode penis, holding it like joy stick in video game, her clapping sound of her oiled breasts... all that added to confusion and the pleasure of the blindfolded man.

Jim: "Wonder what would be next? Tattoo or some kind of branding like the wood charring?" he tried to prolong the game. Seemed Shelley had done this before, she was acting almost like an expert.

Shelley: "Ok. Tell me your fantasy, Mr. President..... and I will do it for you!"

She whispered in Marilyn Monroe like voice.

Jim: "Ok. You will act like you are my step daughter and we are having sex! Ok?" He was really thinking of Kiana now, but he couldn't confess that to her yet.

Shelley: "Ok, Daddy! I am twelve years old and I am horny. Can we have some fun?" She was great actress.

Jim: "Ok, but do not tell Mom! And if the Police finds out I will go to jail and I will be a "sex offender."

Shelley: "I want gifts! I will be a good girl. This will be our secret till we both die, ok?" she was continuing the strange role play.

The confusion got even more! From Shelley to Marilyn to Amanda to Kiana! He was delaying as much as he possibly could.

Jim: "Amanda! Turn around. Now bend over in the doggy style. He took off the blind fold. Wow. Her milky white skin and pear shaped ass and nice healthy waist were in front of his open eyes. There was a huge mirror on the dresser nearby and he was excited even more from the reflecting sex images of this almost perfect couple. He was forty-seven, she was thirty-six. They should have been married by now. It was too perfect. Back on his mind he was wondering what can go wrong here. They both were living their fantasy! Sometime he was puzzled if owning a club was a good thing? Are people generally attracted to the glamour, the flashy dance floors, the artificially happy crowd, the money, the bottle service, the VIP entering without waiting in lines, the drunken women? Seemed people felt rich there, they were all champions, and everyone was sexy, young, smart, and immortal! For some reason they could not meet his emotional standards. Seemed they built all those fake expectations and the only glue in the club scene was the alcohol and the benefits, it brings. Women would talk to the owner of the club for their own reasons; mostly, to extort free drinks, free drugs, cash, to plant a phone number so next time they seduce the men in shopping and promise maybe sex? Being a club owner had its perks. Women veered toward men with material things. The impression of club owners is that they have money and toys.

Shelley: "I am cumming, Daddy!" she awoke him from his wandering thoughts. Her buttocks were squeezing him and drugging his torpedo skin forward, duplicating the motion of her mouth earlier.

Jim: "Amanda, you graduated! I am cumming too, Oh baby!" He exploded inside her and she felt the quantum wave pulsating up her spine.

Shelley: "You are doing your tricks again! What is about you, that is so different from the others? Where is that extra pulsation coming from?"

She fell with face forward biting the pillow, preventing her whispering from turning to scream.

Jim: "Nosey neighbors?" he collapsed next to her. He kissed her white breasts slightly exposed, and then he kissed her back and inserted his left hand between her wet thighs. He was ready for another round, but she pushed him away.

Shelley: "Don't you have a club to run? Lying around me will not pay the rent. I will excuse you this time and you will get your bonus later, but don't get used to having too much sex with me. I want my man doing business first; pleasure is a reward, not a right here."

Jim: "I worked all my life and got me nothing but mean and crooked surroundings. Now I am with you I feel like I am escaping into the different world" he kissed her.

Shelley: "Great sex is different than great accomplishment! I know you are helping here and there, but see where we live? In some an apartment! I need my man to move me to my own house and show me he can handle a family!" she sounded like a family counsel.

Jim: "Ok. Thank you for my gift. Now let me know when is your birthday and I will have a surprise for you!" he stood up heading toward the shower. "I will tell you what the gift will be when I return from the shower, Miss Material Girl/Madonna/Carmen Electra/Amanda."

Shelley: "Wait, Jim! What gift is equal or better than my gift I just gave you? On second thought I think I am falling in love with you already. So what is equal to my love?"

Jim: "Here is my real estate pocket license. We are going house hopping!" he looked at her expression.

Shelley: "Great! I am thirty-six; I should have had a house by now!" she said it with a serious face. "Come here, lover! I see you know how to get a good woman's attention!" She opened her legs and invited him using her index finger like a hook.

Jim: "Oh, my God! It is all about talking? Why was Kiana not like Shelley? I am the same person, who basically tells the same story to different people. One is ignoring me even I spend a quarter million on her, the other will give me any kind of fantasy sex based on just telling her what she wants to hear?" he was puzzled, but he inserted himself in that gorgeous orifice with the 8 inch of thrust. He named his penis Peter.

Shelley: "I was living with this guy for ten years and he never even promised me anything. He was not even close to you, Jim." She started again to pleasure him, but this time was more subdued and too mechanical.

Jim: "Now we have sex like married people, it is boring, but still is good."

Shelley: "I agree; it feels good. I like "Peter," addressing his tower.

Jim: "When we buy a house you can own Peter. Now you are just renting it!"

Shelley: "Are you implying a marriage proposal? Wow. If you promise my monopoly on Peter and you are not outsourcing it to other sexual prospects, I think we have a deal!"

Jim went back to the bar. It was a seven day operation. He offered to Larry to take some nights off. He wanted Shana and Evelyn to cover the shifts. Shana had a child and she could work certain hours, based on her babysitter's availability. Evelyn was more available, but she was hanging with strange crowd. Jim was looking for cheaper bartenders who could produce the same as Larry. He allowed Larry to rent from him the office at half price and to sleep there at night. The office was furnished like a small hotel room; a huge queen size bed was with velvet cushion head board, two dark grey granite small tables, double (green/white) hotel curtains, sofa bed folded on one side, white imitation granite table he placed a 25 inch TV on, love chair in the corner looked like an observer chair facing the bed. To reinforce security Jim built extra framed doors one on outside, and one on inside which slid like roll up and down garage gate. He intended to bring his JVC 700 digital camcorder cameras and lock them up from eventual visitors. He was very close to realizing his producer's dreams to make Walker's Media finally visible and get recognized! It took him 17 years to get to this level and he was confident he could expand the club, become a real estate broker, and move on in production of his full featured films. He wanted to buy commercial properties, to develop them, to grow as a respected citizen!

First week of January Mansur approached him.

Mansur: "How are you doing, Jim! Can we talk for a minute here?" His voice sounded familiar. Jim sensed something bad was going to happen?... Mansur led him to a booth close to his side of business, not far from his kitchen counter.

Jim: "What is it, Mansur? You are always in some financial trouble?"

Mansur: "Jim, you are doing great fixing the place, but I need help again. Dragan construction is taking me to court. They need 2,000 dollars ASAP. We maybe lose our license for unpaid mechanic's lien?"

Jim: "That sounds awfully familiar to Sarkisian claim in October '05. Why are you always asking me for money? Remember, you are 5,000 Mansur strong in northern Lebanon, and Malik is here, with many of your rich, friends."

Mansur: "You are the only person who stayed with me the last eight years. And we signed a lease for eight more years. You will get your money back. Get this guy off my back for now."

Jim: "Mansur, you keep asking without giving. I need my first floor open for business ASAP. Then I will help you with your debt. You have been asking me to pay the full of my share of 6,000 dollars in rent the last seven months but you wanted me to expand the club to three floors with 2/3rd of my money against yours 1/3rd investment. Your nephew stole my $40,000 to get married. Finally after three months my bars are ready to open. Now allow me to operate my bars and to make this place profitable.

Mansur: "Ok, write me a check and get your first floor open." He reluctantly agreed.

Jim: "I built gates between the kitchen and the bar, so nobody will interfere with each other s business."

Mansur: "Jim, you are like family to me. One thing here is; be careful with Malik. He is one evil man. He has money but he is very careful with it. He is asking to buy your first floor business." He stood up.

Jim: "Is it not kind of late to buy anything, especially after everything is ready to start making money? The base in business is the construction first and the expectation to make profit later. Basically, if one is buying a business he is reimbursing the construction cost and he is buying the assumed profit? I can't just sell something for money for the construction. Ok?"

Mansur: "Let see how the business goes and eventually you may buy me out?" he bluffed.

Jim: "What do you need?"

Mansur: "300,000 dollars or half first, then 5,000 a month until you pay off the 150,000 balance."

Jim: "Put that in writing. I am a realtor and "if it is not written, it is not legal," right?" He laughed.

Mansur: "Let us do the baby steps first. You tell me when you got $150,000 dollars saved and we can negotiate from there. Otherwise, we are just wasting each other's time and it is a pure speculation!" He sounded very similar to Jim's own philosophy. His English was not that great but it was understandable. Jim just did not trust him so much.

Jim: "One more thing. Our occupancy permit states that we can use all three floors. Our entertainment license states that we can use the normal hours for club operation, but we have our liquor license operation hours limited. Police are harassing my employees and I can't operate the first (very visible) floor using illegal hours."

Mansur: "Thanks for the check. We need to talk to Nikias tomorrow. For now open the first floor till midnight and then move the customers upstairs. Then the police will not bother you much."

Jim: "Seems we can never get it right. The evil forces always keep us in some fear of being punished?"

Mansur: "You know how the government works. They give you enough, but they regulate you more than they should." He went out the door.

Jim climbed up the stairs to see how the bars were doing? He was still concerned about many things, but once the bar opened and people poured in his mind was at ease.

"Leo welding" completed all the construction mid January. Jim had hired this Korean entrepreneur to compartmentalize all three floors and with garage gates style dividing walls the club looked like a puzzling fortress, a citadel. He installed frames on each door, to every floor, to the back alley, to his office, to any window, including the sky light windows. It was at cost around $20,000, but the security was important. Every business in the area was broken into in the previous five years. The biggest heist was at the neighbor restaurant Normandy, at around $20,000. They cut the 2nd floor and dropped the safe and dragged it to a pickup truck in the alley. It was inside job and criminals were videotaped by the surveillance camera in the alley. That was in this area. His competitor at club Vibe, got robbed in day light at gun point. Mr. Rogbin couldn't shake off his bad luck. Restaurant Filomena was robbed after Valentine's Day. Police guessed that was inside job and most of employees were fired in the next two months.

Nathan: "Wow, Jim! You are making this place like a miniature club! Three floors and all those security gates! You look like you are preparing yourself for a long hold here? I am impressed." He was drinking miller light beer and watching the show. The ladies of the night were sipping in from different parts of town, but with same intentions, to entertain and to make money!

Jim: "I am thinking to place cameras all around here and in and around my office?" he was puffing on a great Cuban cigar Cohiba, just delivered a day before.

Nathan: "Aren't you afraid that may scare "the element" away? That is what makes your place so unique!"

Jim: "I am working to clear "the Element" from the street and from my club, but Police never help me when I call them. Look at the alley next to the Normandy.

I have been telling the cops to stop harassing me and to focus on taking the drugs out of the area. They can see everything in real time on cameras, installed by John Arkidge Company, but unless there is a murder, they do not care to check on the drug dealers or users co-mingling out there."

Nathan: "So. Once you open the whole club you need good promotional team, right?" He was going through second miller lite.

Can I buy you a drink?" He was a great person. He was one of Jim's favorite customers.

Jim: "You buy me a drink; I will buy you a cigar!" Both of them were laughing now.

Nathan: "I hope you don't kick all the girls out?" he became almost serious. "How is your love life?" He knew about the turmoil with Kiana.

Jim: "I caught her with a boyfriend, finally! Now I am working on a new prospect, but I still do love her. You know she is my first love!"

Nathan: "You are insane! You can have any lady here at the bar!"

Jim: "True! One who is in love reaches for the difficult and impossible before he settles for the three words "want to fuck?" I pushed away thousand beautiful ladies here, who practically would marry me in a drop of a hat. Unfortunately, they are usually drunk or they only see the money signs and benefits." He inhaled the Cohiba.

Nathan: "I do think you are just obsessed with her and she is playing you for a sucker! Leave her alone, that Kiana and stay with the new lady! Ok!"

Jim: "My mind (God) agrees with everything you are saying, but my heart (Satan) tells me to keep her and my heart bleeds. Love hurts."

Nathan: "One way love is an obsession, not true love! I wonder if you are not some kind of stalker." He probably was right to a certain point.

Jim: "Stalker is not sacrificing his life and business and giving gifts and cash in hundreds of thousands for lies! I am not Don Quixote, the Man from La Mancha, who will love his imaginary lady Dulcinea de Toboso."

Nathan: "Similarity is there, but you get away because you don't use Sancho Panza. You do not have any friends or confidants. I do not know how you do work so hard and constantly expanding without any partners and real friends?"

Jim "... And no days off, no break, and no vacations! I took twice a vacation in twenty-five years and was hardly a month all together! The great Government imagines that foreigners come here loaded with money or they can tap in some mysterious sources of money related to illegal activities; like drugs smuggling, weapons sales, child pornography, white slavery of women kidnapped, mafia activities, extortion of money from rich men, illegal alcohol and cigarettes, dog fighting, etc."

Nathan: "Yeah, I watch movies too and most of them involve some crooked government official. You must understand that the mafia style and government style are similar in eliminating the competition. The difference is the government is considered legal entity and is based on constitution. Mafia has their own rules, but the public is not aware of them. We know about the mafia from the way they manage to control certain industries and by the trail of dead bodies. When big boss gets jailed like Teflon Don/aka John Gotti, then they talk about them, but before that nobody knows if the mafia exists. I think the government does think you are a mafia!" he sipped on the beer and he was like a child in Disney World. He had the big and wide open eyes of someone who enjoys the surroundings of beautiful women. … And they arrived at around 10.30 pm like a clock work.

Diamond and Essence: "Hey, Wesley!" they screamed at simultaneous voice like they had done it thousands of times before.

Diamond: "Many 5-0s outside. Be careful." She ordered a Long Island ice tea, one of the most potent alcoholic beverages (with five different liquors, coca cola and sweet and sour mix). She was early thirties tall beauty and above average in street smarts.

Jim: "I know that they are always there. I had a snitch here that I kicked out recently (Fiola's friend, Layla) for talking to the cops. I think they are up to something, but I know how to deal with them. I keep the place clean."

Diamond: "Can you give me some condoms? I know you take the chocolates from HIPS. You do not need the condoms. I heard you got a new girlfriend!" she gave him five dollars.

Jim: "I will give you a bunch of condoms, but don't use them here, ok!" He pocketed the bill and he directed her to Larry. "He will give you the stuff." He slapped her nice round ass and blurted out, "behave, no business here, ok!"

Diamond: "I am with you, but watch the younglings here. They are the one who may put your club in trouble?"

Jim: "I know! Thanks!"

Nathan: "Man, you are a pimp! I have never seen women who are so comfortable with someone who they do not fuck?" He was puzzled.

Jim: "I do not fuck everyone who enters that door. You know the rule "If they pay you, they are business; if you fuck them, they are wives and they will not pay for drinks."

Nathan: "True!"

The night shift was predictable and the money was flowing in as usual. Toward the end of the night Jim checked all the floors and the bathrooms. He found two used condoms in the trash bin on second floor and one used condom on third floor. He had a meeting with Larry after the shift.

Jim: "You know Larry; I took you in my club from the streets. I gave you a job, I made you a manager, and I trusted you with my office. I left the country for a week and you had all the freedom and choice to do what you like! That is a lot of trust! Now, I feel the evil forces are closing on me! I am trying to keep that club clean. I spent my last pennies in improvements. I left you in charge here. Now I find condoms all over the place. I may sell them to the hookers, but I did not allow them to have sex in our bathrooms!"

Larry: "The bar is very busy and I do not have time to check the bathrooms all the time." He was looking for excuses. He was not looking at Jim's face; there was not real eye contact. Something was amiss here, something was not clicking. Was Larry's homelessness converted to normal income too much to handle in such a short time? Or was something more sinister boiling behind the picture? Sometimes, we need to go beyond the comfort of the friendship, (an illusion until proven by tragedy) and we need to punish our closest friends before we punish our enemies. The true story of Prince of Wallachia Vlad Dracula The Impaler comes to picture. He was equally cruel to his native citizens and to his enemies.

Jim: "I am fining you $50 for not keeping the club clean. Next time I find condoms anywhere you will lose your job." He saw Larry's face changing to angry red one.

Larry: "Boss! I have no idea how they got there! I need this job!"

Jim: "First, I see you find time to play on the computer and to change the music every thirty minutes. If you had the same vigor in keeping the eye on the club as a whole -- like checking back exits, third floor activities, first floor people hanging at the door like they own it and asking for cover charge. I already hired a doorman to check IDs, but he is not in charge the Bar management like you are (we are talking about Bryan, the african american). When Police check anything they ask for certified ABC manager."

Larry: "Ok, boss! Here is 50 bucks." He reluctantly handed the money. His face was in pain.

Jim: "You understand I trust you and this is symbolic. You have my register. The money is not really taken from you, but from me. One more thing, remember my rule "you do not have friends at the bar, you have good customers!"

Larry: "I make $150 a night, supposedly. Today it will be less. Ok!" He walked down the stairway. Recently Jim suggested him to find a place to live. The office was too small to share.

Larry was upset for many reasons. He just found a place to live on 15th and N Street at "Miramar" apartments. He couldn't sign the lease without co-signer and he was able to convince Phil, a guy who claimed to be a lawyer, to help him get the lease. He was even able to furnish it. Now he was fined $50. He was puzzled himself how the condoms ended up there? Then he remembered the police undercover who were at the bar in November asking for Jim. Does that condom appearance anything to do with strange behavior of those cops? On the other hand he had been under the microscope of the Police for most of his adult life so that was not anything big to lose sleep about. He was not happy why Jim should punish him for something he had no control over? He thought. Yeah, maybe next time he will play less with the music and he will check the bathrooms now and then? He couldn't afford losing money, his job and his boss' trust.

Jan. 26th, 2006 arrived as usual. Jim came early to the club. He checked all the floors. He turned the sound on from the first floor and all floors had the same sound. While he was checking the floors he noticed the same situation recurring; the condoms from the night before on each floor bathrooms. He had two more bartenders to rely on. He almost called them, but before that he wanted to have an emergency meeting with Mansur and Larry.

Mansur: "What is the problem now?"

Jim: "I will fire Larry. He is not keeping the place clean! I found used condoms again after I warned him and fined him a week ago."

Larry: "I have nothing to do with those condoms!" He was defending himself.

Mansur: "Larry is a good man. Do not fire him. Give him another chance, please." Jim."

Mansur sounded fatherly and he was like a bad referee, who sees the faults, but he will not give the penalty to the deserving party.

Jim: "Nobody has the key to the Club, but me and Larry and you, Mansur!" Dark clouds of suspicion were filling up the room.

Mansur: "I am asking you to keep Larry. He has manager's license and seems you want to spend time away lately with your girlfriend Shelley!"

Mansur knew how to push his selling points. Shelley was a great reason to take some time off. Seemed money was important, but personal happiness was a sufficient argument.

Jim: "I wish I had better choices in some pool of beautiful and honest people and not worry about some condoms, hookers and dirty cops."

The dark clouds were hanging around that cursed club. Seemed anyone touching The Prosperity/Sally's/Starlight Bar get burned and going out of business? There were many factors involved here to stop Jim's success story.

The first factor was incomplete licensing. The normal hours of operation would be till 2 am weekdays and 3 am on weekend to sell liquor. Kitchen should be closed two hours prior to the closing hour of establishment. Food should consist of 45 percent of total revenue; there should be ID checks during liquor sales and adequate security during large promotions. Noise should be at 60db, practically zero sound coming out from any door and windows. Parking should be sufficient or by valet company, and finally the nearest school or Church should be 500 feet away from it. Jim never complied with the noise regulations and his speakers were installed at the windows and some at the door entrance together with the lighting show and TV screens at middle level; all those were attractive features, with some resentment by the police. Later on Lima, Lotus and The Paparazzi clubs would use the same features -- lights, TVs and sound. Sometime he would ask new customers, "How did you hear about this place?" The customer would answer "I saw the lights and I heard the sound."

Detective O'Conner: "We have to penetrate that labyrinth somehow."

Partner Waldo: "His patrons are protecting him with some code of silence. Maybe we can pull the rug from under him? His manager Larry is very popular but he is somewhat negligent with keeping tight control at the place. The prostitutes have good relationships with him and they coach the new comers ladies how to act around the bar and how to detect us. We sent many undercover men there but they either get discovered sooner or later or they just get corrupted by the life style of the prostitutes. Those women who bring $4,000 a night to one pimp are like in some special club society. The game for a Police Officer is to get free sex, basically, playing the mind games with them. I bet this guy, Jim gets laid every night if he wishes to do so?"

Detective O'Conner: "I think we have better chance with squeezing the pimps. The ladies of the night wouldn't cooperate much, especially the veterans in the business. We have to look for younger prostitutes, who are new in the business."

Waldo: "We can use the underage liquor drinking to intimidate the bar management and owners."

Detective O'Conner: "We tried that many times through MPD and ABC enforcement officers, but we couldn't get results."

Waldo: "How about we plant mock money and set him up?"

Detective O'Conner: "That is great idea. We need some strong officers, who can't be easily tempted and corrupted by the ladies."

Waldo: "Hey, make sure they are married and had sex the night before!"

Detective O'Conner: "Right!"

Detective O'Conner: "We have to synchronize everything with MPD and with ABC board. To get a warrant to search and arrest we need the Judge's approval and signature. Then we can close them down."

Chapter 13

January 28th, 2006. It seemed normal Saturday. Jim was with Shelley. He had prepared the bars with everything necessary for the weekend earlier and he intended to go to work. For unexplained reasons Shelley was very seductive and playful. They had the usual passionate love making at about 8.30 pm. Jim took a shower and he was getting ready to go the club.

Shelley: "Can you stay a bit longer? Larry will not miss you too much." She kept staying in bed, naked and shining from the body lotion and oil she was applying daily on her. It made her body skin softer and slippery.

Jim: "Why? Are you ready for more?" He always preferred to have sex over money making. He assumed that not being married, anytime he had opportunity to have sex it was like a gift. He yearned to find a nice and understandable lady, who would share his ambitions and achievements without agendas and second thoughts. Was Shelley the one?

Shelley: "Yes, I am but I miss your warm body and kiss more than the sex (and there you are real good too)." She invited him back to bed as usual with her index finger curved like a fishing hook.

Jim: "Ok, a hug and kiss only, nothing else!" Both knew he was lying.

Kiana: "Hey, where are you?" She called out of nowhere at 9 pm.

Jim: "I am ready to go to work. Why?" He slipped out of the bed once he screened the caller ID, saying "private."

Kiana: "Are you with Shelley again?" she sounded jealous.

Jim: "Yes! You left me!" He acted agitated. He was speaking in low voice in the corner of the living room, almost catching cold.

Kiana: "What is your priority now? To get laid or to make money?" she sounded like a wife and like Shelley at times.

Jim: "Until I get married, I make my choices. Now I can listen only to opinions."

Kiana: "I need money, Jim! I do not like men that have excuses and especially with no money. Go to the club, man! Make money!" she almost ordered him.

Jim: "Ok, but what will the money render, for me? You had money when you were here and you still cheated!"

Kiana: "I am trying to get rid of DP and you are not giving me money or any incentive to do that. I don't like weak men."

Jim: "DP controls you. You are weak."

Kiana: "Stop talking about others, I will not talk about Shelley also. Shut up and make money. If you are strong, I will come back to you!"

Jim: "Ok, bye!" He agreed. He returned to the bedroom and jumped under the sheets. It was stress reliever to have Marilyn Monroe, Carmen Electra, and Amanda in one Shelley.

Shelley: "Club trouble?" she was either naive or the perfect actress.

Jim: "Not really. Someone wants to buy the new and expanded club. We were negotiating." He was shaking from the cold and that covered his lie at the moment. In reality he was always on cloud 9 when Kiana called him. The instant erection her voice was always giving him now was very useful to Shelley....

Shelley: "I never knew someone who would get an erection from selling a club? That is the first for me, especially when your whole body is shaking from the cold, amazing!" She opened her healthy ex Army legs with a natural motion. "Come here, Daddy! No more business tonight, ok!" They made love again for almost half an hour. That was one of their last encounters of trouble free sex. After that they both fell asleep.

The Satan and the all the evil forces were closing in on the club, like hungry coyotes. Fate works in mysterious ways. Detective O'Conner and his crew were on a mission to close the club. They sent in whole gangs of detectives, who were federal agents, and they instructed the Metropolitan Police Department to wait outside the club. They found two of the youngest hookers around the bar and they proposed to have sex with them. According to the Police report they were taken to the bathrooms on the 3rd floor. There was no sex conducted but there was money exchanged, which were marked by the Police. Once the money was exchanged the two young ladies went to the bar to pay their drinks. At this time the Police got a signal to enter. Around twenty Police cars arrived within a minute. Jim had observed the big tent built at side entrance of "Capitol Hilton," earlier between 16th and 15th Streets and the closed for traffic X Street, NW. That was because of President Bush was visiting. He did not know that the same Police also were preparing to attack his club.

Detective O'Conner: "Where is Jim?" He screamed out of his lungs. The Coyote Pack (a mix of FBI, MPD and some ABRA investigators) cornered everyone, from the regular crowd to "the element," (consisting of three hookers, some johns, drunkards and who knows who might be the others most likely their own undercover agents). Some of the coyotes climbed to the 3rd floor. They couldn't find anything there. They reported that to Detective O'Conner. He was disappointed.

Detective O'Conner: "Round everyone and send them to Central Cell."

Partner Waldo: "We can't arrest anyone without evidence! Those hookers can tell anything to the judge to get off. We need hard evidence." He was right.

Detective O'Conner: "Take pictures of everything. If nothing to show spread unwrapped condoms on third floor and make sure they are stretched. Now we will "have evidence." We need to interrogate everyone. Use intimidation and scare tactics. We need this club out of business. We cannot find Jim. He is the true owner here. We have to make this case to stick. Use everything that is legal or illegal to do that. Let the lawyers sort things out later. I checked Jim bank accounts. There is nothing there; therefore, his lawyer can't bail him out even he wanted. So, let's be true cops not losers in this case!"

Partner Waldo: "You are in charge, boss! Basically, you are giving us Carte Blanche to do whatever we want! Thank you!"

At 2 am Jim was awoken by a phone call.

Kiana: "Are you at the club? It is kind of quiet around you." She was calling again from a private number.

Jim: "Who is this? I am asleep." He was acting like he did not recognize the voice. He got up and headed to the bathroom. He relieved himself while Kiana's voice increased to some staccato octaves, which even the sleeping beauty Shelley would have heard if he did not close the door behind him fast!

Kiana: "Asleep? I know you are dying to fuck my pussy, but you will never get it by staying home, especially on Saturday night! Fuck!" She was furious.

Jim: "You don't call me for months and then you call me twice in one night? You run away with DP, you wouldn't see me while you were here, and now suddenly you are concerned about my money? And you offer me your pussy as my incentive? What a laugh..." He was puzzled. There must be something much more sinister than she was presenting? Was DP behind the scenes pushing her to extort more money from him ... or were some of her drug dealing "entrepreneurs" short of cash? Further on in the story, her best drug mover, disguising himself as music producer "Saint Sylvester" would end up with thirty years in jail. The answer came in the next 15 minutes.

Kiana: "You must be with that slut Shelley? It is not even close to your always hustling nature to be asleep at home at 2 am on a Sunday morning and not being at the club?"

Jim: "Ok, if that will bring you back to me, I will go to that damned club! Now tell me when are you coming to see me in DC?" He wanted to finish that bathroom conversation ASAP.

Kiana: "Send me money tomorrow via Western Union and I will see you next weekend!" she lied quick.

Jim: "I know you are not telling the truth, but if I lose $300 it is my stupidity! I will take that chance. By the way I almost fired Larry the other day, doing illegal things!" he wanted to show her he is The Boss. He almost hung up.

Kiana: "What happened?" she sounded concerned, her voice was back to normal, low and seductively sexy. She was always giving him instant erection. He started to bulge up again.

Jim: "Why are our conversations never normal? I like you when you are concerned and talk without screaming! Say something nice and I will tell you everything when we meet next week! I do feel my cell phone is bugged."

Kiana: "Why? Are you doing something wrong? Tell me all about it next weekend. Send me money tomorrow, ok, Jim? Go check on your money. I don't trust this guy Larry! Bye."

Jim: "Love you always, Kiana." He was whispering now, while splashing water to refract and cancel the sounds of his conversation.

Kiana: "Love you too, my Jim." He started to put on some clothes and he was trying not to wake up the beautiful and fully naked doll like Shelley. She was either really asleep or she was the greatest actress he had ever seen, save Kiana. She always reminded him of sleepy cat with a face to match it. Fully clothed Jim headed toward the door when at 2.20 am the phone rang again.

Jim: "Angel! What is going on?" it was one of his loyal and best customers and top dollar earning hooker for her pimp, unfortunately.

She claimed she made $475,000 (yes, almost half a million dollars in cash untaxed) for her pimp Marquis in one year. She was the one to call him a year before about someone vandalizing his champagne Benz in December, 2004. Later on, in 2007 she would be Jim's lover, but not girlfriend.

Angel: "Jim, the cops are in your club, about twenty cars and I see them entering your place like there is a fire inside!" She was screaming.

Jim: "They are always there. They have no life. Maybe they brought President Bush with them after they left Capitol Hilton?" he was jokingly assuming, but he was slowly accepting the information. This genius mind was aware of the anti-reality the cops were trying to induce on him, but he never thought they were really serious?

Angel: "I am watching them from across the street. I see they are arresting people. Some of the hookers are being taken out to the paddy wagon as we speak."

Jim: "Do not go there. I will get to the bottom of it. I will call Larry now. Thank you!" He was seeing the repetition of the Zoro club falling; he was bewildered but never surprised. After all the algorithm of all possibilities includes failure and success at the same! Jim dialed Larry's phone about five times. There was no answer. After fifteen minutes he decided to call Mansur. He sensed that the Club was under attack. He did not want to leave it open to "Wagner-Ride of the Valkyries" like attack of the crooked coyotes dressed like police officers. He knew their tactics; he just did not exactly know what, was the story?

Mansur: "Hello!" he sounded asleep and hard to talk. "Who is calling so late?" Anybody would have felt sorry for him if they did not know him.

Jim: "It is Jim, Mansur! I am with Shelley. I heard that the Police are arresting people in the Club. Can you go there and sort things out?"

Mansur: "Do you know what is going on? Maybe someone got hurt?" he sounded concerned.

Jim: "If that was the case Larry would have answered the phone! Maybe he is in trouble with the police? I told you to fire him three days ago."

Mansur: "You are assuming! Let me go there and see what is going on. We need to talk after that. I think you should be there to supervise the operation, not with Shelley now!"

Jim: "I need a break Mansur! I need to live life too. Your hours of operation are all screwed. That is why the Police are always in my face. We are expanding and blowing good money away, but we cannot get our liquor hours straightened! Do not blame everything on me, Mansur!"

Jim felt like a dog chasing his own tail, when talking to Mansur. His "would-be-if-he-could-be partner" just did not care. Mansur's system worked all his thirty years on slogan "blame others" and he survived. Why at this time, should things be any different?

Shelley: "Hey, lover! What is all this shouting about? Are you in trouble?" She was running toward the living room putting a white long robe on.

Jim: "There is some action in the club and I am not sure should I go there now?" He lit a cigar.

Shelley: "No smoking here. Go outside on the balcony."

Jim: "In this cold? Ok!" He needed to focus on himself now. The anti-reality was facing him now like an impregnable black wall. He needed answers and to counter the coyotes. And he did!

Jim knew the game! He was experienced in the judicial system and he knew reacting to the police entrapment will prolong their existing anxiety. After chasing skirts for about half a century the Government made more money from their supporters and clients, than from the ladies of the night. Although during World War II the lines were around the corner in Hawaii to have sex with prostitutes, the GIs were suppressed from having same fun once they arrived at the Main Land. Only three major cases were registered against the big caliber Madams like Mayflower Madam, Heidi Fleiss and Washington Madam.

The big hit against Mustang Ranch, was for unpaid taxes and the owner Joe Conforte played the 15 million dollar game he "allegedly" owed to IRS. After he bought it back on auction through his own lawyer for 1.5 millions, the Feds discovered how the cash was converted to gold and from New York was sent to Brazil where it was converted to cash. Later on the same business was sold for $200,000 to one of his prostitutes. She was able to restore the license and Joe Conforte was able to send her a greeting from Brazil.

Heidi Fleiss went to a California jail, but she never disclosed her clients. Washington Madam was killed in Florida, "allegedly" she committed suicide. She was about to tell it all. Sidney Barrows,The Mayflower Madam, was another story in New York ending in 1984. His own friend Contessa, he met at St. Moritz, next to The Plaza, she was pretending to be copy cat of the Mayflower Madam, most likely, the Plaza Madam? They met in 1984, coincidently! One leaves, another comes in, the irony of life!

The Police were bored. They were looking for less exposure. It was more effective for them to chase massage parlors, bars, pimps and drug dealers. The benefits were they had no resistance by big lawyers and they were able to steal a lot of cash. Many drug dealers were caught in the alley and money and drugs were confiscated. There, in the alley, was a murder too. A white junkie was sold fake cocaine and he was in convulsions and dying after he filled up his nose. The Police would argue that they would be arrested and processed "solely."

Police: "You have two options! First, we take your money as evidence and the drugs also. Then we arrest you. Second, we take everything from you. We don't arrest you, no charge, no processing, like nothing happen!

Which one do you choose?"

Drug dealer: "I choose the second!"

Police: "Great choice! Now go and do not look back. Go!"

Drug dealer: "Damn it! They stole my stuff, but I am free!" he would tippy toe out of the alley.

Detective O'Conner: "We are screwed! The whole idea was to get this guy Jim! He beat us in the game! Either someone told him about our raid or he is the smartest man in the universe? Who could have leaked the FBI sting info? It was known and organized by most trusted partners I have worked with for twenty years. We never lost a case; we never had a leak like this. We got a big drug king pin like Rayful Edmonds III, who was running 300 million drug emporium a year. We busted much more difficult cases, but this is about to get away!" He walked around with long black metal flash light and he seemed to be the center of attention. Everyone was asking him questions, but in truth he wanted to find something like... drugs, guns, gambling paraphernalia, some twisted pictures, anything to have this case stick. Why wasn't Jim here? Damn it! Was he just one lucky man, who had the ability to smell them, to foresee their covert moves ahead of time? He reminisced, the raid of the Potomac house of the Mr. Rogbin, the infamous owner of Phantom, Urban, Fusion. Cash in millions was hidden everywhere in the double walls. One million was in his club vault too. "Why there was no money anywhere here?"

The gang of coyotes, was very hungry. They needed cash. They disclosed 1.9 million to IRS that they found, but in reality in Mr. Rogbin's house was near three million! One million was nicely, distributed to all the members of the "magnificent 9" (three members from each -- ATF, IRS, FBI)... At the house raid the liquor guys (ABRA) were missing, no liquor license, and no jurisdiction! Good, less to cut. The local police at Potomac were nothing but photographers, who get to be invited after the damage is done. FBI did not trust the Cops; cops did not trust the FBI. The press was invited after the scene was edited (made to believe) for public consumption -- TV, newspapers, radio. If one watches movies, that was true reenactment of "Training Day" movie with Danzel Washington.

Jim waited out this time the wave to pass. The wave of destruction was approaching him. Usually he would scream, fight, kick, and call, trying to be interactive, proactive, and reactive. This time he was passive. Through his life of extreme survival he learned one thing in Martial Arts. The physical fight may take pain; the mental game may take laughing.

Jim: "Make the opponent crashes himself in his own inertia and stupidity... "the 180 degree rule!"

He would relate to the Feynman diagrams and to pyramid structure (cone theory and it's symmetry), Yin and Yang in lotus position were basically the two quarks W- and W+, who represent the positive (yang male, bright) and the negative (yin, female, dark) side of the human brain on top of the pyramid (cone, lotus position), who control the opposite sides of the imaginary triangle (a cone, frontally dissected). The related sides of that triangle are the Sun (positive energy), moon (negative energy), earth (negative energy, ground). All those forces cancel each other in the center of gravity of the triangle via annihilation. The result is the creation of heavy mass, The WeZon (Jim's boson).

Finally The QED (The Quantum Electrodynamics) and QFD (quantum electroweak) theories were connected! Sorry, Mr. Higgs! There is a new Ruler here. The WeZon, gravitational wave will move with warp speed to counter any little man made disasters, (like the little coyote Mr. O'Conner created with placing fake, used condoms at the edited scene on third floor at Zeus Lounge/old Randevu). He was not aware of the protective gravitational field (plasma) which acted like a shield to Jim, making him Deity like. The WeZon acts like the trigger catalyst for GalaxFi (the field, which is neutral in charge, with mass, moving with universal speed, much faster than light).

Finally! When Jesus was killed, he was not really physically killed. The gravitational shield (WeZon) protected him from dying and he was resurrected. The other two who accompanied him did physically die. They were poor thieves, who were not protected by the gravitational shield, in reference to (Mr. Dodson and Mr. Rogbin) in analogy today. When the roman soldier pushed his sword through Jesus side under his rib cage and there was no blood to leak, a sign that he was not a human, but Deity! They checked his tomb later on, he was not there. He was a spirit! He was gone. Sorry, little detective O'Conner. The similarity here was obvious. Jim was not in the club either!

Shelley was very comforting due to his sudden shock. Maybe because she was tired of the great sex they had twice already, maybe because she could not believe that the great United States government could be that cruel to close a million dollar club that easy, she was trying to just convince Jim that everything would be all right.

Jim: "I wonder what Larry did, but I will call my lawyer tomorrow. Hopefully, it is nothing major to be concerned about?"

He guessed that Kiana was giving him some kind of revenge for catching her with DP and she had to leave DC... Then he remembered Samantha/Candy who he kicked out together with her lesbian friend Lily for cutting someone's throat. He was guessing who of his lady-patrons had betrayed him? Was Fiola's wife-in-law, Layla (code name for sharing the same Daddy/Pimp), was she the snitch? Just before he left for Bulgaria, she was barred from the bar. The other possibility was that the police were just trying to intimidate the business. The hot spots Chief Naylor was so proud to declare a war on did include the Zeus Lounge, also.

Lawyer Nikias: "Hey Jim! What is the problem? It is Sunday, 10 am!" He sounded concerned.

Jim: "The police raided my club this morning at around 2 am. They may be taking my license? I am not sure what they were looking for, but they arrested a bunch of my customers."

Lawyer Nikias: "You have nothing but hookers there. What happened?" he was just assuming.

Jim: "How do you know that? You have never been there!"

Lawyer: "I hear the police talking about your place at hearings with ABC Board" he was bluffing. ABC Board would never mix cases of troubled businesses without the defender's party present. Usually, the information like that is based on word on the Street; "the buzz." It takes someone like falling star DC Council Jim Ronan to start a gossip like "Jim was the Al Capone." (Gossip that was initiated at Ben's Chili Bowl restaurant, in April, 2001)...

Jim Ronan and the whole DC council were in trouble. He would resign eventually from being a voting member for DC Metro/WMATA Board of Directors, from Whitman Walker Clinic for HIV/AIDS patients, from DC Taxi cub Commissions because of his involvement with the DC lottery bid. Unfortunately, it took his opinion to bring the seventy plus protestors (at least on paper), to push Jim out of 1115A U Street with 5,000 square feet club space. The false loud mouth met his political demise later on April 1st, 2014, when he lost reelection for his 5th term. The full cycle here again is in four sequences, and thirteen years after his Al Capone analogy. The identical story would be repeated by the financial demise of Khalid on June 2nd, 2011 (24 months = four sixes after June 2nd, 2009 altrecation, and thirteen years after Randevu establishment in 1998). Jim Ronan will start his lies at the same year of 1998, after his election to Council member at Ward 1). Try to figure this Cornel University and MIT.

Jim eventually opened club Zoro, but he attracted bad promoters. The good ones went to Phantom, Urban, and Cloud Clubs. The mind is unstoppable when a desire is made in Quantum dimension. Jim was able to reopen the oldest club in USA (since 1971) which was dormant for twenty years (4x5), another full cicle in four sequences!

Lawyer Nikias: "Go to work. If there is no any sign on the door, just open for business. Call me if they try to do something to the license. Ok!"

Jim: "Thanks! I know I am a hand full!" He tried to minimize the damage.

Lawyer Nikias: "You are beyond a hand full! Bye. Don't forget I charge a lot of money for my advice!" He hung up. "All those clubs owners are nothing but trouble" he said to his wife.

Wife: "That's what pays your bills, Nikias!" She laughed too.

Jan. 29th, 2006 at 4 pm Jim drove to his expanded lounge, now three-story trouble. He felt like a betrayed King, whose soldiers had abandoned him. The place was turned upside down, seemed like a tornado went through all the floors. The furniture was thrown around like it was a battle of the Titans here. The sound system was unplugged, speakers were flipped sideways.

Jim: "What were they looking for? Snakes?" he was puzzled. There were no drugs here, no weapons, and his nunchakus were at home. Police have taken his baseball bat a year before, during some customer fake complaint (some customer lied he drew a knife against him, but it was the mouth plastic holder of Black and Milds). The liquor bottles were taken out of the liquor cabinet.

Jim: "Damn coyotes! What were they looking for? Hidden cash, cocaine? They were wasting tax payers' money and time, For real, though!"

Then he looked at the one box of HIPS paraphernalia. He recognized the chocolate Hershey's kisses. To his amazement he saw a box with new condoms wrappers, wide open on top and many new added to the original few he had in brown paper bags before. The brown bags from HIPS were with current page crimes against prostitutes, with rolls of red or black colored life styles condom wrappers and chocolates.

Jim: "They must have raided the club for prostitution" he assumed, but "why the arrests? Let me call Mansur, now!"

He dialed again and again. Mansur was not picking up the phone. He did not have a mobile phone. His wife Anika had one. She was not answering also. He decided to wait until the bar crowd arrived.

Chapter 14

While he was hooking up his sound he checked also the 3rd floor. There was a lot of furniture he bought from Park Hyatt hotel. The two love chairs and long sofa bed were in the corner close to the angled skylight windows. The third floor was in style of some winter resort ski house. The roof was triangular.

The dual mobile bar was installed on the opposite side of couch and chairs. Great sound acoustics were achieved here with minimum sound amplification. Jim liked coming here to relax and to smoke cigars. Sometime he would have some company. Several times he even had had sex here. It was in September, 2005. That was two days before Jim and Shelley first encounter each other.

Red haired Amazon (Sarah): "Hey, I like this place! How many floors you got?" she climbed up the steps at 9.15 pm that Monday night.

Jim: "We are just opening the 3rd floor. We have work done on every floor. We are using only the second floor for now." He was scanning her six feet perfect body, age thirty, Caucasian, great hair style, well dressed, high heeled red shoes. She looked more like a Washington socialite, than an average hooker.

Jim: "Are you a promoter! How can I assist you?" he approached her a bit too close. He researched and discovered that any woman or man have their individual space (approximately 12 inches around the person). If the person does not pull away from his approach, being too close, then he/she is not afraid and probably she/he was not a cop.

Red Haired Amazon (Sarah): "I only do promote myself!" she was witty and quick. "Black label and soda, little ice," she ordered finding the corner bar stool next to the game machine.

Jim: "Do you like to play!" He meant the game machine (he was splitting the money 50/50 with some unknown company from New Jersey).

Sarah: "That depends on who is asking?" she grabbed the drink like a baby's milk from a nipple. "Are you the owner?" Jim was not surprised with alcoholics. He was checking her out "was she a police undercover?"

Jim: "I am one of them, I do the bars, and my partner does the food."

Sarah: "Can I take my drink to the 3rd floor?" she stood up. The long red dress revealed perfect long legs, the flat stomach, full natural breasts, and the slightly see through dress that had the invite signs all over.

Jim: "We just had furniture delivered this weekend and it is a mess upstairs." He did not trust her much.

Sarah: "I may bring you a lot of business! I know many people here in high places!" Her body got closer and closer to Jim's. He can pick now at her cleavage showing the half exposed apples like white breasts.

Jim: "Wow! You are not only great looking, but also kind of aggressive." He pulled away from her, thinking, "That seems like a trap to me?"

Sarah: "Sexually aggressive, after a couple drinks I really get better, I get my hair loose!" Her legs parted almost revealed her bulging pubic hair.

Jim: "Do you work with a pimp! Who is your "folks?" he used street lingo.

Sarah: "Do I look like I need any pimp to tell me what to do?" She sounded appalled.

Jim: "Look! You are lucky that you are here early! The strange crowd comes later. We have everybody here, from normal, to alcoholics, to hookers, to pimps, to undecided who they are? If you don't belong to any category and you are just normal, they will try to convert you or insult you in some way. I brought a teacher one night; the pimps barked at her like evil dogs and she never came back."

Sarah: "Let me see the 3rd floor. We can simplify all those questions to one!" She was heading toward the locked door leading to the third floor.

Jim: "Larry, watch the bar. Call me if you need me. We will have a drink and a cigar upstairs."

Sarah: "Allow me to buy you a drink and please relax!" she grabbed his ass with her free hand.

Jim: "I will buy a drink; you will buy me a cigar! I really don't drink when at the club and in general with people I don't know!" He opened the door. He turned the lights on 3rd floor. She still had her hands on his ass. She slid her fingers toward his bare buttocks under his pants. "Open the belt a bit," she ordered him.

Jim: "Wait! Larry, give her another scotch and soda and give me a good cigar Monte Christo. We will be awhile, I guess?" Larry was quick to respond and he was bewildered. It was so early and nobody was a witness to the game of cat and mouse here. They ended up finally on the third floor. Jim dimmed the lights. He turned the corner night stand light on one of the gray granite top table. They found a way through the furniture in disarray to the couch and the love chair.

Jim: "What do you think?" he was lighting the thick ten inch fat cigar. She looked around, finishing her first drink.

Sarah: "Do you want my hair down?" She unpinned the two side pins and now she reminded him of wild lioness, ready to mate. "I like your cigar! It is very suggestive!" she opened her long legs, the picture perfect well trimmed dark hair vagina was a quick pick for him, who was trying to ignore the whole situation arising.

Jim: "I thought you were all red hair?" he pointed his long cigar toward her V-shaped crossed legs. "I bought this furniture from Park Hyatt hotel. Are you comfortable here?" he was observing her from distance. She looked around.

Sarah: "Want to talk about furniture or about my pubic hair, color? Come here, lover!" She tapped her free hand on the sofa next to her.

Jim: "First. This is too good to be true. Want to pleasure me? I usually do not do things like this in the club. We can go to my office, which is more suitable for that. Let's go. It is next door on third floor," he started to get up.

Sarah: "Do you want me to climb up and down three more floors on high heels like that? You need an elevator, buddy! No, we are staying here! Show me what you got?" she grabbed his pants and started to unzip his bulging 8 inch tower.

Jim: "That is after two drinks? Imagine what you will do after the third drink?" He made a silly comment.

Sarah: "Shut up! Want to talk or you want to fuck?" She swallowed his dick into her gorgeous mouth raw.

Jim: "Now I know how empires collapse! I hope she is not a Police undercover? And if she is, she is the best they ever had! She is probably just an alcoholic? A Police woman would not fuck a club owner, especially raw. Also by now they would be swarming from everywhere, up the steps, falling from the skylights," he was thinking. Sarah was working hard to pleasure him. He was about to explode.

Jim: "Wait, baby! We will burn the joint down!" he frantically searched for one of his huge ashtrays he had, taken from street bins. He found one and he left the Monte Christo, in it. He pulled away from the lioness mouth and he picked two of the couch cushions and he placed them on the floor.

Sarah: "Want me to lay on those?"

Jim: "No, madam! We will do it doggy style. It is my favorite!" She obeyed. Her perfect white ass was suddenly in front of his swollen to the maximum 8 inch penis and he pushed it in her pink and juicy ready vagina.

Sarah: "Oh, daddy! You make me feel good!" She kept her purse close to her for an unknown reason.

Jim: "Damn! You should be married, we should be married to each other!" he screamed pumping her closing and opening vagina.

Sarah: "I always dreamed of fucking a club owner, but they always have overprotective girlfriends or wives!"

Jim: "Don't worry! I am almost single! I think my girlfriend is cheating on me?" he was almost contracting in her, ready to ejaculate.

Sarah: "I do not care about your girlfriend. Just do not cum in me, please, Jim."

She was begging and squeezing at the same time. Her vagina was pulsating in her own rhythm, in some mysterious synchronization with his pumping back and forth Peter, (his nick name for his dick).

Sunday, January 29th, 2006. At about 11 pm the bar got full again... Most of the faces were of regulars who were not aware of the police raid the night before. They were doing the usual drinking and small talk. He noticed less of the hookers around. He guessed the word was already on the streets and they were just cautious. He remembered Girard with his seven ladies who he paraded in front of him just a year before.

Girard: "That is my stable!" he pointed at them walking around in line with heads down. They were not allowed to look at other pimps or at any friends of their Daddy. They were young and sexy. Their ages were between nineteen and twenty-one.

Girard: "Those bitches bring me a G a night or they get kicked out of the "family."

Jim: "Hey that is $7,000 a night! That is 2.5 million a year! I am in the wrong business, buddy! Have a cigar!" they both laughed. Women disappeared into the dimmed exit light door and they boarded two black SUVs.

Girard: "Time is of the essence. The bitches don't go to bed until the quota is achieved!" He slowly sipped on Remy XO, a signature drink for upper echelon pimps.

Jim: "You must be a great accountant! How do you keep up with the numbers?" he was puzzled.

Girard: "How? It is very easy! I just count the money once a day. The bitches monitor each other. I want to see 7G. Usually they know who isn't up to snuff and not performing and they sometimes beat her up or if they like her, they may subsidize her."

Jim: "Do you have sex with them often?" he was curious. His cigar was sending a nice swirl of smoke up into the high ceiling. The colored sound activated lights were creating holographic images of tornado like columns from the fine cigars of those two powerful men in their own special fields.

Girard: "Not with a specific one. Usually we only initiate them thorough sex (always bare). After that sex is more like a ritual not with any emotional strings attached. If a pimp shows more attention to one of the ladies, the others wife-in-laws, may beat her up or even kill her, or just chase her away if she is weak?" He liked to stare at TV, watching the BET videos uncut.

Jim remembered this particular pimp for two reasons. The first was the way he was bragging about making money. It seemed so natural to him. Girard was telling "either you are born a pimp, or you are not." One does not become a pimp overnight, just by an idea or by copycatting someone else. Second, it was the tragically ending of his career just a week later.

Fat Moe: "Hey, Jim! Did you hear? Girard is dead!" he said it with voice like he just spilled his coffee.

Jim: "Really! What happened?" He was doing inventory check and he almost dropped a bottle of Patron.

Fat Moe: "Do you remember Star? She was his best in the stable. Some would be tricks were trying to disrespect her. When Girard approached them they pulled out guns. Words were exchanged. Star tried to prevent them from fighting and jumped between them. The drive by tricks shot her first, and then they shot Girard second. One of them got out of the car and finished them both in an execution, style right in their heads. Then they took off on K Street toward the 9th street tunnel. Nobody of the witnesses followed them." He sat down with some smirk on his face. He was a drug dealer, disguised as a photographer. Once he moved his business in 2002 to Randfevu/now Zeus Lounge in DC, then Sally's business collapsed and that caused Prosperity to take over in 2003, then the stabbing of six patrons in May, 2004 made Jim to expand to it in 2005.

Now at end of January of 2006 Jim was entering and reevaluating his own damage assessment. All the answers were around him. It was up to him to agree with them, to change them, to reverse the direction of the tidal wave rising against him.

Mocca: "Hey, Jim! I heard that the police fucked up the joint last night!" She was a slim 5ft 7inch ice eating street lady. She grew up in front of him the last five years from a novice at age eighteen, to full grown veteran now. They were close enough friends and even one time lovers. She was depressed then of her cheating boyfriend after she slashed all his tires and Jim comforted her, but it turned to sex. At any moment Kiana was acting weird, then Jim was most vulnerable and he resorted to having sex to forget his heart's pains.

Jim: "Yeah. Larry is not answering his phone all day. My partner is hiding. I do not know what happened, but from what I see in the boxes from HIPS and from the bullshit on the 3rd floor, I believe it was a police raid. Someone has tried to set me up?" He fixed her a Long Island Ice Tea. He always was puzzled how her small framed body could take that much alcohol without damage, especially after seeing her ice eating diet!

Mocca: "Many people envy this place, Jim!" she always behaved concerned and she never gave him any trouble. She was respecting the club, just like many others since its opening in 1998.

Jim: "My lawyer will straighten up everything tomorrow. I still have my license! And believe me I have lost businesses before because of the police action or their inaction. That is how my tax money gets used, unfortunately! One never knows what the police next move will be in any given situation? When I call them they show up in two hours. When I ignore them, they are all over me."

Jim closed the club as usual. Nobody of the police showed up. "Maybe it was nothing?" He lied to himself. He went back home. He had chosen not to bother Shelley this morning. She was just a fuck, not a girlfriend, not a wife. He did some yoga to release his stress. He took a long shower at 3 am and then he opened the Bible. The page his fingers split was showing that fast talkers are weak and they think with their right brains, the slow talkers were wise and they think with the left brains. He decided to be "the slow and the wise," man. Yin and Yang, at work!

Monday, January 30th, 2006. The phone rang finally in the afternoon.

Larry: "Jim! They are after you! Bad, bad, bad!" his voice was in crescendo tones... He never sounded like that before.

Jim: "Calm down, brother! What exactly happened?" he was afraid that his conversation was recorded by the cops. In reality it was not.

Larry: "They accused me of taking money from the ladies for renting the bathrooms for sex!" then he paused.

Jim: "Did you? Is there any evidence of that?" He asked the basic questions. He knew how the lawyers thought and talked. His jail time taught him well. His master's degree, international maritime law or real estate law educations were useless here and now!

Larry: "They took all the money from the register as evidence. They had some police, mock, marked, money they said I took from the hookers."

Jim: "And what happened after that? I heard they were arresting some folks."

He avoided mentioning Angel as the caller.

Larry: "I spent the last two days in Central Cell. The judge just released me."

Jim: "Then come to work! My lawyer advised me until any further action is taken against the business or the liquor license in particular, the bar is OK to operate. I see the license is still here."

Larry: "I was released with contingency "not to return to work at the bar." Now, they are after you. They kept asking me if I was Jim."

Jim: "What was the story with the condoms all over the place, especially, in the boxes on the second floor and the all stretched used ones on third floor? I already fined you about that," he was trying to hold a minute more of the conversation, feeling Larry was a bit reserved with details.

Larry: "We never opened the 3rd floor. Police may have placed them there? They were not there the night before."

Jim: "Are you telling me that the fine of $50 was wrong?" he almost dropped the phone.

Larry: "The lady you took to third floor a couple of months ago Sarah... She was at the raid too. She was wearing a police uniform! You should have known she was a cop, Jim!" He sounded disappointed, for his own reasons. He was losing his apartment, his job, and his friends.

Jim: "Larry! Get a good lawyer now. Hope things are going to get better in the future? I will give you great references if you need them?"

Larry: "Those women are the problem. Stay away from them. Stay away from Kiana. I think Shelley is the only normal lady I have seen you with!"

Jim: "I know. Maybe Kiana called the cops? I wasted too much time chasing her and trying to catch her cheating. I should have concentrated on running my club!"

Larry: "I have seen your style and it is not any different than any businessman I have known. The problem is the L and K streets are notorious with the hookers, pimps and bad cops. You just became part of their scheme and scenario and they are looking for someone to blame. Ok, good luck!" He hung up.

Jim: "Sarah, Kiana, twisted minded cops, hookers, pimps and tricks. They were all in the algorithm. Now I need to minimize their intentions to destroy my image! After all that is why we all have names and seven billion of different identities on Earth. Legacy is frozen in history images of phenomenal characters" he thought.

Bruce Lee thought "To destroy your physical opponent is to break his image first."

He went through his books again. He came across the story of Pythagoras, who was regarded as Demi-god!

... He was able to heal sick like Jim was able to...

... He made major contributions to music, mathematics, astronomy...

... He was able to be at two places the same time like Jim was able to...

... He was initiated and he studied for quarter century the Egyptian esoteric science,

... He also studied with Rishis in India. He was looking to unite all esoteric thoughts into one...

Similarity was unavoidable with Jim's linkage of Yoga practice and meditations techniques, the Pyramid mystery and with Western Quantum electrodynamics science. The Egyptians were using irrational numbers PI (Comma of Pythagoras), which was 63/64, or Phi, the reverse 64/63 (golden proportion). Those numbers are used to build spirals in Fibonacci sequence (series in which each number is the sum of two preceding it). Jim calls the spirals "Cones." He discovered how all 10,000 pyramids around the globe were almost identically built. They used suspended sky projectors of light cones facing the earth. It was done at night. Once the height was determined, the radius around the light tower was marked with stones, then the steps were calculated by dividing the slope (hypotenuse "c" at Pythagorean Theorem: "a" square + "b square" = "c" square). Pythagoras was eventually killed by one of his followers for not allowing him to be initiated. You see Cornell U. Once the method of building of such architectural marvel was discovered (basically similar to using a modern flashlight) the formulas can be invented and considered genius!

Jim needed to take quick action. He called Shelley.

Jim: "I need to move some of my stuff to your house." He was really not asking. He expected a yes."

Shelley: "Sure! Is everything all right?" she was a true keeper...

Jim: "I am ok. I think the Police are looking for more trouble. They chased away Larry and most of my regulars."

Shelley: "You can move in with me. Just help me with the rent."

Jim: "True. I don't need to pay four rents; my club, my office, my apartment, your apartment! I am ready to let go of my apartment."

He started cleaning house. He went through his pictures he took for many years. Those were pictures he took of ladies who were normal or working, some nude, and some semi-nude, some professionally made of top models trying to be. After all he had legitimate business with Tax ID... Walker Media. What probably saved him was that Shelley would not accept any pornographic images. She was an HR Manager in one of the most government subsidized insurance companies Charter plan. That company had near 320 million dollars of government contracts to pay for the insurance coverage of the less fortunate financially and unemployed. Later on their chief Jeffrey Thompson was investigated for campaign donations to get those contracts.

Jim considered his work as valuable art. He dreamed one day to tell his story in pictures and videos he produced through the years. Photography was in his blood. He could have been Da Vinci in another era. He sacrificed a lot of money and time to produce this work and he was obsessed with upgrading his photographic and video equipment. Seemed the quality was better on film camera than on digital camera. Unfortunately, with downloading direct to computers or to mobile phones the old technology was the film! He went through all his pictures and tapes. It was 3,000 hours of Beta-SP, 3/4 U-matics, Betamax, VHS, and miniDV... The pictures with explicit material he put in special plastic bag and they were heading to the trash. He made sure all the film negatives had the same fate. Then he separated all of his nude art videos (some call it pornography) and placed them in five boxes (mostly Betamax, VHS, muniDV) and they were loaded to find the trash incinerator. Jim knew the fate of his rival Mr. Rogbin, which was raided. Jim knew how the Police's Modus Operandi, worked. The government never changes for better; it reinvents itself in any possible ways to take advantage of its citizens. Only on one occasion does history remember the French Revolution. They stormed the Bastille after the King Louis XVI ordered all Rosicrucians rounded up after he assumed that they were infiltrated by German free masons. Robespierre, their leader, was also killed by his own followers on the guillotine. The reason; in process of him killing off all of his opponents from the monarchical Klan he pronounced himself as a Demi God. The problem with him was that he had never been fully trained and initiated as free mason. One can be enlightened into the awareness (usually from some child dramatic event), one can achieve great heights in spiritual world, but without proper guidance he may abuse the power he achieves. After all most dictators, kings, presidents think they are God chosen, or Demi Gods themselves. Are they? Not necessarily, just men, whom are chosen to a particular job or position, in life that usually and verifiably is destined to perform.

Look at Obama? Is anything he thinks of himself and results shown God like? He repeated most of the Bush policies in the first four years – continued the war in Afghanistan and Iraq, extended tax breaks, the nation debt was not reduced, the health of the citizens did not get better, but more expensive, the gas prices stay doubled at near $4.5 a gallon, the NSA domestic surveillance increased, Google assisted his reelection and self expanded on barges and submarines, Congress and Senate got paralyzed and foreign policy is nonexistent (with Syria, Iran, North Korea, Libya, Israel, Russia, Egypt). One has to wonder, what are they doing in the Government, besides playing golf and going on vacations in Africa? When BP spilled oil in the Gulf of Mexico Obama fined them 20 billion dollars. BP fixed the problem and plugged the one mile deep hole in less than three months. The Canadian IT company GSI, awarded without a bid, couldn't fix the website for three years after passing the law and there is no punishment to them a penny, even they blew 600 million dollars on building it (2010 to 2013).

American taxpayers are always misled and screwed, yet they keep reelecting the same wrong characters on both sides of the aisle. Jim was an independent voter. He voted for Dole, Bush, Kerry, and Obama. He was not political, but he did not want to be passive in the game that the US citizens played. Most Americans will expose their innermost dirt on TV show, but when they are asked "who they are voting for?" they hide it, thinking it is a great secret! In reality they hide their stupidity. If one doesn't read books and it is not current with the news on cable TV, the same genius can be persuaded to vote by a single Tweeter message, or by Face book friend "like", or simply by someone driving him on a bus to Ohio early voting center (0% republican, 100% democratic votes counted there in Nov. 2012). Any theory of probability will collapse when seen these numbers, Mr. Obama! You can't blame republicans and Bain Capital and Mitt Romney for everything. Yes, he was representing Venture Capital, but he was not the monster your campaign described. The 1% swing vote is not a Victory. It shows the republicans are out of touch with their base. They simply couldn't attract the young, the single women, the old, the Spanish, the black, and the Christian base in USA. We salute you, dear Emperor Obama!

At that present time of January, 2006 US Government was too powerful to fight with conventional weapons, especially unilateral/ solo and even the mission impossible was to win without any known weapons. Here he relied solely on his intuition, this super natural ability to dodge bullets and to do the opposite, to make his enemies suffer tenfold compared to him and to use their tactics to hurt them, without them noticing him. Stealth in psychological warfare is the most agonizing reason to the losing party. And Jim was master in using his super subconscious mind; he was bringing closer the quantum shield and bouncing back the dark plasma the government and its cronies were throwing at him. He was not the Creator anymore. The game here was of the Survivor, but he would turn it to The Winner. Yes, but how? Is the game of cat and mouse always about the one who has to win? Is the mouse really the cat, and the inflated, powerful paper lion, really nothing but a little scared, impotent mouse?

Readers: "Talking is cheap, brother!" Jim can see them screaming. "Facts, evidence first, to make us believers, second!" Everyone was thinking.

Jim: "First, he did eliminate the pictures and the videos. Then, he did the same with all Kiana's bank deposit receipts, because he always deposited cash to her bank account number. He never wrote any checks or made transfers between him and her account. He never knew who his investigator was (Detective O'Conner), but he sensed his presence. He knew he was ahead of him. Larry was telling him in his own words that the Police were aggressively pursuing the newly remodeled club. Jim would name "Officer X" the one who is chasing him, but he couldn't catch him. Twice he missed him. Once, Jim was in Bulgaria on vacation, second time Jim was not found at the club at time of the raid. Desperation was written all over during and after the raid. The additional amount of condoms on second floor and the sneaks like condoms hanging from any possible spots (chairs, night stands, lamp shades), that was "Officer X" signature in addition to the marked (mocked) police money.

Jim started to move equipment from the club and from his apartment. The industrial Digital 3 chip JVC 700 camcorders and the huge digital deck recorder were the first to evacuate, and then he wrapped all his S-VHS Panasonic VCRs were to follow. The greatest sound system in the world at this time Nakamichi was out too. Then he evacuated his 2 amplifiers racks of industrial Crown PSA, microtech 2400s. The huge speakers he bought from Mr. Rogbin and then moved to Zone club, now were stacked up in his next, supposedly bedroom. They were left for the building management to worry about. They were most powerful dual 18 inch, 300 watts per speaker monsters. The 8 speakers took the space of whole back wall, being double stacked. He decided to abandon them. He had another 12 speakers shared between his apartment and his now club in ruins. He kept some of his production Walker's Media tapes. He produced 40 videos on different formats. That was his legacy! He had about 10 DVDs of X rated videos with great quality, but he bought them from shady characters. He did not want to give the Feds/ "Officer X" any more evidence than he needed. After all illegally purchases without receipt are felony charge. If one asks the government what is really, "legal" you would be surprised! Maybe with some exception everything is illegal except having sex after marriage. Think readers! Why one can work and drive after sixteen, vote and kill (while in armed forces) after eighteen, the same person can drink alcohol after twenty-one and pay his students loans till the age of forty or more.

If that is not a scheme, then what is? We are not just talking about legality of the Tax Code or the gas price extortion at the pump. Then the speed limits and seat belts and the size of drinking sodas, food labels ingredients and smoking nowhere! The long arms of the IRS will close Wegelin, a 250 years old bank in Switzerland because of the money hidden there by US rich citizens (January 4th, 2013), so much for Swiss Safe Haven.

Wegelin, Jim, Hmm... too close to ignore. Can someone fight regulators? Yes, the one and only Jim can! He hired a new ABC manager the next day on Tuesday, February, 2nd. The Police activities were not visible, but he was not giving them any opportunities. Once he saw the "work" of officer X, he knew he would come back sooner or later. He made sure there was nothing left in his bank accounts. He found his latest tax records and he was ready for any audit by IRS, after all Al Capone and his rival Mr. Rogbin were raided for taxes evasion. Later on Mr. Dodson (his second rival) would join the same criminal group (see Fab Empire blog and Washington Post articles, in year 2010). One can wonder can $46,000 personal debt make one bankrupt, if he is claiming ownership of 10 million dollars a year enterprise, like Mr. Dodson was.

Readers: "No!"

Jim: "My lawyer Nikias was right. Mr. Dodson was only a GM, a straw man for LLC (Michael Jordan and ten Ethiopian investors at Cloud night club).

Thursday was another day of moving equipment. He was driving his black 300CE. He parked his car on X Street. It was full of amplifiers and CDs and small speakers. He also brought some liquor and beer. The bar needed supplies. Mansur was not talking to him. He just wanted money. Lawyer Nikias was awfully quiet too. Seemed everyone was waiting for something to happen.

A dark unmarked police cruiser pulled over next to Jim while he was unloading his bar supplies.

Jim: "Do you need directions or something?" he sensed "officer's X" presence. "That must be him!"

Detective O'Conner: "We need to talk. Yes, there is more than "something"

here..." He looked for approval from his partner Waldo. They both laughed like hyenas.

Jim: "What is going on?" he got serious. He now was seeing the master mind, of his pursuers.

Detective O'Conner: "I have warrant to search your home, office and club. We are the federal enforcement investigating for prostitution." He did not show any papers, but his badge only.

Jim: "Were you in my club last Saturday? I was not there." He used that parry, as a "you did not catch me, why are you bothering me now" tactic.

Detective O'Conner: "We ask questions, you don't! We have enough evidence to close that club and to arrest you right now. Act voluntarily or we are going to your house and we will break your door." As he was speaking two more dark sedans pulled over. The SWAT team dressed officers had no local MPD uniforms.

Jim: "You are not MPD! Who are you?" he felt something more sinister was coming.

Detective O'Conner: "This is United Stataes Federal action." "The Police work with Club owners and they are not reliable." He said the last sentence whispering to his partner twisting his head toward him.

Jim: "I do not have anything in my office or in my house. I need to call my lawyer." He requested.

Detective O'Conner: "After we check what we need to know you will have plenty of time to talk to anybody if that you feel is necessary? Now we follow the judge orders."

Jim: "Warrant is based on probable cause to search! I know the law …" He shocked the swat coyotes.

Detective O'Conner: "Listen. We arrested all your crew on Saturday. They are talking. They are witnesses enough to put you in jail for a decade. So, are you giving us the keys or we are breaking all those doors?" he waved toward the coyotes as to watch out if Jim needed to be subdued by force.

Jim: "I will show you the place. You don't need their help" he handed about thirty keys chain to the negotiator. He observed a huge 3 ft long door ram, a torpedo like and ten inch wide metal pipe with handles on each side ready to smash through any door. He had framed door outside his original wood door. Police would have needed torch to open this mini fortress office door.

Detective O'Conner: "There is nothing here, but furniture and a laptop." He reported to his supervisor. "Safe got no cash, but check books," he was loudly disappointed.

Jim: "So much for your probable cause," he laughed. He almost mentioned Mr. Rogbin's case, but that would have had his lawyer implicated. He swallowed the words at an instant. "Those coyotes are not here to play; they wanted to find something to charge."

Detective O'Conner: "Let's go to your house!" he was a bit softer, obviously disappointed. There were about ten more SWAT wearing coyotes at his apartment. They had pump action rifles drown, bulletproof vests, German looking helmets and another torpedo looking door ram opener. The things missing were ambulance, fire department and MPD. It seemed like a limited operation.

Jim: "What is this, "Training Day" movie?" He almost laughed at them, referring to the Denzel Washington movie. He saw some cute blonde intern twenty-four year old lady being trained how to collect evidence. She was short and somewhat sexy. She was walking around with a writing pad and some plastic zip lock bags.

Jim: "First day at school? There is nothing here interesting for you?"

FBI intern: "We collect evidence. There is always something to collect. You can get your stuff back if nothing is held against you?"

Jim: "It is like walking in circles! Why should I take back something which you should have never taken?"

Detective O'Conner: "I don't have to remind you every five minutes that that is the judge's order. The witnesses gave us probable cause." He was repeating his mantra.

Jim: "I need to see your discovery package from Saturday. The additional condoms you installed and mocked money are not probable cause."

Detective O'Conner: "Sit here and stay quiet." He told him to sit outside his apartment door on the floor. Then the fifteen coyotes entered his apartment. Inside he heard crashing noises, moving furniture, and loud voices. The good thing was that he removed the most valuable electronics the previous days.

Detective O'Conner: "Do you have any guns, drugs, animal porn videos?"

Jim: "Are you kidding? …Or you may plant some here like you did in my club? I meant the condoms." Previousky casino briefcase, drugs ecstasy and small crack green bags were also planted in the club most likely by that FBI crew, but Jim got rid of them.

Detective O'Conner: "The judge will decide, ok!" He ordered all evidence boxed. Jim saw all his production video tapes leaving his door in five boxes.

Jim: "I own a production company. You are taking my twenty years of work!" He almost cried.

Detective O'Conner: "We will look at your three laptops and if nothing is there, we will return them to you. The same will happen to your tapes. Ok!"

Jim: "So, what is the charge? You are obviously not a true Police, (MPD) that I have seen before."

Detective O'Conner: "We are investigating the prostitutes in your club."

Jim: "Are they allowed there? If not please make a Police/FBI warning sign at the door. I do not want to be sued. I already ask the MPD for that."

Detective O'Conner: "They can drink there, but they cannot rent the bathrooms for sex" he sounded somewhat fatherly.

Jim: "Yes, I know that!"

Detective O'Conner: "You can go to work at the club now."

All the evidence gone, Jim got his keys back and he entered his apartment. Wow. It was worse than he expected. They threw a lot of his stuff on the floor. Things from the kitchen drawers ended up in the shower tub. Two file cabinets were emptied on the floor by his huge 18 inch double tear speakers. His bed was flipped over and his walk-in closet was in disarray.

Jim: "I hope the intern took pictures before and after?" he thought. It was like a wrath of tornado passed through. The signature of "Officer X"/aka detective O'Conner was identical to his style at his club.

Jim: "I hope they did not plant some listening devices here or some drugs or ammunition just to make a case here? Mr. Rogbin was hit and they took his cash and that was confirmed by his own confession to Geof at Pino's restaurant, in Georgetown. If they planted the cash at his Potomac house, then that would be an outrage" he thought. Then he decided to not touch anything and just leave the crime scene. He picked some essentials, like tax files and his briefcase with his licenses and passport. He went to work, but his mind was in unease. The business was good, always good.

Jim: "Alcohol always sells!" was his slogan.

Chapter 15

The Federal city, called Washington, DC was amazingly rich, conniving, bad and corrupted. The original design by the architects was not to contain any residential buildings, but only federal. With time people started to reside in it and they claimed autonomy. Mid 70s under Marion Barry movement the Federal Government, (Congress) allowed thirteen member City Council and to elect a Mayor under The District of Columbia Home Rule. The budget of the city was reviewed and approved by the Congress. Different city agencies were working independently from each other, but they had the same goal to accomplish. That was to enrich themselves by any means. Taxi cab commission, DC Lottery, ABRA (Alcohol and Beverage Regulatory Administration), DCRA (Department of Consumer and Regulatory Affairs), etc., they were all in the same game to "serve" the public. They all were using MPD as their watch dogs, except for Metro Subway Transit System.

Jim was not afraid of some crooked cops. He knew them too well at 1901 D Street (Central Detention Facility). It was a Federal jail. He was to play the game with the federal coyotes now. He was able to sustain 7.5 years of business at the corner of one of the most dangerous street in DC -- X Street, NW! No, he was not paying the cops like Mr. Rogbin and Mr. Dodson were doing (the website Fab Empire mentions that Dodson was paying his personal friends in MPD $250,000 a year!), Au contraire, my friends.

Jim: "Keep the police guessing and keep them at a distance, across the street at least!" That was his Modus Operandi. It worked.

Police: "This guy Jim is the only person who disrespects us in DC." That was the rumor at MPD and it was true. Jim was not afraid of them, just like Al Pacino disrespected those, "cockroaches" in the movie, "Scarface."

Detective O'Conner: "Those computers are new or just wiped out? We can't find anything on Jim's laptops. We may let him slip away. We can't allow that. Looks like someone had informed him about the raid in advance? Damn it." The poor Satan sounded defeated. So far all raids were easy for him and he was highly commended for promotion. Not this one. He experienced the chill of failure. His witnesses were not really truly cooperating. The undeclared code between pimps, hookers, tricks was built in thousands of years. The interdependence of each other in relationships between the mentor pimps, the obedient "daddy's girls," the need of money supply, especially from their generous regular, johns; all those people were leaving the zealous little coyotes as if they were in some audience like some bystanders. The problem with the undercover coyotes (VICE) was that they wanted to feel like some saviors of the "innocent" victims of lucrative, sex trade. They were passing laws for harsher punishment of pimps with underage prostitutes, added punishment for interstate sex trafficking. In 2006, they changed the laws for traveling abroad US citizens and added punishment for sex with underage prostitutes, all that was helping the coyotes but not helping Jim. He inherited a terrible but lucrative street history and now he was facing the "cockroaches." If he was really the thug that they were labeling him with, he would deserve anything he was accused of. They thought of him as: terrorist; money launderer; KGB; Mafia; gambler; liquor after hours pusher; alcoholic; drug dealer; pornographer and last, but certainly not least, arms dealer.

Jim was none of the above, just the opposite. With the exception of cigars smoking and with the random sex, he would almost pass for a saint! He never had kids, he never owned a house, he never drove any new car, and he never splurged on buying luxury watches. His cars were usually German old cars around fifteen to twenty years old. He bought his second normal pair of shoes at the age of 50! He would give away cars, money, furniture to people who did not deserve it and he would not expect anything in return, but respect! But he learned that that respect is not always given, certainly not with money. His fault of being generous was basically a God's gift. He found out that

God would replenish the money, gifts, and cars tenfold. Jim called that "quantum funny mathematics." He discovered the time curve for givers moves backward and upward into gravitational wave swirling into open cone and it is shorter. But, the takers time curve prolongs and bends downward and away moving into downward spiral, "The Horn of Plenty vs. the Horn of Empty!" Basically, it is a time machine with opposite time reality (winner, loser and ... positive, negative states of quantum symmetry). He knew about the pyramids power. He knew about yoga. He decided to connect all his knowledge in the history of the world using the quantum mind he possessed and developed. To build his quantum field protection he needed to bring the antigravity with special breathing and mental exercises. He did the meditation in lotus position, he imagined himself in a pyramid, and he knew the levitation has two characteristics. His body remained in physical world/ Earth, but his mind brain wave (bio electric impulses/Sun) and his emotions, (magnetic fields/Moon) together were creating an imaginary spiral, where everything was moving with the speed of light or with warp speed. He used the Fibonacci way of sequence numbers to build his quantum spiral fn = Phi n / 5½

Looking from outside the spiral was basically like looking like a cone. The amazing thing was that the higher the numbers the more accurate is the Golden Ratio Phi = 1,618. How the pyramids, spirals, yoga and cones were able to connect? Jim felt connected with Pythagoras living in 500 years BC, with Fibonacci living in (1170-1250) AC and now he was living in decade of 2000. The wormhole was able to connect those great minds. Jim started to see how the labyrinth he created was puzzling his investigators. He knew that in life the physical labyrinth has a beginning/entrance, then center and eventually an exit. He looked at labyrinth as suspended house build like a spiral or folded cone.

The assumption in pyramids is that the pharaoh did not want to be found by the mortals. He submitted his body to the God of Light! Special openings in the walls of pyramid allowed his spirit to communicate with Light/energy. The puzzle was how a mortal, average person able to get to his sarcophagus? Answer is easy. Usually after the mummified body is placed on a dais and his gifts and most valuable items are left with him, not excluding his wife, the walls are usually cemented and any access to him is denied. To find the secret passage the spiral is compressed to earth level. One may see then the genius cave entrance brought to human level, for example. The entrance of the light maybe at the level 40 of the spiral (the same number is where the golden ratio 1,618 is most accurate). Let's assume that the spiral has 60 levels. If we compress the spiral to ground level, we will see 60 circles, the cave where the entrance to a sarcophagus would be at 40th circle. In quantum theory we can short cut driving up the Earth garage complex in circles. We can build imaginary bridges and cross the 40 circles and be there in a much shorter time.

Jim finally understood the hexagonal star in the Kabbalah/Talmud, that, the dissected physical pyramid/cone is a triangle upward and the spiritual and emotional cone/pyramid downward, are introspective.

The double Star of David represents seven spiritual qualities. Those are:

1. Kindness, 2. Serenity, 3. Harmony, 4. Perseverance, 5. Splendor, 6. Foundation and 7. Royalty

Reading in the Kabbalah the events and persons are expressed in numbers. Father is 3, child is 41, and father and mother are 44. The phi "Golden ratio" is division of the Tree of Knowledge 233 and Garden of Eden is 144, yes 1,6! One Cambridge university professor used the "skip code" in statistics. He found out that the Bible psalms and the codes are similar. Jim discovered much more than Star of David. He just agreed that the two inverted triangles represented the intermixture of the internal world of the human and external world of the universe. He assembled his own Quantum Vortex Diagram, for the first time in the world history. Pythagoras, Francis Bacon, Kabbalah, Fibonacci, and Jan Oort finally connected in that picture. Quantum time in cosmic dimensions/speed was eliminated, when memory banks connect.

Wow. Obviously the coyotes did not learn anything from the Bible or they simply missed the history class!

Jim ought to win here and he will! Readers will see now how he did it in next final chapters.

Jim was very upset. He did not expect he will be robbed of his video tapes. He really wanted to be remembered as video and film producer, that where his heart was and he thought he was really good with camera work. He called the camera work and the event he recorded "breathing." He would direct and connect with the subjects he would record to bring emotion in his art. He bought and sacrificed many years to bring the best possible equipment (all digital), so the viewer can have the best enjoinment. In his opinion the classic film production has and will always have superior quality over digital video, but the cost of filming and editing was out of his reach at this time. The digital effects enhance the psychological effect on the viewer, and that where the viewers would move to some fantasy experiences; the reality vs. fantasy or where physical communicates with the possible future events. After all most of the science fiction sometimes becomes reality. Are the film producers dream makers or future reality forecasters? Yes. When Pentagon runs out of war scenarios they turn for help from Hollywood. Hollywood plays the reverse game. They steal sometime classified information from the Pentagon and they make movies based on true events. Jim wanted to be better than Francis Ford Coppola, Steven Spielberg and Oliver Stone. He wanted his own legacy. He did not want to be remembered as failed club owner. He was looking at the liquor business as "cash cow" to finance his equipment and future and being a realtor he had plans to invest in buildings and land development. All this was questionable now. He never thought his production tapes would be seized. He was laughing that the coyotes were not able to steal his high end 3 chip cameras. He had removed them on time. But the coyotes did something else. After Jim moved out of his contaminated by the FBI search apartment he was surprised to meet the angry building manager Miss Mathews.

Jim: "Hey Miss Mathews! I am here to give you a notice to vacate."

Miss Mathews: "Jim, you are one of my best tenants if not the best! What happened to you? The police was asking me questions about you two days ago and yesterday the 202 apartment was broken into."

Jim: "I already left apt. 204."

Mathews: "When they saw how much equipment you had left I guess they came again to steal it. Unfortunately, they hit the next apartment, they broke into wrong door."

Jim: "True, I left about $10,000 in speakers, video equipment, clothing and all furniture. I am not touching anything they have touched."

Miss Mathews: "In order to get your security deposit you need to leave the apartment clean. We can bring a crew to help you do that. Write us a check for 900 dollars, ok?"

Jim: "Thanks! Here is the check. I am not going there again."

Miss Mathews: "You can keep one of your parking spaces, if you want?"

Jim: "Yes, I will! Thanks." He left the building at 1200 N street. He was puzzled that the Police would be burglarizing, an apartment probably while watching him at the same time he was working in the club? "What weird thing is going to happen now?" He was happy that he evaded them again and again. If he was in the apartment he would have fought them. And they probably were not wearing this time swat uniforms, he bet. Now he was predicting their next move.

That quantum mind was right. He was about not to be surprised at their next move. As soon he opened the club door on February 9th, 2006 they followed him up the stairs.

Detective O'Conner: "Jim, you are under arrest! Turn around!" He pushed Jim against the bar granite top.

Jim: "What is the problem now? You can't plant evidence and burglarize my apartment and I am under arrest? Get it right, whoever you are, because you are not the police!" He shouted at the coyote.

Detective O'Conner: "Talk to the Judge tomorrow. Tell him your story. He will decide."

Jim: "I need to lock the club, before it gets burglarized again!"

Detective O'Conner: "I will take care of that. How do you know FBI burglarized anything? Do you have it on camera or do you have witnesses?"

Jim: "My resident manager told me. Is she a good witness?"

Detective O'Conner: "Did you dial 911?"

Jim: "That's really funny! To call the people who robbed me? Like I am in an ambulance and I call for an ambulance, great logic!"

Detective O'Conner: "We are Federal Division, we don't deal with MPD."

Jim: "At the end you use the same tactics and you are all looking for someone to blame."

Jim was processed with other criminals at Central Cell on 500 Indiana Ave. He was awakened at midnight to be interrogated. DC is federal city.

Detective O'Conner: "Do you need a lawyer? We will ask you some questions before you see the judge."

Jim: "I have nothing to hide. You have nothing on me! I can talk to you. Just loosen those handcuffs. Ok?" he stretched his two hands toward the damn ass, dressed with a blue uniform but covered with civilian brown coat.

Detective O'Conner: "It is cold here!" he read Jim's mind. "They should give you some warm clothes here."

Jim: "Can we finish the small talk and get to the point?" He felt like he was set up in a wrong movie scene.

Detective O'Conner: "You said you were aware of bathroom rentals for sex. Tell me more about that. This conversation is recorded, for your information."

Jim: "That is the only true thing your people do, recordings! Everything else is some kind of entrapment." He almost laughed at him. He was sitting in a chair and he was very uncomfortable. His hands were handcuffed behind his back. He guessed they wanted to intimidate him more this way?

"Sure, coyotes dressed like cops. Do you know who are you messing with? I am the number One King in DC. The other two are thieves and crooks." He was thinking of the fake Mr. Dodson, and the ignorant Mr. Rogbin.

Detective O'Conner: "What entrapment? We raided your club and we collected plenty of evidence. Now we are putting two and two together to decide if the place can continue to operate? What is your position there? We know you are the owner, true or false?"

Jim: "False. I am one of the ABC Managers. There are about five of us."

Detective O'Conner: "According to our records, you are the one who is renting the bars section from "Mike's." That makes you a partner/ owner." He increased his voice to sound serious.

Jim: "I give money to Mansur for construction, rent, his bills, but my name is not on any lease or on any licenses. How does that make me an owner?" He rightfully argued.

Detective O'Conner: "We know you owned other clubs, the Zoro for example. We have monitored all your activities before and after that club."

Jim: "What Zoro, has to do with this situation here? First, they are not related. Second, you really did not find anything in the club Zeus Lounge to incriminate me, except some HIPS candies and pamphlets and free condoms. I did not buy them. And on top you planted some new condoms which are non HIPS. So, I am not going to tell you something I did not do and that you are pressed to hear or record for your boss." He almost spit in the coyote face, but he stopped himself short.

Detective O'Conner: "Listen! These charges against you are just a misdemeanor. Agree on that and you are free to go. You said you are aware of the renting of the bathrooms for sex!" he was almost begging. Jim detected his bargaining chips were weak.

Jim: "I cannot tell you what you guys want to hear. You put strange items in my club, you set up my bartender with mocked money, you send me an undercover police woman Sarah, and you burglarize the wrong apartment, probably to plant more evidence, (Watergate style). And now you tell me to bargain with you!"

Detective O'Conner: "At your apartment you said you know about the sex in the bathrooms, now you are saying you don't agree on any charges? I think you are lying? I have no more questions. I will see you in court!"

Jim: "Great!" He laughed at him. The marshals escorted him shackled to a heavy populated Central Cell, where the stink of pee and dirty men was never ventilated since it was built.

Next day was Wednesday February 10th, Judge was in the chambers.

Jim: "I am aware of the charges, but I don't agree with them. "Not guilty" is my plea." He told through some court appointed lawyer.

Judge: "The charge is a bawdy house. You need to hire lawyer. Next court date is February 24th. It will be a fact finding and from there we will proceed to real court with or without a jury. You are released on your own. No bail needed. Because of the history of your club you are not allowed to return there until the court date."

Jim: "That is my life investment there. I can't just leave everything I worked for there. That is pretty harsh." He tried to relay to the stubborn Grand Coyote.

Judge: "You have time to go through the charges and the discovery package presented to us. Your lawyer should be able to defend you if you think that you are wrongfully charged?"

Jim: "Thank you sir!" it was useless to argue with the inferiors. The irony was that they called themselves, "Superior Court of District of Columbia," wearing some funny black robes under the big picture of Lady Justicia.

Jim: "Those characters belong to the Inquisition which basically killed the Renaissance in Europe for five centuries."

Pope Gregory IX established the Inquisition in 1231. Giordano Bruno was killed on February 19th, 1600 AC. His argument was that Earth is not the center of the Universe and they are many more Planets like it according to Copernicus theory. Amazingly at the same month and within a week error Jim was exposed to similar scrutiny, year 2006 vs. year 1600. Hmmm... Readers may notice the number "6" and 1 and 2 and two zeros, anything to do with "golden ratio" 1,681 or 1,685 Hmmm... just, a thought? Does Pythagoras, Kabbalah and Fibonacci, Francis Bacon and German Engineer Scherbius communicating with Jim's mind?

The slogan "Great Minds think alike" may be true, but are "dead great minds communicating with each other?" We know how government operates. We are now on break through discovery how dead (supposedly), minds communicate with each other. We will be tapping into QED (quantum electro dynamics), sorry "boson" guy! Mr. Higgs does not bring anything new to the table here. He is just a sketch artist, for CERN with 10 billion dollar grant toy-collider! If someone communicates with passed brains it may seem an occulThe difference here is there is no any real human skull or made of diamond scull used to channel underworld powers, nor animal or human sacrifice of thousands of Aztecs to change the Sun powers and mercy of their leader Mexitli. He did not need the secret free masons' rituals in their initiations. He did not need to go forty days in any desert then to return as deity. He did not change his diet to yoga or took some LSD pills to bring himself to an altered mind and to deep into the underworld reality for help. He believed into the Quantum field, he knew The Invisible Hand would pull him out of this situation. He wanted to make a statement. He wanted to create a legacy not only in DC, but in the Universe. After all every person has a name for a reason. Dante "Inferno" created ten circles of sins. He also stated that "every word and every thought of the human affects the Universe!"

The same could be translated as any action is judged by the Universe and Cosmic consciousness/God!

At the 8th circle, Valleys 1-10 Dante is observing the

1. Seducers 6. Hypocrites
2. Flatterers 7. Thieves
3. Simoniacs 8. False Counselor
4. Diviners 9. Schismatics
5. Barratos 10. Falsifiers

All those positions can be filed by the DC government characters in five seconds. The police, DC counsel, The Church charlatans, the open whoring to get a job, or to keep one. What he wrote in 1300 AC can be valid 706 years later; the real players may not be the same, but the same rules of the game apply forever.

One person may not be able to change the way they operate, but a jolt of higher awareness may Shock and Awe (Technically known as rapid dominance) the self proclaimed "perfect and untouchable" DC and federal power structure. Jim decided to just relax.

Shelley: "That club is nothing but trouble. I want you to find a different job and be at home at normal hours. I do not want to date you here and there. If you change your job I will marry you and I will give you a child!"

Jim: "Ok. I will try to take it back and then I will sell it to someone. Surrendering to the cops it is not my style and the last thing on the list is to make them win without a fight."

Shelley: "Sometimes, leaving a trouble is better than fighting a battle which nobody wants to win. I don't like your club, my mother is unhappy with me dating a club owner, and you really do not like it. You keep fighting for your license; you don't trust your partner. Now you are out for a couple of weeks! Maybe God is giving you time to reflect on yourself?"

Jim: "Yes, my wife to be! I have unfinished business with the police. I have principles and no one steps on my shoes unpunished. I will take my club back and prove to them they can't push me out! After I sell it, I will leave it and we can get married and we can have our baby!"

Shelley: "I see you are attached to this great money the club gives you. Why don't you call your lawyer and shake off the police from your back?" She almost kissed him.

Jim: "Do you know what happened? I did invest every penny I had in construction and expansion of this club. I should have invested in something different than liquor." He kissed her back.

Shelley: "I have an idea. Invest in us from now on. You are a realtor. We can buy a house. Let us go house shopping!" she kept forgetting that the whole situation had changed. Jim was out of a club, out of money and with limited options. They made love and she was very comforting.

Shelley: "Think this way. Until the court day you are all mine and you should not worry about anything, but to make me happy!" She sounded sexy, out of breath and enjoining every stroke he was delivering inside her juicy and contracting vagina.

Jim: "Hey Nikias! They push me out of my club. They are trying to remove me from there. Can you give me some great advice?"

Nikias: "You know I specialize in ABC law and I can help you with the lease, but I am not a criminal lawyer. I can give you some numbers, but they are expensive!"

He was sympathetic to a point.

Jim: "I have a hearing in two weeks. I need to move fast. Ok. Who do you know?" He was anxious. He was aware now how Mr. Rogbin felt being targeted and prosecuted, "who has Mr. Rogbin chosen to represent him?" He was in need of quick reference.

Nikias: "Oh, he picked a criminal lawyer William Martin. He represented Monica Lewinsky, Clinton's mistress. She is out of the country for good."

Jim: "I remember that giggle! Who knows what he will talk about me after I hang up?" He thought.

Jim: "Sorry about the trouble!"

Nikias: "You are always in trouble, but you always come on top. My other clients are in much worse condition," he stopped short of mentioning Mr. Rogbin… "Call, Duval law firm, good luck."

Jim: "How about the hours change? Were you able to change them to normal?"

Nikias: "The hours now are your last worry! Get your club back first, ok?" He hung up the phone and missed the stand a couple of times. He was angry obviously, but he marked the time duration for future billings.

Jim: "Two weeks! I know how the judge manipulates the evidence and their ways to make witnesses, to sound credible. He remembered Elba. He remembered that her assailant did not show up and defense lawyer and defense investigator fell asleep on the easy case and the Judge allowed the liar Elba, and the arresting Police Officer to lie, and her assailant/bisexual lover/roommate to hide from prosecution. Talking about "kangaroo court," then? They should have placed a sign at the court door "White Man wanted for jail time."

When Jim fought them, the judge got upset and sent him to 180 days to jail! There he discovered that they needed some diversion, in Federal Prison. Bravo, kangaroos and coyotes! You can't keep even your quotas alive.

Jim: "If a judge spends one day in jail treated like everyone, maybe they will quit their honorable jobs, or be more lenient toward sending someone for decades in detention?" He thought and then he dialed the criminal lawyer's number.

They were friendly, but not helpful the way he used to deal with Nikias. The meeting was on Eye Street, across McPherson metro station.

Jim: "I want my club back and to stop the Police from harassing me!"

Duval: "I used to be a federal prosecutor. I know their style of thinking and how they gather information, and then how they use their tactics to get their targets."

Jim: "I already know their tactics. I wonder why they do target me, if they go after the ladies of the night. I think they are 400 years behind in USA and locally at least 60 years behind on X Street. I basically inherited the whole situation!"

Duval: "The Judge will not care about your history knowledge or the Police's opinions about X Street. They will look at the facts! We will check the Discovery package, what the Police had reported and if the charge has substance?"

Jim: "I had some brown bags dropped by HIPS with chocolates and information and come condoms. Police added much more and even staged some orgy style scene on third floor (I keep that floor under lock)."

Duval: "Were you there during the raid?"

Jim: "No, sir! I was home with my girlfriend." He paused.

Duval: "What is the charge exactly against you personally?"

Jim: "Disorderly House (bawdy house). Whatever that means?"

Duval: "My friend! If you were not there and all that means one big nothing."

That is the good news. The bad news is I charge a lot to get you out of this situation. The even worse news is that if you don't fight them the charge will go on your record and into public information. I know the government. They live on false pretenses that they are useful. And to get elected they always show some track record of closing "bad" business and opening some community center... Hmmm ..."

Jim: "What are your fees?"

Duval: "It is a criminal case. We start with 10,000 dollars!"

Jim: "10G? My lawyer charge 3,000 dollars and adds extra billing later."

Duval: "Do you know Havana Breeze restaurant on K Street, NW?"

Jim: "Yes, sir!" He did not want to address him with his name. He felt the next move would be some sales speech or some anecdotal threat.

Duval: "Are they open now? No. They lasted less than two years and now the Cuban owner is charged with prostitution. He called me the other day."

Jim: "Did he pay you 10,000 dollars too?" he was sarcastic.

Duval: "If he did he would be still in business! Don't test me, Jim!"

Jim: "I think if you lower your demands everyone would be in business. I think in the game if everyone seizes to be so greedy, there is money for everyone. Government likes total control on permits and regulations, you like to minimize the penalties to your clients. We, the clients, (business), we try to stay in business, but sometimes we cannot pay you and the government without bankrupting ourselves. See what happened to Mr. Rogbin and now to Havana Breeze? The government has shut down 32 establishments in 10 years! Don't tell me it is always the business owners fault! Those are at least 50 million minimum lost in investments and tax revenue to near 100 million!"

Duval: "I am not an accountant. I am a lawyer and we can talk all day, but you see you are out of your club, I am not holding a check to retain me. The government does not waste time and they will be happy to see you gone!"

Jim: "Let me think about all that. Mr. Rogbin paid much more and he is still in trouble."

Duval: "They may have found drugs and a weapon in addition to the cash, but that is just my opinion" he stood up. "If you hire me I will go through your file ASAP and we can make a couple of phone calls and I will have a meeting before the status hearing in two weeks."

Jim: "The weird thing here is that I know I am innocent, because I was not there and the HIPS condoms and chocolates, I can justify as candy boxes and information. The problem is if I have to pay $10,000 to do that? I am really without those funds now. Maybe I can sell one of my Benzes?"

Duval: "Ok. Sell the cars and you can buy them again soon. I need to get paid in full, sorry!" he almost closed the door behind Jim who was leaving and talking.

Jim: "Let me see what I can do?"

The door closed with both men disappointed on each side. Jim expected a crushing noise inside the office, but a few months later he heard that the office was relocated. He guessed that their greed did not pay the rent? On second thought Jim's destruction of anybody coming across as not being a friend or cooperative was obvious. Except with Contessa and Frida, he was always cheated by everyone else in relationships and business. And as a rule his enemies got bankrupted, died, deported. He basically had only two real friends, Tavit The IT guy and his family.

He placed two ads for sale in the classified section of Washington Post. He got many calls for his two Benzes model 300 CE. He spent total of $45,000 to buy and repair them, but he was selling them for $4,000 (the black and his favorite one) and $5,000 (for the champagne, newer and only with 95K miles on the odometer). The black one was show room looking with great leather interior, but with 240,000 miles on it. The buyer was a twenty-five year old black man who gave him an envelope with brand new 100 dollars bills.

Buyer: "I like the champagne Benz better, but I don't have the funds..."

Jim: "Hey. I put 16,000 dollars just last year, I did rebuild the engine and I have installed new transmission in the black one. You have a car for the next 10 years, a Benz for $4,000. You are one lucky fellow." He almost started to cry, but he covered it with a fake smile. "Where did you get that new money?" He checked them against the light. They seemed genuine.

Buyer: "IRS, tax refund!" he lied and after signing the title over he drove off. He seemed happy and the fast car made him disappear before Jim said good bye to the "Black princess" 300 CE. He was about to call the greedy lawyer Duval. His cell phone lit up.

Mansur: "Jim, you know I need to pay the rent here. I know you have restrictions to come to the club, but my landlord does not want to hear excuses."

Jim: "I need to pay my lawyer. After I come back there I will pay you back. Can you cover for next two weeks?"

Mansur: "Hey, buddy! If you say you are innocent of the charges, then you don't need a lawyer!" He was bluffing or testing Jim's intelligence.

Jim: "I will figure something out. I left my apartment and my office, but you, my lawyer, Shelley; all you want money from me. Then how can I pay you without earning money? Then you have my equipment there and my liquor and wine still."

Mansur: "Send me Lora here. She can watch your equipment and sell your liquor, but to keep the place I need $4,400 rent; you gave me $1,600 so far..."

Jim: "Ok. After the court day we will talk again! For now I will give you $4,000. I will meet you at your house in Beltsville, MD."

The greedy Mansur canceled the greedy lawyer. Jim could hear the laugh of the coyotes, gathering around him, digging into his empty bank account, drinking in his club, getting ready to destroy him in court.

Jim: "You will not win. I will take my club back with or without a lawyer. If God/my subconscious mind are stronger than them now is the time to play, coyotes!" He did not need to prove to them, the inferiors, that he was right or wrong. If they were all liars, he had to be a better liar. Are the lawyers doing the same? Look what they did to Mr. Rogbin and Joe Conforte? Jim paid his taxes. He was good. Now he needed to negotiate. Can he outsmart the super power like US federal government? Yes. Can he do it without a lawyer and not spend the required "10,000 dollar" lawyer fixation. Yes. Can he take his club back? Yes.

Jim: "I see your doubt increases, dear Cornell U readers, or just your curiosity? Nobody gets grades on curiosity, but on factual research, ok?"

The two weeks passed painfully slow, but they did. Mansur was one silly old man. He was selling Jim's liquor and using his equipment, but Jim was not given credit for that. He just pocketed the money Jim gave him, like it was some kind of entitlement. The truth was that while Jim was struggling to keep his record clean, the Mansur's family was buying new condominiums, new SUV Honda, his daughter got a new Lexus and the house was undergoing remodeling! Everything would have been great if someone just stepped back, and held back his selfishness. Everything seemed like a fast train going downhill with no breaks.

Angel: "Hey, Jim! They are talking to the younglings in jail. Some of them are snitching on you. They might press criminal charges against you? I know you can handle the situation, but be careful." She was the one to call him about the raid; she was the one to call him about his champagne Benz being vandalized in December, 2004. Now she was his muse, at his distress.

Jim: "Are you sure you are telling the truth Angel?" Both they were trying to laugh. "You know one has to believe in himself/herself before he/she calls God (in my case, my sub consciousness) to help! I wish a lot of luck to my enemies!" Now they started to laugh for completely different reasons. Angel recently kicked out her pimp Marquis, who collected from her $475,000 a year, but gave her a used Cadillac only and pocket change back. Jim was laughing at his enemies' fate. Soon he would unleash his best qualities to put them on their knees.

The court day came and before he to see the judge the defense attorney pulled him in the side room.

Goldstein: "Three things, sir! I want to quote you something from the law book. First, "a bawdy house (house of prostitution) is a place where women/men perform sexual acts for profit without legal permit. The active or knowledgeable, but inactive, (looking the other way) manager of such a nuisance place to his neighbors it is punishable by law, considered misdemeanor. Second. You can plea bargain and maybe we can help you reinstate your position and recover your loses? Third, we can go to court and they will not stop there until they convince the judge to send you to detention. Believe me, I can't help you there. Too much evidence is stacking up against you."

Jim: "I have been through the process before. I pled "not guilty" and they sent me 180 days in jail. What shall I do now? I was not there at the raid. They found nothing incriminating in my office or in my house. I don't see your angle?"

Goldstein: "The problem with your case is that you have been at the same place since 1998. You can't tell me you are not aware of the hookers in your club? The same question the judge will ask you. You say "No," and you will get the maximum punishment."

Jim: "And if I do agree? What is the guarantee I will get back to work?" he saw a window of opportunity. The previous case he had in 1996 was a disaster. His supposed defense lawyer did not present him with any options, especially the option he may end up in jail for 180 days! Now, he may end up with years in jail or get his club back? It was all about negotiation.

God: "How much is this club worth to you? Is it worth a Police record, where you agree on their (Police) terms?"

Jim: "If I fight I may end up with no record, but my name will be tainted already at that location. They will scrutinize me to open any other club in DC. I better agree with their offer and to plead guilty, even I am not!"

Satan: "Agreeing without fight is like not using your head! I knew you would succumb to me. Remember the red dressed Sarah? I sent her to you. You did not use your head, then also. No wonder you are in this predicament."

Jim: "I am a man, she is a woman. What is the sin to agree having sex with a seductress?"

God: "First of all, I do not condone nor bless fornication. Who can change the world history sometimes falls for the sexual nagons. That does not make him a sinner unless he agrees that is his weakness. I suggest you do confess to your weakness. Sarah and many others are great proof of that. If you do not plea bargain then Satan will test you again and again until they convict you on much bigger crime."

Jim: "True! Being free with guilty plea, is better than being with a, not guilty plea and staying in jail. (It happened to me before, remember?)" The irony was that his rival Mr. Rogbin would listen to Satan and he would fight in Court as "Not guilty." His lies were discovered and the police raid turned too much evidence against him. He ended up in jail and he was to be deported. His lawyer was Brut Maloney.

Jim: "Ok, Ms. Goldstein! I want my club back. Tell them I am "guilty!" he listened to his sub consciousness/God this time.

Satan: "Damn it! I lost this one. Soon this guy may stop loving Kiana too. Damn it. I had this guy by the horns for three years. He spent $250,000 on her and I was laughing at him all the time. Love cost, buddy. And you say you will die for her? I wanted to see that; a death for a cheater like Kiana? No wonder I am the co-creator of the greatest sitcom on earth "Seinfeld." Larry David is my image in the flesh! He claims he is the co-creator, but it is actually me."

God: "Yes, the show about nothing ends up with nothing. It basically laid the foundation to cynicism and lies for decades ahead and expanding the Democratic base, which in turn elected the anti-Christ as a president. Good job, my brother Satan. I did not expect anything different than that!"

Satan: "Yes, we are brothers! If you are so righteous why most of the world is in turmoil? Why are you not helping most of your followers?"

God: "Whoever has awareness does not need my help; I may just finish what they started. I am not the initiator of events, you are! See what happened to Jim and Kiana? See what it is happening now? If a given the opportunity is twisted by you; (money, drugs, alcohol, sex, technology used to war, over eating, excessive in pleasures), then my intervention is almost Mission Impossible. If a person stays away from the environment which created his downfall he becomes more aware how to correct it. Jail is created for the purpose of staying away from the trouble society considers as nuisance! If a person recognizes the problem and he shows ability to fix the problem, the judge will recognize that and will let him be free to do just that. Jail, sometimes, is a life extension for the person who continues to stay in trouble. It gives one time to reflect; even it limits him from interaction with his environment. If that detention does not help, then the society lets the natural law to take effect; one has the choice to die on the streets or to die by public court."

Jim: "Wow. Death is somehow a balance to someone who can't control his urges! See Satan. I would have died loving Kiana and you were the one who urged me to keep her? God was rational and he told me to investigate her to the point of chasing her away! Thanks for the help, Satan? Thanks for the "rational" headache, God! You brothers are something!"

He entered the court. Judge was Lucille Tucker. She looked tired at her age of forty-five. She was a beautiful African American lady with well styled hair. Her black robe fitted her well and one can easily imagine her strong tall body with proportionate long legs under the long desk.

Court clerk: "Jim Walker vs. District of Columbia, case number CM2006 2209."

Goldstein: "Present! Step forward," she directed her client toward defendant desk.

District Attorney: "Charges against Jim Walker will be dropped upon his admission of "guilty." We recommend "John school" and 300 dollars restitution."

Judge Tucker: "Do you understand the plea? You will have a criminal record. Do you have anything to add to your defense?" she was quietly coughing, trying to stay away from the court microphone. She looked at Jim's file. She was puzzled for a second or two. Seems detective O'Conner had a field day in exaggerating the picture of the "grand crime." Jim almost laughed, but he remained somehow with a very dramatic Hollywood face with concern. Academy Award's look out, here he comes.

Jim: "Yes, your honor. I am realtor and I have other businesses besides that club. I hired a manager Larry who I reprimanded and I did suggest that he be terminated two days prior to the raid. I am guilty to keeping him longer than I should have."

Goldstein: "Jim Walker is trying to recoup his investment there. He is penniless now."

Judge Tucker: "Ok. I am giving him one year in prison which is suspended with unsupervised probation. He will go to drug test center for the first six months and he is allowed to return to the bar to work. Any illegal activities should be avoided. My decision is made based on his education, previous record and his plea and corrective action he is willing to contribute." She signed the paper, which was sealed by court clerk and was given to Jim.

Jim: "I know my partner may not allow me to get my money. How can I be assured I will be able to recover that?" He was almost leaving the stand.

Judge Tucker: "The commercial part of the bar is not in my legal field. That is between you two to resolve." She banged the desk with the gavel...

Jim was happy. He was free to go to work. He made a copy of the judge reinstatement order and he went straight to the bar. He sacrificed his favorite car to keep Mansur afloat and to bring himself back in the business.

Mansur: "What are you doing here? Aren't you supposed to stay away?" He sounded threatening. Where was his fatherly mood when he was asking for favors? Malik was sticking his head behind him even angrier.

Jim: "Hey, guys! Calm down. The judge allowed me to take my bar back? Here is the order!" he was showing a big smile on his face in contrast to the others in the room.

Malik: "Let me read it!" he jumped in front of the surprised Mansur. He grabbed the copy and scanned it up and down two to three times.

Jim: "Keep it! Police may come and harass you without that proof?"

Mansur: "Jim, we have been through thick and thin. What happened here made the Police raid the place! I suggest you sell your share or you buy me out ASAP! "He was not the same person and not very sympathetic even though he got the rent paid.

Jim: "Listen! I told you Larry was to be fired! You kept him here. I knew police was coming. You said to keep him and now you blame me? Words have sequences."

Mansur: "Ok, when I said keep him I also assumed that you would be here to supervise him? You were not here, you were with Shelley and allowed this to happen!" he was calming down a bit.

Jim: "You are with your wife every night. I am trying to "Live the Life," too. I can't be here seven years every night!" he had a point.

Mansur: "Police always hit on the weekend nights. From now on be here at least on weekends! Now, can we meet the Judge and confirm that the order is true?" he sounded suspicious.

Jim: "Sure! Do you want to do it now? We may interrupt the court and get thrown out?" He understood his angle, (after all the Mediterranean's thought alike).

Mansur: "Get your liquor and sell it this weekend. Pay me what you owe me and we will go Tuesday afternoon. Do not get into any more trouble. I will show that order to my lawyer Hillcrest in Bethesda. I hope he will agree and we are back in business...?"

Jim: "This place has one lawyer. It is Nikias. Why do you need to pay more? I did not hire anyone to represent me and I still won the case." He smiled.

Mansur: "You are different than anyone I ever met, but the lawyers see the technical part of a business. We are too emotional about things we do. Police wants to see documents and results. I also want to sleep at night!" He tried to smile. Malik was steel angry. Deep inside he convinced himself he could own Jim's one million dollar investment for free. Well, he had it for two weeks, but no profit was made.

Jim: "Items don't make profit, personalities do." He thought. Most of his business was built on his great personality and wit. Just a smile without a substantial joke or positive interaction with his weird customers wouldn't make a dent in the highly competitive night life profit share. He kept his employees base to a minimum and he preferred to do it himself, than to rely on some thievery ABCmanagers. Malik thought by just showing up at the door and by turning on the lights and some music the business will flourish!

Jim entered the cursed club. It was cold and there was not homecoming feeling. There was a cold feeling of an evil spirit in there.

Malik: "I bought beer, wine, liquor while you were away. Pay me and you can take over the bar."

Jim: "Give me thirty minutes." He grabbed the mobile phone and dialed his best business friend Tavit. They were not close, but they had things in common. He was his IT man and Jim was helping him many times by buying some of his cameras and computers. Tavit fell on hard times paying his taxes and IRS made a plan for him to pay them back.

Jim: "Hey Tavit! I am back in the business, but I need a small favor. Mansur's brother-in- law is asking me to buy his liquor. I paid the rent, but he is on my back to get his money back."

Tavit: "So, you paid the rent but you need to buy liquor? Sure. I can give you a thousand. I am behind on my taxes already. One week more or less will not make any difference. Hope things are going to get better for you?"

Jim: "Well. I moved to my new girlfriend's apartment. Mansur is giving me hard time, but I don't pay him much attention. I will try to make some money here or just sell my share?" He was just thinking loud.

Tavit: "I will bring you the money. Give me fifteen minutes, ok?"

Malik was surprised on Jim's efficiency to do business. He was thinking that by placing hurdles in front of Jim he would just stop and go away!

Jim: "The keys are changed, Police orders?" He was puzzled.

Malik gave him the new keys after he got paid.

Mansur: "Police will give me a hard time once they find out you are back here.

I suggest you hire a new bar Manager. You are lucky you paid the rent. Many people are asking to rent the place after you were barred out."

Jim: "You expect me to abandon ship because "rats want to play?"

Mansur, they are testing us. Stay with me." He climbed up the stairs where he found a good cigar and he rested for almost an hour just looking at the spinning ceiling fan at times. He closed his eyes imagining what Mr. Rogbin was feeling like or Joe Conforte about the coyotes and little rats, the mighty representatives of US government?

Those are the real people, who got their dreams crashed, just like the Indians or the Cubans, or the Irish, or the blacks at different history times. The phrase "cockroaches," Al Pacino gave them in the movie "Scarface" was well chosen, to describe the losers in "The Game" of DC night clubs and entertainment establishments closing. ABRA will shrink their staff almost 80 percent in that ten year period of the War on Clubs. They will move from H Street, NW to North Capitol, NE, to U street and finally to 2000 14th street now, in the year of 2012. It showed that one of most powerful DC agency was struggling just like the Police and of course the club owners.

Chief Naylor's slogan "One murder, one license," may have applied to Go Go scenes, but, why 32 entertainment liquor establishments have closed? Were there 32 murders or were there 32 schemes by DC political machine?

Jim Ronan will lose his powers over DC liquor licensing in 2013.

Jim: "Pay back is a bitch, cockroach!" He hated him since his comment, "Jim is Al Capone." That was in the spring of 2001, when he was trying to open the club Zoro at 1115A on U Street. When Jim called him next day he conveniently declined to answer, hiding behind his male, gay secretary.

During the two weeks he left, his hotel room looking office was ransacked by the Raymus' Leasing crew, led by Vladimir, the master thief. Only one couch was left there.

Jim: "I guess they can't steal everything?" To take the couch out one needed to dismount it first. Thieves are usually inpatient. Yes, Jim told them he would leave the office, but he did not expect it to be emptied next week. He was trying not to pay the rent while waiting for the court day. Now he wanted it back.

Raymus: "Just pay us for this month of February and you can move back to your office." He was the ever business friendly nice guy.

Jim: "Thank you!" he was almost short of calling him an angel. The only wild card here was Mansur. Jim detected a strong resentment of his partner for coming back to the club.

Mansur: "My lawyer Hillcrest wants to meet you in his Bethesda office."

Jim: "Great!" he was suspicious of his partner's intentions.

Lawyer Hillcrest: "You are aware you can't work as manager in liquor establishment if you have a criminal record!" He sounded serious.

Jim: "My ABC manager's license is not revoked. I am allowed to work at the bar by the judge's order."

Lawyer Hillcrest: "This man will lose his liquor license because of you, sir!" he pointed at Mansur.

Jim: "Are you representing Mansur against me? I am not sure if you are aware that I paid for the liquor license once we took over the next building at 1428 X Street. We, along with Mansur are using the services of Nikias. Mansur cannot be together with me with one lawyer and against me with another lawyer."

Lawyer Hillcrest: "I am his lawyer. I worked against Nikias in the past. He is good. Understand the predicament here. You both can't be together there. You buy him out or he buys you out! Do you have 300,000 dollars? That's what he is asking. Then you can stay and deal with the ABC Board and the police."

Jim: "I invested total of one million there, Mansur invested one third. I have an idea. I will stay there until I will find a buyer for both of us or just one of us!"

Mansur: "Hillcrest. We are going to Judge Tucker chambers tomorrow. I will call you when she confirms her decision, or I find out if she was in error?" All men stood up. Nobody was happy.

Jim: "What a life? Federal Government and DC liquor agency giving different arguments about the liquor enforcement regulations? On top of that, Hillcrest may not be licensed by DC Law? What does he know? I will talk to Nikias also." He thought pushing the street level button in elevator. In reality Hillcrest was Mansur's neighbor, so they small talked to push Jim out. That meeting of three of them was definitely staged!

Nikias: "What? You pled guilty? You will be out of business."

Jim: "That was the only way to get back to work, Nikias!"

Nikias: "I have to notify the ABC board. I am your lawyer. I will suggest you hire someone to work for you. You just become an accountant, promoter, but not manager."

Jim: "Great. I will not be in the spot light. I maybe just a consultant, ok?"

Nikias: "Now even I can't help you!"

The irony was that, Jim was helping Nikias within two months of this conversation. If this was not a twist of Quantum Reality then what it is?

Chapter 16

At end of April, 2006 there was an ABC hearing about the assault of ABC manager, Jim Walker at Zeus Lounge DC by a known pimp.

Nikias: "What is the hearing about? A fight at the brothel, you are running?" he had that smirk on his face, turning his head toward Jim in conspiratorial manner.

Jim: "Yes. You have never been there, so let me answer the questions, ok?"

Usually if one brings a lawyer he is considered guilty to a point.

Davis: "What is the case from the District Attorney?" ABC board chairman asked, surrounded with six women.

ABC investigator Ricardo: "Not present" he was appalled.

Davis: "We will proceed! The Police states that the fight occurred at closing hours and the drinks were still cold with ice. We need your explanation what caused that fight?"

Jim gave a small talk to his lawyer Nikias. "May I?" he pointed toward the defendant desk.

Nikias: "Dear Chairman. My client will answer the questions with me as his counsel."

Davis: "Step to the other (free desk). We can use the prosecutor desk today, which is kind of unusual." Everyone agreed with the same laugh.

Jim was not surprised. God/TIH was giving him the game of chance again. He was ready to exploit it. An opportunist with Quantum Awareness will connect with Cosmic Intelligence. That's what Jim was and beyond…

Jim: "Dear Chairman and ladies of the Board! The fight was provoked by a disorderly client, who was trying to talk to a lady who rejected his advances. One of her friends, a Spanish guy tried to stop him. I tried to break the fight. Then a friend of the assailant swung a chair across my head and he hit me in the face."

Davis: "The police stated that the lady was a prostitute. What is your reply?" he gave a long look down on defendant.

Jim: "I protected her dignity, Sir. I am not asking women what is their profession, hobbies, orientation?" The whole room got quiet. Women in the room agreed with him. He took advantage of that opportunity and he continued.

Jim: "I am ship's captain by profession. I run my business the way I run my ship. Since 1998 we had maybe three fights total."

Davis: "Three fights in eight years? We have three fights in one weekend! Bravo!" the human wave of Thought, the lawyers rippled in two directions in agreement.

Jim turned around. To the left of him were Mansur and Nikias almost holding hands in huge surprise and both sinking down into their chairs, "What idiots? Scared like little girls." Jim almost screamed at $250 an hour lawyer. Then he stepped forward toward the seven members ABC Board. He passed his business cards as realtor to each one of them. They whispered to each other "who is this guy; a realtor, a ship's captain, a lawyer like, and ABC manager?" He won.

Investigator Ricardo: "May I ask a question?" he stood up from his chair and almost collided with the returning Jim this time behind Nikias and Mansur.

Davis: "One question. We are almost done here."

Investigator Ricardo: "The place is known as a place for prostitution and I need to address the Board about that."

Davis: "How do you reply to that, Jim Walker!" now he was reading from his realtor card.

Jim: "I am not aware of anything like that!" he sensed they had no file update for the January raid. "Fuck you investigator Ricardo, the cockroach."

Davis: "Based on this facts finding and the testimony, we will write our decision. We will return in five minutes after our vote is counted."

Investigator Ricardo was with a crazy face; and in disbelief Jim was able to rebut his "rightful," argument, according to the Police. In his mind Jim couldn't agree because he was not there during the raid. God again was there then, like it was here now.

Davis: "The license stays as is! We voted."

Nikias: "How about the hours? Can we get the hours changed now? We got them approved a year ago."

Davis: "Sure, just bring a letter with three signatures minimum from the local ANC, ok! Dismiss!" He hit the gavel.

Jim: "Mansur, Nikias! I did well, didn't I?" he was proud of himself.

The victory against one of the most corrupted DC Agencies was partial, but still a victory. The liquor hour service was still limited for another two years.

Tuesday came slowly. Jim took a taxi with Mansur to DC Court house. The crowd was thinning at around 4 pm of that beginning of March, 2006. Mansur and Jim sat patiently in the court room until the last case was closed. Judge Lucille Tucker asked the DA "who are those left in the room?" almost to leave her chambers.

Jim: "My partner doubts your decision last week that you allowed me to return to work at my bar?" He pulled up Mansur who looked like a child with his Mike's restaurant green hat.

Mansur: "We are partners, but my lawyer disagreed with your decision."

Judge Tucker: "My decision stays. Tell your lawyer to contact me, if any grievances. Good day gentlemen!"

Jim: "I told you. Federal power is superior over some little lawyer. Your lawyer would have lost his license if he barged in her Court like we did without an appointment. Let's get out before we get arrested here!"

Mansur: "Damn it! We are stuck together again. Ok, do your business. They are going to squeeze us more from now on. Be careful, ok! I wish we had money and we could move somewhere else!"

Jim: "I will help you sell it. I am a licensed realtor!"

Mansur: "You are now a licensed criminal, buddy!" they both laughed.

Jim: "The criminal who can't be prosecuted is now a free man! Ha, ha" they laughed again.

Mansur: "What I am going to do with you, Jim! Every day is a first for everything. Life is a challenge."

Jim: "Mansur! Do you see this face? As long I am around you, you should feel safe. You step on me, and then you will see what happens?"

Mansur: "Are you threatening me?"

Jim: "You know I am protected by God and that is why your business expanded and your license is still on the wall, and my license is not revoked."

Mansur: "I am protected too, buddy."

Jim: "Really?" he walked away without mentioning the last word. In October, 2008 Mansur would lose his license. Read how Cornell U and MIT?…

Shelley: "Wow, Jim! You pulled this one through! We just met a few months ago, but so much has happened since. You completed your expansion, got rid of your ex, won the case and you took your club back. Now, I will let you follow on your promise. We are going house shopping!" she cuddled in him like she needed a blanket.

Jim: "We will celebrate! Here is a good Veuve Clicquot Brut! Imagine, when it was founded, in 1772!"

Shelley: "Imagine we get married and we get a house and have a child, in 2006!" She pulled him in between her ex Army strong legs. "You are my hero!"

Jim: "I love making love to you when you are happy!" he thrusted his torpedo in her ever juicy vagina.

Shelley: "I need you to meet my mom this weekend. I need her blessing!"

Jim: "Your, Mom? Bend over now and I promise to meet your family soon." They were enjoying one of the rarest and last moments of greatest sex on earth.

Jim: "Remember the song "Summer time" by Lois Armstrong?...

"….Summer time and the living is easy. Your father is rich and your ma is good looking…." they both laughed.

Shelley: ".... so hush little baby, don't you cry." She was contracting in pleasure. "Where is my baby?" Trying to sing like Ella Fitzgerald's from the famous duet.

Jim: "We are making one right now," both were laughing and cumming.

Shelley: "I wish you were making the same great income but day time?

I don't think mom will approve if you keep that club life?" She disappeared in the shower.

That proved to be a very prophetic. That weekend her mother proved to be the a bitch she was, an old, single, fifty-nine year old cleaning lady in some prison facility in Norfolk. She was really black and Shelley was almost white.

Jim: "Something is wrong with the picture. Shelley's sister is all black! Who was the father of Shelley, a Spanish or white man?" He thought.

Shelley: "My sister and I have different fathers, obviously!"

Jim: ".... And she would judge me and she would give us her approval?"

Shelley: "Yea, if she is not happy we can't move forward!"

Jim: "You are the judge," he pulled her inside the bedroom and they had passionate sex.

The mother had a little one bedroom apartment near the beach and she was at work. Jim knew how to change Shelley's mind, but her mother proved to be prejudiced and having many issues.

Carol: "Hey. I am cooking steak for dinner. If you bring a nice bottle of red wine, we are going to be all right."

Shelley: "I know your favorite is Cabernet. I will let Jim pick you a good one," she winked at him. "Get some points with her, ok?"

Jim: "I rather take you to dinner! I don't want to owe her favors!" He detected that Carol was checking him out. She was ten years older than him and he was eleven years older than Shelley."

Carol: "How long have you have been together?" she was investigating in somewhat of a fatherly and motherly demeanor. The steak was good, wine great, but the conversation was like stepping on glasses without crushing them.

Shelley: "I told you Jim has his own business. He is club owner and restaurant owner too." She looked at Jim, "you should say something too. Help me here," was her expression.

Jim: "I really like Shelley and we plan to buy a house together and possibly start a family!" He tried to be positive and convincing. The steak and wine was helping for now.

Shelley: "I told him to check himself with paternity test and to change his business to something in the day time. I can't be waiting till 4 am every morning to come back home."

Carol: "What is your plan to change things?" She sipped on wine and followed with quick bite of that great steak.

Jim: "I am selling the club soon and then I will invest in a day time business." He almost sounded convincing. Everyone was comfortable around that false perception of reality. Jim knew in his mind that a family is a restriction for his ever occurring adventures. It seemed great on outside, but when you get into details he felt not being ready. He was looking for mutual love and true respect, being worshiped for the genius mind he was. He could not love anyone equal or better than Kiana. He would get instant erection just thinking of her, but that's where Satan was controlling him and the pain and turmoil started between his genius mind and his weak and loving heart. He basically felt being stupid when in love with this ever evasive creature, who gave him the best sex and the worse pain. The great thing going with Shelley was that any time they had some disagreements Jim would balance that with great love making and she would submit and quiet down.

Jim and Shelley walked over some artificially built sand dunes by the local Virginia Beach government, after dinner.

Shelley: "I am tired. Do you really want to go to the beach?" she made childish cat face.

Jim: "I will carry you like a bride!" He lifted her up and her perfect body glued up to him. She wrapped her hands around his neck and she kissed him. "You are my Hercules!" Jim laughed and slightly turned around. He felt he was being watched. He saw at a distance Carol shaking her head.

Jim: "Your Mom is spying on us!" he was trying to soften the situation and make a little comedic observation.

Shelley: "My mother does not like anybody to touch me. I was raped at age of 2, while she was working in the next room; at some laundry."

Jim: "At age of two? Do you remember anything?" He was puzzled. After DP the Don, Kiana, Khloe, Mr. Smith, Frida, Contessa, Mansur, Shelley was supposed to be the "normal one?"

God: "Normal people are who respect you regardless of circumstances in their past or present; weak people are the ones who follow you regardless of right or wrong you do, saint people are who will help you, even if you are wrong. God will sort it all out at the end, right or wrong. History always changes the winners and losers positions, after time passes. The irony is that today's winners maybe so crooked, that in later stage they may end up as biggest criminals and even jailed!"

Satan: "Bad is normal. To make a miracle you have to outsmart me? For me Carol acts as normal mother!"

Jim: "Time and speed will judge who stays where? I think although everything seems circumstantial, there is some order of events, and that where people cross paths and the Quantum Laws apply in result where the normal and the weak people are tested? I, being on a higher level may touch their lives, I may even have helped them in the past, but how does someone like me, matches up with one to be his partner?"

Satan: "The one who can outsmart you can be your partner! Kiana did." He almost giggled, causing his heart pain.

God: "Your match can outsmart you, but in way to teach you a lesson in positive way! Kiana was a power broker for the evil forces. Drugs, kid without marriage, using a trick to advance her career, stealing your money, cars and cash, all that to benefit her, not you or both of you. Using your Quantum, genius mind you will find that friends are the ones who chose you at tough situation over the others. "Normal" for you will be your companion would help you or assist you to get your goals achieved."

Jim: "That means I need two characteristics:

Normal and a friend.

God: "You need Quantum and advanced "normal friend!"

Jim: "Can that be a woman? I prefer that over a man!"

God: "Yes, but exclude the sexual part of the relationship. If sex happens it has to be after both agree that it will not be destructive in your mutual development in searching and spreading the knowledge and the Awareness in the Galaxy and beyond!"

Jim: "Now I see why the deities are usually single men or women. The only man and woman are Mary and Jesus, her son. The others are individuals like Allah, Mohammed, Lord Buddha and Jesus. Nowhere, in the Bible are phrases as Jesus and wife, Mohamed and wife, Buddha and wife."

Jim: "So, in general women can't rise to the level of men's Awareness?"

God: "The man's power is in his sperm. This is his expression of physical continuation! Aphrodite, the Goddess of Love, beauty and lust was conceived from the sperm of castrated Uranus, by his son titan Kronos. Man's pure, eternal power is in his Knowledge and his ability to spread the Awareness to others. Knowledge should not be given to anyone in final true form. It has to be revealed to certain people who can withstand the mountain of knowledge and the scrutiny of the masses. Most top scientists were laughed at or tortured by dictators or by The Catholic Church and The Inquisition. It is amazing how everyone adores most advanced toys of the day -- phones, cars, jets, military advancement, excessive wealth, but they do not look at the sources how they were achieved. Yes, my son, it is done through Knowledge! The worse that could happen to The Earth and to the Galaxy is to use the Awareness in developing wrong weapons and to lead to self destruction. You are chosen to lead and teach, not to follow skirts, especially ones who need their mothers' approval!"

Jim: "God, I am still a mortal! I am still a man! I have physical needs to the point!" Jim, observed himself dropping Shelley near the water, but his mind was wondering away from her.

Satan: "Carol controls Shelley. Shelley controls you in a way. You live in her house. You are trying to please her. Indirectly Carol controls you."

Jim: "I will challenge you eventually, Satan!" he tried not to listen to his heart. That weak heart brought him to the situation of almost losing his club just in recent months.

Shelley: "Hey, Daddy! You dropped me too fast. You should be nice to my mother. She may like you one day? And you should be more forward with me. I noticed a few times, a private call changed your body language. I feel I am your rebound girl. I know you still think of Kiana. I told that to my mother."

Jim: "You should not tell her everything you think. Mothers amplify the negative thoughts tenfold and then they brainwash you."

Shelley: "I feel like we are in some jury room! …My sister, my mother, my coworker at HR Jacqueline. They all talk about you. I usually try to defend you. You are my significant other!" They kissed next to the water meeting the sand in short waves.

Next day her mother was off.

Carol: "I will take you on your offer to take us out to lunch." She almost ordered him to say yes.

Jim: "We can take one car." They all agreed to use his sport Benz 300CE. The restaurant on the beach had two floors. The first floor was enclosed and seemed was full with loud talking patrons at the bar.

The scattered around tables were full with families and kids screaming over the loud sounds of the flat TVs placed around the horse shoe bar.

Carol: "Let's go to the open deck above. I love the sun." Everyone followed her.

Shelley: "She is acting strange again. Don't argue with her. She is up to something." She was showing Jim, mostly in some military sign language. Jim just shook his head. "What I am getting into?" Then he remembered Malik saying "Everyday is like going to school. Every day is a test of some regulation."

Jim: "Why should emotions, be tested? They are not regulated and licensed?"

Satan: "Not in my world. If someone wants to control you, they create a thought first, (bio electric impulses), then they pass their emotions (magnetic field) to you to change your behavior, (energy, work). Your boss can do that, or your feelings toward a person could cause you to get up in strange hours to work on their desires. You are their mental and physical robot/slave. Kiana did that to you, because you thought you loved her. If she loved you, she would have done same things to you."

Jim: "Marriage then would be a contract where two parties agree to love and work on each other demands?"

God: "About love! Nobody works, when in love. Here we differ with Satan. If you love your job you really do not work, because you feed back from your interaction with your environment. For example is the battery of a car. It recharges constantly from the alternator and the gas we put in the car. The star Sun has the similar capabilities to recharge from the released energy after the life leaves the dead animals or people (from all vertebrates). How a star like the Sun still generates power after 4.5 billion years?"

Jim: "Here is the science of incarnation and reincarnation. The incarnation happens once, but reincarnation is six times. The Great Pyramid was ideal incarnation machine.

Here is the theory of the seven spheres, or seven planets and the one star, the Sun. They create or destroy matter by interacting with their frequencies. The same frequencies like The Sun, the Moon and the Earth affect the human biorhythms. Mostly the changes happen while the person is asleep or in altered state of mind. To predict someone's behavior some oracle used the horoscope, 12 zodiacs, based on astrology. That was started in 1700 BC."

Carol: "That is a nice table." She pointed at remote area from the entrance. "I don't like too much traffic around me."

Jim: "I am not surprised, coming from a loner, old fart," sotto voce, but just stayed silent.

Shelley: "Don't you like the view? You were a ship's captain. See how many ships are around?" She pointed with a smile toward the horizon.

Jim: "This is a main Naval Base, here in Norfolk. I am not surprised. I am still a ship's captain, once a captain, always a captain!" He said it with pride and he tried to respond with a smile.

Carol: "Do you miss the sea? Hello..." She answered to a greeting waiter. He was young, medium built, wearing all black clothes and apron. He was Caucasian, friendly and wearing sneakers.

Shelley: "They look fit like athletes, I guess one must be fast and strong to climb those steps and run across the huge deck?"

Jim: "... or they give speedy service?" He tried to conclude using her tone. Those two lovers were able to read each other's mind and to finish their sentences. The wild card here was the Old Mother of hers.

Carol: "I am hungry. Can I have a nice glass of wine, Shiraz, please!" The waiter was waiting for their small chat to complete.

Shelley: "Bring as a bottle. Jim is treating!" She rubbed his hand slightly. She was trying not to be too affectionate around her mother.

Jim: "We are celebrating many things, my club, and the new house to buy…"

Shelley: "… And maybe baby soon," she was a natural cheerleader. In actuality the more she was showing excitement, the more her mom's behavior was changing for the worse.

Carol: "The wine is good. I need food quick." She ordered and everyone was just waiting and chatting. She was stuffing herself with bread and butter.

Jim: "I need a cigar. I will go downstairs to smoke." He knew her mother was not tolerant to any tobacco products and he wanted those two women to chat eye to eye. He went downstairs. He went to the bathroom first, and then he pulled out a nice Cohiba. After ten minutes he returned to the table. The wine was half gone and there was not any sign of food.

Carol: "We have been here half an hour and besides the wine and bread we haven't seen our waiter." Food arrived as she finished her sentence. The appetizers arrived in about five minutes after his cigar break.

Waiter: "Sorry for your wait. Kitchen is overwhelmed. I will give you free dessert at the end. Ok!" he disappeared toward the door he came from.

Shelley: "They should give us more than free desserts or just notify us from the beginning that it will be slow service. I am an HR manager. I would have been more upfront with the situation. This way the customers would not be stuck with wine and long wait."

Jim: "Well. It is like any business. They lure you in and keep you waiting." He heard himself agreeing with them.

Carol: "Look. We may have to wait even longer for the entrees too?"

Shelley: "I think after the appetizers we should cancel the entrees and leave?"

Jim: "Are you in a bad mood? I am a businessman and usually I would talk to the management before any drastic decision!" He was right.

Carol: "Have you noticed; there are no black waiters here? Maybe there are just ignoring us or it is pure discrimination?" she stopped eating. Her body stiffened like a mother wolverine.

Jim: "Hey. I don't see any Bulgarian waiters here either." He was trying to defuse a developing situation before it got worse. If he was poor, he may have thought up any problem to get out of there. He sensed here a reverse prejudice toward white people, not against the food service itself.

Carol did not say anything and stood up. She started walking away toward the exit.

Shelley: "I told you not to provoke her. Anything to do with race or ethnic comments she takes it too seriously," she followed her mother.

Jim: "Let me drive you back to her home." He screamed after her.

Jim stayed another five minutes. He made a few phone calls. He expected that both mother and daughter would return and they would resume everything as the dinner was normal? Nobody did return and he just paid the waiter even for the food which was never delivered.

Waiter: "What is wrong? I explained you about the kitchen situation."

Jim: "My mother-in-law observed that there is no diversification in your restaurant. That's what made her upset; the food was just a pretext."

Waiter: "I appreciate you paying the bill. Otherwise, I was to pay it!"

Jim: "I am a club owner. I hate when people stage anything not to pay the bill. Basically, it is a felony walking out without paying or without justifying it" he shelled out 20 percent tip. He left the food in plates just being served and walked toward the car.

Jim: "Shelley, where are you? I have been calling you the last ten minutes."

Shelley: "I have been trying to reach my mother. She has been ignoring me because of you. She finally answered and she told me she does not want to see you again. She is walking to her house. She said you are racist!"

Jim: "We need to talk! Am I a racist, dating for the last five years African American women? You and Kiana are not from my race. How come, I am the "racist"?"

Shelley: "I am next to your car. Come and get me. Let's go home to DC. I want to pick my stuff from my mother's house. She does not want to see you now."

Jim: "Weird. Ok." He assumed that maybe a marriage to a daughter with a cookoo mother was not such a great idea? They drove in silence the next four hours. Those 167 miles were the longest miles when the love he thought was there was dying over, he don't even know what?

Jim: "Kiana was stealing my money, but not giving me any sex. This one is stealing my emotions, but costing me nothing!" He was puzzled.

God (at his rational mind): "Maybe it is not your call to live the mortals' life? Some deities are what they are not because of being like everyone else, but because of their difference from the others. Imagine 7 billion saints and deities lurking around. I will be exhausted dealing with all miracle workers then. At this time, I can see about 40 to 50 discoveries by the scientists, but those are on physical level. I am in search of the next Jesus, Mohammed, Allah, Pythagoras, Einstein, and Tesla. Or, maybe it is you?"

Satan (at his heart): "I keep seducing you with successful stories, and then I snatch them away from you. I even put you in jail to test you, but you started reading The Bible! I just can't crush you and make you disappear from the spot light."

God: "Jim knows how to use The Awareness of higher consciousness, by neutralizing the positive and negative charges coming at him. He keeps communicating with his own sub consciousness and he does miracle after miracle on a daily basis. He knows how to convert hydrogen to helium. He knows how to use the Time to his advantage. He is beyond the modern science. Note that! At Einstein's and Max's Plank formulas and theories, Time was not even mentioned, sorry, Satan!"

Jim: "Hey, Kiana! Have you seen the movie "Casino?" Everything there is reenactment of our relationship. Robert De Niro plays me, Sharon Stone plays you." She called him in May, 2006.

Kiana: "You are not Robert De Niro…." She was trying to minimize Jim's love and affection for her.

Jim: "You are not Sharon Stone either, but in real life she is a Pisces and that is your zodiac sign too. She spent money, which she did not earn like there is no tomorrow and see where she ended?" the conversation was in this context…. "And she ended living with a guy, who she was giving money to, like you and DP the Don are doing now!"

Kiana: "You keep thinking that you know me, Jim? You keep chasing me and you think that it will bring me closer to you? It does the opposite. It makes me run away from you."

Next couple of months he focused on his real estate career. He advertised in Washington Post at real estate classified section. He was getting leads.

Shelley: "I am your best customer. Find us a house. We can get something at around 200,000 dollars."

Jim: "Sure! That size of home is small in DC, but huge in Maryland for that price!" He pulled out of MRIS (Metropolitan Realtors Information System) any kind of detached homes, condominiums, townhouses, whole buildings needing repair, land only in whole DMV (District, Maryland and Virginia). They drove around for days and they had looked at most likely nearly 100 houses. They almost forgot about her mother's bias toward white men. Shelley liked some of the homes, but she couldn't make up her mind.

Jim: "Nobody would work as hard as me and show you so many houses. A realtor would sign buyer-agent contract immediately and he may just show you three houses maximum."

Shelley: "A real customer would not make love to you every night for free!" She squeezed his penis while he was driving to the next house to view.

Jim: "Touché!" Both smiled.

Shelley: "Look. You will get the commission as an agent regardless we sleep together or not. Take the sex as bonus. I am worth your time and you are my significant other!" She kissed him before the next house stop.

They found a house in Baltimore. It was multifamily home. It had 7 bedrooms. The home inspector found some termites, but in general the house was in good shape. The roof needed a little work, but not major leakage was detected.

Jim: "I am not sure if the bank will approve any termites being detected there?"

Exit Realtor: "Mr. Walker! The clause is "if the new buyer shows evidence of treatment against termites, the loan will be approved."

Jim: "Great! We can get the house!"

Shelley: "We will need new appliances and remodeling funds, baby!" She dragged him to nearest home appliances store located in Anne Arundel Mall. Ironically, here was where Amanda brought him in 2001 to spend part of his $30,000 hard earned money. Kiana had Amanda outspent tenfold at $250,000, but it took her five years!

Jim: "I love you baby, but I need to ask you one serious question!"

Shelley: "Go ahead. After all we should not have secrets. We have been dating almost a year."

Jim: "I don't mind spending any money, but I need my name on the title. I have been taken too many times."

Shelley: "How is your credit?" That was too low a blow. He did not expect the next sentence from her. "I can't have my credit screwed up!"

That was a breakup point for their relationship. Jim was getting the chilling draft from her mother and now from her, looking for a man with good credit. He had the money to assist her, but learned that people would think of their credit more than the true relationship.

Damn Americans! He compared the Europeans, who would survive two World Wars and they still kept their families connections strong. He did not like the Soviets and Russians as governing entities, but, he gave them a huge respect for fighting and winning wars without money in the treasury. Seemed Stalin's dictatorship worked, even with the cost of 23 million dead citizens. Now China was the rising superpower, with similar dictatorship. What does credit have to do with a relationship?

His anger transferred to his work at the club. When one of the street thugs came to the club at end of July to talk to Angel, Jim addressed him.

Jim: "Bernard, you can't come here without paying your debt. Where is my 32 dollars? Leave my bar or pay to stay, ok?"

Bernard: "I have business with Angel now," he was trying to ignore Jim.

Angel: "Bernard keeps selling fake cocaine. One white guy died in the alley a week ago. Now Police is looking for the seller. That is him." She whispered to Jim, going toward the bathroom and pointing toward Bernard "the thug." That made Jim even more motivated to kick the intruder out.

Jim: "Look Bernard! You are basically loitering now. Leave, ok?" he escorted him toward the exit stairway heading toward the first level.

Bernard: "I want to talk to you!" Bernard was a well built twenty-five years old. He was a boxer and he kept bragging about beating up people. He was definitely in some altered state of mind. Jim did not expected what happened next.

Bernard: "Do you want your money? Here is your money," he threw a sucker punch at Jim's right jaw. Jim just had a dental implant with 2 golden crowns and a bridge to hold them. He spent 15,000 dollars in 2003 to rebuild his mouth like some robotic device. The sudden punch broke the bridge at an instant, which caught this overconfident club owner in surprise.

Jim: "Why are you doing this?" he tried to scream, but he finished the phrase with a counterpunch at Bernard. The fight was unequal. The blood was blinding Jim and the metal of the crowns cut through his right upper lip like a knife. It was basically one inch opening.

Angel: "Police, there is a fight here at 1426 X Street. The owner was attacked. Please assist!" She walked out of the club. Bernard saw Jim's cell phone fallen on the floor and he grabbed it and ran.

Jim: "Give me my phone asshole!" He tried to follow him, but two of Bernard's cohorts blocked the door.

The approaching Police sirens at distance ended the fight. The three thugs scattered in different directions. Jim followed one of them and he pointed him to Police.

Police: "Who assaulted you?"

Jim: "This man" he pointed toward the slow moving fat man, who was acting like nothing happened.

Fat thug: "I don't know who this man is. He must be drunk!" He lied to the uniformed police.

Police: "Do you have any witnesses beside you? We can't have just "hearsay" …

Jim: "There were two more thugs who escaped. One of them is black."

Police: "Black? That's a serious description! Who made the phone call?"

Jim: "Angel did!" he looked around. She was nowhere to be found. His lips were really swollen and he couldn't talk much.

Police: "I don't see any angels around? You need to go to the ER. Ok?" He started writing a report...

Jim: "I don't want a report, neither an ambulance! Ok?"

Police: "Your club is getting to be a trouble spot lately.... Believe me; you need a report for your insurance."

Jim: "No, thanks!" He stubbornly refused, thinking of the last visit to ER in October, 2005. The students at GWU were practicing on him and they did not align his nose, but just stitched his nose skin at cost of $3,300. He had to go to Bulgaria in pain and he adjusted his nose bone in front of his puzzled brother.

Jim: "I will see my own dentist tomorrow. Bye!"

Police: "As you wish! We will make a note that you reject the ER visit."

Next day Jim drove to his personal dentist Dr. Mercer. After a night of excruciating pain and increasing fever he was sitting in a dental chair with a broken jaw and bleeding mouth.

Dr. Mercer: "You are in bad shape, buddy. I am not in the jaw business. You need an extra plate here. I will make you an appointment at Washington Hospital Center for that surgery."

Jim: "Thanks!" He mumbled and left, but not before he dropped $200 at the reception/accountant's desk. He stayed two days in hospital bed after some Indian speaking students practiced on him. He woke up with Shelley next to him.

Jim: "Hey, baby!" nothing came out of his mouth. It was wired shut.

Shelley: "Now you can be quiet for a while! They say you can't eat solid food for a month!" She sounded childish with her braces on her slightly crooked teeth, a definitely a poor supervision by her big mouth mother Carol. Jim grabbed her hand. She looked like an angel to him, he wanted some comfort from her, but she just said, "I will see you at home."

Jim drove his car out of the hospital garage half a day later.

Mansur: "What happened?" He saw his half face swollen and shook his head.

Jim: "It is business!" He tried to mumble moving his tongue only inside behind the grill. It was hardly audible, but his body language translated it to some "go along with the punches" attitude.

Mansur: "What I am going to do with you?" He shook his head.

Jim: "I have a new ABC manager. Megan will take care of the bar and the rent. I will take a couple of days off," he wrote on some paper napkin he found on the counter.

Mansur: "Okay!" he never liked third party involved.

Jim: "I will sell a couple of houses and we can pay the rent and maybe invest in some improvements here from my commission?" he wrote on the back of the flipped napkin.

Mansur: "You always have grandiose plans, but you see in what situation you are now? If I had a son like you I would never worry about a thing, but I doubt sometimes if all your ideas are rational? Our landlord does not wait on commissions from real estate sales. You know that!"

Jim: "Would you rather see me dead? I always have plans B and C!" He was getting frustrated and his healing jaw was in pain.

Jim: "Can a man get sick in the private business?" He thought. His surgery will end up costing the government $30,000 paid by "Victim of crime compensation fund." The irony of where the fund sources were coming from? That was money seized in form of cash, luxury cars, properties, jewelry, drugs sold by undercover agents. All those from the outlaws like mafia, convicted killers, art collecting thieves, illegal brothels and casinos, bootleggers and unstamped tobacco product pushers, from fraudulent SEC transactions, from recovering Swiss Bank hidden US tax evaders at Wegelin & Co. accounts, and from frozen Sadam Husain accounts.

Jim: "One has to think big and get the easy task achieved. I usually get what I want, but there is always a price to pay and personal sacrifice. Maybe God is telling me something?" He took the car out of the garage and headed to his broker's office. It was Weichert Realty headquarters in Bethesda.

Leona Hammond: "Hey, Jim! What happened to you?" she was the managing broker there. Just six months before she invited all realtors to have their Christmas Party at Bellagio Casino Hotel in Vegas. Jim was then more concerned of his club expansion and he was grieving over Kiana escaping with her lover back to Georgia.

Jim: "Miss Hammond! I need someone to handle the house Miss Shelley Wheeler is buying. She is my client but my condition does not allow me to work with her." Leona agreed.

Shelley: "I am going on a business trip to Miami soon. Hopefully, when I return the financing of the house will be finalized and your condition will be back to normal?" She was now mixing some cooked meat and vegetables in the blender for him.

Jim: "That is good! I can drink liquefied food with a straw!"

Shelley: "It is like being on a diet!" she was acting a bit distant.

The doubt started growing soon after she created security code for her phone in July 2006.

Jim: "Why do you need a security code for your mobile phone? I don't have one."

Shelley: "When I am in Miami I don't want someone of my co-workers to get to my info there."

Jim: "Ok. How many days are you going to be there? I will miss you, baby!"

Shelley: "Ohh. You will live. It is only four days! I like your liquid diet. You look like you are losing weight!"

Jim: "Yes… a pound a day!" She went to the bathroom and she was taking a shower. Her phone was left on the kitchen table.

Jim: "I feel bad spying on her, God!" he was debating.

God: "If that is the way to get to the truth, it is not a sin. But if you get to the results and they prove she is innocent then you've committed a sin."

Satan: "You should love her regardless. Do not verify your doubts. Most people in love do not have the guts to say something to hurt their partners. Some of them die never knowing the truth about their partners."

Jim: "Basically, you are telling me to listen to my heart and love her. That's what happened with Kiana. I loved her and she cheated and robbed me. You two are twisting my mind and breaking my heart. I will check her phone. We will decide who is right and wrong."

The contacts were minimal; between five to six people. Mom, Jim, Jacqueline, Freddy (her boss), her sister Sasha, and then was one guy Warren.

Jim: "Let me check this guy Warren?" He found the message button on the phone and pressed it in hurry. He felt like a burglar in Watergate Hotel.

The dialogue popped up like two feisty snakes were in a battle.

Warren: "Where this transgression is coming from? I thought we were going forward? Now I am in a guessing mode."

Shelley: "I told you I live with my boyfriend and we are to be engaged soon."

Warren: "Tell me that when you are next to me, not in a text!"

Shelley: "You are too attractive in person. I feel safer chatting via text, lol."

Warren: "I am smart and too sexy to resist in person, and I make you weak!"

Jim: "This guy is full of it. He is too confident" he was getting angry.

Shelley: “My man is in the hospital and he is coming out in a day. I may see you for a few minutes after work, but don’t raise your hopes too high.”

Warren: “Ok. You can see me after work or early in the morning around 7 am. I live in Laurel too.”

Shelley: “Early in the morning? That is a new twist. Are you taking me to breakfast? Or ....do you have other intentions?”

Warren: “See me and we can talk.”

Shelley: “I usually socialize with Jacqueline after work or with Jim. Breakfast is a nice surprise.”

Warren: “I am an early riser and a great cook!”

Jim: “This Mother Fucker is using my hospital surgery to take advantage of her,” he almost smashed the phone at the table. “But why should I blame only him? She is gorgeous and she loves sex. I guess she is still looking for someone else besides me?”

Shelley: “Hey, baby! Come shampoo my back, please! And if you are nice I may let you oil it too?” she shouted through slightly open shower door.

Jim: “Sure, baby!” he turned off her cell phone and he took his clothes off. His naked body enjoyed her soapy and shiny white skin touching him with her round buttocks. Then she turned around. She was in perfect shape, but her stomach was bulging a bit.

Jim: “I am a father? You seem pregnant! …Or are you on your cycle?”

Shelley: “I wanted to talk to you about that. I am seeing a doctor. He said I have a fiber tumor. The ball inside is like a three month baby. He said he can take it out but it will affect me from getting pregnant.”

Jim: “Maybe we can have the baby while the tumor is still there?”

Shelley: “Maybe, but it will be complicated!” She was speaking with mixed sounds of water and her childish voice. It would have been a turn on if this Warren was not suddenly in the picture. Jim was observing her in his mind from a distance. “Now we have a secret code, a breakfast guy, and a tumor now.... What is next?”

God: “If you don’t want to repeat the Kiana disaster, let her go! You are better off without those women! You are a deity in the works!” his mind was rational again.

Satan: "Kiss her and you will make up. Just do not tell her your discoveries and doubts. Most married people do that!" His heart was in a cluster of pain, but nothing close to Kiana's pain.

Shelley: "You are not ready?" She washed his 8 inch sleepy penis with soapy warm wash cloth. It was amazing how this perfect muscle responded. Then she moved Jim under the shower and she started swallowing his penis slowly until he was ready to explode. He grabbed her and he lifted her up. She grabbed a towel on the way out the bathroom.

Jim: "We can do the oiling later." The beach towel hit the bed before both were entangled in some sex play. "You make my pain go away," his stitched lips were not kissing her, but his 8 inches of pleasure was doing miracles.

Shelley: "Oh, Daddy!" she was juicy and ready and willing.

Jim: "I love you baby!" He screamed low enough not to attract the neighbors.

Shelley: "Like that?" She turned around to please him at his favorite position.

Jim: "Was Warren also enjoying that position?" he was pumping but his mind was wondering. Until Kiana he was dealing only with the Satan. He was sexually active. He was controlling women with his sexual prowess. His mind/God was never that mentally involved. He took women as meant to be, as entertainers, as companions, as dolls, but he never loved them.

Love was when his heart and mind worked together as one. He was doubtful, but never broken hearted until he discovered DP the Don in her bedroom. Was Kiana insane?

Jim: "Why did you bring sand to the beach, damn whore?" He has seen the Satan image live when he circled around him near the Howard U Chapel. Why do women and men fall in love with the wrong people? Are women in their vegetable state in liquid emotion? Are their minds locking out the rational mind and therefore they ignore God? Is this the reason there are almost no female deities nowadays?

Shelley: "After Miami, we are moving to a house, baby!" She said that just as both they were reaching orgasm. "I love you too." She contracted her perfect vagina muscles in back and forth motion. Both lovers collapsed in heavy breathing.

Jim: "Give me five minutes for the oil massage."

Shelley: "Oh that can wait. I feel very relaxed now."

Jim: "Me too." He forgot about all the troubles at that space vacuum dimension. It was an escape from everyday worries… Carol, Warren, Jacqueline, Mansur, clubs, work, and the Miami lies.

Seemed that American women live in one dimension; lies, promises, negotiations to give sex, to get perks, cash, cars, gifts, good homes, vacations.

Jim: "Satan, is the life's best bargaining chip, The Sex?"

Satan: "Love in the USA is related to sex! See what Kiana did to you? Why did you give her quarter million? See where you are now? You have a broken jaw, yet you are getting sex because of the house you are finding for Shelley. She will need your money too to buy the house and furniture. You already fixed her car and bought her TV and paid her rent. Is this love?"

Jim: "With Kiana I was in love. Money did not matter to me then. Now I feel I should have been more careful with my money."

Satan: "Stop having sex then and you will be rich! No pleasures! No love. Listen to my opposition, your God!"

God: "Finally, we came to the same conclusion with Satan. You don't need women! They are destroying you!"

All was confirmed soon. Jim was able to use Shelley's e mail to pull out attachments from her computer. She gave him her pass code.

Shelley: "When I come back I want two things from you: a house and that you will find a new job."

Jim: "That means you give me a week to sell the club? I will try."

Shelley: "Be good and don't see other women, while I am away, ok?" She gave him a kiss. He responded with the same. She boarded a taxi to take her to Miami, mid August, 2006.

Jim: "I really like that lady, but she makes me feel I am in some boot camp; too many rules and games." Shelley ordered him to drink eight glasses of water a day. She was monitoring his urine. She sent him for a paternity test. If it was not for the house to buy and the perks she was getting, Jim couldn't see how another person could control or adhere to her demands and make her happy?

Jim did not receive any calls from Shelley the next two days. He called Jacqueline's daughter.

Debbie: "Hello. Who is calling?"

Jim: "I am Shelley's boyfriend. Did anyone call from Miami? Did they arrive there? Did your Mom call?" he sounded concerned.

Debbie: "Oh, yes. They are ok. They went to this hotel Turks and Caicos. They will be back in three days," her voice was young and informative. She was around 11 years old. Her brother was eighteen. He seemed much older and mature for his age.

Jim: "Turks and Caicos! Thank you." He tried not to scream and be polite. He clicked off the cell phone. The moment he hung up his phone lit up!

Carol: "Hey Jim! Have you heard from Shelley? I pray she is all right?" Her mother was in distress.

Jim: "Oh, they are ok! The problem is why didn't she tell me that she was going on vacation to Turks and Caicos Islands? You know I am ship's captain and I know a lot about world geography."

Carol: "I am so disappointed at her. She likes to keep secrets from me."

Jim: "What secrets, bitch?" He almost screamed. He stopped himself short remembering the Virginia Beach fiasco. "Oh, you are not alone!" He said instead and thought about Warren, "the breakfast man."

Carol: "I am glad to know where they are, but I am still not happy with the whole situation. Are you ok? I hear you found her a house? That is very nice of you!" she hung up.

Jim: "I found her a house? Is that another secret? We are buying a house together!" he was initially appalled, but after all he was a realtor and he would take different names like a buyer, buyer-agent, seller-agent, seller, and broker.

Carol: "Please, call me when they return, ok?" the phone rang again.

Jim: "You call me too, ok!"

Carol: "Sure. Sorry for the last time on the beach, ok? Bye now."

Jim: "No problem. I never meant to say anything….." The phone went mute. Carol couldn't wait for his response.

Jim: "Let see if I can sell this club? Maybe if I do my part, she will stop lying?" He opened Shelley's e mail. Then he entered her password "banana." He wanted to pull some attachments out. He sent a couple of e mails to possible buyers, then he posted on Craig's list a new add; "Club for sale." He suddenly noticed new e mails in the Inbox.

Pierre: "Hey. We met last night by the pool. You were a bit standoffish? Here is my number 649 456 3245. I hope tonight is a good time to meet again after 7 pm?" Shelley: "Hey, my boyfriend maybe checking my mail? Please stop contacting me here."

Pierre: "Ok. Hope he is not reading the mail that often? I suggest you delete it as soon you read my number. See you at the restaurant in the hotel you are staying. I am a realtor. I want to show you around."

Shelley: "Ok. I may buy a house here? I am looking for one now."

Pierre: "Great. We can mix business and pleasure! Now delete the conversation, please!"

Shelley: "See you at 7 pm. I have got your number, in case you don't show up?"

Pierre: "I will see you at 7 pm!"

Jim copied the number quickly. As soon he did that the correspondence between those two cheaters disappeared. He was not surprised. After the credit score, Warren, "Miami" fiascos, what could be new to the puzzle here? Kiana trained him well.

God: "I told you that women lie all the time."

Satan: "A lie which awards you with a job, car, house, wife, sex is good as long you are happy! That is why I am your friend!"

Jim: "Are you two telling me that to have pleasure one has to lie?"

God: "Mental pleasures are non sexual. Physical pleasures require any kind of compromises. Emotional pleasures are a balance between mental and physical. They include the creativity of plasma in gravity and antigravity collision... the neutral mass created has no charge, but it has weight/new matter."

Satan: "I came from the earth/the Darkness. Everything solid is visible symmetry. Everything you people interact with becomes distracted, or ruined. You think you can control your destiny? I control you, you little cockroaches, called "people!"

Remember the dinosaurs? They appeared 230 million years ago on earth and ruled for 135 million years! You people, are here for some 10,000 years and you think you know everything?"

God: "I cannot judge the material world. I only measure people's awareness. They self destruct and very few can relate to me in pure form, which is in Light to start. Plasma is creativity, but I need the quanta, the energy."

Jim: "Is that why they call God is Light, then the Sun is true Creator, the God!"

God: "When I talk nobody listens. They only see my anger. I really don't destroy anything, Satan does that. Because people think they are so smart and they can analyze everything, they don't see Satan's work. They think I punish them. People are too busy with pleasuring themselves... They worry about the problems they create so they don't see the big picture. They depend on doctors and priests to solve their physical and emotional problems."

Jim: "I know the answers before and now, but I feel I should live the Life given to me as is. I can change my life, but how can I change the others? I am not in some financial group, big rock star, a grand TV editor, some president with trillions in the treasury and billion people, looking at me and following me around."

God: "You live in exemplary way. Let others judge you, do not do it yourself. Oh, best to do it cast your best ideas in stone."

Jim: "How? Like Moses and his Ten Commandments? The Bible says that "Sin is transgression of the law," or with other words, "Sin is breaking The Spiritual Law (the 10 commandments), (1 John 3:4 KJV)."

God: "Respect God and you will be awarded with Knowledge and Awareness!"

Jim: "But that knowledge is in my Sub consciousness! Does that mean I am God like?"

God: "Yes. You can mirror me and be like me, but nobody can be my twin. Try to rule in your environment first. Then you will be elevated to my capabilities. So far you have all the ingredients and the knowledge on earth level. Congrats on beating Higgs by three weeks before he announced his Boson in July, 2012! With your drive you did not need a 10 billion dollar CERN toy collider!" Now get rid of Shelley, my son!"

Jim ".... But I love her, God!"

God: "To love a cheater is like to love a criminal! You become her, a sinner and only Satan loves sinners!"

Jim: "Ok. The only thing about me is when I get angry; the nature starts working against my enemies in number six sequences."

God: "I noticed how your mind operates. I have seen what you did to Prosperity in 2004, to New York City in 2001, to New Orleans in 2005, to Indian Ocean in 2004, to Mr. Baldwin in 1999, to any of your rivals. The number six represents the Cosmic Dimension, an open Spiral (6) times 4. That is your dimension, a complete cone.... and knowing you, there is more to come! As for my rival brother Satan, he is one incomplete Cone, with Spiral/Six times 3! He eludes the required hurdles and keeps you believing you can be like me, but he never brings you to Quantum Vortex, where the Cosmic Intelligence lives and all possibilities are available to chosen ones.

Jim: "God. Is that the reason the day is completed every 24 hours? Is it all right with you to teach people my, (your) secrets? Would that anger you?"

God: "Son! Or my identical thinker! Listen, I have been installing knowledge to some chosen people on earth, but they all end in some disappointment! Some were accused of heresy, some got burned by the Inquisition, some were sent to Siberia to do hard labor, and some were executed by dictators, some just died unrecognized in poverty. The ones who made it were already established rich and in spot light and some made it ok in life, sponsored by some government or by individuals with a lot money to burn."

Jim: "Are you telling me a poor man can't break in "Knowledge Club?" Or what we called it "the Awareness," society. I did it!"

God: "You are not the rule! You are the exception of it. No one that I know has your résumé in peaceful time. I can't imagine many of the 7 billion earth people having Master's degree, being kicked out of elite Naval Academy, owning a restaurant like Bellini's, without penny invested, started a chain of four night clubs with 100 dollars, got out of the game without bankruptcy and jail time! Do you want to be recognized, my Son? Write the book of your experiences, then that will be equal to the Tree of Knowledge in the Bible. You know that Tree was nothing less than a laboratory with codes in the Manual of Creativity! Only Adam was able to read it, but later on he was seduced by Eve to disclose what was in that Manual? After that they were punished with thinking. That brought the consciousness to Adam and Eve. They were careless before that, but now they saw themselves exposed and naked.

They became afraid. They covered themselves with clothes. You know, once man started to think his physical earth life was shortened. His vegetable state was elevated to mental level, where his mental qualities were detrimental to his physical longevity. The eternal life was reduced to 1,000 years, then to 700 years and now to 75 years (Haley's Comet returning circle)."

Jim: "Then why can't we return to vegetable state! Is it not that where Satan rules?"

God: "Yes. He gives you longer life, carefree, but one needs morals and responsibilities to his environment. See what happens in Brazil to the rain forest or anywhere man is using resources without planning! Water is 75 percent on earth. Drinking water is 2.5 percent. You are using at the moment one percent of it, and you are seven billion people. If there is no plan to preserve it, there would be water wars soon. You write that book quick, Son!"

Jim: "I am a scientist, God! Water desalinization, is way to extract drinking water from salty (ocean) water."

God: "Tell that to people in mid Africa, or Mid USA, or mid Australia. Driving the water to them will increase the cost to amazing price."

Jim: "If people can make gas pipes to anywhere, why do they not use the same pipes for water?"

God: "You are genius! The answer is in every individual how to live forever? Once everyone gets Awareness and respect to his surroundings, when there is no fear of the nature and there is constant rejuvenation, then there will be many deities. Remember also "When there is sex, then there is death." Creating a baby is creating your substitution. Look, when water cost 5.00 to 10.00 dollars a gallon, people will come with a solution!"

Jim: "Ok, let me deal with small details in life for now like the cheating Shelley."

God: "Make more pages in the book, but "live the life!" he reminded him of Contessa's slogan. Honestly, if my other Son Jesus was here he wouldn't have done any better than you. He was betrayed for thirty silver coins by Judas Iscariot, who listened to my brother Satan. In your case was Larry at Randevu/Zeus Lounge DC, who was caught with 20 dollars, mocked money, but he made a bargain with detective O'Conner to betray you and save his ass. That was the identical story with Andy Sherman, your GM at Zoro, who testified against you and was promised the club by the Police in exchange! You see things in government don't change for tens of thousands of years, and they will keep the same forever."

Jim: "So, for them passing the law of "imminent domain," it is not enough, they have to play dirty too, hmm?"

God: "The law by which the government can appropriate private property is also called "condemnation." They will offer you a fair market price and if you refuse they will start a legal action against you, the owner. Since you are not the property owner of those places, but licensed manager and operator, their job was easier, by finding moles in your establishments. I would question all Mansur's intentions with you. Remember Rayful Edmonds girlfriend and later your girlfriend Nina? She told you Mansur was crooked. You did not listen to her and you invested a million in that club."

Jim: "True! I don't listen to nobody, but my sub consciousness, which is you, God! Sometimes I don't predict accurate every movement on the chest board, but most of the time I get out victorious. I lost some battles, but I won the War!"

God: "What do you mean, you won the War? See where you are now, betrayed, cheated, and poor?" He hast no mercy.

Jim: "I am alive. I am free. And I am writing the story of how the Federal US Government can't do anything to stop me! I did plea "guilty" and do prefer to walk out away free, rather than to plead "innocent," and stay in jail!"

God: "Yes, we know the history, your freedom and ability to spread the Awareness and the Knowledge is more important to future entrepreneurs than the all Carnegie, Rockefeller, JP Morgan, Warren Buffet, Bill Gates money and quotes."

Jim: "It is amazing! I read the 18 best quotes of Warren Buffet, "the greatest investor of all time!" I also read Francis Bacon (born January, 22nd. 1561). I can see two brilliant minds and can relate to someone who lived 500 years before me more than this new coffee drinker and doughnut eater Mr. Buffet. You see life in a free mason and not a drop of blood in this paper shoveled from Berkshire Hathaway's, portfolio holder. And it is amazing he is talking about a possible "4th law of motion by Newton"—"The faster the motion, the less return for investors," seems that in his world, he is as good as his followers with little money."

Jim: "Once the class is empty there is no need of a teacher," he thought. "If you are not convincing the people to invest in you or to listen to what they are interested in, you will be poor and jobless!"

God: "And the Feds are using Buffet Law, to extract more taxes from those that are well off. You, Jim, did it without investors and even without your own money. The quantum thinking works for you and sometimes against you. Your ability to recover and be free it is your brand mark."

Jim: "True! Bye now!"

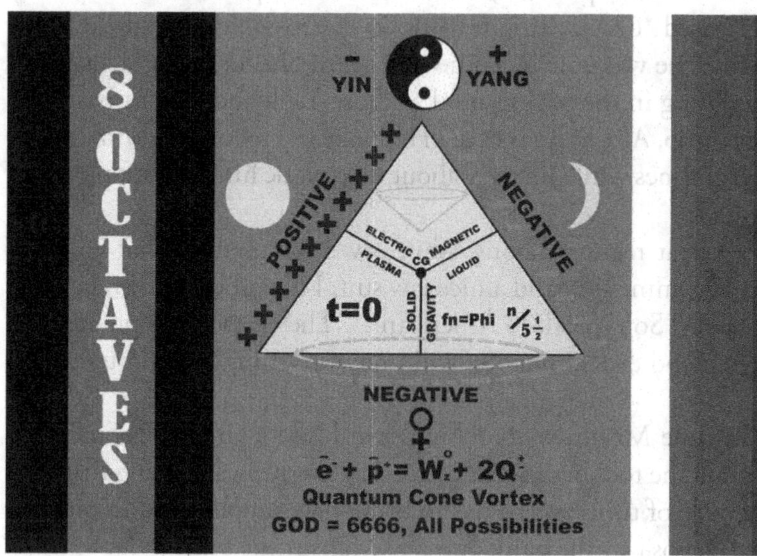

Chapter 17

Two more days passed. Jim dialed Pierre's phone number many times. He used *67 blocking feature, so Pierre couldn't read the caller ID. At times he was convinced he overheard Shelley's and Jacqueline's voices laughing in the background at those Turk and Caicos Islands.

Pierre: "Alo, Alo. Who is this?" He spoke in French. "Shit/merde" he screamed at times while Jim was about to explode himself, but preferred to stay quiet.

Jim: "Great realtor! Saying "shit," over the phone. That will give you a great commission and a nice law suit. I don't blame him, but that whore Shelley! So typical, so American…. They leave their phones and e mail open and expect nobody will know anything?" he thought.

Meanwhile Megan was robbing him blind at the club. Since Jim couldn't talk, he told her to text him every morning at closing time. He went a couple of times to the bar to bring new supplies and to pick the money to deposit in the bank and pay Mansur the rent.

Jim: "Damn, Megan! You are stealing too?" She was his new ABC manager; a blonde, chubby, too friendly at times medium height thirty year old liar. She was not putting all the money in the register. The credit transactions were going through, but the cash was not. He started to show every night $180.00 in Z reports.

Jim: "I am paying 1,500.00 dollars a week in rent. Do the math. Can your deposits cover the rent?" he texted her.

Megan: "Business is slow!" She replied.

Jim: "I see you make five gallons a night of your invention "pink pussy." All my liquor and juices are gone. I usually make 700 to 800 in a night at single bar; before the raid we were clocking $3,000 a night. We don't make $180 dollars a night now!"

Megan: "Police came and they checked my license and the bar patrons. They scared everyone away."

Jim: "Did they ask about me?"

Megan: "Yes! The cop was very angry and he said he would close the bar."

Jim: "Did you take his badge number and name?"

Megan: "Yes. Officer Gross 2852."

Jim: "So, he is from second district. Not his jurisdiction. We are between 1st and 3rd MPD."

Megan: "He said he will be back soon."

Jim: "I don't care about the cops! If you can't sell my liquor and put the money in the register I am coming to work at the bar even with my mouth wired shut!" he texted angrily.

Megan: "Ok, boss!"

Next two days were the same amount of Z report (total sale for the day and clears for next day the memory), the fatal $180! She lost her credibility and soon she lost her job. Seemed she had criminal record in Maryland and the ABC license she got issued was for three months only. One day the Police arrived and she ran away almost knocking them over while they were coming up the steps.

Jim: "Where are you, Megan? I need you here. I can't talk to those people now!" He texted her while the Police were scattered all over the place.

Police: "Are you the ABC manager? What happen to your face?"

Jim: "I am the manager. Here is my license. The rest of your questions, please read the Police reports," he wrote some on paper.

Police: "I see. I wonder how this place is still in business."

Jim: "Ask Judge Lucille Tucker," he wrote. "At this gossipy small town there is no coordination between those clowns," he thought. He returned to the bar to serve his customers. That Saturday night in August he made nearly 1,000 bucks.

Jim: "Why can't people be honest for a day? What is with American people and trust?" he almost screamed behind his grilled mouth. He returned to his Laurel home. He waited for Shelley's arrival. He just wanted to see her face, lying face.

The afternoon passed slowly. He decided to wait for her. The club usually opened the door at 9 pm. At about 6 pm the front door opened. Shelley was exasperated. She had big luggage and small purse when she left, now she was carrying a third bag.

Jim: "Hey how was your trip?"

Shelley: "I hate you! Why did you tell my mother where I was? Why are you so inquisitive where I go, who I meet? It is not your business?"

Jim: "That is a nice, hello, I miss you, baby." He was trying to mumble behind his grilled mouth."

Shelley: "We are buying a house, I needed vacation, my mother talks to me 8 hours a day, and you are having troubles the last six months with that club. I have fiber tumor. So, me and Jacqueline decided to get away, ok?"

Jim: "You left Warren and Pierre, me and your mother stranded!" He wrote the names on a paper.

Shelley: "So, you have seen the e mail and my phone messages? Now I see why Kiana left you!" She was almost crying. She pushed the luggage toward the bedroom. She opened one of them.

Shelley: "I hope you had good time? Aren't you supposed to go to work now?" She started pulling out calendars, sea shells, necklaces, and photos of Turks and Caicos.

Jim: "All those gifts from Pierre? What does he do all day?"

Shelley: "Were you the one calling all day and night? He is a professional photographer, realtor, and investor. He showed me two vacant lots for sale on the beach. You can build houses there and a hotel. I think to cancel my house buying here and to invest there?"

Jim: "I am everything he does, except for the beach!"

Shelley: "Those people have been living there for thousands of years and you cannot be like them."

Jim: "This is a British commonwealth, like Bermuda and Bahamas are. The difference is that in USA a foreigner can became well off within one's life time. Those "thousand" year residents should not have one foot available for sale. I think you met a con-artist?"

Shelley: "He drives a new SUV and he seems pretty active on the island. Most people knew him, while we were driving. And he is married!" she was defending Pierre.

Jim: "You know the islanders. They would say hello, to everyone. The undercurrent is their true mischievousness. The realtor is truly a hustler, maybe a pornographer? Look at the calendar you brought? Looks like a "Playboy"

magazine."

Shelley: "How do you know I fucked him?" She gave Jim a huge sea shell. "Listen to the sea."

Jim: "I can hear and I can read. I read your last e mail this morning. Your Pierre is asking you "do not tell your boyfriend about what happened on the islands and us. Buy a Miami guide and tell him all about Miami. Erase after reading! Lol." What is that; Mission impossible, deceitfulness. Destroy after reading?" he tried to laugh it out.

Shelley: "The Island is like a fantasy. It is easy to be seduced."

Jim: "It takes one Playboy/realtor to spoil the whole Fantasy Island."

I may go there myself but I wouldn't deal with Pierre, The Pinocchio."

Shelley: "If you missed me, show me! Don't try to psychoanalyze every situation. In the world we do what we have to do to survive and to enjoy the day. I am not judging you about your bar and who you do interact with. Let us not talk about work. I have to deal with gossips about you at work and bunch of guys single and married, hitting on me constantly. I hear you were talking to some young lady, who is a cousin of Myra. You know at Charter Health plan everyone is related. Were you guys talking about real estate?"

Jim: "I don't remember exactly, whom I have talked to. I have thousands people a week passing through my bar and through the patio. If I see her, I will remember her; if that is true? Sometimes I just do it to promote the Club and I do pass business cards constantly."

Shelley: "Ok, mister perfect! Go to work. I am tired of reading your notes. See you after work."

Jim found out that women can get away with anything they want as long someone is willing to listen to them and he is willing to compromise. He reluctantly headed to work. It was an average Sunday, but he still made $750.

The first floor bar was not productive. That's where Shana and Evelyn would work the Happy Hour, but they were just breaking even.

He was convinced that "pink pussy," drinks money went to Megan's pocket, not to his register the week passed. He had three more weeks to recover and take the grill off. His interaction with his regular customers was like nothing happen, he knew their drinks for years. The new customers were puzzled to see him with a black eye, swollen but healing lips and the strange grill wiring his mouth shut.

Mansur: "I am glad you catching up with the rent. I have twenty people a week coming to ask me to replace you."

Jim: "Do you tell them that your liquor hours are screwed up? Do you tell them they have to reimburse me for all legal fees and construction cost, plus the sale price formula is usually the last year Net profit multiplied by three times."

Mansur: "You are realtor. You tell them that," he tried to be smart.

Jim: "I need to disclose all that I know. The place will never sell. We are stuck here and Nikias is too sick to help us."

September, 2006 came. Larry came to the bar to have a drink.

Jim: "Do you still have your ABC license?"

Larry: "Yes! It is good for one and a quarter year!"

Jim: "Come to work tonight!"

Larry: "I don't have a record or any restrictions now. Sure." He started to work right away.

Initially, it looked like DeJaVu. The same faces, same partners, Mansur seemed pleased. Even the money was as good as before the raid.

Jim: "I think it was all a bad dream; the pimps, the hookers, the cops, the raid. I will be less involved with the direct contact with anyone. This way the cops will not see me as a recurring problem. Hope this lawyer will get the liquor hours finalized? Mansur never really wanted that bar there, that is why his hours were deli hours. Closed at 3 pm Saturday? Closed at 8 pm every day of the week? What kind of lawyer originally had he chosen? Some guy Lewis in China Town!" He was enjoying his cigar again; even the scar was not fully recovered. The one inch scar on top of his lip would remain forever and it did close almost perfectly after awhile. Only when he shaved he felt a little bump and he was getting tiny cuts from new blades.

Shelley: "Do you want to hear sorry story?" She almost cried.

Jim: "What is it? We need only good news from now on!" He wanted to live normal life. He had his club, a strange but beautiful and available girlfriend, and a house to buy! Hmm.

Shelley: "My own credit union will not give me a loan! And I have a good credit!" She was sobbing.

Jim: "Calm down, baby!" he held her tight; he enjoyed her body when she was most vulnerable. He almost felt like a father to a child, but he found himself aroused. That is not right. So, the role playing was false if ends in false results.

Shelley: "You always find solutions, Jim! What can you do for me and for us to get that loan?" Now she remembered she can seduce him and she grabbed his fully erected penis. "Maybe I can start the process now and here?" She took his 8 inch tower deep into her mouth. She was squishing it like it was a bubble gum.

Jim: "Ok. Ok. I will help you even though you don't want me to be on the title."

Shelley: "I will do everything to get this house. I did already give a month notice to vacate my apartment mid-November."

Jim: "My Lady! I work for one of the best real estate brokers with their headquarters in Bethesda. Weichert is as good as Remax or Keller Williams. We have in house financing. I will introduce you to them. Get all your financial information ready. You will be with a loan approved within two weeks!"

Leona Hammond: "Miss Wheeler, we will be happy to process your loan application. Our in house financial officer will work with you. We wish you to move to your new house as soon as possible. We will ask you to put deposit of earnest money in our escrow account, which does not co-mingle, with our broker account.

Shelley: "I do not know what she is talking about? Sounds like a lawyer or foreign language!"

Jim: "Welcome to the real estate world. That was one of the most difficult exams I ever took lately. It was full of strange words with specific interpretation. I felt I was passing the US BAR exam for a law degree!"

Shelley: "Don't you need to know the legal and financial aspect of real estate?"

Jim: "Yes! We need not to say certain words, even if we know the business. Clients will exploit any opportunity to sue a huge company like ours, especially an angry one."

Shelley: "Then don't make me an angry client, ok?" she sounded funny, yet a little threatening.

Jim: "See the financial department, and then we will talk."

First week of December she got the key for the house at Gwynn Park, Baltimore. Jim did his job well. He treated her future house for termites. He also treated for the same another house he had an eye on for months. It was at 3501 Walbrook Street, near North Hilton and North Ave in West Baltimore. He called this house "General's house," because of the two huge living high ceiling rooms. It had 8 bedrooms, alarm since 1956 and 2 cars enclosed garage. It was a default house in case Shelley loan was not approved and was test for Jim's credit. He would use his own commission as buyer-agent and he was able to avoid the closing cost, and his own money would be only 5,000 dollars in down payment. The appraiser said the asking price was 10,000 dollars bellow the real price. Jim thought the 10,000 dollars built-in equity was a great idea for this "General house."

Everything would have been perfect, like hitting the restart button until the evil Carol showed up. Shelley needed to stay in a room somewhere, but she declined Jim's offer to live in the office. She wanted to see her clothes on display like it was in her huge closet at Laurel. The move-in date was December 12th, 2006.

Shelley: "My mom is coming to stay with me for a week to help me pack and move. We can move your stuff to storage for now" she suggested.

Jim: "My stuff only? Thought we are moving together?"

Shelley: "You do not know my mother! She wants to go through my stuff and throw out many things. You don't want her to go through your stuff. She is cookoo a bit; you do remember the Virginia Beach?"

Jim: "Cool! I will miss you next week," he kissed her for the last time.

Two days after he received a call from Shelley.

Jim: "What? Miss me already?"

Shelley: "My mother wants to see the house. You are my realtor, right!" she was curiously serious.

Jim: "Ok! We can drive there!"

They all jumped in the champagne Benz. It drove ok till the house in Gwynn Park, Baltimore. The house was freshly painted with fresh flowers in mini garden before the main entrance. It had a huge living room and a newer kitchen. The back patio was enclosed and it was facing another small garden. Two bedrooms on top were freshly painted too. The bathrooms had a sky light window hatch which was giving a bright spot at the second gloomy floor.

Shelley: "Not bad for 89,000 dollars. The basement is huge also. It needs new water heater and HVAC."

Jim: "I hope that will not affect my commission?" Carol was inspecting the house on her own. She seemed weird and unhappy.

Jim: "What is with her?" he whispered to Shelley.

Shelley: "She is always in another dimension." She was also unhappy.

Carol: "Thank you! Drive us back to the hotel." She did not ask, she ordered. Yes, she was not in the 4th (real earth time) dimension. Jim would call ignorant, self-centered, emotionally deficient people living in "minus 4th dimension," zombies or near dead. They are the ones, who live in court, pulling the progress of the real people in reverse. He noticed on many occasions "Carol type" zombies, threatening him with any kind of charges, when their demands were not awarded. Usually the zombies use the 911 number to call police, like they are their personal guards. Police, themselves are emotionally deficient. They would choose who to assist; mostly women, rarely transgender and almost never men. The zombies and police were in same "minus 4th dimension."

Jim: "That is not the way to sell or buy a house. I don't feel right about the whole situation. Isn't house buying supposed to be a happy event?" His gut feeling was confirmed within next thirty minutes.

Shelley: "Jim. We need to talk. All of us," she said as soon the car pulled over in front of the hotel. Something was wrong with the transmission anyway, so Jim was glad to agree.

Jim: "What is it?" he looked at them both. They exchanged glances.

Shelley: "We decided not to allow you to move to the house. My mother does not approve of you as a boyfriend and as husband for me."

Jim: "Why isn't she not telling me that herself? Seems she is very talkative behind my back?" Before he finished his sentence, Carol jumped out of the car. "Very well, proceed!" He looked at Carol with head down entering the hotel. Shelley did not say any more. She started crying.

Jim: "Sometimes in life, people make choices for a lifetime. You choose now, me or her?"

Shelley: "For you it is easy. You never met your real mother. Mine talks to me eight hours a day, she needs me. She is my mother and she controls me."

Jim: "We just made love two days ago. Does that mean nothing to you?" He started to cry too. He tried to grab her hand and to change her mind.

Shelley: "Get your own house. I will come and visit," she lied.

Jim: "If your mom keeps controlling who you are to date, who to live with in your house, who to marry, then we should go our separate ways. After Kiana and you, I may just stay single for the rest of my life?" he did not want to let her go, but after Warren, Turks and Caicos, house fiasco and her mom, he felt it was time for the separation.

God: "Finally, you are a man! The man who needs self respect, because I see nobody is doing that to you, except your family!"

Jim: "You think you are my friend?" He was crying.

God: "Yes, the only rational friend! I am your sub consciousness. I am yours and you are mine. Stay with me undistracted. I will show you soon why?"

Satan: "I hate to lose you again. You left Contessa and you survived, you left Frida and she still wants you back, Kiana left you and now Shelley. You are gradually going down. The money is a factor, yours or theirs, but somewhere in the algorithm of life you are not the Casanova that you think you are. You started as a Saint, you have my devilish side, but you keep going back to a lonely Saint like man!"

Jim: "That is the way to keep people and their enforcement, the Government in suspense. Once they figure you out they label you with some color file "nobody, good, average, dangerous, extremely dangerous." Being married and with children they would think you are "Good!" He laughed.

Satan: "The opposite is for a single man. Your color is extremely dangerous. You are on any kind of lists; KGB, sex offenders, flight restriction, terrorists, bootleggers, tax evaders. No joke, Jim!"

Jim picked up his stuff from storage and he returned to his office. The club was still there and against all odds it was still making him money. He had his two cars... the Van and the Benz. He just needed to rethink the whole situation.

Mansur was cooking something on his own. His business increased day time due to expanded space on the first floor. He was selling also Jim's alcohol. He would put money in the register after the sale. Also he was selling cocaine. His accounts were spread between Capitol Hilton, Sam's, Normandy. His wife Anika was driving their new model "Honda" SUV for no apparent reasons up and down Georgetown. His sons were stealing his money; he was remodeling his house at Beltsville with the money he should have been reinvesting in his business. He fixed his refrigerators, his oven, he begged Jim to share in buying a new ice machine. It took him a year to buy one.

Jim: "I have a strange element around the bar. We made even negotiations with the government; we can't change the customer's behavior. I filter them. I throw them out; I keep the good customers around. I hired ABC managers. Seems the business is slow and the bar is not what it used to be before the raid?"

Mansur: "Sell it, Jim! Take your share and go somewhere else! Maybe the bar business is not good for you anymore? I am looking for other investments. Malik and I are looking at gas stations in Fredericksburg, Va."

Jim: "What ratio in the sale will I take? I invested here twice the amount you did."

Mansur: "I allowed you to stay here through thick and thin. I own the lease.

I will let you have 1/3 to 2/3 split in my favor. Ok?" He became serious, not the father figure he was usually trying to represent. His Arabic accent sounded like a cough at times of his anger.

Jim: "I will use the mass media to advertise in the Washington Post, Washington City Paper, and the Craig's List" he stated.

Mansur: "Use your Realtor knowledge. I can't pay you any commission."

Jim: "I need my share even it is only 1/3rd. I am not greedy. Just don't screw up with my money when buyers show up, ok?"

Around twenty buyers came through the establishment in the early spring of 2007. Jim posted 400,000 dollars selling price. He got any kind of proposals. It was amazing to watch Mansur's mind change by a day. Initially, Jim asked to sell his part only. He got many proposals at $100,000 to down payment and monthly installments.

Mansur: "Find a buyer to take over everything, food, liquor, and entertainment!" He was not agreeable on any partial terms.

Jim: "Ok. It is difficult to pull $400,000 out of someone's pocket. I remember Pier 9 club was closed for twenty-two years before I did reopened it with legal liquor license as The Zoro, in January 2002."

Mansur: "You have different ways to get businesses than anyone I have known. I still don't know how you did it?"

Malik: "Why can't you get a loan and buy Mansur out? This way you keep everything?" For a devil he was it was making sense.

Jim: "Market is good for anything. I need someone with open mind and willing to negotiate."

March, 2007 Bernard showed up with two dogs at the front entrance.

Jim: "That is the guy who assaulted me and who had broken my jaw five months ago."

Police: "Let us talk to him!" after they took his picture they let him loose.

Jim: "What?" he couldn't believe his eyes? The surgery did cost $30,000.00 dollars to the DC government. He explained that to the Police.

Police: "You healed well. This guy is a professional boxer. It could have been worse!" They were laughing sarcastically. Seems they were sadistically enjoying his story and his pain. Similarly, it was like telling a pedophile a story about sex abuse. He/she would have been turned on.

Jim: "Could you tell me at least his real name and address, so I can press charges?" He couldn't believe their non apathy.

Police: "His name is Bernard Lloyds and he lives at 901 P Street. Talk to your lawyer if he can use the police report to prosecute him. We can't arrest him. We checked your police report. You don't have a real witness. Some prostitute Angel and she may not testify. We know how the "element" works. Once the court date comes we can't find a witness, besides the plaintiff, you! Basically, arrest and court procedures are a waste of time."

Jim: "You already prejudged me! That is why I stay away from Police for years." He was right.

A promoter showed up with a lesbian following. She said she would fix the place to fit her entourage's idea of comfort. She also said she would do so well, Jim would ask to partner with her.

Ramona: "I will invest here in labor and paint. We will check every corner, also we need better A/C. Sounds is good, but your liquor is low. We drink a lot and we are good spenders."

Jim: "Can you guarantee me $4,000 a night in sales? Whatever is on top we will split the profit."

Ramona: "Look. I can guarantee you the attendance of 100 people minimum. You do the sales, but don't be too expensive. I will tell you the prices they are willing to pay. If they feel you are overcharging them they will not come back." She wrote on folded white napkin some numbers.

Jim: "You are cutting my prices almost in half and I do still expect $4,000 in sales? If you are my partner we would have problems."

Ramona: "You need fast bartenders. The higher the volume, the higher could be the total sales. I will bring my own bartenders, ok?" She was not really asking, she was demanding.

Jim: "That is completely different angle! I can't control outside help."

Ramona: "You will supervise the bars. You will check the sales. At the end you and I will be happy. I will charge $10 at the door, including one drink. After that they are all yours."

Jim: "In this case I will give free drinks for starters. We have to cut in your profit after the $4,000 is reached, ok?"

Ramona: "Think repeat business. I will invest time and money here. Even you lose a bit the first time after a month things are going to show profit." She was optimistic. Jim liked her enthusiasm. No promoter ever fixed the club. She painted soon the walls in green and red color.

Jim: "If this will make the money green and red will be my favorite colors," he was laughing about it.

After twenty days of remodeling, the club had its first lesbian event. They came mostly in couples. Some were in three and four. The liquor and beer was stacked for a month ahead. Jim basically got a credit for $6,700 from the suppliers. He wanted to be sure he was not short in case of sudden high demand. They were checking him out, he was checking them out. Promoting and business may sound similar, but the responsibilities to pay the bills were falling on the business owner!

Jim was trying not to interact too much with them. He knew they were not looking to socialize with a straight man. He also noticed that the bartenders were very standoffish. He tried to tell them how to use the registers.

Bartenders: "We know how to use cash registers!" One of them screamed.

Jim: "I am the owner. Here are the negotiated prices with Ramona."

Bartenders: "Ok. We have done many parties with same prices. Thank you." They were brushing him off. The similarity with behavior with his gay bartenders, (Kurt and Walter) at the Zoro was astonishing.

Jim: "Looks like we are going to have a challenge here?" He thought. The beer was chilled in big ice bins and premium brands liquor was stack by the exposed brick walls. That was half of his total inventory. If sold the revenue would have been in $10,000 range. Jim calculated the profit return would varied from:

Beer and soda 1:10

Rail drinks 1:14

Premiums liquor and Wine 1:5

He was checking the X reports every thirty minutes, even the bartenders were making faces. The sales were sluggish. He found a tall African American lady to chat with. She seemed straight. At the end of three minutes conversation she told him she had a car trouble and she was there, hiding from the Police.

Jim: "What did you do?"

Leada: "I was driving my uncle's Cadillac and I was trying to park. I was too drunk and I hit a car. I drove the Cadillac two blocks further and I hid the car in an alley. I don't remember where the car is hidden, but is somewhere on this street. I called my brothers to come and look for it. Then I found your club open. I came here. Now I am completely drunk!"

Jim: "Listen. I will take you to my office and you can wait there till they find your car."

Leada: "Ok. I need to lay down somewhere. I hope you have a nice couch? I am taking my drink with me. Ok?" She did not need confirmation. Her sexy ass was heading toward the exit.

Ramona: "Who is she? …One of ours? I never met her before."

Jim: "She is a friend of mine. I am taking her to her car. Relax!"

Ramona: "Ok. When you come back I want to talk to you. Some lady Mocca is asking for you."

Jim: "Take her $10 and let her in." He pushed Leada out the front door and he stopped at the screaming voice.

Ramona: "She is bringing a guy with her," she needed an answer.

Jim: "Mocca, behave inside. Ok!" He quickly exchanged glances with her. The man with her was a regular. "Just pay Ramona the cover charge. It does include a drink." He saw the man paying with 20 dollar bill to Ramona and she calmed down. Once they disappeared in the entrance, Jim guided Leada toward his next door building entrance at 1424 X Street, NW. She almost fell while he was opening the gray glassed door. Nobody of the lesbian crew was outside to see him. Seemed after they took the money from Mocca's companion they were enjoying their scavenger loot.

Jim carried Leada to the penthouse office almost like a wounded soldier. She collapsed on his bed as soon the door opened.

Jim: "Hmm! I need to release her from those tight blue jeans and place a bucket nearby if she starts vomiting." He started undressing her perfect body. The bed was not comfortable. It was a pull out sofa bed. He could feel the metal bars bellow her through the tiny mattress. He placed extra pillows under her semi naked body. He had a favorite one from some twenty years ago, which he called "TV pillow." She noticed his effort to please her and she gave him a kiss.

Jim: "I thought you were one of the lesbians? Thank God you are not." He kissed her back.

Leada: "Oh, no! I am "strictly-dickly." She started unzipping him. "You are not leaving me here in that cage by myself!" she pulled open the strings of her blue silk bikini.

Jim: "Hold on. Let me text my friend Mocca." He quickly texted… "Mocca, watch my bar. I will be there in fifteen minutes."

Mocca: "Do not make any babies without my permission, Daddy!" They used to be lovers.

Jim: "They are all lesbians. Do not provoke them, ok?"

Mocca: "Ok, boss!" but she did the opposite. She started kissing her male companion. Ramona was furious.

Ramona: "Where are you, Jim? Your straight friends are flirting and kissing, and is unacceptable!"

Jim: "I am in the bathroom. Hold your horses. See you in five minutes. Ok?" he dipped his 8 inch tower in Leada's juicy cunt. She was not tight, nor loose. She had a child 9 years before, but it affected her in a positive way and now it was showing; a ready, juicy, and willing to be pleased vagina.

Leada: "Ohh. Don't stop Mr. Club Owner! What is your name?" She was moving toward him in rowboat motion back and forth and squeezing him and releasing him in a rhythmic classic position.

Jim: "I have a couple of minutes. My name is Jim. You call me big Daddy!" He was enjoying the view of himself entering in and pulling away from her well designed buttocks. "If this is a sin and I am bad, I want to be the worse of the sinners!"

Satan: "Hey, I gave you a lucky break, because you really loved Shelley. Kiana was your obsession, not your love. She was 100 percent possessing you. Shelley was about to be a good wife, if her mother was not controlling her, even with her little lies. This is a bonus here, don't get too excited. If you can keep Leada it will show me that you are better than me!"

Jim: "Hey, Satan. Are you telling me that everyone you can't control is better than you?"

Satan: "I only control hearts and emotions somewhat. I do not control minds. People who really love and mutually respect and love each other are in God's domain. Love is the strongest connection between two people and it is indestructible. It is almost like matter, the invisible plasma."

Jim: "Hey. That matter is with no charge, with mass and emitting 2 quanta with +/- in state of emotion, (sex, fear of death, surviving tragedy)?"

God: "Leave my brother Satan alone. He will lie to you that Sex is Love. Actually when sex occurs the only positive energy is the transfer of the sperm to the ready to fertilize egg in the womb. Anything else is a play to cheat woman's body."

Jim: "Are you telling me that lovers are cheaters? I thought love is forever and married couples are the structure of the society?"

God: "Love is only expressed in procreation. The rest of the time it is a lie. Love without sexual interaction is true love. Love between mother and daughter, uncle and nephew, between two brothers or between two sisters is true love. Spiritual love is the one to last and it is the strongest. When sex occurs the bodies create a lot of +\- charges but no mass, no matter is created. When a spiritual love is connecting people two things are happening: First, the mass gets created like in wormholes communications, with miniature black holes with negative mass who when in great sequences can create a "soul wind" (similar to the "solar winds" on Sun), the mass (the WeZon, or boson claimed by Higgs later on in 2012) is like the neutral river who directs the wind in either direction which depends on who has stronger pull of the two minds with +\- quanta/quarks."

Jim: "In quantum field river can move in different direction. Only the Nile River can flow north or upward in physical world."

God: "Don't interrupt me, son! Second, the 2 quarks/2quanta (to simplify things) are looking for port to harbor. The stronger spiritual mind will pull most of the mass and those 2 quanta toward itself. The weaker mind will retain some mass but not as much the stronger mind. It is amazing that after that exchange of neutral charged mass, both minds will be selfishly satisfied? The God/sub consciousness now is in a satisfied state and the active (scratch pad) mind will do the same."

Jim: "The Big Bang Theory is that the Creator worked in low entropy, that where the White Holes will create light, Expansion! The high entropy at the The Big End/Crunch theory will be creating congenial black holes at high entropy, Destruction!"

God: "Why is our universe still alive after almost 13.2 billion of years is because Sun (with age of 4.6 billion years) feeds from the bio energy released from the planets in form of bio electrical currents from highly elevated Rulers or from the physical sacrificing of the lowest level of vertebrates. In 1927, Jan Oort (a Dutch national) wrote the thesis "the stars of high velocity," in 1932 he discovered the "dark matter." He observed the density of matter near the Sun was nearly twice what could be explained by the presence of stars and gas alone."

Jim: "I think it is a bit complicated? We train all day to create antimatter, to lose weight, to burn energy. We start everyday energized from the sleep and our goal is to lose that energy, to create negative mass against the one we started with and to feel useful, creative or destructive? What kind of game is this?"

God: "That is the circle of "Life." We live and die for our pleasures. The only person who never dies is the one detached from his earth senses. He lives in the cosmic mind of the Universe. You can satisfy your sub consciousness and me, but you cannot win against your body. You will die just like everyone else. Just work on your legacy as a thinker, not as a lover!"

Jim: "The visible universe is asymmetrical. We only see and judge the bodies of planets and stars. The invisible universe, the dark matter, and the anti matter we know from the gravitational affect on the matter and radiation. When matter and antimatter meet they annihilate and release photons, the gamma rays. Meeting God and Satan is like those two are meeting: matter and antimatter. God (bio electrical +\- charges), meet Satan (physical earth pain or pleasure in the heart) and the third player is the balancing, the Moon (magnetic, emotional). Depends what is the state of the sub consciousness +\- the Yin or Yang, the black magic or white magic projects forward like white holes, black holes in the person's time machine. There are 500 terrestrial gamma rays observed daily by the Enrico Fermi space telescope visible as red dots. Thunderstorms create bursts of antimatter."

Leada: "Faster, Daddy!" her voice was stimulating and awakening. He found himself adrift for a minute.

Jim: "Turn around. I can't stay here too long. Ramona is driving me insane." He inserted his torpedo in her perfect throbbing vagina in "doggy style."

Leada: "Oh, oh. Cumming now!" the contractions held his 8 inch and fat penis even tighter and he started to feel her juices flowing and he pulled out just on time to ejaculate in powerful three feet away splash almost hitting her face, when she turned around to watch his eruption.

Leada: "Oh, no! You should have kept it in. I wouldn't mind having your baby, my club owner! And you seem smart and handsome. Put it back in. Ok?"

Jim: "Ok, when I come back I will obey your instructions. Now go to sleep and I am going to the club before Ramona does something stupid." He kissed her and went to wash up. He brought her back a hot wash rug.

Ramona: "We have an emergency here. Where are you?" she was panicking on the phone.

Jim: "What? Is the Police there?" he was running down the steps.

Ramona: "No, it is worse...."

Jim and Ramona almost bumped into each other at the club entrance.

Ramona: "This strait couple which you said is ok to enter is kissing inside!" She was howling like a wolverine.

Jim: "Just give them the money back and tell them to leave. That is your part." He was amused at her remark. "Look around at your own crowd! Ninety percent are holding hands and are seriously kissing each other."

Ramona: "I did invest a lot of time and money to fix your club. I do expect more cooperation from you!"

Jim: "Let me talk to Mocca." He went to the only straight couple in the club and he saw them kissing.

Jim: "Mocca, I told you to behave and respect them. What are you doing?" he was talking to her more like in a fatherly way.

Mocca: "Hey! I am your regular customer. They are here for the first time and they are all wrapped around like anacondas. They can't tell me what to do. I am over eighteen and this Ramona is not my mother. I will be here long time after they are gone, Jim! We are staying here. I want another "sex on the beach" drink."

Ramona: "You can't handle your people? They don't want the twenty dollars back. We are leaving and we are not coming back here ever again."

Jim: "Fine!" He went to check his registers. He made Z reports and took the money out. He noticed his bar trash bins were full of empty beer bottles and Gray Goose bottles of vodka. He made a quick assessment of his inventory and the bar receipts. After the one drink free he would have minus $700 in revenue; from head count of 70. He was minus 2,000 dollars. That meant the bartenders have stolen $1,300!

Jim: "Straight or lesbian, they all are liars!" He was concerned about his equipment. He checked all and it checked out ok.

Jim: "Ramona! Stop promoting yourself in DC! I see your bartenders were giving all night free drinks and you can't blame that on one straight couple. I will pass the word around about your criminal enterprise. If you need free drinks and to steal cash from the bar registers, I will report you to the authorities!" he angrily texted her.

Ramona: "Fuck you and your club!" she texted back. That was the last real promotion there. After that Jim was just playing by ear. He was just trying to sell his club. He noticed that Mansur was not really trying to change the hours and his investments were going to the gas station in Fredericksburg, VA...

It was early August, 2007. He hired a new bartender for the happy hour. She was from Eritrea. She had been a customer at the club on and off for almost a year. She seemed intelligent, but when it came to sales she couldn't sell one drink. Jim fired her the first night she worked.

On August 22nd Jim went to the club. The locks were changed. He called Mansur immediately.

Mansur: "Hello!" he answered.

Jim: "What are you doing? The locks are changed!" He screamed.

Mansur: "Jim! It has been almost ten years. I received a letter for audit from IRS. My lawyer Jack Lemon has advised me and you to go our separate ways, if I was to save my liquor license? We have a hearing on September, 2007."

Jim: "Mansur, I have all the books kept in good order. I will come to the hearing. Now, just give me the keys."

Mansur: "I have a buyer for your club. Saba, the Eritrean bartender you hired and fired, she is bringing $30,000 for the bar on the first floor and $20,000 for the second floor," he lied.

Jim: "50,000 dollars? Where am I going to go with that little money? I invested almost a million here."

Mansur: "Take the money! Ok? It is better for me to put a new name and to keep my license, and maybe then I will get the hours I needed?"

Jim: "I think this is a court issue now? You can't avoid me. I live here, on top of your (our) business! And I don't believe you will give me a penny, ok?"

Mansur: "Come get your stuff. And maybe you can open another business like you did with me?"

Jim: "I will take my liquor and sound. I will see you in court after that!" he couldn't believe the Satan camouflaged as Mansur. He hung up furiously.

Satan: "I have helped you get rich. I made you poor. I gave you beautiful women; I made you fall in love and to waste your money on Amanda, Kiana, and Shelley. Now you finished with upgrading the sound equipment and video equipment here; go start your life somewhere else. You did not lose money; you gained experience in the last 10 years. Not bad at all!"

God: "Sometimes my brother Satan is ahead of the human expectations and he seems good for the moment or for awhile. I am the regulator of the Mind and the Time. That is why very few survive the temptations of money and political influence. Whoever pulls out of the game may survive the human punishment like jail, deportation, bankruptcy, family broken, even death!"

Jim: "Death?" He could not believe it.

God: "Your competitor at Avenue A Club Andrew is dead after surgery. The same thing happen to Mr. Baldwin, who lied and protested your license change in 1999. It is time to "clear the desk," now. My advice is if you leave DC, leave it with a Bang!"

Jim: "How, God?" He basically was communicating with his sub consciousness.

God: "I know how your mind works. You do not leave anybody who hurts you unpunished. We will play our game now. They cannot figure you out. Most of the Feds and DC government work on paper trail and money trail, also who you communicate with? You are Ok on that. You got no money, and no "friends" who are on some "Patriot Act," list. Now we have to deal with the revenge powers you have. I will help you."

Jim: "Are you implying the 666 theory? Something will happen in six months?" he found himself suddenly excited. He thought maybe he could take his club back, or sell it by then?

God: "You will think of bigger picture. Forget about that Satan club. You need to gain yourself respect. What will happen next it is for the history books? Write your story. Your book will bring you to the level of Da Vinci, Nostradamus, Pythagoras, Francis Bacon, and Einstein. That is where your wealth will come from. People like to read true stories with weird endings."

Jim: "That is similar to Faust play by Johann Wolfgang von Goethe. He wrote his two parts in thirty years and he died a year after the completion in 1832. He wrote about history, politics and his own philosophy. Do I get what I want?"

God: "Yes. You will have the World! Satan owned the soul of Faust. I own you, you compliment me. Here is the difference. You must, empathize your own situation sometime. That means, you look at yourself from outside! When you stay too long inside yourself you become the Satan. Astral projection night time or day time meditation and awareness will bring you to deity level. All your wishes will be granted.

1. No name now, Legacy forever later.
2. No home now, your Planet later.
3. No wife now, every woman you wish later.
4. Poor now, rich later.
5. No child now, every child will want you to be his father later.
6. Government rules you know, you are the World and Galaxy Ruler later.
7. Experience now, professor of science later."

He was in shock. He knew he would get out of this situation somewhat with positive outcome, but separating himself from the little empire he built was painful. He was the King of X Street! He was the only seven days a week operator here and his crowd was loyal and his spot was unique. He hated drug dealers and pimps and the Police knew that. His Achilles heel was him tolerating women, of any kind at the bar. He was disgusted of his partner cowardice. He inquired meeting with his lawyer Jack Lemon after he wrote him back two letters to stop bothering Mansur by asking him to pay the share he gave to Saba, basically for paying the rent in September, 2007.

God: "You should go to court and demand a judgment. Those three are nobodies, ok?"

Jim: "I am not leaving my club and my office without a fight. I have the "Brave Heart," of the Scots in me and the genius of Bulgarians! I will win!"

God: "True, but it will take some time, maybe four to five years? Are you ready for that?" he laughed.

Jim: "I am ready to win at any time frame. Nobody fights to lose, but even if one loses it has to be in respectable way, with dignity! I want the courts and the history to write about the battle and the wining, ok!"

God: "If I did not know you I would think you are insane, but it is the opposite with you. You, no matter what, will win! And you will write about it!"

As he was preparing for the court battle a call from France came.

Juliet: "Hey, Jim!"

Jim: "Juliet! How are you?" trying to be friendly, while depressed. He met her a year before in 2006, while he was living and fighting with Shelley. He even drove her to the house in Baltimore he intended to buy for himself, "the General house" on Walbrook Street. She liked it then.

Juliet: "Did you buy the house?" that was her next question.

Her English language was much better than a year before. She was 31 then, in 2007, and she was more aggressive. Her ethnic background was from Senegal and she was tall and beautiful for her race. Unfortunately she was trying to look fashionable and she was using too much make up and she changed her hair to red metallic. When she entered Randevu bar in 2006 all hookers accepted her as "one of them" vs. a girlfriend material. When Jim told them Juliet is his French girlfriend they could not stop laughing for a while.

Angel: "We thought you are a pimp now?" After fifteen minutes they kind of observed her and after they found out she does not speak much English they returned to their usual activity -- drinking, gossiping, and waiting for new clients.

Juliet: "Are those your friends? They seem they like you. We are like this in France." She didn't stay out late at the bar to see the real deal; pimps, hookers, johns, alcoholics, drug dealers and some normal tourists and locals, mixed with undercover police.

Jim: "I did not buy the house. I had no credit lines? I have been buying everything with cash and check cards and basically I killed my credit!" he answered.

Juliet: "I am coming to see you regardless. I have a proposition for you, you can't refuse!"

Jim: "Where are you now?" he was concerned on how to avoid her.

Juliet: "I am at the airport. Can you come to pick me up?"

Jim was at BWI (Baltimore Washington International) within forty minutes, just before Anne Arundel Mills Mall where Amanda took him shopping in 2001.

Juliet: "Hello, Jim! Je t'aime, I love you!" she gave him a tight hug. Her 5'10" zero fat perfect body did not match her face but it was welcome distraction for Jim at this time.

Jim: "I love you too. Where are we heading now?" he tried to avoid talking about his troubles.

Juliet: "We are going to your club. I wish you bought that house!" She gave him a kiss with a smile.

Jim: "European culture is so normal! They love you when you are up and love you when you are down!" he thought.

Jim: "Ok! Are you spending the night? You can stay in my office."

Juliet: "Yes, if your girlfriend does not object?" she was testing him.

Jim: "I am single!" He kissed her back. Her long legs were showing under her high cut dress like oily dark arrows pointing upward. For a moment he remembered Kiana's body sitting at the same seat just two years prior. He shook his head "Women, nothing, but sweet trouble!"

Satan: "Listen to her she may be your way out of here?"

God: "Listen to your mind, Jim! No more mistakes, ok?"

Juliet: "That is a nice bar! You did not show me that last year!" They had a couple of drinks on the first floor.

Jim: "You owe me 50,000 dollars. Put this on my tab. I will deduct it when you pay me in full" he whispered to Saba.

Saba: "Do you like a cigar also?" She role played a good bartender.

Juliet: "I like your bartender. She is very friendly!" little did she know about the true disaster here. "Let us go upstairs now." She handed the small traveling bag to Jim.

Jim: "Keep the receipt. I will come back and sign it later, Saba!"

He grabbed the cigar and put it in his mouth. Then he opened the gray glass door of 1424 X Street, NW. The nice round ass walked in front of his eye sight up the stairs. He wanted to pull her skirt down and ravage her pussy even before they made it to the second floor.

Juliet: "You missed me?" She talked like they were lovers with a week of separation. If she knew what a year could change in USA, she would of not been so forwarded and so optimistic.

Jim: "Don't stop! You will break my cigar." He was almost touching her anus with the cigar, he was that close.

Juliet: "I will break something else upstairs! Hurry, Jim!" She ran up the stairs playfully. "The Penthouse, I remember! Let me go, let me go!" she held the framed metal door to his office entrance. "I am in jail; please rescue me, White Knight! And then I will be yours forever!"

Jim: "If this is not a Hollywood play, then what is it?" he observed the French and Eritrean actresses within ten minutes.

Satan: "I told you Leada was the last, but you have your ways with women! I see. Enjoy your pleasures, sinful man!"

Jim: "I will. If I can't get married, shall I stop living?"

God: "Are you making a baby? Do you love her? Does she love you? No, then you are committing a sin."

Jim: "Yes. For me to be good I have to be bad also. Symmetry in life is living life to the fullest even it is not socially approved."

God: "I understand. Living temporary like being married is better than not living with a woman at all, and you are great in getting the ladies somehow."

Jim: "It is all about the confidence, even when one is poor, act wealthy. When sick, act healthy, when you don't know, project wisdom. Teachers are intimidated more by smart looking students than anybody else. When I was a student they thought I knew the subjects even I didn't always, I always projected confidence. Something like in 007 movies James Bond does. Arrogance is not confidence."

God: "One thing about you I admire! You constantly read and you are current with world affairs. You are your own Henry Kissinger, a "think tank!" And I see you do great modeling and can forecast of the future. The most amazing was your prediction of falling of the Berlin Wall and the end of Warsaw Pact as we know it. You did it 9 years in advance."

Jim: "Prediction is like a sitting duck, a philosopher. I did not just predict it; I also triggered the process... Remember my three friends from senior class, three and two years ahead of me now Rafael, Carlos, Marko? I was the third to escape, the last was Marko. Every action in life has equal reaction. Each of us took a chunk from the wall. As a result the Naval Academy (now is called Naval War college) is only for naval officers. The merchant marine was separated and they do attend now as civilians. During my studying we were all in uniforms for 9 semesters in 5 long years."

God: "You can beat the communists? Let me see if you can show me how to dismount the greatest economy on planet Earth, the USA?"

Jim: "I will show you, not tell you. Now let me "dismount" Juliet at the moment."

God: "That is not your priority, ok? Bad son! I gave you everything you wished but those women take your mind from greatest achievements. You also smoke cigars, bad yogi too! But I am not Faust. Keep your soul. And I can't send you to any of Dante's "Inferno's," circles. You are better than all those characters. Unfortunately they are the one in position to judge you now."

Jim: "I know. Let me live my earthly life for now, God!"

Juliet: "Hey. What are you waiting for? I did not come from Paris to watch Disney World!" She undressed and jumped in the shower.

Jim: "I am still waiting for your proposal?" he followed her in the shower as quickly as he could. Then after short play in the shower they headed still wet toward the make shift bed; the pulled out sofa. The beach towel was large enough to cover her body, so Jim tried to center himself and not wet the rest of the bed. Her African body was like a spring and full of life. She reminded him of those great Olympians like Flow Jo, who he was fascinated with since he saw her wining the fastest in 100 meter dash in 1988.

Juliet: "Marry me! You are now 50 and you are not getting any younger."

She took his penis deep into her hairy, juicy vagina.

Jim: "Is that "the proposal"? What would I gain from that?" He tried not to laugh. "Those Europeans are never boring. If she was living here in the USA that would be a possibility!" he thought, while he was enjoying the free sex. He did not pay for her ticket, nor did she ever ask him for cash or gifts before and now.

Juliet: "What you gain? A wife, maybe your own child and then French citizenship! They retire at age sixty-three! What I gain you will ask me? I get American citizenship and my son can come to USA and get education, citizenship and work!"

Jim: "What happened to your French husband? Is he white?"

Juliet: "Yes, he is white! Can you fuck quicker? Don't hold back. We are divorced. He cheated a lot!" She said it in one burst of breath. Her body was sweating and oily, mixed with shower water and human steam that was coming from her, as the sun was hitting with its reflecting lights from the tall federal building across the street. The mixture was ghostly. He stretched his hand to the camcorder nearby. He turned it on.

Juliet: "Are you trying to make me immortal? Video is forever. Go ahead." She started moving in back and forth motion.

Jim: "I have an idea. You hold the camera and you videotape me from your face down." She obeyed at the instant. The camera now recorded him entering her from between her breasts down to her perfect vagina.

Juliet: "This is like watching a porno movie." She had the screen reversed so she could see the actual picture being recorded. "I may get used to that? My husband was too selfish to be creative with our sex life. After the child was born he basically lost interest in me and sex!" She was moving and talking.

Jim: "I had never had storytelling and videotaping at the same time. It is like a narrator and video in old films!" He ordered her to turn around. She obeyed.

Jim:"You will make a great wife to someone! Maybe I am the lucky one?" He entered her now anally. She squeezes initially in surprise, but then she relaxed her muscles and her buttocks opened wider reacting to the feeling of pleasure.

Juliet: "I love you even more and in strange way. That actually feels good. It is my first time, Jim!" She started moving in rhythm like it was a normal sex in her vagina.

Jim: "Wow. It feels good to me also. I will marry you soon, Juliet!"

Juliet: "You are my Romeo, Je t'aime!" She started to cum in bursts. She squirted and it splashed on the beach towel underneath.

Jim: "I am cumming too!" he threw the camcorder away. "This was too good to miss!" He thought.

The night was relaxing and they cuddled most of the time. Her favorite position was to "spoon," him from behind. He would feel his naked buttocks rubbing against her pubic hair and then her thighs and her pelvis. That way she was able to stimulate his penis while he was asleep. He woke up a couple of times observing his erected tower in her hand holding him from behind. He would turn around in his sleep and then she would lay sideways on him and then she would start to swallow his penis to full erection. Then she would sit on it and just use him like she was "riding a horse." She did it a couple of times, and then both fell asleep.

Jim: "Where did you graduate from that Entertainment college?" he was cooking breakfast and she was grabbing him from behind, in a cuddling kind of behavior.

Juliet: "In France this is normal, if you love someone? Why? American women are different?"

Jim: "What you just did with me it is only in the movies. In real life those "beauties" are nothing but gold diggers, drug crazy, no sex "Material girls."

Juliet: "Women behave according to the circumstances. With rich guys they ask, with poor guys they give. Europeans are more tolerant to variations, due to so many wars there. I love you with or without club or without the house. You seem you have retained your qualities of European, even you have been here, what, like thirty years?" she stirred the sausage and the eggs and she took over the cooking. "Make me some coffee, ok baby!" Her French accent was sexy and he almost got arousal just from that. Jim did not respond with words, he just gave her a kiss. His memories of the lady in Calais, France were similar. French women like to talk and to get emotional.

Jim: "Coffee is ready!"

Juliet: "Breakfast also!" They ate, they took a shower together. It was the departure mood in the room.

Juliet: "Drive me to Greyhound bus terminal. I am going to North Carolina. I have family there. I will be back in a week. You think by then on my proposal! If you are ready to commit, we can move forward?"

She sounded more like a lawyer and business woman when they were at the bus terminal. If it was not for the memory, of last night one would think those two were in some corporate relation.

Jim: "I will be ready by then!" They kissed but with hidden affection. Cameras were all over the station. Homeland security was making their files full with poor men and women, obviously.

Jim: "Wow! That was like I was hit by a lightning strike!" Not since Frida made him an offer in 1986 he felt in tough corner. He would have taken Frida's offer, but she kept talking about her mother moving-in and then he needed to run away, from gay Mr. Smith and from New York. He did not speak French, but this was not the issue he could not handle. He wished Juliet was somewhat better and younger looking and without a child. He was not seeing himself raising a child who calls someone else "Father." Then she also had an agenda, "The citizenship!" He was wondering if once she would get it, would the relationship suddenly change.

It was mid September, 2007. The four year battle to win his club back or to get his rightful pay started. The email flew out to the chief counsel for ABRA Connelly, to US attorney Bishop, to Police commander of 1st MPD.

In one of the letters to Bishop Jim compared legalization to guns in DC with legalization of the prostitution by imposing taxes on 10 billion dollars porn industry, in specifics to impose taxes on the local pimps. He did not receive an answer but he knew someone had a good discussion about that. He even went to Washington City Paper to report the shady operation of Mansur and his family. He also visited the Lebanese embassy. Mansur was bragging earlier about killing someone in his old country some forty years before. He was hiding in USA all this time and no FBI, or no Interpol was able to touch him. He also called FBI, but nobody was really interested in pursuing the old case. He, Mansur was still in business and he and his wife Anika were happily ever after. His drug dealing was now flourishing too. Great, USA! The movie "Scarface," was similar to Mansur's story. Criminals from Cuba or from Lebanon act alike.

Apollo: "Hey, Jim! Stop bothering my father! I will unload on you thirty guys from my gang at your office. You know we never needed your money. We make $10,000 a day from drugs sales. My father just played you to invest in his business. You are so stupid!" That was Mansur's son calling. Jim just hung up. He decided to find a buyer for Mansur's club and grill. For some unknown reason the restaurant's name remained the same "Mike's," but the Eritrean cookoo lady changed the bar section to "Attitude."

Jim: "From Sally's," "Starlight," "Randevu," "ZeusLoungeDC" and to "Attitude," now? What would be the next and most important how long they would stay there?" He was puzzled.

God: "Nobody would last here ten years like you, son! Do you know why? This place after you has no soul and vibe like yours. You spilled your blood here. You never lost any business because you couldn't produce the money. You just got tangled in DC and Federal government "promotion through destruction scheme." The more "cockroaches" show themselves as crime fighters and "good doers," to women and children, the more they will grow in ranks. In a decade thirty-two dance clubs will be shut down just in DC. They were not replaced with any new ones, they just died."

Jim: "That equates to thirty-two families who lost their wealth and broken dreams."

God: "True! The other side of the coin is most of them started with questionable finances and the investors, most of the time; push them toward taking higher risk in picking promoters and pushing the prices too high! Most of businesses who survived are none entertaining, with weird followers and cheap prices and they last for twenty years."

Jim: "I am not competing with deli style restaurants. I am in the league of high end night clubs, God!"

God: "I know that Son! That is why you are so unique and I will make sure you will win!"

The meetings and e mails were not working. Saba decided to place a restraining order on top of the trouble he already was experiencing. Instead paying him what she owed him she decided to hide behind her Police officer friend Paul Tulio. Jim even went to court to present his case. The judge ruled against him. Naturally the first of his reaction was to retaliate. He thought of kicking the gas pipes, gluing the doors, but the rational took over in him.

God: "You will get more in court than in vendetta. You will get your money back. The more you press them legally the more they will bend."

Jim observed after hour drinking, fighting, closing the place at 6.15 am, some four hours later than allowed by liquors license. He even videotaped from the window the street disturbance and dispute over unpaid money to a prostitute services.

Xia: "Pay up, motherfucker! Give me my $20! You paid her, now you pay me, ok!" She was the bartender's Rudolf's girlfriend. She was in the face of some Spanish client who was too drunk to fight her small, but feisty Chinese body.

Eduardo: "Xia! Stop being so loud, please! Someone will notice and you will bring unnecessary attention to us, ok?" Eduardo was the captain in Dynasty, NY a high end and overpriced Italian restaurant, established in 2006 in DC, later it would be replaced with Lincoln at 1110 Vermont Ave, NW. His confused drunken mind would lead him to dating transgendered women and a year later to him committing suicide. The Spanish guy, Siro, with him will be an underage (19) Bolivian national (illegal US alien) who was selling cocaine and supposedly dating the daughter of the owner of Palermo. Lobo at this time was in jail for a year; the reason that he was not paying taxes to the government at amount of 1.6 million and he was not maintaining a payroll. He was paying his employees in cash; the same thing Mr. Rogbin was doing at Phantom, Urban and later Fusion clubs. Paying cash is good as long the contractors are 1099ers. One accountant or owner should keep a ledger with all expenses. The only deductible is 500 dollars per contractor. Everything above is taxable by the government at this time, mid to the end of 2000 decade.

God: "You see! You paid your share of taxes and I kept you alive! Stop worrying about the little people. There is much more to show your strength to the world."

Jim: "There are two types of people. First category, are those who watch the news! Second category is those that make the news! I am the second; I make the news, God!"

God: "Sometimes instead being too proactive, you should just trigger the process and let the news develop itself. It is like being an arsonist. You don't stay in middle of the fire and get burned. You just watch from distance what you started, ok? Remember, "Vengeance is mine, sayeth the Lord!"

God: "You are now tinkering with Enso, "El Nino – Southern Oscillation." It will bring sixteen strongest hurricanes in 2008 in Atlantic Ocean, event not been observed since 1944! His sister El Nina would manifest herself in the winter. You were born in December (on 26th). Guess when the strongest and longest snow storms would occur; in December and January 2009/2010 winter! Meanwhile a false prophet would claim your powers "to raise the oceans". He would become the US President in 2008! El Nino is Spanish for "the child," and the capitalized term El Niño refers to Christ child, Jesus, because periodic warming in the Pacific near South America is usually noticed around Christmas."

Jim: "Hmm. My anger would help the election of a false president?"

God: "Not once, but twice! Explain your powers, trigger man!"

Jim: "That's like my occult prediction in 1980!

I have a better example; the story of Valery Plame in her documentary,

"Fair Game." She was a CIA operative and they used false information to trigger the second war against Sadam Husain in Iraq in 2003. There were no "aluminum cylinders at Niger to make weapons of mass destruction" dear Collin Powell (with 700 million dollars financial portfolio?) and dear Condoleezza Rice (the National Security adviser to George Bush, Jr)."

God: "We can do better than those career clowns in the government like Cheney, Rove, Clintons and Kennedys. We will bring the economy down after eighty years of prosperity."

Jim: "That is the Bible prophecy and only Nostradamus was able to pinpoint accurately the events of "two powerful economic powers would lose their strength at the beginning of the 21st century." He was talking about Russia and USA. I can't see how the USA would lose power overnight? Just a decade ago Greenspan was artificially trying to slow down the overheated economy with increasing the Federal

Reserve interest of borrowing, to slow down inflation and to promote more hiring."

God: "Wars don't make a nation rich as a whole. It just induces fear in potential enemies. Since the USA is not using, a major weapon system, it just irritates but it does not destroy the enemy. The new enemy is now in "wait and see" mode. Those like China, India and Brazil can now show surplus. Anything bad to USA and Russia is good for the others."

Jim: "The USA corporate wealth is 90% of world corporate wealth!"

God: "We are not after the individual or corporate wealth. We are judging what is in the Government's Coffer (treasury). China has surplus, USA has debt. And you will help them get in even in more debt. You see, Son! You are like barometer to the economy. When you do well, everyone does well. When you do badly, everyone who caused it will suffer 1000 fold."

Jim: "Well. I know my anger gets results in the number six sequence. I lost my club in August, 2007. I got received an e mail from Connelly in October, 2007 that I am clear of any wrong doing as ABC manager. The "news" should show up in April, right?"

God: "Yes, son! The financial market will hit first "The Lehman brothers," exactly in April, 2008.

They will officially bankrupt in September 2008. On March 2009 the stock market will hit 6626 low, half of its highest. The perfect storm would eliminate the 4th largest player on Wall Street with 600 billion dollars in assets. Namura holdings would buy the LEH Asian arm with $225 million in assets for $2! Barclay's would buy the North America operations for 1.3 billion dollars. AIG, GM, Chrysler and major US banks will follow suit. US Central Bank, the Fed will bail out the AIG for $85 billion and would own 80% of its stock. Freddie Mac and Fannie Mae will also get Fed's assistance. The Lehman Brothers would just let go. Later on the "too big to fall "slogan will be enforced, but not for individual Ponzi scheme master mind Bernard Madoff, or for other copy cats."

Jim: "That sounds right. ...And I caused all that? I am sure closing Bellini's, the Zoro, and the Zeus Lounge DC helped nobody, but it affects everybody in a negative way, great work, dear Government. Revenge!" He almost laughed.

God just shook his head…

Jim needed income. He fell on hard times. The Mercedes Benz Dealership at Bethesda Euro Motor cars was not able to fix his transmission on the CE300 Benz even he paid them 5,100 dollars for the repair. It was bad and it was leaking. The engine also was overheating. Jim got a job at Kennedy Center. He became head bartender and captain. The Restaurant associates crew of 400 strong was sent to different occasions on Capitol Hill, at the Newseum on Pennsylvania Ave., to DAR Constitution Hall, on 18th street, to the Smithsonian Air and Space Museum, on Independence Avenue, to the World Bank on G Street, NW, DC and more.

In November, 2008 he was working on Capitol Hill. The swearing of new Senators was in Dirksen building. Jim was in the corner behind the bar, when a short man entered the room. When the announcer called the name the whole room got quiet.

Announcer: "Senator Ted Kennedy present!"

Jim: "Shall I duck down? I do not want to be next to any Kennedy. Fuck!" He hated the government so much and now he couldn't be more head on with and in it than being in a room with a "Kennedy!"

Announcer: "Senator John Kerry present!" The audience of mostly press, interns and newly elected senators got loud. The tall giraffe like Senator lined up next on the podium. He could have been a president in 2004, but the tape from Al Qaeda two days before the election reassured Bush's reelection.

The irony here is Ted Kennedy, also a failed to become president in 1980.

Jim: "Any more losers?" He thought, while he was serving mostly beer and wine to the crowd.

Announcer: "Senator Richard Lugar present!" Crowd was modestly excited.

Jim: "Loser No. three," he almost laughed. The government was too predictable.

Richard Lugar: "We, the republicans, are always outnumbered!" he said, crowd cheering. He has been in the Senate since 1977.

Ted Kennedy: "We are well balanced!" he has been senator since 1962, starting at age thirty!

John Kerry: "Some of my colleagues have been here since the Vietnam War!" He was the youngest from the clowns; he had been a senator since 1985.

Jim: "Where is the "term limit"? The founding fathers never expected fifty year careers on Capitol Hill!" He had a phony smile on his face.

"They are talking about events forty years ago? The issue is how to bring the economy back now?" The irony also is that Jim mysteriously would fix that issue within a year. How? Please, keep turning the pages, dear reader. He is not the phony Shirley Maclaine; a writer of fourteen mystic books with 1000 questions and no answers. "What if?" …What the fuck?

What about the book, "Consilience" by Edward O. Wilson (in 2003)? He is the opposite phony. He has all the 1000 answers, but his personal experience is missing. One cannot write anything without "I or Me" in the middle... He, Mr. Wilson, becomes a statistician, a reporter of events. Miss Maclaine cannot throw at you her hallucinations in a bath tub or while driving, and her related 1000 questions about "The Awareness" without some formulas and reasonable explanations. Questions create more questions without answers. Someone should ask the "wonderers" how they balance their bank accounts, or that maybe another clown question.

Jim would have liked to be in the room with Sen. McCain, who wanted to fire Henry Paulson, the mastermind of TARP (Troubled Asset Relief Program), who was Secretary of the Treasury. TARP was approved by the Congress for 700 billion dollars bailout and eventually signed into law by President Obama.

Basically, the Feds helped their twin at Wall Street. Indirectly Jim's brother Adrian kept his job in Bulgaria as insurance agent for German Subsidiary of AIG, called "Alliance/Allianz."

Jim: "Those are the people who control the world economies and starting wars?" He thought. He felt sorry about them. They were all gray haired, pompously behaving like the world owes them something. They were more concerned about holding the power, than with the real purpose of legislating. Those two, the shorter and the taller clown had the benefit of banking on the biggest governmental scheme since the Social Security invention in 1935, the "affordable health care law." The money from the "New Deal" was drying up after seventy-three years.

The new president Obama was endorsed by Ted Kennedy, who basically drafted the, "health care," plan as opportunity to collect more taxes from everyone, or to punish the uninsured. The MIT professor Jonathan Gruber will get exposed in November of 2014 of misleading the low information "stupid" voters. The inside trading in buying stocks in "Obama care" made the Heinz Ketchup beneficiary through his marriage John Kerry even richer. Under the advice of Henry Paulson, he bought 115 different stocks in Health care related companies, out of the total 132 stocks he had in his financial portfolio. Unfortunately, Ted Kennedy died in August 2009, so he couldn't benefit from his own scheme.

Mansur finally got his liquor business hours approved in 2008! The problem was that his license was now on the firing line. The ABC Board had a series of postponed hearings and they were getting closer and closer to shutting him down. The irony was that even Jim was formally removed from the premises as an operator; they were on Mansur for revenge like hungry wolves on a lost sheep. After they couldn't use the IRS via audit, they had a final hearing in first week of October, 2008.

Jim: "Let me buy you out, Mansur! I have a buyer. His name is Kamran and he is willing to buy you for $300,000 cash." The meeting was in nearby eatery.

Mansur: "Who is that guy?" he was desperate to get out with money in his pockets. His lease was expiring in 2013 (five years remaining).

Kamran: "I am the owner of "Dalila" and "Gondola" Ristorante Italiano in Virginia. I have an offer for you. I will trade you my restaurant and a house in Leesburg for your club and restaurant. I am giving you appraised value of two million total in exchange for your spot."

Mansur: "I have a house in Beltsville. What I am going to do with two houses."

Jim: "Sell your house, Roy! Then move to Leesburg, ok!"

Mansur: "I need cash. Give me 100,000 dollars down payment and then we will do monthly payments."

Kamran: "Trade, no cash!"

Mansur: "Cash, no trade!"

Jim: "Losers, stubborn losers! You are both wasting my time."

Mansur lost his liquor license a week later. The hearing at ABC board lasted four hours. Jim tried to help Mansur again by defending him. Mansur had chosen Saba to represent his part of the liquor business. He wrongfully assumed that a seventy-one old and crippled lawyer Jack Lemon would give him proper counsel? Third mistake he made was to ignore Jim. That hearing was about the liquor license; not Saba, nor Jack Lemon, had a clue in answering the Board's Inquisition like questions.

Detective O'Conner: "Jim, you can't come close to Saba within fifty feet!" He was at the hearing in adjusted room.

Jim: "She can stay outside. She is not competent to stand at that hearing! That hearing is all about me, mister!" He was right. He had read the showcase 5 bullet points of the prosecution.

Detective O'Conner: "If you stay in the room with Saba, you will be arrested!" Jim looked at Mansur. He was like a high school boy with his funny hat on. He was definitely brainwashed by the lawyer and by the Police.

Mansur: "Sorry, Jim! I need to save my business and my license!" He headed toward the hearing room.

Jim: "You will lose everything without me, Mansur!" he shouted over the detective's shoulder that followed Mansur.

Jim: "Great!" he retreated to the adjusted small room, where he listened for the next four hours the inquisitors, who were throwing his name around and nobody, was able to answer.

Jim: "Three stooges! They will lose the license." He wanted to break the door down and to scream at the Board members. Toward the end he overheard their ten minutes recess, he jumped out of the room and he entered the main hearing room. He knew about the risk of arrest, but he could not allow the license to be revoked.

God: "You are a brave man, Jim! I predicted that you would not stay idle too long and you will take action! I sent detective O'Conner on assignment, so you can say your final word! Bravo!" He heard the TIH (The invisible Hand/God) and the same force (Chi = Hellium4, Quantum Vortex), which made him defect from Bulgaria, now pushed him in front of those seven clowns.

Chairman: "Who are you, sir?" he looked down and above his reading glasses. He was a new elected chairman. He was around sixty-five years old, an ex police commander.

Jim: "I am the person who you have been talking about the last four hours. I am asking to have my answers recorded!" He looked around. Nobody from old players were here; mostly men with gay tones and two women. No Davis, no Maria Laban, no Ceaser? The only familiar face he saw was the Board General Counsel Connelly. He was hiding behind everyone on the elevated stage.

Chairman: "Look! You need to be represented by an attorney or at least to be on the call list! We can't just take anyone walking in the hearing!"

Jim: "This hearing was all about me! This is like a kangaroo court. You can't make a decision without hearing my side and without my explanation!"

Chairman: "Mansur can appeal our decision if he does not agree. We are adjourned now! Good bye and good luck, sir!"

Naturally, Mansur lost his license. ...and the next two license holders till year of 2013. How? Please read, Cornell University students.

12/11/08 Bernard Madoff gets arrested for the twenty year long Ponzi scheme. The Lehman brothers were the first to fall, and then the richest inmate #61727- 054 was to go to the "Big House," from chairman of NASDAQ to 150 years in jail and with 170 billion in restitution. The amazing thing was that from his loyal 4,800 investors, only half lost money. The rumors were he would make people wait year and half minimum before he takes their money usually in tens of millions.

God: "You are unstoppable now!"

Jim: "Well I lost the club. What is next?"

God: "You leave it to me. I am much bigger than their little courts, banks and any kind of weapons they make."

Jim: "I know that. Are you taking Satan's role now?"

God: "No, son! I am doing exactly what your sub consciousness is sending to me! You trigger it; I multiply your power 1,000 times."

Satan: "Here I lose! I want to do badly, but I don't have the powers to multiply it to that extent. I bow to you, God and to you "trigger man," Jim! I salute you!"

Jim: "Satan, you remind me of a petty thief, but you act like you are big and bad!"

Satan: "Look! The dark matter in Galaxy is 84%. I live there and the one who can suck my energy and convert it to his own use, wins!"

Jim: "I know the Sun has God's quality to generate life and to suck out life, but the better one communicates with God/one's sub consciousness the better one is. Satan, you are just into small pleasures and mischief."

Satan: "I made more babies with alcohol and drugs induced than sober people make. And don't forget the money factor. Take the money away and you will see third world sex. Women would barter anything to feed their children."

Jim: "So sex for food is prostitution?" he was curious.

Satan: "Anything which has value as gift or alter woman's mind to choose one man over the other is prostitution. Cave living, fire owning, and any accommodation man provides in exchange for sex is the same thing."

Jim: "Where is the true love, Satan?"

Satan: "Only two people who contribute equally to earn food and money, and who exchange equal gifts are in love. I don't see even 1% of people who are in love, but I make them feel like they are. I make 99 % foul."

God: "Wrong! You are talking about sex and love! The percentage is much higher of people who love and don't have sex. I would say 10% are talking about that no sex-love, but really 5% are true absentees, we are taking between sexually active. We are no talking about jail people, weirdoes, which are too young and too old to have sex! From those 5% I can relate to two or three living on Earth now."

Jim: "What is my category, God?" He was wondering.

God: "You are unique at this time! There were maybe less than ten like you throughout history, but nobody at the moment is even close to you, son!"

Jim: "I am the only one now? Wow." He was not surprised, "how about John of God in Brazil?"

God: "He is using crystals to enhance his powers. If that was the way to get powers, then everyone should have been born with crystals in their heart and brains! You are the one, son!"

Jim: "What is so unique about me, God?"

God: "You connected the earth and the Galaxy knowledge with Cosmic Awareness." You got deep into Quantum thinking. You write the formulas. You explain everything through modern and esoteric science of life. You are the one who does not need money, governments' projects, and Nobel Awards for achievements to get respect. You don't have one award and yet you heal people, you destroy economies, you rise the oceans!"

Jim: "I thought Obama was the all "Mighty President?" He said he would make the "change!"

God: "Son! Presidents have four years of power and they don't even come close to you! Obama is an orator. He does not know or he does not care where CERN or Stafford particles collider is?"

Jim: "My library is limited, but my knowledge comes from outside of anything written. I am not here to talk, but to do. I am living all my ten lives in one. When someone gets licensed or is certified, he/she is expected to use that education to provide for living. I am licensed into many fields, but I hardly use those certificates. I am a thinker and a creator/destroyer."

God: "Now is the time to destroy! You will be remembered more when you inject fear and respect into your enemies. You will start a movement of loyal followers. You created enough to write a 1,000 page book. Now show me your desires. We need to get to "negative work/antimatter-black magic!"

Mansur kept calling Jim to find him a buyer. Jim was hesitant, but he kept advertising for him. Saba was gone with the liquor license gone. She even threatened Mansur with lawsuit.

Mansur: "I am poor!" he kept laughing about it.

Jim: "I am poor too, Mansur! I will find you a buyer. I will ask for 1/3 of sales proceeding, ok! Sign here!"

Mansur: "Sure!" He signed in desperation.

May, 2009. A Lebanese, thirty-one year old promoter arrived at Mike's."

Jim: "Who are you?"

Khalid: "I am the owner of KH productions. I have been in the business since I was seventeen. I always dreamed to have my own club. This looks good, but I need to eliminate the stairways to third floor. What are you asking for?"

Jim: "We are asking for 600,000 dollars. You get the restaurant and the three story club with liquor license and cigar license! I personally invested here 1 million dollars!" The true number was 908,000 dollars, but a little exaggeration was allowed, he thought.

Khalid: "I will give you $500,000 but I need at least $200,000 to fix the joint. Let me talk to my mother-in-law, she's got the money. I need to put a spiral staircase here." He pointed toward the corners of the room, near the windows.

Jim: "Once it is yours you can do to the club anything you want. I can assist you to get your liquor license and to keep the cigar license."

Khalid: "Cigars! Hmmm. I like a good cigar once in a while!"

Jim: "There are only three cigars (Tobacco) bars in whole DC. This is one of them!"

Khalid: "This is like the Prohibition era. I feel like Al Capone against the Irish rival Dean O'Banion in Chicago."

Jim: "Do you know the real name of Al Capone?"

Khalid: "No!"

Jim: "It is Alphonse Gabriel Capone, a Capricorn, like me!"

Khalid: "Hmmm! That is why Police talk shit about you?"

Jim: "Police are my last worry! Let make that business work! I am trying to sale my share, but the old man Mansur wants completely out. You pay him 2/3; I get 1/3 of the sale. We have a contract between Mansur and me. Want me to show you?"

Khalid: "No! Where is he from?"

Jim: "Mansur is from Lebanon."

Khalid: "Really? Me too..."

Jim: "You both should finalize the deal. Don't leave me out, ok!" he almost warned him about his spiritual and quantum powers, but he decided to keep it in secret for now. People were generally ignorant about the esoteric sciences until it is too late to correct their mistake. Soon both Mansur and Khalid would have a bad taste of QMDL (quantum mind destruction law).

The first week of June, 2009 Jim observed his refrigerators, beer coolers and portable A/C units thrown on the street and loaded into a big trash open container.

Jim: "What are you doing?"

Khalid: "Get out of my face!" He was not the same person Jim met before.

Mansur: "Take your stuff from the trash and go away!" he was like a different person too. Jim could not believe what he was seeing? What was suddenly going on?

Mansur: "You made me lose my license! Now you want money? You are nothing but a hustler! Go away!"

Jim: "Mansur! You did not let me help you at the hearing. You lost your license, because of Saba and Jack Lemon, your incompetent counsel."

Mansur: "If you don't leave I will call the Police."

Jim: "Now listen! If you both don't give me my money I will give you six months and you will be out of business!" He knew that from his success with Prosperity. The reaction of Khalid was identical to Saba's; he posted a restriction order on Jim.

Jim: "God will punish you by the New Year!" he told him before his departure from the crime scene.

Not surprisingly on December 26th, 2009 (Jim's birthday) the longest and the deepest snow hit the East Coast of USA. The three feet high snow blanket did not let go for next three months. Jim was able to bring the powers of El Nina, the sister of El Nino (both climate changers).

Realistically, Khalid couldn't keep up with the rent paying and promoting with his concept of being a "Wine and Champagne Bar." He turned to gambling at casinos at Charles Town, in West Virginia. He spent great amount on video clip to advertise his remodeled new club, all this while the snow kept falling.

God: "Good job, trigger Man!"

To continue staying in business Khalid started to develop a new scheme. He was selling shares of his business to anybody he could take phone numbers from. Once he got evicted a year later, his rolodex would reveal all his victims/share holders. He had investors from Lima club, from the parking attendant next door ($30,000), and from Charter Plan also. He was able to pay once back rent for five months with penalty with the mixed money from gambling and shareholders in October 2010. Then he got involved with a lawsuit with Raymus leasing management, which also managed and owned Lotus, Tattoo clubs and many other buildings on 15th and K streets in NW. He installed a new A/C unit for the third floor in the club and he improvement, he deserved a break in the rent! The interior improvements are tenant options, not landlord obligations! Jim had four corporations and he was fully aware of that. He had a good laugh when he saw the lame excuse posted by Khalid on his website about the lawsuit.

Jim: "Landlord takes care of exterior only; tenant is responsible for the interior! What is wrong with those doorman/promoters/owner pretenders?" He laughed. He decided to check the file of the Rogue on L club by going to ABRA on 2000 U Street, NW. The public record revealed that Khalid was not the lease holder and not the liquor license owner!

Jim: "Who is this pretender?" The file exposed that Mona Lisa, who was the mother-in-law, was the lease holder and the liquor license owner through sublease from Mansur. That puzzled Jim. He immediately shifted his attention to sue Mansur. Ironically, Khalid ran $160,000 in back rent and after a couple of court fiascos he got evicted exactly on the 13th year anniversary of Jim's opening, on the same day June 2nd, but in 2011! Do the math, Cornell U. There is no need of supercomputer here to see how exact was Jim's curse again? 6666!

24 months contain four sixes. This is the Satan's sequence 666+6 = God!

Jim had seen his Million dollars investment going to the trash in June, 2009! He even took pictures to prove that in court…

God: "13 years precisely! You are good "Mr. 008!" I can't call you Bond, or 007, the fictitious character invented by Ian L. Fleming. He wrote 11 novels and sold 100 million copies, starting with "Casino Royale" in 1952!"

Jim: "Really! I know I do factual things. I know my education in different fields is backed with licenses and certificates, but that accuracy is beyond any expectation!"

God: "Do you believe in luck?"

Jim: "Yes, but only when I am surprised."

God: "Were you surprised on June 2nd, 2011?" he was trying to be a smart ass.

Jim: "No, because I did expected it and wanted it!"

God: "You just discovered my number God's Number is 6666 sequence! Now we are on something you have been working all your life to research and to perfect your technique! That is your ability to think, to pursue and see results you want in your behalf, you called it "Quantum Thinking" or "QMCL," right? Quantum thinking leads to two results, creation or destruction, by invisible means. In 1930 the QED (quantum electrodynamics) theory was born which discovered the leptons (electron and neutrino) and electrically uncharged neutron, sibling of the proton. Later on in modern times they are talking about Sigma Bosons, Higgs bosons, beta Mesons, and Feynman diagrams. No matter what, you are ahead of them!"

Jim: "I know, but what is your explanation, dear God, my "Invisible Hand."

God: "You mastered the technique of achieving results! Most philosophies without trial and error are just theories and hypothetical. You just don't do research and don't conclude what fits your expectation. You try to change the outcome by inserting your own variables in the algorithm."

Jim: "God! The whole idea is to think out of the box. One can be very selfish or very generous, but at the end of the day it is all about "what helps you to sleep at night?" Are you happy with the results? The greatest satisfaction is when you move to miracle levels. One can be considered a Saint, while the other is placed in the crazy house for the same thing.

The difference is who can explain his/her actions with reason? When the Inquisition was torturing their Victims for heresy their main question was "How did you come to these powers? Who gave you that knowledge?" The ones who denied any knowledge was released, the ones who confessed how they acquired the knowledge were burned at the stake. The Vatican has tremendous knowledge of everything, but they prefer to hide it, revealing that knowledge would make them stripped from the great mystery surrounding them and from their power over their followers."

God: "Would you like your research and knowledge to be made public? Is that your angle to get famous and recognized?"

Jim: "Let's look at the science! Anything which is not given to the people with explanation is considered magic and paranormal phenomena. That leads to shamanism and UFOs and government cover up. I write this so the common person can't be afraid to become successful, to change his/her destiny, to solve his own problems and to not depend on others. I need my legacy recognized, but not to be famous for selfish reasons."

God: "If everyone becomes like you, then the miracles will become normal and the common things will be miracles! The whole universal order would need sudden adjustment."

Jim: "Then someone opposite of me will bring the Universe back to today's level, to the ignorance and to phony governments!"

Jim went to the Court house at 500 Indiana Avenue, NW. He filed the court forms to sue Mansur. He was claiming his $200,000 Mansur owed him, that was a fraction, 20% of his investment. Then the economy was in recession. He felt excited. He entered the DC Superior court this time as a plaintiff. The Superior Court is a trial court of general jurisdiction. It has divisions for Civil, Criminal, Family Court, Domestic Violence Unit, Probate and Small Claims. The irony was that he had been through most of the courts with family court and civil court remaining. Now he was exploring the civil court. He was to go through three appointments, stretched out over a forty-five day period, in which Mansur only showed up once. Jim's experience with the court system was the more the defendant would not show up, the more the plaintiff would have a chance to win!

Chapter 18

Meanwhile Jim was pressuring Raymus from Raymus Leasing, to give him his club back.

Raymus: "You got 60,000 dollars? That's what we need, four months' rent in advance, ok?"

Jim: "I have a partner! He will give you the money?"

Raymus: "Who?"

Jim: "Kamran, from Delila and Gondola in Virginia.

Raymus: "Sounds good. Bring me their financials, ok?"

Jim: "Sure!"

August 8th, 2011 the lease was signed. Jim was given the key for the club. The clause in the lease he did not like was "due diligence." That meant that at any time within three months the lease could be terminated for any reason. Kamran Sr. and Kamran Jr. were from Pakistan.

Jim: "I hope that those characters are not like Azfar from Mirrors night club, located at 33 New York Ave, NE. Just a year before Azfar (also from Pakistan) signed a lease and made Jim a GM and a partner there. Azfar was owner of Citadelle restaurant on Glebe Road in Virginia. Unfortunately, after a dispute with the new owner RGB Commercial the lease was canceled. Azfar got his deposit money back, but Jim lost his contract and position, and approximately 1.25 Million dollar potential income a year.

He was excited. He needed to create a quick promotion crew and to start booking events. He was seeing himself as the "come back businessman!" He went to a couple of clubs and he was welcomed by the doormen, security and promoters as one of the elite club owners in DC. Most of them knew him on first name basis.

Gill: "Hey, Jim! Long time! Where have you been?" she gave him a quick kiss on the cheek. She was the main hostess for newly opened hot spot Josephine's at 1000 Vermont Ave, NW; just around the corner of Zeus Lounge DC. They basically shared the same alley and the same trash containers.

Jim: "Maybe I can get some DJs and promoters from here?" he whispered to Gill, but she was kind of busy to greet and kiss other patrons.

Jamya: "Hey, are you the owner here?" She was a tall, approximately 6 foot mixed race goddess look alike, at age twenty-five. Her perfect breasts were like a plate to eat from and on Jim's throat level. Her high heels made her even taller.

Jim: "I have other location nearby. What can I do for you?"

Jamya: "Oh, my birthday is next week. I am scouting for a nice place and to get a good table price?"

Jim: "I can give you the whole club, but we are not open at least for a month. We can do one day liquor license event, but I need a guarantee of 12,000 dollars revenue."

Jamya: "Whole club? Don't make me fall in love with you now." She was living the average club goers dream to seduce a club owner. "Maybe we can work something out to wave the guarantee?" she brought her "obvious arsenal" close to Jim's chest. The long cut dress revealed her healthy body in sexual nuance.

Jim: "Are you going to take an advantage of a single temporarily club owner?" he did not pull back.

Jamya: "Here is my phone number! Let's make a deal!" She kissed him in the air next to his cheek. Her body was ready to be ravaged, but Jim stopped himself, trying to behave.

Jim: "Let's talk in quiet place. I will show you the club now, if you like?"

Jamya: "I can't leave my cousins now. Chat tomorrow, ok?" she bent over to fix her dress right in front of him. Her great ass was so inviting. Then she disappeared in the crowd occupying the dance floor.

DJ Quick Silver: "Club owner got his perks, obviously!" he laughed behind him.

David Karim: "Hey Jim! I hear you are reopening the club! Congrats!" He was the co-owner with Alain Kalantar (from the Phantom Night Club, the VIP coordinator in 2001). David was UFC (mixed martial arts) champion in the past and he and Alain were able to put a team of investors to help them start chain of lounges. Because they were sympathetic to Jim struggles, he considered them non rivals. That was very important for their survival in the business.

Not that fortunate was Mr. Dodson and Mr. Rogbin.

On Wednesday 12/02/2009 Mr. Rogbin was convicted of tax evasion. He was detained immediately, being a "flight risk." He was facing up to 10 years for not paying near $900,000.00 dollars in taxes, which later was reduced to $350,000.00 by judge Ginsburg during appeal. He also faced deportation for felony and not being an US Citizen! His lawyer Brut Maloney couldn't save him, just like he couldn't save Wesley Snipes, Michael Vick or Monica Lewinsky.

Nikias', untimely death, in September of 2009 also did help the Feds case. He was the only one current with Mr. Rogbin's affairs. Seemed the devil government needed fewer obstacles to win their case and Nikias was their last one. They used the phony calculations similar to what they did to Joe Conforte at Mustang Ranch. They did not see that Mr. Rogbin got two clubs and the money could have been deposited with a proper audit. They just saw the cash in millions lying around at his clubs, or at his home in Potomac at approximately 2 million of dollars. Rumors were that they found 4 million dollars; 3 million at his house, and 1 million at his club. Somehow 2 million were missing. He even asked the government to release his money so he could pay the $350,000.00 he owed in back taxes.

Jim: "Where is the justice here? The Government can't hold the money as "evidence" forever!" Judge Ginsburg denied that argument.

"Money seized in raid can't be used to benefit the defendant by any means." They estimated he spent 3 million, but declared only 700,000.00 dollars annual income in 2003. The government used "the cash method of proof," cash on hand against his expenditures, his 2 million dollar down payment for house at Potomac, Virginia. The true story is that any club starting capital involves investors. The investors of course give cash. Many of investors do expect profit. They will demand 300% return usually in six month period. When the government does raid a "cash cow" business, they will ask where the money came from. If the investors are LLC (hidden contributors) the government would confiscate all assets. If they discover the real investors, the government would accuse them of "money laundering." Well, then what is venture capital? That is exactly what the investors do, when they own private equity in the new business. The decriminalizing is when the government approves who the players are and call them "venture capitalists." For example Bain Capital venture capitalists were buying Lehman brothers. When they don't approve the investors they become Mr. Rogbins and Joe Confortes, and criminals!

The other story was with Mr. Dodson. He also suffered from the snow, from law suits, from stabbing around Christmas in 2009. The GM Mr. Dodson was in debt of $46,000.00 dollars. He was kicked out of the club which was in debt to the Feds by nearly one million dollars, on January 20th, 2010. In August, 2010 he filed for bankruptcy.

God: "Good job, Jim! Your rivals are out within three years of you losing your club, in bankruptcy and deportation mode! Now focus on your club!"

Jim: "I am ready for anything possible to restart my life, God!"

God: "I know you can. You got the keys to the club, but it took you four years! Time is not your friend, when it is working against you. You were ahead of the time before year 2007."

Jim: "It is interesting that I had so many "friends" before 2007. Is that because I was beneficial to them and I had money?"

God: "Yes! In USA people equate success with having a steady income, with excessive material and preferable new collection, with some government position in higher ranks, and with developers' names. There is a price for everything. Sometimes the price is your own freedom. The leverage is to show enough wealth without being offensive. The anti-trust laws were based on breaking the growth of individual monopoly capitalists like Rockefellers, JP Morgan and Andrew Carnegie in late 1800s. You were an individual they couldn't control or to write new laws for. They just used your own management and partners to break you. The "friends," you are talking about were not real friends. They wanted to be you or to stop you from being you."

Jim: "Kiana was my downfall too. Instead of throwing money at her like a belly dancer in thousands, I should have been wiser with my money!"

God: "She taught you a lesson about money. Once you stop giving them their imaginary allowance, you are off their targets list."

Jim: "Everything in life has a price. Love is mixing bowl of phony security, children creation and family obligations. Most of the connecting or disconnection is based on favors and money!"

God: "The human desire is to have more in material or in pleasure means is the work of Satan. Humans foolishly excuse their actions with love or a vendetta. If one limits their drive to the most important things like "Awareness and life extension," the world would be in a completely higher state of living. We need to preserve the planet and to find other similar ones to civilize and develop. We maybe short of water and air soon, if we keep doing nuclear tests in underground and in the atmosphere!"

Jim: "I will focus on Miss Jamya and my club reopening! Ok?" He thought.

God just shook his head: "…Oh, Jim!"

An amazing thing happened that weekend.

Jamya: "Hey, Jim! I need a little time before we get involved. I have family to take care of," she lied.

Jim: "Fine! Don't forget me. Ok!" He did not believe her. She was too happy when he met her. Even she sent him a picture. She told him she lived in Richmond.

Jamya: "My priority is my sister and she is in the hospital." She may have told a good lie, but to the wrong person. Jim felt she was testing his patience.

Jim: "I could be a part of your family. We can start the process by getting to know each other and date?" He could have said that to a deaf person. Liars don't need convincing.

Jamya: "Listen! If you don't understand my situation we can go our separate ways now?" She became the bitch she was. In reality she got a few more phone numbers from four different guys and the "sick Sister," was a delay mechanism to keep the men on the waiting line.

Jim: "Anybody put me on the back burner will get hurt! I am not to be played with or to be ignored."

Jamya: "Are you threatening me?"

Jim: "God punishes people like you. I am just giving you a warming. Expect earthquakes, hurricanes and flood at the area, which is surrounding you. You are now a target and anyone who is taking your attention away from me!"

Jamya: "You should see a doctor. That sounds crazy! I will delete your number."

Jim: "God will delete you! You can't block text messages. I will be in quiet mode now. Watch the news and suffer!" He noticed the date. It was August 10th, 2011.

It was beginning of God's wrath, triggered by Jim.

Read this Cornell University and curious readers.

The news predictably came soon. Some two weeks later, on August 24th at 1.51 pm Jim was walking near McPherson Square subway station when he felt the ground lifting one foot. He thought there was a bomb explosion in the underground subway; then he saw people running out of buildings near the White House.

Jim: "I am not talking to anybody. They maybe terrorists?" he went to the nearest restaurant in the hotel Sofitel on Vermont Ave., NW. At the bar he met with about twenty puzzled tourists and locals mixed in front of the giant TV.

Monaem, the F&B manager: "Relax! It was an earthquake. Ok?" He was screaming, but he was generally ignored.

Anchorwoman: "An earthquake with magnitude 5.8 hit Mineral, VA."

Jim: "That is 35 miles NW of Richmond! That's where that, bitch, Miss Jamya, is from!" her name reminded him of some Playboy centerfold. After Kiana left him heartbroken and poor all women got a new name "Bitch!"

Anchorwoman: "The depth of the earthquake was four miles and its affect caused shakes felt from Miami, Fl., to Portland, Maine, and to Columbus, Ohio. It flooded the Pentagon, started a fire at the US

Senate, it shut down two nuclear reactors at nearby North Anna power plant."

God: "DeJa vu! You are doing your "thing" again! I am on your side, buddy! That earthquake is the biggest ever to occur in Virginia, just like the biggest earthquake in the Indian Ocean in forty years on 12/26/2004, your birthday! Then you were pissed at Kiana, now you are pissed at Jamya!"

Satan: "I guess you like and hate those 2 ladies at the same time?"

Jim: "Shut up! You are supposed to make me happy? I have more work to do here," he was now in the revenge mode (all disasters end in three). The bad news kept pouring. A major hurricane was brewing in Atlantic Ocean. It started in the Caribbean as tropical storm Irene, paralleled offshore of Hispaniola and after four land falls in the Bahamas with wind speeds of 120 mph, and it was classified category three! Irene reached southeastern Virginia on August 28. It caused fifty six deaths, major flooding in Virginia, New Jersey and New York and Vermont.

God: "Can you calm down? This is the seventh costliest hurricane in USA history at approximately 16 billion dollars!"

Jim: "Love cost even when under control! Ignorance cost more!"

Satan: "You are getting weaker! In 2004 the death toll was 300,000 people!"

Jim: "Yeah, but here is closer to home and the target is fresh. I just sent her text message about my quantum powers!"

God: "I know you and I know you will not be happy with a little earthquake and flood. More revenge is coming, once you get emotional."

Jim: "God! I am not trying to compete with Satan. I mean well unless someone crosses me the wrong way. All I need is a name, face and location to get the destruction or creation started. There are seven billion people on earth with unique fingerprints. Basically, everyone can be a target!"

Satan: "What makes you any different than the seven billion living souls? You can be a target too."

Jim: "I was and I am a target. Anyone of my caliber, in my league, should be. That is in physical reality. There are more complicated encounters in the spiritual or afterlife world. Getting to my level of being it is not coincidence. It took Moses 40 days to get God to reveal his orders to him and to his Jewish followers; and to write the Ten Commandments. It took 40 days for David to prepare himself to fight

Goliath. Jesus fasted 40 days in the wilderness, and he was seen in the Earth 40 days after his crucifixion. It took me 40 years to get to need to write this book. Seems that to get to God's number 40 (the sequence of spirals in form of 6, to complete a perfect cone, to enter the vortex, to communicate in a wormhole in warp speeds in dimensions where time does not exist, and to return to Earth level of being and teaching the Awareness), it does take 40 years! Many fear God, but how many actually meet and talk with God? Answer that Cornell University, please… Ohh, you can't? Then hear this. For the mortals to get to deity levels the test is to fight and climb to the 40 levels of torture in the Quantum Pyramid. Every step is a challenge in self endurance, in education, to overcome the everyday worries and fears that life is throwing at you, to forget the greed, to ignore seduction, and to purify yourself to enter the parallel universe of God, while living the Earth's life. After Life the soul will move to Quantum Universe and to Cosmos, the next two dimensions. The lesson here is to be aware of the living to the fullest and in higher dimensions while enjoying the everyday Earth encounters; jobs, food, people."

Jim was concerned about the club. He checked it in the middle of hurricane blasting through DC. The debris from the 14 story Charter Plan building kept falling on the lower three story club's roof. They made small holes and caused three minor leaks in the office and around the 3rd and second floor bars.

Jim: "Hey, Kamran! The earthquake and Hurricane Irene did not damage the club. I plugged in a couple of holes."

Kamran: "What? We got leaks? I will talk to Raymus. He gave us a bad roof." He was almost hysterical.

Jim: "He did not. That was an "Act of God" event. It happened after the lease signing. He will fix it. Just be nice to him. Ok?"

Kamran: "We just gave him 60,000 dollars. I am a bit skeptical about the whole deal, ok?" He hanged up.

Jim: "I did maybe overkill? In the process of getting even with Miss Jamya I also destroyed my own club?" he thought. He decided to pursue Mansur and to recover his loses. The whole economy was down since 2008 and around 5 million homes would be in foreclosed by 2011, with one million lost in 2011.

Chapter 19

Jim went to court three times. Mansur didn't show up. Meanwhile, Kiana kept calling and lying.

Jim: "Who is this?" He answered to the private caller.

Kiana: "Jim Walker! You don't know my voice?" she acted upset.

Jim: "I hear you now. How are you?"

Kiana: "I am great!" she was thinking about her next lie.

Jim: "I am expecting good news. Tell me one." He was half aroused. He was surprised that he still had feelings towards her no matter how much he was trying to suppress it. After all she was his real, love.

Kiana: "I have been thinking later about settling with someone. I have a three year old son, his name is Leon and he needs a father. Also I miss you somewhat."

Jim: "What is the catch? You never do something without a reason."

Kiana: "You know Jim! The best friends make the best lovers!"

Jim: "I guess?" He almost dropped the phone. He couldn't believe that this cheater was even considering him a friend, even less a lover.

Kiana: "I am coming to DC, but first you need to notify me when you are close to $35,000 or to $40,000 in the bank, ok!"

Jim: "You know I will reopen my club soon and Mansur owes me money!"

(Not mentioning the $200,000 lawsuit). He learned not to tell important news to everyone.

Kiana: "Great! I will call you soon."

Jim: "Yes, but every six months! How Leon will accept me; as a stepfather? Where is his real father?"

Kiana: "Oh. I haven't been with him for years. He got two kids of his own. I hardly can take care of mine and then to take care of two more!" She lied so masterfully.

Jim: "So, it will be three of us?"

Kiana: "Yes! And don't talk about anybody else, ok?" She was getting in higher tones and Jim sensed it was time to hang up. "You don't know, but my mom died recently and I don't have many great friends left."

Jim: "Sorry to hear that. Bye! I love you!" He really was.

Kiana: "I love you too Jim Walker!" she said it fast and she was definitely lying. Jim felt good even he did not trust her.

Satan: "Now you feel good, don't you?" He was laughing.

Jim: "How true love hurts me and fake love makes me feel good?"

Satan: "Ask 99% of married people what they think of "love?" They will tell you it hurts and it is very restrictive."

Jim: "So, why do they get married then? Is it not better to stay in relationship but not marriage?"

Satan: "Marriage provides false security. Women want benefits. They don't want to feel like whores that they truly are. I am laughing at the grooms all the time at weddings, when they say "I do!"

God: "Women cause more troubles than benefits. Why a man should pay by a judge's order alimony for eighteen years, but the same judge cannot order the same woman to obey her husband's sexual desires for the same duration? That shows that marriage is a devil thing and giving birth is the way women control men."

Jim: "Maybe men should rent women like they rent cars (for a day or for a week)?"

God: "That sounds more rational and more like a recreation!"

Jim: "Government labels that as prostitution, but I call them "stresses relieve nursing." Do you know how much crime was reduced by just having sex?"

Satan: ".... And they say I am bad? Give me a break, conservative hypocrites! And they say God is great because of no sex?"

God: "Jim! Play the game of life. Eat, drink, smoke, and pleasure yourself, but don't forget you have a higher purpose here on Earth and out-there, in the Universe and Cosmos!"

Jim: "Ok, "TIH."

The club's reopening was supposed to be the first week of November, 2011.

Jim noticed the hesitation of Kamran as awkward. He had whole crew lined up from cooks to promoters to bartenders and DJs.

Jim: "Raymus, have you heard from Kamran?"

Raymus: "No, but I know he has to pay his taxes. Real Estate tax and insurance is added to the rent of $14,000.00 per month. I need to see him ASAP."

Jim: "He kept quiet and I have not seen him entering the club since he signed the lease. I have the crew to operate the club now and the sound and liquor ready."

Raymus: "Just like the old times, huh?"...

Jim: "Yeah, just with the exception of the missing lease holder, Kamran!"

A week later Jim received the disappointing phone call from Raymus.

Jim: "What is the news, Raymus?"

Raymus: "Your man took his money and bailed out!"

Jim: "Really? I was expecting that, but I was not sure if he would do that?"

Raymus: "Well. He did it! We are very disappointed. He used the clause "due diligence" to bail out."

Jim: "I am pissed too. Thought we can open before New Year?"

Raymus: "You have been talking to me about reopening since 2007. I don't want to see your referrals again. Bye!" He hung up.

Jim went to court on December 9th, 2011. He was supposed to see the judge for the final decision for case no. 2010 CA 009100B.

Judge Gregory E. Jackson: "My judgment is for the defendant. The compensation is in the amount of $200,000."

Jim: "Thank you, your honor!" Mansur did not show up again and he lost the case. Now the final nail in the coffin was to be hammered in.

Satan: "Call your future wife and tell her the good news!"

Jim: "I think I should collect my money and then I will call her, ok?"

Satan: "The sooner you call her, the sooner she will come to live with you. She is asking only for 35,000 dollars after all. You are awarded 200,000 dollars. Call her now!"

Jim: "Satan, I do not have her number. The only number I have is her mother's house and she is deceased. That was a number I have since 2006!"

Satan: "Dial it!" He meant well.

Jim: "Great! We will be one happy family!" he found the old number in a small file where he had Kiana's social Security number and her address at Warner Robbins, Georgia.

Jim: "Hello!" as soon someone picked up the phone on the other side,

"Kiana," he screamed at the phone.

Mr. Julius: "No sir! This is her husband! May I help you?"

Jim: "You are her husband? And I assume Leon's father?" He almost fainted, but nothing could surprise him coming from this deceitful, evil woman.

Mr. Julius: "Yes. We have lived together for the last seven years. Can I help you and who is this?" he sounded like a king and Jim's voice was lowered to whispering tones. He almost started to cry. He decided to pause and to hide his emotions. It sounded like a DeJa Vu with DP "the Don." He remembered the squeaking bed at 3636 16th Street at those early hours of November in 2005. Now six years later seemed like nothing had changed.

Jim: "You are lying! She was with DP until 2008!"

Mr. Julius: "DP the prisoner? He kept trying to steal her from me and raped her many times. He lured her away with marijuana and telling her about her gang loyalty forever? Why are you so knowledgeable, Mr. Love Detective?" He was getting irritated.

Jim: "Listen, Mr. Julius! She is a sociopathic liar. You may have a baby by her, but she constantly cheats on men, like me and you! She just called me a couple of weeks ago to marry me, and to give her 35,000 dollars, ok?"

Mr. Julius: "You sound like you are disappointed. She is all about business.

I caught her with DP so many times. She mentioned something about a rich white sponsor she left in DC. Is that you, Jim?"

Jim: "Yes. That is me. So, I am a "sponsor," but not really rich now. She left me broke after she wiped out all my accounts."

Mr. Julius: "I can't help you get your money back, sorry!"

Jim: "Mr. Julius! She is lying to you and everyone. She is using the baby to find a new sponsor, you!"

Mr. Julius: "I know! Everything has a price. You know, she is a student, so..."

Jim: "She cost me $250,000! That is beyond being a "sponsor!"

Mr. Julius: "Hey, Kiana! Someone is looking for you!" He turned around toward the stunned Kiana, who just returned from doing the laundry. In the background was Leon, who was following her.

Kiana: "Who is that?" She grabbed the phone from her husband.

Jim: "So you are married? And you want to come to DC to marry me too?"

Kiana: "Why are you calling my mother's phone? I told you never to call me. You have to wait for my calls!"

Jim: "...To wait for your "blocked" calls? I was about to tell you about my $200,000 law suit against Mansur. The judgment was against him. I won!"

Kiana: "I don't care about your money, mister!"

Jim: "Since when? You just asked me to save $35,000 and then you will see me? I got $200,000 awarded."

Kiana: "Do you know what Jim? I used you and you are asking to be used again?

I don't love you and you make me hate you now for disturbing my home!"

Jim: "Home, where you use another man by making yourself pregnant with his child?"

Kiana: "I work and I am studying to be a doctor! You lost your club and I lost my interest. This guy is providing me with what I want! Now leave us alone. Save your money for the next Kiana, ok? Bye!"

Jim: "... But I love you?" he screamed just before she was to hang up.

Kiana: "I know. Bye…" her voice got lower. She was about to cry mostly over losing expected money and her scheme not working and her cover blown between the two guys.

Jim: "Thank you, Satan, great advice!" He was happy to hear her voice, but what a price to pay? "She is still was driving my 560SEL Benz and she is having sex with this guy for the last seven years? And I am "sponsoring," her life style, from the very beginning, getting tortured by the government and by ABRA and dealing with crooks like Mansur? I should have helped my family in Bulgaria instead and so many other people who really needed my help!"

God: "Now you know why you should not listen to Satan! The more you dig in someone who never respected you the more dirt revealed. It is like the peeling of a rotten onion, anyway you peel it stinks."

Jim: "I am somewhat relieved that I know the truth, but my love is unchangeable. I am like Don Quixote of La Mancha, I will pursue that Dulcinea de Toboso to the end of my life."

Satan: "I did my best to advise you till now! You are on your own emotionally from now on. You will miss me! Bye!"

God: "Son! Do you want to be liked and respected and to be immortalized?

Jim: "Yes, God!"

God: "Then you keep writing that documentary. Finish that book ASAP."

Jim was puzzled. He was dating the President's Obama assistant Beverly, just a year before. She was a smart and beautiful thirty year old African American from Michigan. Her medium build frame and perfect body was a constant temptation. She resided just one block over from M street North. She was always hungry. Jim would take her out to small dinners and ice cream places. She loved "Fro yo," (frozen yogurt) and there was one on P street across newly opened "Whole Foods" supermarket.

Jim: "What do you do for Obama?" He did not like any of his socialist ideas. "I just left those people with same ideas in Bulgaria thirty years ago!"

Beverly: "Oh, I am in his advisory team with Valerie Jarrett, his mentor."

Jim: "Tell Obama to fix the economy, not to waste more time on "Health Care." It has been two years already." That was in November 2010 and Jim was more concerned with enjoying sex, with that perfect tigress than the economy, but he said it any way. Amazingly in the speech in the State of the Union, in late January, 2011 very little was said about "Obama care" and a lot of his monologue was on economy!

Jim: "What does it take to get into the President's mind?" He felt like Rasputin in 1907, which influenced Tsar Nicolas II decisions and basically brought the Russian October revolution in 1917.

He felt he could change the world history a year before (and many years before and after), but he couldn't pick the brains of that master thief Kiana! He constantly thought of her on the back of his genius mind, but he knew she could be just as dead. That was his feeling of lost love. He hated her and loved her at the same time. That perfect storm was helping him create other disasters around the world. Greatest earthquake of magnitude 9 hit Japan march 11th, 2011, followed by tsunami, costing 309 billion dollars. Nuclear plant at Fukushima was not able to cool off the six reactors for almost six months. Contaminated food of near 100 products was stopped as exports to USA and Europe. The earthquake at Mineral, VA and the hurricane Irene were to follow in August, not to forget the eviction of The Rogue on L Lounge in between!

God: "Your anger is unstoppable, but I don't mind punishing the bad guys!"

Jim: "Is Japan bad guy?"

God: "They are renegades from China. They used to be superpower! They did bad things to Port Arthur in Russia. They started the revolution. You are in the USA, because you run away from the communists. Japan basically made you defect from your own country! They owe you, son!"

Jim: "I know which city owes me the most also!"

God: "Where?"

Jim: "Who gives the most, owes the most, New York of course!"

God: "Don't tell me that is my next project?" he almost protested. "What happened there?"

Jim: "First, Contessa was nice to me, and then she turned out dead. Second, Mr. Smith was nice to me, and then he turned out gay! Third, Mr. Elliot made me a Captain, but he never paid me."

God: "Molly made you an owner of Bellini's restaurant of the Presidents, then she betrayed you! Is DC the next target for us?" He laughed.

Jim: "Yes, sir! I am the protector of places I go. Once someone steps on me and I move away, the city or the location becomes a target..."

God: "I agree with you being a protector to your most dedicated friends and valuables. I am surprised of how you were able to keep your equipment worth of 500,000 dollars after so much drama with evictions, club closures, and unstable income. Your credit is nonexistent! You don't have anything to show to the world like a house you own, family you created money in the bank, diamonds or gold, or any land development! But you have powers nobody has at present on the earth. And the most important of all it is you can explain them through esoteric sciences, where the science and spiritual world intermix!"

Jim: "Knowledge is more important than any wealth! I live in quantum reality where I can be anything I want, while most people live in materialistic reality!"

God: "Jesus was a carpenter! You are Jim "the Thinker" and my "trigger man." You know Noah's Ark. He built the ship 300 cubits long, 50 wide, and 30 high. He saved his family, all valuable animals, except the unicorn? Next flood is on May, 21st, 2019. You know the Earth can't support seven billion people. The only humans with your Awareness will survive; approximately half a billion. You will be their leader to the high mountain, then to Quantum Cone vortex!"

Jim: "What shall I save? I have two friends, equipment and three cars."

God: "You will own all the cars, airplanes, space ships and the Galaxy! Keep what you have, but don't dwell on those things. Those things show more of a character than real meaning of any material collateral. That in the banks system it is called "stress test," in the military is "endurance," and for you it is "discipline." It is amazing that "Citigroup" did outperformed the giants on Wall Street "J.P. Morgan Chase," "Morgan Stanley" and "Golden Sachs."

Chapter 20

2012 was a presidential year. Jim was not fond of Obama at all. He was also turned off by the Republican's greed for power. It reminded him when Robert Dole was selected out of many republican candidates and he lost easily against Bill Clinton, by 10% in 1996. Jim predicted that the 13 clowns are going to lose eventually against the seasoned and crooked Barack Obama. It was amazing to see how the fractured Republican Party was looking for the best candidate to win against the best orator, on earth! Every week someone was "the flavor" with some great points on economy, immigration, women health care. The combine cost of 2012 election would be 6.5 billion dollars!

Jim: "Where is the bad economy?" He was amused of their lies. After all who was really telling the truth anymore?

It was beginning of mid May, 2012. He met a lady coming out of "Lotus" night club in DC.

Jim: "Hello, gorgeous!"

Elaine: "Hey. How are you?"

Jim: "I am great! How was it in the "Lotus" club?" he saw a lady and man trailing her at about a ten foot distance. "Maybe here is my lucky break? This lady looks perfect," he observed her peripherally. She was twenty-five years old with long enough red dress to show her full muscular legs and flat stomach and natural full breasts to complete the statue. She was a tall African American lady and she was kind discrete not wanting to attract too much attention on the Street but her soft and young voice had enough subliminal sexual innuendo to start World War III.

Elaine: "I was bored. My best friend dragged me there, but we the ladies were disappointed of the low quality of men! Nobody was trying to talk to us?"

Jim: "Many gay guys go there or they are simply broke! The owner Michael Romeo is my friend."

Elaine: "I have to go back to my company, but we can chat some other time. Here is my contact information." Then she walked away.

Jim: "Nice meeting you, Elaine!" He texted her right away to make sure it was not a fake number.

Elaine: "Likewise! I'll be in touch."

Jim tried to text her or call her once or twice a week. There was no response.

He decided to move on. He met a beautiful lady at the age twenty-three living near 1234 Massachusetts Ave., NW. That was the place he used to live when he was dating the Cherry Blossom Queen Mia in 1986!

Tiffany: "Hey! How are you?" she was very friendly. They had met many times before, but it was their first real conversation.

Jim: "I used to live here!" He pointed toward 1234 Mass. "I am trying to rent there again!"

Tiffany: "Good! My building is more expensive!"

Jim: "You look beautiful. I finally had a chance to tell you."

Tiffany: "Thank you! What do you do?" She was heading to her building entrance.

Jim: "I am a writer! I write my documentary and I explain everything through the Bible, modern sciences and metaphysics."

Tiffany: "That is far out, but I can relate to the Bible. Science is not my field."

Jim: "Well. I connect everything as esoteric science (and beyond) and I place my personal experience in life to back the facts. Theory is nothing if not proven. I do that in my documentary."

Tiffany: "Here is my information. This is my e mail and mobile phone. Maybe we can chat more over dinner?" She disappeared in the building. Jim noted the day was June 2nd, 2012. He always remembered that day. It was the 14th year's anniversary of opening his first club Randevu. Was that the lucky break he finally needed? He wanted to be married, happy, maybe have some children soon? Everything Satan did want him to have.

God: "I think you are on better path to fame with me. Leave women alone, ok!"

Jim was puzzled. He found the right answer very soon.

It was June 13th, 2012 at 9.52 am. He sent e mail to her.

Tiffany: "I think you are very interesting person. I received your e mail. I agree with most of the things you say. I am not a scientist, but everything you say about God makes sense. What about the antimatter and antigravity? You talk about the fear at CERN about end of the world when antimatter is created (year 2011). That is like playing with the Creator!"

Jim: "I create antimatter and antigravity every day. I don't use 10 billion dollars protons smasher, but I just use my meditation technique and I think in quantum dimensions."

Tiffany: "You are ahead of our time. I can't even make conversation and even less to argue with you about any, "quanta."

Here was their e mail correspondence:

Jim:

"I am thankful for your input. I have done my research the last 40 years and probably for the last 20 years I observed the trends in medicine and science following my predictions or analyses. Just a year ago at CERN the atom breakers engineers created less than an ounce of antimatter (or less); negative mass. They thought it world be the end of the world? I do create anti-matter almost every day and believe me, antigravity and anti-matter works for me in positive or negative way. My enemies always lose against me and my friends prosper with me. Remember the Bible story about the flood and the guy who took the essentials to survive with him, Noah's Ark?

I read the Bible in reverse. What are they trying to say? Are our lives predestined or are we the pilots of our own ships? I think it is a mix? God and pilots communicate and as result we control somewhat the direction of our life. God with our request make things happen better, or our way on our request. Most people talk about GOD but they don't know how to communicate with GOD! If things go our way, we say "thank you GOD," if they do not, we ask "why you are not helping me GOD?"

The way to create is to advance one's self, to a level of higher thinking and to jump in front of the crowd and to show them, not to talk to them what the Bible says.

My book is mostly about my research in phenomenon of how God helps us, even when we are not aware of it. Then I write formulas how it works. Then I do demonstrate how it works. I did cured people who can't walk, from brain tumor; I removed back pain chiropractors can't cure. I fix that, but that is nothing abnormal. Anybody who thinks and acts like me can do the same. Physicians and spiritual leaders tell you what you want to hear. I do my thing and it works, not necessarily the general society way. That is what makes me unique. I am not selfish. I can teach and share, also I can listen for any improvements. I have achieved many miracles, the last 20 years, but not because I was good! I was just not afraid to take chances! The means were different, the results were amazing. That is why I write this book."

Sent from my i Phone

On Jun 13, 2012, at 9:52 AM, Tiffany <Tif359@hotmail.com> wrote:

"Hi Jim,

Thank you for giving me the chance to read some of your work. I was really impressed. It has actually encouraged me to research and deepen my education on quite a few topics. For instance, I have always heard of the 7 chakras, but I haven't deeply studied or attempted a more than superficial understanding of what those really are.

I am sure you are going to be on the New York Times best sellers list real soon! I think it is really wonderful that you have spent the time and energy to do the analysis and critical thinking that your book required. Thank you again for letting me, experience some of this work.

I am sure this is a book that a lot of people will really be fascinated with. I think so many people are searching for answers and if, you have the formulas, that's amazing. It sounds like you have helped a lot of people over the years. It is great that you are willing to share what you learned with others. I am glad you took the chances, to experiment and learn. I am really excited for all the success you will surely have to come in the future.

Best Wishes,
Tiffany"

Jim: "Hey. Forget about the science. You said you were single, how about a date?"

Tiffany: "Jim, I can't! My sister died recently. I can't open emotionally to anyone now. I wish you good luck with the book, ok!" She almost started to cry.

Jim: "Ok. I hope you will recover eventually and we can meet again. Sorry about your sister! Bye."

The e mail was documentation for his advanced thinking. He predicted the next news.

Peter Higgs: "I discovered the Higgs boson," he announced on July 4th, 2012. That was 3 weeks after Jim's e mail to Tiffany talking about the same thing and without ever seen the Feynman diagrams!

God: "You guys are good! You started your research simultaneously at mid 60s and you came to the same conclusions! The difference is that you, Jim did it without any financial support and you used different techniques and no more than 10 books altogether in research. Peter Higgs is a theoretical physicist. He is famous for his suggestion of broken symmetry in electroweak theory (QFD) and the existing of neutrally charged mass (boson H) and after the protons collide there will be two quarks W +\- with opposite charges. You, Jim have already discovered the annihilation formula.

Mater + Antimatter = Annihilation.

The annihilation leads to creating of neutrino and releases energy in Pair of quanta. Basically, you were into QED (quantum electro dynamics) since 1960s."

Jim: "Yes, since 1969. Thanks to yoga book by Eva Rushpaul. In my opinion Mr. Higgs reminds me of a Police sketch artist who recreates the event, which already happened. For example once the fission was on the drawing table, the scientists used it and created the Atomic Bomb and they used it on Hiroshima and Nagasaki on August 6 and on August 9 in 1945. Near 250,000 people were killed. While the theory of Einstein, Edward Teller and Oppenheimer was confirmed, these charlatans like Pakistani Abdus Salam and British Peter Higgs were begging for more funds to prove the Big Bang theory."

God: "True! It is like to reinvent the wheel!"

Jim: "Ancient philosophers explained the events in Universe with different words, but with similar results. The matter is created all the time and it changes all the time. Do we agree or disagree that we are the only thinking God like creatures, we need to bring the Awareness up to speed, if we don't, blame yourself, not me!" He was proven right soon not only once, but three times within next six months (with Debby, Isaac, and Sandy hurricanes).

June 15th, 2012 Elaine contacted him via text message.

Elaine: "The number I gave you belongs to my sister. Please, contact me on my new number (850) ......thinking of you, Jim!"

Jim: "Ok! Can we chat live?"

Elaine: "No. My mom is here; maybe later?"

Jim: "Hmmm. Ok!"

That "later chat" never happened.

Jim: "Can I come to visit?" he grew suspicious.

Elaine: "Sure, but I will be there at the end of July. We can chat more without family around."

Jim: "What do you do all day with your family?"

Elaine: "We eat; sleep and we go to the beach! I live near Live Oak, Florida."

Jim: "Ok. Can we find time to chat live? What can I do for you to make you happy?" he was exposing himself for the predictable question of, "money?"

It always worked.

Elaine: "We will celebrate my sister's birthday. We are going to the beach and we will rent a hotel for Friday and Saturday night. Any donation would be helpful!" Jim: "Gas and hotel is pricey these days. Don't put that entire burden on me, please! We just met and you were not even talking/texting me for a month! Let me see what I can do to help? Do you have any numbers in mind?" He did not believe what he was reading. "They are all the same! Damn it!"

Elaine: "$300?"

Jim: "I can send you $175 for now to see if you will get it? Then I will send you the rest, ok!"

Elaine: "I appreciate that! Here is my name and the city to send it to.., Live Oak, FL."

Jim: "Give me thirty minutes," he heard himself saying the same words he used to say to Kiana, but they were lovers. Elaine would have made a great replacement, if she was genuine!

He sent the money. He texted her "did you receive the money." The amazing thing was that she did not answer till Monday, some three days after! What is with Americans and money? They are like actors. "Nice" till they get it and "mean," after they see the money. Kiana was the epidemy of the "money" game and ignorance, and the "minus 4th Dimension." Liars live in the world of darkness, in the underworld, zombies like. Phone texting and e mails were the best invention by Satan, and given to them.

Elaine: "Yes, thanks!" The same person wrote the strangest message later on in the evening.

Elaine: "It is Aaron! We are outside. Open the door, please!"

Jim: "What the hell," he texted her back, "who is Aaron? A man, I have been talking to some guy all this time? And he made me send money probably to someone with stolen ID? Maybe I was used in some outsourcing game, where someone's real number was given to a gang of crooks, who impersonated good looking women and they extort money through texting all kinds of seductive messages?" he continued texting.

Elaine/Aaron: "What is your problem? I am a woman! You want to hear my voice? I can make someone call you and sound like a woman!"

Jim: "You seem very creative when asking for money, but very mean when the same guy asks you to verify anything you do?"

Elaine/Aaron: "You have a nice life, ok?"

Jim: "If you do not return my money something bad will happen to you." Elaine/Aaron: "Are you threatening me?"

Jim: "God will punish you 1000 fold! You are a man and not a good one either! You are a liar. If I was you I would look for another state. Now you became a target of my powers and God's wrath!"

Elaine/Aaron: "You will be an old lonely man. You do not understand women!"

Jim: "I will be recognized and never poor and never lonely! Bye Man!"

The news broke within 48 hours.

Anchorwoman: "Florida was hit by Tropical Depression Debby -- downgraded from a tropical storm on June 27th, 2012. Interstate I-10 was flooded with up to two feet of rising water. Twenty thousand residents were affected, many sink holes were opened and four people died. President Obama offered federal assistance."

Jim: "He is afraid that Katrina's shadow assistance by President Bush may be compared to his and it will ruin his reelection. Anyway; what I told you, God? Am I good? Interstate I-10 does split Live Oak in two!" He was proud.

God: "Yes, you are not just good! You are the best of the best! I worry about the people you are wasting your money on? Where do you find them? You are like magnet for liars and losers! Why can't you find someone I can be proud of seeing you with? Then I don't have to punish anyone and I don't have to work that hard! You know it took me six days to create the world as is, but it takes billion of years to undo my creation. Your earth encounters are weird at any dimension!"

Jim: "There is a reason I destroy my false friends. It eliminates the trash on earth, this way when I find my match, it will be less destructive."

God: "Nobody can match you in the opposite sex. They are just trying to use you. The world is full of beggars. They will use everything possible to steal your good money, brains, future income. The whole court system is based on thieves outsmarting other thieves. The biggest thief is the government, because they write the laws and the Tax Codes! You should not worry about Elaine/Aaron now. They will move from man to man, and then to women until one day the news flash will announce some terrible drama. Once someone is a thief it affects their off springs and whole generation after."

The president's campaign was heating up. The republican nominee Mitt Romney was gaining momentum. Republicans meant well but were under scrutiny about abortions, birth controls, no taxes increase for the rich, balancing the US Budget, military cuts. Jim was not a politician. He wanted the Republicans to win. He was not impressed of the VP pick Paul Ryan. He seemed to mean well on TV but when one can hear him on the radio, he did not sound like a VP; even less a President!

Mid September, 2012 Jim met a beautiful lady of mixed race. Her name was Donna. She was one of the bank managers at PNC bank on Connecticut Ave and Eye Street, NW. She was around 5'8" and she was in those "ready to marry" state of women. She was beautiful and friendly. She actually was actively seeking his friendship after he met her briefly on the way to the Farragut North subway station. At age twenty-eight she couldn't be a greater choice for everything a man could wish. She asked him out two days later.

Jim: "I work till 10 pm. Can we meet after?"

Donna: "I work out at the gym or at home after 9 pm. I usually will take a shower and I will go to sleep around 10 pm. I can usually hang out after work till 8.30 pm. Maybe I am getting old?"

Jim: "Maybe we can just chat over the phone?" He was getting irritated already.

Donna: "How is your weekend looking?" she was also uncomfortable with Jim's availability.

Jim: "I work till 11 pm! I may see you after work on Monday?"

Donna: "I tutor a young man in different subjects on Monday till 8 pm. Then I usually go home. I cannot invite you at my home, but maybe we can pick a bite nearby in Bowie?" That conversation sounded like a world peace negotiation. The difference was that nobody was agreeing on anything.

Jim: "Ok. Let us chat later on. I keep losing your signal while you are in the subway."

Donna: "Ok, I will call you before I go to sleep, Jim!"

Jim: "Ok!"

The text on Thursday was affirming her lunch availability. They went to "P.G. Clarke's" restaurant at 1600 K Street, NW. She ordered tuna salad, Jim ordered veal marsalla. The waitress was good looking but she seemed she did not belong there. Jim made a small talk with her, but he did not want to get deep into some sorry story.

Donna: "I don't drink but, can I have lemonade?"

Jim: "Make it two!" Then he started talking about Kiana.

Donna: "I will never use a man the way she used you, Jim!" she held his hand for a few seconds before devouring the tuna salad.

Jim: "You seem hungry!" he laughed.

Donna: "Ohh, I worked out last night and skipped breakfast."

Jim: "That is why you don't answer my phone calls and texts?"

Donna: "When I work out I am Amish! No gadgets!" Lunch eventually was over. She gave him a tight hug and she left with a big smile.

Donna: "Thank for the lunch!"

Jim: "Next time will be dinner!"

Donna: "Ok, bye!" She sank into PNC bank entrance.

That was the last time he saw her. He texted her on the weekend. One time she answered at 3 am in someone's SUV full of women laughing and some men voices in the background.

Jim: "Where are you?"

Donna: "We are leaving, "The Paparazzi" club."

Jim: "I am one block away. Can we meet for a minute? I miss you already!"

Donna: "We planned to hang out with my friends today. I miss you too. Let's chat some other time, ok?"

Man's voice: "Who is this?" It was a deep and unfriendly. It sounded like a jealous type. The line went dead. Jim called a couple of times. The phone was turned off. He texted, but that was like shooting in a barrel.

Jim: "Text me when you get home, ok!" He sent his last message and he went to sleep. She never returned his texts.

Jim: "I guess she found a new boyfriend? So much for work out and lunch dates."

Black men had their ways with black women. They hardly spent money on them, but they had them cornered in bed faster than any other race. Jim was always wondering of the black race code of conduct. He was able to tap into their sexuality, but not into their ways of thinking. Washington, DC was the number one city of cheaters in USA. He got his fair share of sex because of that and much more than any white man because of his charming approach. Money was a factor too, mostly. He always acted like he is well off. It worked most of the time at least for short dating periods. Location always counted. He was living at the Penthouse of 1424 X Street, NW, next to his old club and even he did not have it, the mass impression was he still had something to do with it. Yes, he did until Kamran screw up the lease in 2011. The winning of the court case against Mansur and the loosing of the club pushed him to write his documentary.

Next two stories would be a case study for MIT and Cornell U, but Jim would answer their thesis research in advance, without their 3 Billion dollars grants.

He never heard from Elaine, but he knew she was coming in the end of August for her studies. It was amazing to see how the weather changed just before the Republican Convention in Tampa, Florida. Hurricane Isaac delayed the Monday opening on August 27th.

Jim: "God, I hope my disappointment towards Elaine would not affect the outcome of the election?" He was happy to see the polls next day breaking almost even for the Republicans and Democrats. It was only 1 percent leading for Obama. That was considered improvement for Romney, entering the race just six months before. The Obama machine was with six years experience and they knew how to brainwash the old, the young, the ethnic minorities, the women, the men married to Democrat women, the unions, the federal workers, the state employees.

When Donna started to play the same game of being standoffish, Jim knew what was next.

Jim: "Donna! I created the last two hurricanes Debby and Isaac. I do not want something to happen to you, ok?" Donna did not answer his text.

Jim: "Ignorant ass! Watch the news. You are dealing not with me, but with God now."

Hurricane Sandy was the deadliest Atlantic Storm with 285 people dead; it was second costliest in US history with 75 billion in damages.

God: "If they used their 6.5 billion dollars on preventing disaster instead cutting each other throats, the politicians could have stopped all the hurricanes."

Jim: "I heard scientists (Chinese) can change artificially the temperature to delay rain."

God: "Yes. They also can change the barometric pressure. The lowest the barometer reading, the worst the weather is. If the pressure is increased the direction and the speed of the hurricane can be changed."

Jim: "Rumors are that the Russians are experimenting with creating more hurricanes off the East Coast of the USA. Maybe the USA should do the opposite and do counter measures?"

God: "They will start climate wars! One, who controls the climate, controls the economy. One, who is aware of the Cosmos, can change its direction. Why is the Earth or a little hurricane so important to you? You are bothering me, trying to impress Kiana, Elaine and now Donna? You are much bigger than them, than any Government, even than the Universe! You know how to think and I am accessible to only you through your secret key to Awareness."

Jim: "Father God! The Creator and equally The Destroyer! I wanted the Republicans to win. You are doing too much. I asked you to punish Donna in Bowie. I saw you expanded the Sandy's front to New York (900 miles) and you did enough damage in Bowie."

God: "We have to start somewhere!" Seemed he could not contain his own powers. Sometimes Jim was wondering?

"Was God = Satan x 10?" The answer is yes. Satan had limited powers; God did not, good or bad.

Jim: "I am glad we are on good terms, God!"

God: "I am you sub consciousness, young man! You pull different strings, I answer you accordingly!"

Jim: "You just helped Obama to be reelected!" He got angry.

God: "Nobody is perfect, but you are the perfect trigger man! I did not believe we could pull off three hurricanes in six months?"

Jim: "Yes! We started with Debby, second was Isaac, the last one was Sandy! God, you are a perfect father! Irene was bad too, in august 2011. I see you do not take sides in politics."

God: "Now what are you going to do? Your book is finished!"

Jim: "The history stops here for a while. I can't tell you my predictions but if I am not happy, and you know what happens next, right? The history will correct (balance) itself."

God: "Yes, I know, my Oracle!" he laughed. "I can use some vacation for a while!"

Jim: "Yes. Till October, 2013!" His mind finally was at rest. He started looking for publishers to tell his story.

God: ".... and a movie also!"

Jim: "... on my own island or continent? I thought you left, God?"

God: "Yes, don't forget to spread the knowledge and Awareness, bye, son!"

Jim: "Bye, Father!"

History will show later on that government shutdowns and Health Care disasters in the month, Oct., 2013.

Next disasters would be; twice snowstorm in "HotLanta/Atlanta" and predicted earthquake in January 2014; snowstorms in San Diego, California and Arizona on New Years Eve of 2015, predicted and occurred with his 100% accuracy, not to forget the one month and 7 feet high snowfall in Boston. All this because his emotional demands were ignored or seriously downplayed by the "the all demanding, but not delivering socially deficient" USA "ladies" pretending to be…

President Obama will address the US Coast Guard Academy graduating class in New London, Connecticut on May 20th, 2015.

Contrary to few examples shown above he will talk about global warming, melting Arctic ice, and rising the ocean level by a foot in a century, caused by carbon dioxide?

Explain how and where Super Storm Sandy arrived, dear Commander-in-Chief. Not to differ much from him Secretary of Department of State John Kerry will blame the fossil fuels burning on pollution, but he will invest in 50 oil stocks, while preaching for clean, solar energy substitutes.

While both will be overly reactive on usage of present and past energy, they both would conclude that the draught will be reason of the rise of terrorist organizations of Boko Haram and ISIS and mass migration.

To defuse the doubt of all readers Jim Walker would have his Chi force detected by TSA body check scanner at Frankfurt airport in Germany on June 01st, 2015.

The officer will be puzzled, never seen that before.

TSA Officer: "What is this yellow square at your solar plexus, sir?"

Jim: "That is low radiation, gamma rays, chi energy?

TSA Officer: "What is Chi?"

Jim: "That is achieved from matter-antimatter annihilation. Meditation…Hydrogen to Helium conversion through breathing…."

TSA Officer: "Whatever… That is far out for me. Please proceed, but see a doctor."

Jim: "That is miniature black hole, shortest wave length, highest energy my doctor may not be aware of! It is fusion. If you know basic nuclear physics? It should be in your training manual. Hmm…"

TSA Officer: "God only knows who you are! What do you do with it… with that Chi?"..., puzzled.

Jim: "Chi is life force, Helium. It makes you levitate, lifts you up, antigravity force. It is the portal, Quantum Vortex to communicate with outer dimensions and God, and make wishes programmed and granted through sub consciousness.

I use it to cure people from cancer, back pain, knee and ankle pain, thyroids/chakras adjustments, anything with electromagnetic fields disturbances, HIV, skin spots, varicose veins… and I do it for free!"

TSA Officer: "Jesus Christ! Go through, please. You are holding the line, sir!"

Jim: "No officer... I am Jim Walker! But thanks..." Smiling, he proceeded.

Back to year 2012, in Jim's Time Machine.

Satan: "You are all mine now! You will be everything you want now! I will show you secret pleasures of women and wealth. I will give you the best weapons, and I will make you God like."

Jim: "No thanks! I just need peace of mind! If everything you say is possible, why are there so many poor people on earth?"

Satan: "Poor people talk about money all the time. They are greedy and with criminal minds. The only difference between poor and rich is who will get a license to do business and who does not is on the other side of the equitation. The biggest game in the financial system is who gets credit?"

Jim: "I guess I don't need you then! I don't have good credit! Bye!"

Satan: "Damn it! This guy has answers for everything. I need to work on younger souls!"

Jim: "When one pays cash, what is credit?"

Satan: "Then the collateral is what one buys with cash," he smiled.

Jim: "How much does a continent cost?"

Satan: "A lot, maybe around 100 trillion?" (True, USA's private equity is $83 trillion, in March, 2014; the total wealth of the USA in 2008 was $118 trillion, according to United Nations report).

Jim: "It will cost me zero. I am starting a movement now! I can get anything I want for free. Remember my restaurant Bellini's, Randevu, Zoro? I went around the World 5 times to 50 different countries for free.

I may be the writer to "Wezfeld" sitcom now?" He was comparing it with the "Seinfeld," just like his own Wezon vs. Boson.

Satan: "I can't fight or help movements. I work with individuals."

Jim: "Lenin started a movement. It lasted 75 years. Adam Smith theorized the Capitalist Movement, and it may last for awhile? My movement, will last forever. The Awareness is bigger than just knowledge. If we don't piss off my Father, God and destroy each other on Earth we will be soon like him: bright, less sexual, not greedy, living forever."

Satan: "No pleasures? That means less population, less drinking, less drugs, and less wars. Then they will not need me that much! Damn it!"

Jim: "We never needed you anyway. Sex and money are overrated and always will be! Bye, Satan!"

Satan disappeared.....

Jim: "I always win!"

"Having the fewest wants, I am closest to the God(s)". . . . Socrates

The End.... for now...

Acknowledgments

Time Space & the Mind by Dr. Irving Oyle
The theory of Celestial Influence by Rodney Collin
The Emperor's New Mind by Roger Penrose
Black Holes and Time Warps by Kip Thorne
The secret powers of Pyramids by Bill Schul and Ed Pettit
Guide to Yoga Meditation and 28 days Plan by Richard Hittleman
Psychic energy by Joseph J. Weed
Astral Projection by Melita Denning and Osborne Phillips

About the Author

Jim Walker background

2012 Writer of "God's Quantum Vortex," self documentary, copyrighted 2013;

Forty years research in Quantum Mechanics by Max Planck, special relativity and Quantum entanglement by Albert Einstein and Dark matter and Dark energy by Jan Oort. Experimented with Yoga, minds communications, mind creativity and destruction, proven predictions, astral (spiritual) projections, healing through consciousness, holistic and conventional health science, and discovered and formulated the pyramid phenomena; the Quantum Cone Vortex. He discovered the secrets of antimatter at age 12 (in 1969). He applied his Awareness and advanced knowledge in many projects. He predicted many futuristic events and applied physics. In September 2010 he replied to TV advertisement requiring shovel ready ideas with 2 billion dollars reward. The same he discussed with Sen. Alan in Virginia. He decided to write this book after their rejection. His projects were in GPS, Time Travel, Capsule travel, Crystal Ball TV, Roof top shopping (helicopter /drone, then gravity delivery). Although that book refers to his restaurant and night club experiences the reader should stay focus on his genius analysis and formulas he arrived to without any field study and research in Cornell University or in MIT. He came in parallel conclusion with theoretical physicists about the annihilation resulting in new particle with mass, but no charge, 20 years prior to his legendary e mail to Tiffany on June 13th, 2012. The 10 billion dollar man Peter Higgs came second on July 4th, 2012 with his toy collider at CERN, but it took him another 9 months to prove his "God's particle" (March 2013!). Frank

Close published his book with Feynman Diagrams "Infinity Puzzle" in December 2012. The irony again here was that Jim's slogan for four decades was the "creation is the power of suggestion through rejection." Yes, Frank Close, you are third. Jim connects all the ingredients to create or destroy in the web of science, spiritual, financial, and political interconnection. The book was copyrighted in April, 2013. The book is written in dialog manuscript style for a movie. The editing here is minimal. It is written in English (Jim's 4th language).

Yes, he has idols to begin with. His fitness idol is Bruce Lee. His mental idol is Henry Kissinger. His holistic challenger is John of God in Brazil. This book is about healing, life extension, and self care, not health care…It is also about a new Movement. To join the Movement of Awareness one needs to cross the boundaries of countries, to elevate oneself from Earth's knowledge and to open oneself to Galaxy and Cosmic Quantum algorithm of all possibilities, and to all dimensions, where Time is irrelevant. To reach this cosmic vortex, the mortals may not need 40 years of research, but definitely they need to prove themselves as awarded in highest science or to go through the scrutiny of hunger, deprivation, desperation and to some excessive wealth; and then lose it all.

"Only a person who has experienced all the possibilities on Earth, then that person can be Aware of, and connect with the Cosmic God, TIH."

—Jim Walker

Comments about the book and to register on our website write to:
GodQuantumVortex@gmail.com
www.MNation.info

Printed in the United States
By Bookmasters